D0409147

MADRID, 1936–1939

LONDON, 1940–1941

Besieged

SINGAPORE, 1941–1942

STALINGRAD, 1942–1943

SEVEN CITIES UNDER SIEGE

WARSAW, 1939, 1943, 1944

JERUSALEM, 1947–1949

BERLIN, 1945–1949

J. Bowyer Bell

MADRID, 1936–1939

LONDON, 1940–1941

Besieged

SEVEN CITIES UNDER SIEGE

SINGAPORE, 1941–1942

STALINGRAD, 1942–1943

WARSAW, 1939, 1943, 1944

JERUSALEM, 1947–1949

BERLIN, 1945–1949

Chilton Books, *A Division of Chilton Company*
PUBLISHERS
Philadelphia and New York

 Published in Philadelphia by Chilton Company and simultaneously in Toronto, Canada, by Ambassador Books, Ltd. Designed by William E. Lickfield. Manufactured in the United States of America. Library of Congress Catalog Card Number 66-22585

For

John Higgins Williams

Preface

THE genesis of this book lies in what for years I had felt was a minor sin comparable to my addiction to the Times crossword puzzle, the reading of military history solely for pleasure. After a time it seemed to me that one of the areas most neglected in theory and seldom exploited in narrative was the siege. Along with the mass cavalry charge and a major sea battle, the siege of a great city, even though a more protracted event, has long been one of warfare's most dramatic confrontations. In our century the siege has often been considered as obsolete as the castle. Originally my intention had been merely to show the persistence of the siege as a form of battle by means of several independent accounts of the more significant modern sieges. Instead, what has developed is seven case studies of seven different varieties of contemporary sieges in what I hope are authoritative, but certainly not definitive, accounts. This external approach, the dependence more on the works of others than on the original documents, was chosen partly at least to appeal to the general reader. Consequently the scholarly paraphernalia has been reduced to a minimum and the sources quoted are works in English. In time these restrictions proved artificial in that many of the sources are as unavailable to the average reader as if they had been left in Hebrew or Japanese; nevertheless, for the most part the book is an essay rather than a monograph.

The mass of material available for some of the sieges is appallingly extensive as is often the case in contemporary history with multivolume official histories, seemingly endless memoirs, and shelves of tangential accounts. In the cases of the seven sieges, no account or study by a disinterested scholar treats the battle purely as a siege, but in nearly every case there is at least one, and often more than one, basic work, such as Dov Joseph's The Faithful City: The Siege of Jerusalem, 1948 or R. G. Colodny's The Struggle for Madrid: The Central Epic of the Spanish Conflict (1936–1937). What is undoubtedly the siege par excellence, Leningrad, has been avoided because of Leon Goure's The Siege of Leningrad.

I am indebted to a variety of individuals and institutions for help in *accumulating the essential, and what at one time were supposedly going to be readily available, materials: the staff of the New York Institute of Technology Library, in particular Richard Griffin and Patricia Rice; the vast and usually anonymous staff of the New York Public Library; the staff of the Zionist Archives in New York, the YIVO Institute Library in New York; and all those libraries, from Harvard University in the north to the Library of Congress to the south, connected with the interlibrary loan program. Finally I should like to thank my wife, who has not typed chapters, read proof (Harvey Fireside did), or checked footnotes, but who as an Egyptologist has with great patience tolerated my misguided interest in recent battles.*

J.B.B.

New York City / St. Mullins, Co. Carlow

Contents

Acknowledgments

PERMISSION to quote from the following is gratefully acknowledged:

The Spanish Civil War by Hugh Thomas. Harper and Row, Publishers (New York), 1961.

Journeys Between Wars by John Dos Passos. Harcourt, Brace and World, Inc. (New York). Copyright 1938 by John Dos Passos.

The Last Days of Madrid by Sigismundo Casado. Peter Davies, Ltd. (London), 1939.

The Winter of the Bombs by Constantine Fitzgibbon. W. W. Norton and Company, Inc. (New York), 1957.

History Under Fire by James Pope-Hennessy. B. T. Batsford, Ltd. (London), 1941.

Their Finest Hour by Winston Churchill. Houghton Mifflin Company (Boston), 1949.

Hinge of Fate by Winston Churchill. Houghton Mifflin Company (Boston), 1950.

Triumph and Tragedy by Winston Churchill. Houghton Mifflin Company (Boston), 1953.

Royal Air Force 1939–45, Vol. 1, by Denis Richards. Her Majesty's Stationery Office (London), 1953.

Civil Defence by Terence O'Brien. Her Majesty's Stationery Office (London), 1955.

"The Burning of the Temple" by Alexander Werth. *The 1943 Saturday Book*. Hutchinson Publishing Group, Ltd. (London), 1942.

Fortress by Kenneth Attiwill. Copyright © 1959 by Kenneth Attiwill. Reprinted by permission of Doubleday and Company, Inc.

The Life and Death of a Japanese General by John Deane Potter. New American Library of World Literature, Inc. (New York), 1962.

But Not in Shame by John Toland. Random House, Inc. (New York), 1962.

Eastern Epic by Compton MacKenzie. Chatto and Windus, Ltd. (London), 1951.

Blitzkrieg to Defeat: Hitler's War Directives 1939–1945 edited by H. R. Trevor-Roper. Holt, Rinehart and Winston, Inc. (New York), 1965.

The Beginning of the Road by V. I. Chuikov. MacGibbon and Kee, Ltd. (London), 1963. Copyright 1964 by Holt, Rinehart and Winston, Inc. (New York) under the title *The Battle for Stalingrad.*

"Stalingrad" by Kurt Zeitzler in *The Fatal Decisions,* edited by Seymour Freidin and William Richardson. William Sloane Associates (London), 1956.

Paulus and Stalingrad by Walter Goerlitz. The Citadel Press (New York), 1963.

Lost Victories by Erich von Manstein. Henry Regnery Company (Chicago), 1958.

A Military History of World War II edited by T. Dodson Stamps and Vincent J. Esposito. West Point: USMA, 1956.

The Story of a Secret State by Jan Karski. Houghton Mifflin Company (Boston), 1964.

The Root and the Bough by Leo W. Schwarz. Holt, Rinehart and Winston, Inc. (New York), 1949.

The Secret Army by Tadeusz Komorowski. The Macmillan Company (New York), 1951. Reprinted by permission of Victor Gollancz, Ltd. (London).

The Tragedy of Warsaw by K. M. Atholl. John Murray, Ltd. (London), 1945.

Invitation to Moscow by Z. Stypulkowski. Thames and Hudson, Ltd. (London), 1951.

Panzer Leader by Heinz Guderian (trans. Constantine Fitzgibbon). E. P. Dutton and Co., Inc. (New York), 1952. Published 1952 in Great Britain and Canada by Michael Joseph, Ltd. (London).

Fighting Warsaw by Stefan Korbonski. George Allen and Unwin, Ltd. (London), 1956.

Sixty-three Days. Democratic Press and Liberty Publications, Ltd. (London), 1945.

The Rape of Poland by Stanislaw Mikolzjczyk. McGraw-Hill Book Company (New York), 1948.

Cairo to Damascus by John Roy Carlson. Alfred A. Knopf, Inc. (New York), 1957. Reprinted by permission of Paul R. Reynolds, Inc.

A Soldier With the Arabs by Sir John Bagot Glubb. Harper and Row, Publishers (New York), 1957.

The Faithful City: The Siege of Jerusalem 1948 by Dov Joseph. Simon and Schuster, Inc. (New York), 1960.

Decision in Germany by Lucius D. Clay. Copyright 1950 by Lucius D. Clay. Reprinted by permission of Doubleday and Company, Inc.

The Forrestal Diaries by James Forrestal (ed. Walter Millis). Viking Press (New York), 1951. Copyright presently held by Princeton University.

"The Berlin Airlift" by Charles J. V. Murphy. *Fortune*, XXXVIII (November, 1948). Reprinted by courtesy of *Fortune*.

We Built and Destroyed by Douglas Bailey. Hurst and Blackett, Ltd. (London), n.d. Reprinted by permission of John Farquharson, Ltd.

Barbarossa by Alan Clark. William Morrow and Company, Inc. (New York), 1965.

Strategy at Singapore by Eugene Herbert Miller. The Macmillan Company (New York), 1965. Reprinted by permission of the Public Affairs Press, Washington, D.C.

The Long Prologue

The worse policy is to attack cities. Attack cities only when there is no alternative.
—SUN TZU: *The Art of War*

TWENTY-FIVE HUNDRED years ago, when Sun Tzu first laid down the rules of warfare, it had, in China at least, become axiomatic that the least desirable form of offensive action was an attack on a city. Despite Sun Tzu's warning, generals in the future continued to attack cities just as they had done for thousands of years. Apparently, urban civilization and the siege entered history almost simultaneously. The great walled cities, particularly in the Tigris and Euphrates valleys, underwent sieges often culminating in nameless and forgotten mounds of rubble buried beneath the dust. In Biblical times the walls of Jericho were not built as decoration nor did they come tumbling down solely due to the efforts of Joshua; in fact, Jericho was reduced many times. The buried, blackened ruins of the ancient world indicate that the envelopment of a fortress city was one of the normal forms of battle. The Greek cities, too, depended on walls or failed to do so at their peril. The most renowned, if not the most militarily elegant, Greek siege is surely the ten-year bungle at Troy, where apparently the tactics of both the mortals and the gods left much to be desired. Although the later campaigns of the Persian War were decided in open battles, often at sea, the Peloponnesian War, the Western world's first great fratricidal conflict, could almost be considered a war of sieges. While the fame of Alexander rested elsewhere, his contemporaries felt that one of the most notable proofs of his military genius was the reduction of Tyre, a city which for centuries had challenged the ingenuity of besiegers. After Alexander, the Romans brought to warfare not only their martial virtues but also their highly developed technical skills. Ancient history from the first mud wall at Ur to the sophisticated weapons systems of Archimedes is studded with sieges. After thousands of years an immense body of knowledge as well as an armory of weapons and machines had been developed for attacking and defending a fortress city. Such an attack, whether the "worse policy" or not, often proved either inevitable or irresistible. Yet all this accumulated knowledge of the ages proved useless to the Romans when the great barbaric peoples of Asia and Northern Europe began overrunning their Empire.

With the disintegration and fragmentation of the Greco-Roman world, warfare fell on evil days. The great battles of Europe were little more than ignorant tribes clashing with obsolete weapons. The great wandering hordes out of the East, sweeping through Europe for generation after generation, produced in response the fortress of refuge, a sanctuary where an embattled rural population could hopefully outwait the barbarian. With the slow development of Western civilization came a limited improvement in the technology of warfare. The crude wood and earth forts became larger and more impregnable. Despite the growing improvements in fortification, the typical eleventh-century Anglo-Norman castle, for example, with its earthwork mound surmounted by a timber wall and its outlying fenced yard, bore little resemblance to the legendary castles of the knights in armor, most of whom still had only chain mail and leather leggings. Not until the first great renaissance of the twelfth century and the gradual introduction of stone as a building material did the fortress-castle begin to resemble the backdrops for Camelot. Many of the most famous castles are of later centuries and were already almost obsolete when built (a long-time failing of the military mind). In any case, the first great vintage years of the siege can be found in the late medieval period, with all its paraphernalia of defense from boiling oil to topless towers and its ingenious devices of attack, the huge battering ram, the catapults, and the siege towers. Few of these devices and techniques were unique. Almost all had a long history stretching back thousands of years before their reintroduction into Europe. It was not until the development of firearms during the fifteenth century that the West produced an entirely new weapon, one which could eliminate from a distance the protection of masonry.

For some time, in fact for a very long time, the major impact of firearms was psychological, for the sound was far more impressive than the shell was dangerous. This was particularly true in the early wars of empire in America and Asia where huge bastions fell before the patter of inaccurate and almost harmless pellets. Artillery remained crude, usually inaccurate, and very often as dangerous to the user as to the enemy. Thus the predicted obsolescence of the fortress was postponed from century to century as the military engineers hurriedly improved their ramparts to offset the slow development of the gun. At the same time the rapid growth of cities complicated the siege with the presence of large numbers of noncombatants. Many of the great battles of the sixteenth century were the result of invested cities resisting under heavy (but not fatal) bombardment.

Perhaps the height of siegecraft developed a century later, at least partly in reaction to the wholesale slaughters of the wars of religion. Military conflict followed a highly elaborate formula with expensive professional armies obeying mutually accepted rules in isolated encounters. The siege became so formal that battles developed as set pieces, more like chess than war. Cities fell on schedule as opposing generals reacted within the narrow, accepted canons of warfare. Apparently a commander could undertake a siege with no more than the appropriate textbook and a loud voice, and, indeed, this appears to have been all the resource available to some.

By the end of the eighteenth century, however, a variety of new factors had removed warfare from the hands of the chess masters and placed it within reach of a new generation of generals, who often used mass armies imbued with revolutionary or nationalistic fervor. Along with new ardor had come new artillery. The scientific revolution, which had lagged far behind the empirical developments of technology, now came to the aid of the generals. No longer was powder so poor that soldiers had to wait to fire until they could see the whites of their opponents' eyes. After the Napoleonic wars, cannons grew larger and larger; the weight of shells increased sufficiently so that no masonry seemed capable of withstanding bombardment. As a result the experts relegated the siege to colonial or peripheral wars; for Europe the theorists could see no place for siegecraft, in view of the prospects for annihilation and destruction by the new artillery. The defense of a city by an army was hopeless, by an insurrectionist mob, suicide. The great siege of Paris in 1870 was more a result of Prussian diplomatic and political tactics than a reintroduction of a military technique by the French. If, before 1914, an army became involved in the envelopment or defense of a city, the campaign was regarded as a historical anomaly and probably a blunder as witness Khartoum or Ladysmith. In the American Civil War, the siege of Vicksburg and the investment of Richmond had little impact on Europe, where the lessons of the American war had far less effect than has often been assumed. In any case the Civil War could be considered both provincial and colonial, and consequently of only secondary theoretical importance.

When the great European war came in 1914, all the expectations of the generals proved wrong. Instead of a swift decision as a result of the immense power of their new heavy weapons and giant armies, the conflict turned into a long and pointless slaughter. In the uneven development of military technology almost all the new weapons proved to be defensive. The machine gun, massed heavy artillery, and barbed wire frustrated even the most determined attacks. The war developed into a great siege with huge armies locked together in a massive cam-

paign of attrition. The generals' blind attacks, repeated in ever-multiplying size, broke down with previously unheard-of losses. All efforts, both tactical and technological, to open up the war to maneuver failed. New campaigns in other zones developed along the same futile lines and failed to upset the stalemate. The German introduction of poison gas proved insufficient. Two potentially effective offensive weapons, the tracked tank and the airplane, had barely been developed. Neither was able to be committed in sufficient strength to outweigh its technical faults or the high command's suspicions. A final decision came as much as a result of exhaustion as of new offensive techniques.

If the 1914–1918 war had developed into a bloody shambles uselessly swallowing up whole divisions in a day, the next war would be different. Almost as soon as the war to end war closed down in November 1918, the pessimists and the prophets began to plan for the next. The massive armies of 1918, equipped with incomparable defensive weapons and slaughtering each other by the millions in static massacres along an unshifting front, would soon be as obsolete as the battle ax or single combat. The rapid development of the tank, the airplane, the advanced forms of communication, all suggested to the seers that the next war would be one of fluidity where maneuver and daring could be reintroduced into military tactics.

Some generals and admirals (as always) insisted that the next war would be an extension of the last, and their numbers dwindled all too slowly. Other than the proponents of mobility, there were two major conventional strategic views: static defense and limited offense. The first, in direct reaction to the Western Front, foresaw a war fought behind elaborate, deep fortifications which would halt any offensive. This view, epitomized in the French Maginot line, to some extent attracted all the armies except the American. The second school favored a limited, conservative offensive by a balanced, mixed force—tanks, artillery, air, and infantry—fighting a series of set-piece battles. The new generation, however, pursued military tactics to the frontiers of technology, proving the battleship vulnerable from the air and the trench to the tank.

To a few the war of the future would be of an entirely different order. The Italian General Douhet foresaw the possibility of destroying a nation from the air without even engaging its land armies. What all the new theorists agreed upon was that the siege had no place in modern warfare. Fortresses would be bypassed and destroyed from the air; enveloped armies would be cut to pieces by armor; and defended cities would become highly vulnerable targets, deathtraps for the civilians rather than havens for the armies. Perhaps a great island bastion like Gibraltar or Corregidor, which dominated a vital seaway, might retain its military value due to its geology and geography, not to mention years of fortification which had made it all but invulnerable. The real war, however, would be won in the field by armored armies clashing beneath fleets of planes.

Much of the acrimonious discussion on the nature of war had to be carried out by necessity in a military vacuum. Although as usual the world was filled with little wars during the years after 1918, no conflict was sufficiently extensive or available for field trials. The Sino-Japanese war was too far away and too primitive. The Italian attack on Ethiopia proved a mismatch. Without first-hand evidence, the next war had to be fought in maneuvers and on sand tables, neither of which produced a definitive answer to a growing number of tactical and technological questions.

Then, unexpectedly, in 1936, in an area long ignored in European councils, a marvelous opportunity to observe and experiment occurred. After a short and stormy career the Spanish Republic finally floundered. In Spain, last touched by serious war during Wellington's campaigns, the military experts of the world found a testing ground.

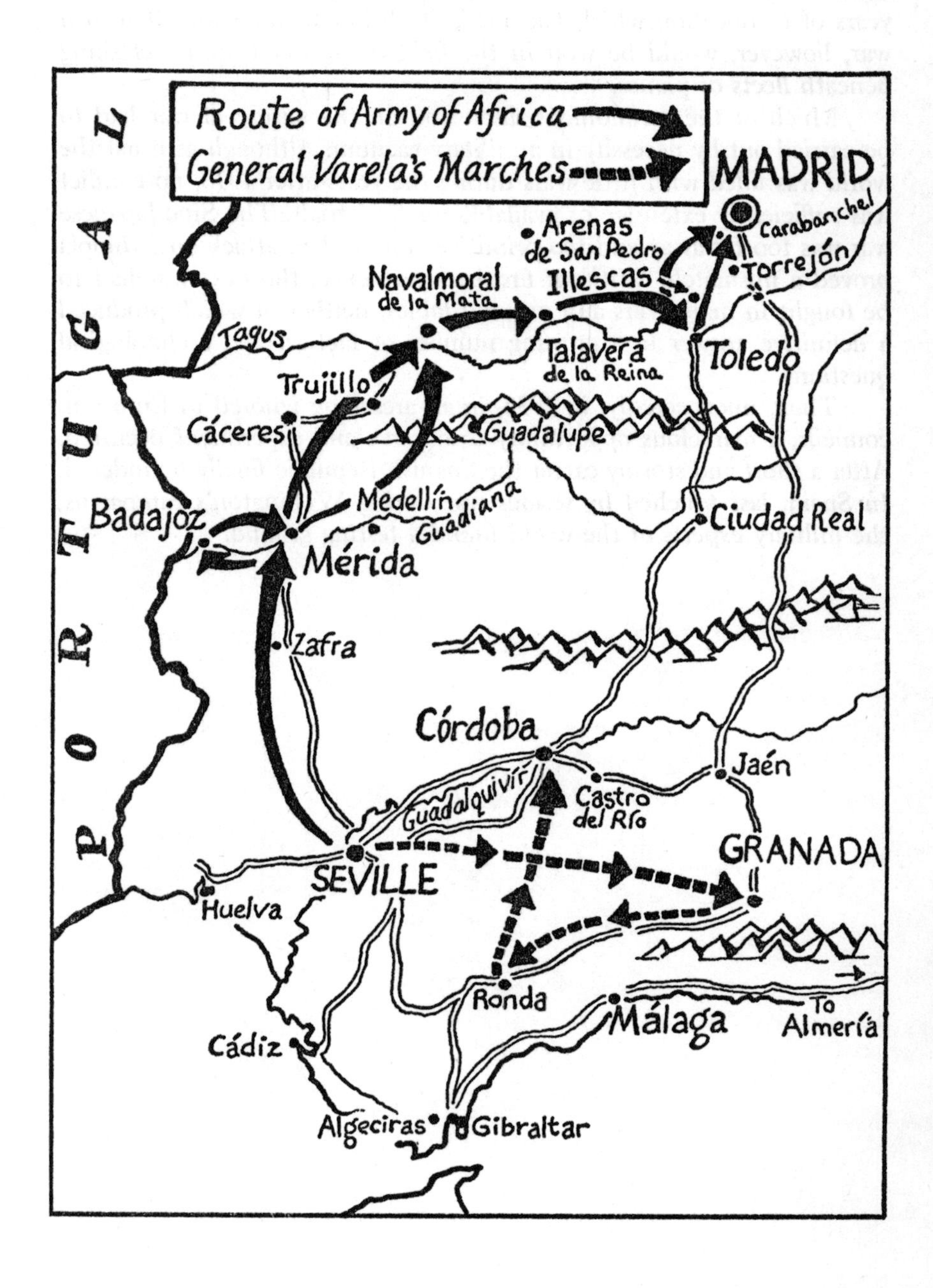

Route of Army of Africa
General Varela's Marches
MADRID
Carabanchel
Arenas
de San Pedro
Torrejón
Navalmoral
de la Mata
Illescas
Tagus
Talavera
de la Reina
Toledo
Trujillo
Cáceres
Guadalupe
Medellín
Guadiana
Badajoz
Mérida
Ciudad Real
Zafra
Córdoba
Jaén
Guadalquivir
Castro
del Río
GRANADA
SEVILLE
Huelva
Ronda
Málaga
To
Almería
Cádiz
Algeciras
Gibraltar
PORTUGAL

1 MADRID: 1936-1939

The Impact of a Siege

. . . most observers have said that there are no tactical lessons to be learnt.
—MAJOR-GENERAL TEMPERLEY

. . . in case of a continental war, the text book most worth of study is the text book of the Spanish war.
—HENRY J. REILLY

IN no other historical field do the manifold causal factors, stretching far back in multiplying powers, seem so limited, so explicable as they do in military history. More than in any other major human endeavor, the battle seems most open to analysis. However complex and haphazard, however open to contingency or fate a battle may seem at the time, the retrospective survey of historians and critics can go far to reducing the confusion, assigning the blame, and portraying the violence of the moment into the framework of a bloody but reasonable game of chess.

The causes of victory, the errors of defeat, the alternatives and options will all be elaborated by later students in closely reasoned studies so that yesterday's battles seem as familiar and obvious as solved puzzles—here Von Moltke went wrong; there Lee faltered. As a result the close study of past campaigns has regularly been instituted in order to avoid the errors of one's military predecessors. When war came to Spain, the opportunity not only to observe but even to experiment was seized by many of the next generation's generals. However, the resulting lessons of military conduct, polished into axioms, did not prove universally valid and swiftly adaptable. The war in Spain was a complex and difficult text and the lessons of 1936–1939 proved not readily digestible.

BY the summer of 1936, Spain had descended once again into violence, discord, and confusion. Early on the morning of July 13, the prologue to the final tragedy began. In Madrid an official Assault Guards truck, numbered 17, pulled out of the Pontejos Barracks. Inside were three captains of the Assault Guards determined to avenge the death of the young Socialist lieutenant, José Castillo, murdered the previous day in the violent campaign of political assassination and terror carried out by Spain's factionalized and warring parties. A few minutes later truck number 17 stopped before 89 Velazquez Street. Here lived Calvo Sotelo, a brilliant and articulate leader of the Right bloc and the hope of many who detested and feared the new Popular Front government. The three captains walked past the night watchman and up the stairs to Sotelo's apartment. After some confusion while the telephone wires were secretly cut, the Assault Guards pressured Sotelo into leaving. Sotelo reassured his wife and promised to call from the police station "unless these Gentlemen have come to blow out my brains." He walked downstairs carrying the bag his wife had packed and got into the truck, sitting next to an Assault Guard and a cavalry trooper. Two captains got in the front. The third, Captain Cuenca, sat behind him. The driver started up and the truck rolled slowly down Velazquez Street. Captain Cuenca drew his pistol, leaned forward, and shot Sotelo twice in the back of the head. They dumped the body near the mortuary of Madrid's East Cemetery. Castillo had been revenged.[1]*

This assassination was not to be toted up and forgotten along with the scores of political murders of the previous months. This murder would serve as "the cause" of rebellion. A conspiracy, mainly of senior officers, had long been planning a *coup d'état* to rid the country of "the Reds." The generals hated the Popular Front government, narrowly elected in February 1936 in one of Spain's rare elections. They distrusted its motives and despised its programs. The generals saw the little group of middle-class politicians as pawns of the great mass parties of Socialists and Anarchists whose alien ideas would destroy traditional Spain. In the meantime, to the army it was obvious that the Popular Front could not keep order. Week by week, Spain had drifted through the chaos of bomb explosions, strikes, riots, and murder, toward anarchy. To prevent a revolution from the Left, the army would act.

In fact, the generals had been patching together their coup almost from election day. No strangers to revolt, the generals had hopefully prepared for simultaneous uprisings in all the major cities both in Spain and in the Spanish colonies. By July 13, all was set. A plane was on the way to move General Francisco Franco from his obscure post as military commander of Tenerife in the Canary Islands to Morocco, where he would lead the Spanish Foreign Legion and the Moorish troops in revolt. General José Sanjurjo, leader of an unsuccessful coup in 1934, was preparing to fly from exile in Portugal to take command

* Superior figures refer to Notes at end of text.

of the rebels. In Spain, General Emilio Mola had finally decided to move. In most of the barracks throughout Spain, the senior officers had spent the summer waiting for the secret password: *sin novedad*—"nothing new." Now it was to be given.[2]

The officers jumped the gun by one day in Africa when their plans began to leak out.[3] The successful rising before dawn on July 17 in the Moroccan garrisons meant the generals had a secure bastion and control of the Moors and the Foreign Legion. On July 17–18, the revolt began more or less as planned on the mainland. Almost immediately much of the Spanish political landscape became a vacuum, out of touch with Madrid and reached only by rumor. Rapidly the vacuum was filled with hastily organized worker militia groups or small bands of rebel officers and politicians. The fate of cities, often whole provinces, would depend on the response of a handful of men. General Queipo de Llano captured Seville with a few score men and a shiny Hispano-Sforza limousine. At Huelva, the Popular Front maintained control. At Granada, the workers demonstrated and the conspirators waited. The Government in Madrid dithered, uncertain as to its first move. The telephone system suddenly became the key to clear the growing confusion. All during the long, hot hours of the evening of July 18, the nature of the slogans used to answer the telephone revealed to the Government the extent of the revolt. On July 18, the coup had neither failed nor succeeded. It had merely begun.

The Popular Front ministers and President Manuel Azaña, fearing civil war, hoped desperately for an immediate compromise. Uninterested in compromise, the masses of Madrid workers began to filter into the streets. They wanted arms and an end to uncertainty. *La Pasionaria*—Dolores Ibarruri—one of the leaders of the small Communist Party, in the first of an endless series of violent speeches, unexpectedly gave the city its great rallying cry: *No Pasaron!*, an echo from Verdun's famous "They Shall Not Pass." Efforts during the day to smash the rebellion by force failed. The crowd continued to demonstrate for arms to defend the Republic. The Republican Government was uncertain as to whether it wanted to be defended. Azaña knew that to arm the crowd would put the power into the streets and ultimately into the hands of the extreme revolutionary parties. Instead of yielding to the masses, Azaña, on the night of July 18, called in Diego Martínez Barrio, a politician noted for his ability to compromise the irreconcilable. The workers milling in the streets of Madrid were outraged. The Government was selling out.

The salesman of compromise, however, found no buyers. The generals saw no need to quit and no honor in negotiation. Answering Martínez Barrio's feeler, General Mola replied, "The Popular Front cannot keep order, you have your followers and I have mine. If we were to seal a bargain we should be betraying our ideals and our men."[4] Martínez Barrio resigned at dawn. José Giral, a moderate supported by all the parties of the Left, took office. Immediately he ordered rifles delivered to the Socialist and Anarchist union headquarters. The armories all over Spain were opened to the people. With the fate of the Republic now in the hands of armed mobs, the new Government could only wait. The hours slipped by and the rumors of heavy fighting and new revolts trickled into Madrid and yet the city remained ominously quiet.

In the middle of the afternoon, General Joaquín Fanjul arrived at the Montaña Barracks high above the Manzanares River on the western edge of the city. He organized a grouping of 2,000 officers and Falangists (Spain's semifascist party) for a sally into the streets. When the rebels tried to leave the barracks, they found their way blocked by huge crowds, partially armed and totally hostile. Fanjul withdrew to the barracks, and his men began firing at the crowd with machine guns. The revolt had at last come to Madrid. During the night the rebels in the Montaña Barracks went unmolested while the newly organized militia vented their spleen elsewhere. Order had collapsed. Mysterious cars sporting revolutionary banners and filled with grim-faced men tore through the streets. Sporadic firing continued all night as many old scores were settled. Erratic and aimless sniping began. Enthusiastic crowds in the traditional, ritual act of Spanish rebellions began to burn churches, symbols of reaction and hypocrisy to the masses. The orgy of violence had begun in Madrid.

At dawn a vast crowd gathered outside the Montaña Barracks. For five hours the crowd fired two pieces of artillery at the barracks. Those lucky enough to have a rifle sprayed the huge stone façade. The rebels held on. Fanjul was unable to contact other troops. Once, over the rooftops, he got a message through to the suburb of Carabanchel, but relief proved impossible. At ten-thirty in the morning, Fanjul was wounded. At eleven a white flag was seen at one of the windows. When the crowd advanced, a rebel machine gun opened fire. Twice more a white flag was reported; twice more the undisciplined crowd foolishly walked into the machine-gun fire. Finally, in a violent rage, the furious crowd just before noon rushed forward and forced the great doors of the barracks. Thirsting for blood the mob rushed into the courtyard to massacre the rebels. Some were smashed to the ground and trampled to death. Many were simply shot on sight. A huge militiaman, high up on the top gallery, began throwing one screaming officer after another down on the swarming mob below. The Assault Guards did manage to save a few of the officers, including Fanjul, but the mob had already slaughtered most of them. Elsewhere in the city, loyal officers and men stormed other barracks. Divided, uncertain, and faced by tens of thousands of howling militiamen, the leaders of the Madrid revolt either surrendered or fled. By late afternoon Madrid was safe for the Republic.[5]

The fall of the Montaña Barracks signaled the end of the old ways. The victorious militia, flushed with success, rushed out to commandeer transportation to take them north to win back Guadalajara. Some drove south to Toledo where Colonel José Moscardó had retreated within the vast stone fortress of the Alcázar with a mixed group of rebels: civil guards, officers, women, cadets, fearful families, Falangists, and monarchists. In Madrid cars loaded with men wearing the insignia of their party and shouting slogans and waving rifles roared through the streets. Huge posters of revolutionary leaders, including Lenin, appeared. The unions and their endless committees gradually took over the maintenance of the city. The parties and unions soon seemed more important than Giral's moderate government. As Azaña had foreseen, the power was in the streets. How long it would stay there appeared to depend more on the success of the generals than on the maneuvers of the crowd; for the collapse of the rebels in Madrid had not meant the failure of the revolt. It had only assured Spain of a civil war instead of a coup.

Although the army had not been able to seize the country as the generals had planned, the rebels did control half the mainland and had the support of the forces of the Right. Some confusion remained, because of General Sanjurjo's death when his plane crashed while taking off from Portugal. No one knew who was to be the supreme commander. More distracting, General Franco could not get his Army of Africa across the Straits of Gibraltar because of the presence of the Loyalist fleet. If the Republic were to be overthrown, these troops of Franco's were essential.

The difficulty, however, was not insurmountable. Agents rushed to contact Hitler and Mussolini, who were certain to sympathize with the general's anti-Red aims. The Italians and Germans were willing to supply the few transport planes necessary to airlift Franco's little army over the Straits. After this was completed, the march north to Madrid would be little more than a triumphant procession against the tattered and undisciplined Loyalists. Then the rebels, who soon adopted the name "Nationalists" for their movement, would wipe out revolution and restore Spain—"One, United, and Great!" German *Junker* aircraft began landing Franco's men on the mainland.

These German planes were simply the first evidence of the growing international complications of what had started out to be a simple (almost traditional) change in the Spanish Government. Soon all varieties of political creeds, all the ideologies of the twentieth century and before clashed in battle. In Spain there were fascists and anarchists, communists and monarchists, republicans and conservatives, often in a variety of small, bitterly jealous sects, occasionally in great, loosely organized unions or federations. No series of events in twenty years would so stir the emotions of all thinking men as this open conflict over all of Western man's cherished and contradictory ideas.

In the early days of the revolt, not only the issues but also the events remained clouded with rumor and propaganda. Germany and Italy were simply the first to fish in the troubled waters where nothing seemed certain but the possibilities. Mussolini, open for adventure, aided the Nationalists more for prestige than profit, more to impress the world than to extend his empire. When he offered the dozen or so transports required by Franco in July 1936, he had no idea that they were simply the first drop in what was to become a very large bucket. Hitler, too, had agreed to help when approached between acts of *Die Walküre* at the Bayreuth Festival on July 26. It was a chance to try out a few planes and make a new friend. Thus, almost from the first, the two great powers of the totalitarian Right were involved in the Nationalist cause by the most casual of decisions.[6] Soon there would be other commitments of all kinds and varieties.

In the meantime, on July 19, General Mola had ordered Colonel García Escámez south toward Guadalajara with 1,600 men. The colonel had stopped his march on Guadalajara to make sure of the rising in Logroño. This was all the time the Madrid militia rushing north in their commandeered cars and trucks needed. They seized Guadalajara. García Escámez pulled back through the Sierra Guadarrama Mountains further west at the Somosierra Pass. At the pass a little group of monarchists from Madrid were holding on to the railway tunnel in hopes that aid would reach them before the Madrid militia discovered their presence. To the southwest of the monarchists, a rebel force under Colonel Serrador was trying desperately to hold up a militia group which had already pushed through the mountains and occupied the Alto de León pass, the gateway to Old Castile. Both sides concentrated their attention on the two passes, rounding up more men and rushing them into the mountains. The rebels, short of men, had the advantage of both experience and artillery. The Republicans were little more than a revolutionary mob led by a handful of loyal regular army officers. Despite the fanaticism and wild courage of the militia, Colonel Serrador took Alto de León on July 22. On July 25, García Escámez captured Somosierra Pass. There the advance halted. The Republican militia were bitter, having expected victory simply because their cause was just. In frustration they shot their own colonel, a regular army officer and hence suspect, and for good measure executed his sons as well. For a week both sides had been shooting prisoners and "traitors" and would continue to do so for some time. After the execution the battle was renewed. Neither side could break through despite costly repeated assaults.[7]

For the Republicans and for Madrid, the bloody, amateur campaign in the Sierras proved of great importance. First it closed the northern gateway to the city, but most significant it converted many of the revolutionists to the virtues of military discipline. Voting whether or not to attack and selecting officers by poll might work in theory, but in the Sierras the result had been heaps of uselessly slaughtered militia.

Some groups, particularly the Anarchists, could not give up the old ways;[8] but the swiftest and most effective response was made by the small Communist Party, eager to become the vanguard of the Republic. Using the Communist-Socialist youth as a base, the Party formed the Fifth Regiment. The other four regiments, now disbanded, were the regular units formerly stationed in Madrid. The new Fifth Regiment was led by Enrique Lister, a quarryman, and Juan Modesto, an ex-woodcutter who had served in the Foreign Legion under Franco. The regiment proved highly effective, mainly due to the ruthless and efficient Vittorio Vidali, an Italian Communist known in Spain as "Carlos Contreras," who modeled the unit on a similar formation established during the Russian Civil War. If the other units still lacked the Fifth Regiment's discipline, their leaders desperately attempted to turn them from political clubs with revolutionary names into fighting units. From the south came word that the Army of Africa was moving toward Madrid.

On August 6, General Franco flew into Seville to take over command of the Army of Africa, which, in part, had been airlifted by the German *Junkers* and Italian bombers and in part had sailed over in ships escorted by rebel planes. With regular officers, Falange volunteers, some new recruits, and the reinforcements from Morocco, Franco's army was the major rebel force. Even so, Franco probably had no more than 5,000 to 6,000 men. Between Seville and Madrid, however, there was almost no defending army. Each town, large or small, that remained loyal to the Republic had an enthusiastic worker population, a ragtag militia, and a hundred potential rebels waiting deliverance on Franco's arrival.

For many, deliverance came swiftly. In the field, the commander of the Foreign Legion, Blanco Yagüe, an enthusiastic and expansive leader, led a mobile column. His advance northward became a whirling triumph. Each attack on a town became a set piece: twenty minutes of air and artillery attack to soften any resistance, then, into the trucks for a charge. If anyone fought back, a regular assault developed; if not, a triumphant parade followed. All those who had resisted, all those who had co-operated too closely with the Republic, all who belonged to "Red" organizations, and many who had simply incurred the personal wrath of the wrong persons, were shot. Nothing unusual was seen in this. The Reds were doing it. Besides, the rear had to be made secure by terror since Franco had too few troops to garrison all southern Spain. After the executions, the churches were reopened and a temporary government was appointed. Then the Legionnaires and Moors piled back into the trucks and drove madly for the next town, the next assault, and the subsequent executions. On August 10, Yagüe reached Mérida, an advance of 300 kilometers in four days. He left behind open churches, piled corpses, and a vast area sullen but secured for the Nationalists. On August 10, the Mérida militia, beefed up by 2,000 Assault Guards and loyal Civil Guards sent down from Madrid, tried to hold up Yagüe's column, but their defenses were finally broken. The next day they launched a heavy but unsuccessful counterattack. After this disaster, the Republicans scrambled back toward Madrid. Meanwhile Yagüe swung around and attacked Badajoz on the Portuguese border. Here, bloody fighting lasted all day on August 14 and through the night in the alleys and cellars of the burning town. With the city secure by the next morning, the "traitors" were taken to the bullring and shot. There were more "Reds" than usual. The executions took all that day and the next.[9]

With the formalities of conquest finished, Yagüe began a new advance eastward toward Madrid. On August 23, the advance column reached the valley of the Tagus River; there were no longer any serious natural obstacles in Franco's path. The columns of Colonel Cabanillas and Major Espinosa Castejón reached the Tagus after crossing the Guadalupe Mountains. On the way they had met the Republic's Estremadura Army under General Manuel Riquelme. The untrained Republican "Army" as usual broke under attack, but the volunteer French air squadron under André Malraux had proved more effective and nearly destroyed a section of Colonel Asensio's column near Medilla. After a pause on the Tagus for regrouping, the advance began again. Once more it was a leapfrogging set piece. The column charged. The Republican militia broke. The Anarchists refused to obey orders, even their own. No one would dig trenches. Panic followed by flight remained the order of the day. Hurriedly, the government in Madrid organized some 10,000 men into another "army" and rounded up some spare artillery. They intended to hold Talavera de la Reina, the key to both

Madrid and Toledo. There, the Republicans had a good defensive position and for once dug themselves in. Yagüe's column attacked at dawn on September 3. By noon the assault had reached the town and the Republican defense began dissolving. By midafternoon, after a brief scurry of street fighting, Yagüe secured Talavera. Between the capital and Yagüe there were no longer any organized defenses.

In Madrid, Yagüe's advance had created an atmosphere of terror and uncertainty among the masses. In political circles the highly volatile atmosphere became charged with bitter recriminations. Defeats on all sides, disasters on all fronts, and the Government still took only half measures, or at least so it seemed to the Left.

Prime Minister Giral had failed to secure aid from what had been thought to be the Republic's allies, France and Great Britain. In fact, during the first week of September, the international situation appeared worse than ever. The British Conservative Government had been concerned that the Spanish civil strife either would lead to a general European war or would so inflame international passions that a negotiated settlement of Europe's problems would be prevented. The French Government under the Socialist, León Blum, fearful of alienating the British, their only major ally against Hitler, and dreading the reaction of the French Right to involvement in Spain, delayed acting on Madrid's request to purchase arms. Finally the French came up with a plan for a Non-Intervention Agreement, which would in effect isolate Spain and allow European diplomacy to proceed along the garden path of appeasement. By September the Agreement was in force and the first meeting of the Non-Intervention Committee to enforce the policy was scheduled for London on September 9. In reality, the Agreement was to be ignored by the interested parties when it suited their purpose.

The Spanish Republican Government, now denied its international right to purchase arms, found that the only possible source of military equipment was the Soviet Union. Stalin, deeply involved in the vast and bloody purges at home and trying to balance a united front policy abroad, decided, probably some time in early September, to aid the Republic by secretly selling it arms for gold. Fearful of international reaction, Stalin limited his aid so that the Republic could continue the war but not smash Franco. In early September of 1936, neither the Spanish Government nor the people of Madrid could see much real hope in the distant and even unlikely arrival of Russian arms. Yagüe's men were too close and help was needed immediately.

The mutterings against Giral's government grew. Already master of the streets of Madrid and director of the militia army, Francisco Largo Caballero, the Left Socialist leader, wanted Giral's job. Hectic maneuvering, constant threats and shifting allies occupied President

Azaña, Giral, and Largo Caballero, as well as a growing school of mysterious, anonymous background figures who seemed to have no official positions, only powers. International revolutionist emigrés, new and unknown politicians, union leaders, and "army" commanders pulled and tugged for control of Madrid. All the while, Yagüe's flying column drew nearer. There was a food shortage. Occasionally Nationalist bombers flew over, terrifying a population innocent of air raids. There was feverish activity as speeches, giant rallies, parades of the militia whipped up enthusiasm for the war. Trials and executions continued. General Fanjul was court-martialed, found guilty as expected, and shot. Others were shot without court-martial. In August the erratic and often vindictive executions started to taper off, to be replaced by rough popular tribunals which at least cut down on accidents and personal spite.

Then, on August 23, the Model Prison caught fire, and rumor spread that the political prisoners had rebelled. With the news of the bullring at Badajoz just in and the fear of Yagüe's arrival growing, the crowd turned ugly. Led by militiamen on leave, the mob stormed the prison. Forty prisoners, those nearest to hand, were shot immediately. The following morning, thirty carefully selected "examples" were also shot. The Government, horrified, determined to stop all such irregular executions. The populace were told to lock themselves in at night and open for no one.

After this the unofficial executions ended; but, what with random bullets and the constant threat of renewed terror, life in Madrid remained uncertain, disorganized and far from secure. The majority of the people were determined to resist Franco but uncertain as to the means. "There was still no cohesion, although there was plenty of enthusiasm."[10] On September 4, 1936, Giral resigned. At last Largo Caballero would have his chance to provide the cohesion needed and to direct the enthusiasm of the masses. The moderates were falling by the wayside as Madrid prepared to receive the Nationalist assault.

Largo Caballero's new Government of Victory included two Communists, the first in any Western government, along with Alvarez del Vayo, a friend of the Communists, as Foreign Secretary and Juan Negrín, another friend of the Communists, as Minister of Finance.[11] As usual, the anarchists did not participate, refusing to contaminate their ideals with responsibility. Except for the shadow world of international revolutionaries gathering in the wings, the new Government now contained the most significant figures of the embattled Republic, and more clearly represented the Republic's supporters than had the Giral government. Whether it would be as ineffective could not be decided that first week of September, but to the outside world it did not look as if the new men would have an opportunity to govern for long.

To stave off attack, the Government of Victory sent Colonel Ascensio Torrado, commander of the Sierras, to capture Talavera with a new collection of militia, augmented by some French and Italian volunteers. Despite the courage of their assault, Ascensio Torrado's men were outmaneuevred and once more forced to retreat. This time the Army of Africa did not follow up the collapse. Instead, the loose ends were tied up: contact was made with Mola in the north, and large areas of nominally-held Republican territory to the west were cleared of "Reds." On September 12 at Salamanca, General Franco was formally chosen head of the new Nationalist Junta. Apparently he had the fewest enemies, the most useful friends, and the best army.

While the Nationalists were consolidating their military position and organizing a central government of sorts, the Republican militia again attacked in the Tagus valley. After a long day's battle, the Republicans retreated, followed cautiously by Yagüe. On September 21, the Nationalists captured Maqueda, and the way to Madrid lay open. Not once had the Army of Africa been checked. By the end of September, an increasing number of observers of all persuasions saw no reason why it would be.

The capture of Maqueda, however, had opened the way not only to Madrid but also to Toledo, only forty kilometers to the southeast. As an alternative objective to Madrid, Toledo would, under ordinary circumstances, have been instantly discarded; but, by late September, the situation in Toledo had altered. Colonel Moscardó remained sealed within the brooding Alcázar. For ten weeks his little collection of rebels had held out. Toledo was no longer simply a provincial city, but the site of the longest and most dramatic siege of the war. The Republicans had even used Moscardó's son as a hostage. When the colonel refused to barter the garrison for his son's life, they had shot him supposedly while Moscardó listened on the telephone. The Republicans then tried again and again to force the fortress. They smashed much of the barracks to rubble, poured flaming gasoline over the ruins, set off a huge mine under the debris, and yet still the rebels fought on. The Alcázar had already become a Nationalist legend.[12]

Franco faced the choice of a sudden dash against Madrid, a city filled with Reds, or a diversion to relieve Toledo. He chose Toledo. There, another victory was probably assured and, with it, great "spiritual" advantages in raising the siege of the Alcázar. Besides, Madrid was too risky. On September 23, Franco's new field commander, José Enrique Varela, replaced the hospitalized Yagüe and moved toward Toledo. The Republicans renewed their efforts against the Alcázar. On

September 25, a giant new mine toppled the northeast tower into the Tagus River. The defenders held on—Varela was only 15 kilometers away. The following day, he cut the Madrid road. On the morning of September 27, the Army of Africa launched a heavy attack against the Republican militia screening the city, and the militia broke and ran. The next day Varela entered the city and raised the siege. For the first time in two months, Moscardó and his men came out into the open. Toledo had fallen and Madrid would be next.

On October 1, General Franco, as Head of State, moved his headquarters to Salamanca to give over-all direction to the war. Varela would remain as commander in the field with Yagüe acting under him. The four columns of the army would be under Asensio, Fernando Barrón, Delgado Serrano, and Castejón. Each of these had about 1,200 men along with some technical sections. This tiny "army" of 6,000 or so men was ordered to advance on Madrid along a forty-mile front from Toledo to Maqueda. With command of the air assured (with their German and Italian friends' aid), and faced by only the Red rabble, Franco and Varela hoped that the march to Madrid would re-enact the sweep up from Seville. The attack opened on October 6. Not unexpectedly the Republican militia broke, keeping to the roads where they were more easily strafed by Franco's aircraft. On October 7, the attack continued and the militia still made no attempt to stand and fight. Planes flew over Madrid dropping leaflets demanding immediate surrender. General Mola, who took over formal command of the front for the final assault, announced he would be having coffee on the Gran Via in Madrid by October 12. All the while the Nationalist advance continued, slowly and apparently irresistibly.

Foreign correspondents, flocking into Madrid, daily reported the fall of some village or other, "the key to Madrid," and the imminent arrival of Franco and Varela. Mola's date for coffee, October 12, came and passed. A sign on a table reserved his chair—no one was quite sure if it were a bad joke or not. On October 17, Illescas, halfway between Madrid and Toledo, fell. On October 19, 6,000 militiamen, in a wild attack, broke Castejón's lines but crumbled under a counterattack. On October 20, General Ascensio Torrado led another disorganized attack of 15,000 militia on Illescas. In Madrid the Republican troops had been piled into double-decker buses. They were driven across the flat plain toward Illescas while the Nationalists watched until their artillery had zeroed in. The ensuing bombardment took much of the élan out of the attack. By October 23, Varela had driven Ascensio Torrado back toward Madrid; and for the first time the rumble of guns could be heard in the city.

In Madrid, President Azaña, despondent over the growing collapse and the fate of Spain (no matter who won), left Madrid without telling his cabinet. He retired to the monastery of Montserrat to sit out the war. For him the Republic was already lost; moderation had disappeared under the pressures of war and revolution. The vise around Madrid grew tighter. The commander in the city, General Luis Castelló, went insane. He was replaced by old General José Miaja, who looked and often acted like a shrewd peasant wearing steel-rimmed spectacles. Many thought him as mad as Castelló for taking the job; however, since there was nothing to be done, Miaja might as well do it. On October 24, General Sebastián Pozas took over command of the Republican Army of the Center. The title and unit names were a hopeful delusion. The Republican Army simply did not exist. With one or two exceptions, the political militia units had proved hopeless in the field. Driven back regularly, these broken units had almost reached the suburbs of the city supposedly defended by Miaja, who had neither the troops nor the equipment to do anything but retreat. On October 24, a sudden advance by the Nationalists threatened the road to Valencia, the escape route to the south. Despite all, the city's population retained their faith, but anxiety and uncertainty increased. The Government of Victory had neither led them to victory nor inspired them to seek it. Except for a few fanatics and optimists, all in power were gloomy, unsure, and wavering. They continued their hopeful speeches and exhortations to resist but in hollow voices. The rumors remained very bad. Then, with the Nationalists almost in the suburbs, the rumors suddenly took a turn for the better: help was coming.

At first the reports of new arms and troops had been discredited as wishful thinking by certain members of the Communist Party. During October the steady trickle of international Communists into Spain had stiffened some militia units. The promises of Russian help or of Comintern help, despite the restrictions of the Non-Intervention Committee, grew more specific. As yet the people of Madrid had seen nothing and heard little they could believe. Some few, however, knew that help was truly on the way.

The longed-for assistance to the Republic would assume two forms, arms and men. The first was modern Russian war matériel, particularly tanks and planes, accompanied by technical advisors and instructors. The Soviet equipment, especially the fighter planes, was first-rate, often equal or superior to the German and Italian equipment used by Franco. The Soviet tank, however, was highly vulnerable to most fire and generally proved ineffectual; but much the same could be said for the German and the Italian light tanks. The "advisors," particularly if they were pilots, often participated in battle despite Stalin's admonition to stay behind the lines. Along with the Russian equipment, from time to time, depending on the delicacy of the international situation, the French Government opened the border to arms shipments. The Mexican Government, in sympathy with Republican ideals, sold what it could, which was very little. As a result of the effectiveness of the arms embargo and the limited supplies available from France and Mexico, the Republic had to depend on material purchased with gold from Russia. The Soviet decision to sell had been taken early in September, when it became clear that without Russian intervention, Franco, aided by Hitler and Mussolini, would sweep on to Madrid. Stalin decided to go ahead, although he did not want the "advisors" to become mixed up in the war. After all, there was no point in annoying the hypocritical Anglo-French Non-Intervention Committee nor in publicly challenging Germany and Italy. The transfer of arms would be enough. Russian ships, carrying military supplies, began leaving ports on the Black Sea. By early October, these ships began arriving at Republican ports.[13]

More dramatic had been the worldwide enthusiasm to volunteer for service in the Republic's struggle against darkness and fascism. Carefully nurtured by the Communist propaganda machine, this enthusiasm had been channeled into what became known as the International Brigades. Despite the fact that the Brigades were conceived, organized, and secretly directed by the international wing of Stalin's government, the Comintern, most of the members were idealists. Many were not Communists; all were true believers in the Republic's cause. The impulse to fight in Spain had risen from a variety of motives ranging from political commitment to boredom. The long-term dedicated Communists simply had to discipline the impulse. Although the total strength of the Brigades at any one time probably never exceeded 30,000 in Spain and far fewer in the front lines, the volunteers, with their ability to take enormous casualties without crumbling and their consequent value as shock troops, were vital. Thus the International Brigade became one of the more curious military units in recent history. With few exceptions its leaders had long careers of revolutionary agitation behind them, and, in some cases, a name and fame to come. A list of brigade commanders during the Spanish War reads like a "Who's Who of the Far Left" after World War Two. Among them were the Czech Gottwald, Gerö and Rajk of Hungary, André Marty and Maurice Thorez of France. The Yugoslav Tito organized aid, and the German Ulbricht was involved in supplying the Brigade. By 1960 in Yugoslavia, twenty-four generals had fought in Spain. From Italy alone came Palmiro Togliatti, future head of the Italian Communist Party, and his successor, Luigi Longo, as well as Giuseppe de Vittorio, who would become Secretary-General of the great Italian union, General Confederation of Italian Labor, and Pietro Nenni, long-time leader of the

Italian Socialist Party. What is perhaps more remarkable is that these men often had to survive the recurring waves of Stalinist purges as well as a decade of war, revolution, and resistance. Their subsequent survival and remarkable success in the tortuous swamps of Communist politics should more than anything else reveal the nature of their success as commanders of the International Brigades. Even the non-Communists or those whose beliefs changed or matured, André Malraux, for example, had the same spirit and determination. Thus, led by the dedicated, their ranks filled with idealists, intellectuals, and exiles holding a variety of beliefs and coming from scores of countries, the Brigades proved to be the Republic's most reliable units. The volunteers often had only courage and conviction in common. Neither boded well for a long life on the front lines, but from such virtues battles are won. Hastily trained during the fall, in camps surrounding Albacete, by the end of October the first Brigade was almost ready to move.[14]

On October 28, on Radio Madrid, Largo Caballero once more promised the Madrileños deliverance, but this time he was more specific:

> *The time has come to deliver a deathblow. Our power of taking the offensive is growing. We have at our disposal a formidable mechanized armament. We have tanks and powerful aeroplanes. Listen, comrades! At dawn, our artillery and armoured trains will open fire. Immediately, our aircraft will attack. Tanks will advance on the enemy at his most vulnerable point.*[15]

At dawn on October 29 after the preparatory bombardment, the Russian General Pavlov's massed light tanks smashed into the Nationalist cavalry and drove them back into the narrow streets of Esquivas. There, for some time, a wild battle between cavalry and tanks swung in and out of the narrow streets, as both sides tried to decide how to attack the other. There was no infantry support for Pavlov. Lister's Fifth Regiment, down from the Sierras, could not catch up on foot. Pavlov saw no future in chasing horses around the block, so he withdrew. On the same day, Nationalist planes began bombing Madrid, the first major city to suffer repeated modern air raids. With the Nationalist bombers flying unhindered over the city and the creeping ground advance again under way, the momentary optimism following Pavlov's tank attack oozed away.

On November 4, the Nationalists took Getafe. Varela informed a press conference, "You can announce to the world Madrid will be captured this week."[16] Largo Caballero had made no preparations for a siege. There were no trenches and still no regular troops to fill them if they had existed. The people had not even erected barricades. The air bombings grew in intensity. Without shelters or proper firefighting equipment, Madrid remained totally unprepared for the raids. With the city burning and the sounds of Franco's guns drawing closer each morning, the battle of Madrid seemed over before it had really begun. The Russian tanks had been no real help. Rumors of more aid were thus not very encouraging.

The world press agreed with Varela, the city would fall within a week. The German Foreign Minister, Constantin von Neurath, drew up a note to send to the Republican Chargé d'Affairs in Berlin, informing him of Berlin's intention to recognize Franco. It began, "Since General Franco has captured the Spanish capital of Madrid. . . ."[17]

On November 5, Varela took the suburbs of Alcorón and Leganés. Russian fighters with red-tipped wings appeared over Madrid for the first time, but the Nationalists maintained control of the air. There was a short breathing spell while Yagüe finished up the staff work for the last great thrust into the heart of the city. Apparently only confusion, despair and bitterness awaited the Republican army.

> *The air of the town was laden with tension, unrest, distrust, physical fear and challenge, as it was laden with unreasoning, embittered will to fight on. We walked side by side, arm in arm, with Death.*[18]

On the afternoon of November 6, Largo Caballero informed General Miaja that the Government of Victory was being evacuated to Valencia. He left Miaja in charge of the looming disaster. If the will to resist existed, let Miaja discover it. Miaja and his officers, particularly his Chief-of-Staff, Lieutenant-Colonel Rojo, felt they could hold, as did Lister of the Fifth Regiment. The Russian advisors, I. A. Berzin and I. Koniev (later Marshal of the Red Army), were confident the city could be defended.[19] Miaja spent much of the night on the telephone rallying support for a last-ditch stand. He told the union leaders he wanted 50,000 volunteers. He told the militia officers that the crucial hour had come. While he promised relief in the future, he did not hide the seriousness of the situation; in fact, he could not have glossed over the odds if he had wanted to do so. All Madrid could hear Franco's guns. At dawn a growing wave of enthusiasm and determination began to spread among the common people. Radio Madrid came on with the news that there would be no retreat. The workers were urged to build barricades. *La Pasionaria* even suggested that the women drop boiling oil on the Fascists. More important than flimsy barricades and passionate speeches was the rapid realization that Miaja meant to stay, that someone believed Madrid could be held. To the west, Varela's bombardment began. At dawn on November 7, the guns sounded very close.

Varela expected Yagüe to drive across the flat Casa de Campo, brushing aside the Republican militia and fording the Manzanares River. By dusk his troops should have scaled the heights beyond the river and occupied Montaña Barracks. After that the city would be his. When the 6,000 advanced at dawn, they ran into difficulties immediately.

The Republicans did not run. Instead of a sudden thrust across the Casa de Campo, the attack ground on in a series of bitter, little battles. For once, the militia, with their backs against Madrid, did not break, but stayed and died. All day, Miaja, in the basement headquarters of the *Junta,* and his Russian advisor, General Berzin, down the hall, sifted the conflicting and emotional battle reports, sent out reinforcements, and waited.

At dusk the fighting slackened. Yagüe had not reached the Manzanares. He had managed only to seize Mount Garabitas in the middle of the Casa de Campo. For Madrid, it was as good as a victory. Michael Kol'tsov, part correspondent and part Stalinist agent, wired *Pravda,* "In twenty minutes it will be midnight. We too have had a holiday."[20]

The next day, Sunday, November 8, Varela attacked again. The air raids on Madrid grew in intensity; large fires burned almost unchecked. The subways were crammed with thousands of refugees. Hurried blackout regulations were put into effect. All the intricate habits of living under bombs, soon to become so familiar throughout much of the world, were hastily developed in Madrid.

It was not only the planes. All morning Varela's shells smashed into the ultramodern University City on the western edge of the city. From the Casa de Campo, the sounds of continuing fighting drifted across the city to mingle with the crunch of artillery shells and the crackle of burning buildings. Just before noon, suddenly, without any warning, the XI International Brigade, dressed in corduroy uniforms with blue berets, their rifles and helmets slung over their shoulders, came marching in perfect step down the Gran Via toward the front. Madrid was not alone. There were 1,900 men—Germans, French, Belgians, Poles, and British—under General Emilio Kléber (whose real name was Lazar Stern). They were immediately spread out as stiffening among the militia holding the Casa de Campo. By dark the brigade was ready.

Varela switched his attack the next day from the Casa de Campo, where the Brigade waited, south to the suburb of Carabanchel. His Moors made little progress in a day of confused street fighting. Back on the Casa de Campo front, Kléber reassembled his Brigade, and in the misty evening charged into the Nationalist positions. The uncertain engagement lasted all night as the Nationalists fought back, abandoning their positions only grudgingly. By dawn on November 10, all that remained to them was Mount Garabitas. Varela temporarily gave up trying to enter Madrid across the Casa de Campo. The Brigade had blunted his attack, but at the cost of nearly 700 casualties.

To the south heavy fighting continued around Carabanchel for three days. On November 12, the new XII International Brigade arrived. It was made up of the usual curious mixture of revolutionaries, poets, and rebels, including Winston Churchill's nephew, Giles Romilly. After an exhausting march, they attacked on the same day, in a babble of languages, across strange ground. Not unexpectedly, the charge faltered short of the objective and had to be called off. The Brigade was withdrawn and moved north.

At the same time, Buenaventura Durruti arrived in Madrid with an independent brigade of 3,000 Anarchists. Miaja was finally persuaded, at this point, by his Russian advisors that the best defense was a series of limited attacks. Miaja and Rojo still considered a bitter defensive war of attrition more practical and productive, but they were willing to back up an attack by Durruti's men with all the artillery and air support available. On November 15, Durruti tried to attack, but his Anarchists would not move into the Moors' machine-gun fire. Humiliated, Durruti promised Miaja that they would attack at dawn on November 16. They never got the chance.

Varela had again switched his main effort back to the Casa de Campo, and *he* attacked at dawn. Asensio's column broke through the Anarchist-held front and reached the Manzanares River. The Anarchists drove him back. Twice more he smashed forward, before his troops got a foothold under the University City. The Nationalists then brought an artillery bombardment down on the Anarchists and attacked again. By this time the point of the attacking force had been whittled down to two Moorish units and one Foreign Legion *bandera.*

When they charged into what was expected to be massive resistance, they found no one. The Anarchists had fled. Hurriedly, the Moors and Legionnaires began occupying University City. They seized the School of Architecture and moved on. By default, the key western heights were about to be occupied by a handful of Nationalist troops. Varela rushed up more men. Columns under Colonels Delgado Serrano and Barrón began crossing the river and moving up behind the Moors. On the Republic's side, Miaja, after a week of successful defense, suddenly found the door to the city open. The XI International Brigade was rushed up to occupy the Hall of Philosophy and Letters. All night, the confused, uncertain fighting continued. Neither side was certain as to the positions of the other. Each building became a fort, every room a strong point. By dawn on November 17, the XI Brigade had secured part of the University, but the situation was by no means stable.

For Madrid November 17 was the worst day of all. The Moors and the Legion were actually in the city, just how deep no one knew. No one really knew what the chances of the defense were, either. The air raids, despite the Russian fighters, had become more intensive. Large sections, particularly in the workers' quarters, had caught fire and still burned. Despite a steady stream of evacuees down the Valencia road, the city remained jammed with refugees. There was no real shelter for anyone. The Nationalist artillery joined the air bombardment. With the troops locked so closely in University City, all of Madrid became a target. The thirteen-story tower of the Telephone Company, the one skyscraper, was hit again and again. No great city had ever been attacked from the air day after day. The moralists were appalled at Franco's brutality, the military observers curious as to the effects of terror, the correspondents fascinated by the casual courage of the civilians.

With his troops wedged into the University City, facing the prospect of one room after another filled with Republicans, Franco threatened to destroy the city rather than leave it to the Reds. On the night of the 17th, it seemed as if he actually would. Stretched far beyond their capacity, the primitive civilian defense organizations could not cope with the situation. The volunteer workers tried hopelessly to put out fires scattered all over the city. The Duke of Alba's palace, filled with art works, was hit and began to burn. The firefighters, determined to show the Republic's respect for beauty, rushed into the burning palace to save the Nationalist Duke's art treasures. In the billowing smoke and flames, the militiamen suddenly realized that they were not too sure just what an art work looked like. They did the best they could. The first "art work" saved proved to be a large stuffed polar bear, followed by several knights in armor, and, somewhat later, the treasured paintings, which were piled up on the wet ground in an untidy heap.[21] The palace continued to burn as did seemingly most of Madrid.

The struggle for the University City became the key, the whole focus of military concern for both sides. Locked together in the smoldering ruins of former King Alfonso's new educational complex, the two armies punished each other day after day. Firing from behind barricades made from piles of volumes on German philosophy and Indian religion, struggling through shattered laboratories and smoldering seminar rooms, the International Brigade held out. Each room became a miniature battlefield. Grenades were rolled down steps or sent up on elevators to explode on the floor above. The Republicans soon discovered one of the key defensive facts of modern city warfare: ruined concrete buildings make an almost impenetrable fortification. Despite the stubborn resistance, the Foreign Legion and Moors pushed on, taking Santa Cristina Hospital and the Institutes of Hygiene and Cancer. There, some of the Moors cheerfully cooked and ate the inoculated laboratory animals, only to die later of a variety of rare diseases. The Nationalists held two-thirds of the University. Some Moors pushed on at one point to break out into the Plaza de España. They were all killed. This was Varela's farthest advance. The Brigade still held on to the ruined Hall of Philosophy and Letters, blocking his progress into Madrid. By November 23, the air raids slackened and the Nationalists gave up attacking, seemingly content to hold their wedge into the city. The great head-on attack, begun on November 7, had ended.

To the more objective observers on the Nationalist side, the growing risk of trying to take Madrid by frontal assault became clear when the breakthrough at University City turned into bloody fighting. There were other factors to consider. On November 16, the Germans had decided to recognize Franco without waiting for the final fall of Madrid.[22] Hitler had thus committed himself to a final, if not immediate, Franco victory. Consequently an immediate victory, even if possible, need not be bought at too great a price. The correspondents on both sides of the battle front were not so cautious. The confidence of the Nationalists, coupled with reports of the burning city, seemed to augur an early collapse of Republican resistance, according to the press in Franco's camp. Within the city, the reporters, cut off from official sources and limited to rumor and uncertain peeks to the west, also decided the city was falling. Their reports, often printed as fact, led distant observers to accept the fall of the city.

But the Nationalist commanders, particularly those tied down in the bitter fighting inside University City, were hardly sanguine. After the failure of the first dash by the Moors into the city, the Republicans were growing stronger day by day. Franco decided to call off the fighting within the city before his small army disappeared in a war of attrition. Depending on the *quality* of his men, he could not afford to trade them with the untrained militia. He did, however, refuse to withdraw from his wedge inside the University City. His German advisors insisted on withdrawal so that proper use could be made of air and artillery bombardment. It would not do to retreat, he said; instead, he would go over to the defensive inside the city. During the last week in November both sides had begun tunneling and fortifying their front lines. The battle of Madrid would take more than a few weeks.

Behind the rubble of University City, a great haze of oily smoke covered Madrid, dripping soot everywhere. Streets were filled with ashes, broken glass, and great lumps of blasted masonry. The fashionable shops, the famous bars and restaurants, were boarded shut, the theaters closed. During the day, the streets were filled with soldiers on leave from the front, workers in bleak clothes wearing bright badges, and an occasional commandeered car. Long lines, especially for coal and food, were always in front of the various party distribution centers. The only touches of color were the huge revolutionary posters covering the free space on every wall. At night there was no color, no light, little movement. The bars closed at eight. Everyone huddled, cold and anxious, at home. The air wardens shot out lights. Since there was a curfew, they might shoot at stray pedestrians as well. Every week more civilians were sent to Valencia, but the huge wave of refugees had raised Madrid's population from one million to a million and a half. Surprisingly few of either the new or the old Madrileños wanted to leave, and many had to be driven away by appeals to their patriotism. There were not enough houses, little food, less coal. A few could be incorporated into Madrid's small but growing war industry. In 1936, however, the civilians wanted to stay with their city or what was left of it. Years later the damage done to Madrid would seem minor in contrast to Dresden, Rotterdam or Toyko, but during the bitter, burnt-out winter of 1936–1937, the ruined city had become a symbol for its inhabitants of their willingness to suffer and to die for the Republic.

Franco's new Madrid commander, General Luis Orgaz, could see little profit in renewing the costly street fighting. The Madrid defenses had *not* collapsed when weakest on November 7, and with growing discipline and reinforcements from the International Brigades, not even heavy bombing and shelling seemed likely to change the situation. The obvious alternative appeared to be an offensive elsewhere. There was a strong possibility that the Republican forces would be too fully committed in Madrid, too slow in shifting their militia troops even a short distance. The direction of the new offensive was 15 miles to the north, toward the Madrid–Corunna road. If all went well, a very swift, sharp attack would cut the road a few miles south of El Escorial. With the road connection broken, the Republican forces in the Guadarrama Mountains would be isolated; further, the Nationalists would be in a position either to infiltrate Madrid's defenses from the north or to draw the net still tighter around the city. Varela, the attack commander, would have four mobile brigades, made up of 17,000 infantry and cavalry. He would face a mixed and unprepared collection of Republican battalions under Major Barceló, a regular army officer who had joined the Communist Party. The Republican line was really not a line at all. During most of the war neither army had enough troops to defend a continuous front. Except for one or two bitterly contested battle areas, the "lines" of the two armies were little more than scattered bands of ill-armed men shivering or sweating on alternate hilltops, more concerned with the weather than with fields of fire. Consequently when Varela attacked on December 13, the Republicans under Barceló were driven back. Varela took Boadilla on December 14, but Miaja had aid on the way. The Russian tanks of Pavlov, nearly useless in Madrid's street fighting, were reintroduced. Both International Brigades were snatched out of the line in Madrid and rushed to the threatened sector. A Republican counterattack recaptured Boadilla, but the Nationalists returned in bloody hand-to-hand fighting and took the village back.

For two weeks minor, confused fighting continued as both sides rushed in men for the decisive moment. General Orgaz ordered in conscript troops and Falangist units, trained by the German officers at Cáceres. The Republicans sent in Brigade units under three odd, if typical, new commanders: Gustavo Durán, a composer; Cipriano Mera, the leading Anarchist general, who lacked the flair of many of his faith, but proved more successful as a commander; and *El Campesino* ("the Peasant"), a huge, vulgar man with a foul mouth and a fine talent for leading his men in action. The Republicans now felt that their northern flank along the Corunna Road had been secured. They were somewhat optimistic. On the morning of January 3, the Nationalists attacked in strength. Within twenty-four hours their point had reached Las Rozas on the Madrid–El Escorial railroad. There the advance finally slowed because the Republicans had hurriedly fortified all the summer villas, almost ideally placed like ready-made pillboxes scattered across the flat plain with interlocking fields of fire.

But the new system of German tactics, the *blitzkrieg*, proved an instant success. Miaja's lines sheared open. The Republicans became confused and uncertain. Ammunition ran so short that blanks had to be issued, and morale fell so low that mock executions were carried out to intimidate potential deserters. To fill the gaps in his line, Miaja began snatching men off the Madrid front. Lister's Brigade was transferred north. Miaja persuaded Largo Caballero to rush the XIV International Brigade from Cordoba.

Nothing availed. The Nationalist advance continued, but Orgaz began to lose heavily in the face of the costly defense put up by the retreating brigades. The Thaelmann Battalion mistakenly held out at one strong point long after the brigade commander had ordered them out of the deathtrap. Although the battalion was destroyed as a fighting unit, its machine guns badly mauled the Nationalists. Despite heavy losses, by January 9, Orgaz held ten kilometers of the highway beyond the last houses outside Madrid, toward El Escorial. On the following day, January 10, the XIV and XII International Brigades arrived in Madrid. With no rest and but little preparation, they were thrown into a hurried counterattack the following morning. Taking advantage of a heavy mist and backed up by Pavlov's tanks, the Republicans smashed into the unsuspecting Nationalists' forward positions. From January 12 to 15 brutal, confused fighting continued along the Corunna Road. On the next day, January 16, both sides began digging trenches and the battle of Corunna Road was over.

Orgaz had lost about 15,000 men in ten days,[23] more than had been lost in the advance from Seville to the University City. His losses almost totaled the number of men he had originally committed on December 13, a staggering cost for ten kilometers of road. Miaja, at the last possible minute, had prevented Orgaz from cutting off the north, but he too had lost 15,000 men, including brutal losses in the International Brigades. Still, Madrid was safe. The November thrust had ended in the ruins of the University City; now the flanking *blitzkrieg* to the north had been blunted.

Despite Orgaz's heavy losses, the Nationalists were far from despondent. Their armies were now better equipped, thanks to the Germans, and far stronger, thanks to the Italians. The Germans, organized mainly into the Condor Legion, with the army forces commanded by Colonel Walter Warlimont, and the air volunteers under General Hugo Sperrle, totaled about 14,000 men. These were mainly technicians, signal corps and artillery specialists, pilots, and, in particular, a group of tank experts under Von Thoma. The Germans, and especially Göring, were quite anxious to try out their new equipment and tactics; for example, how effective would the new Messerschmitt 109B prove, and what would be the best formation in fighter actions? The Italians were less pragmatic; Mussolini wanted glory, not statistics. During the fall and winter, he sent in "volunteer" formations until his commitment ballooned to some 60,000 troops on the mainland, with full supporting equipment, and an occupation force on the island of Majorca which numbered 10,000 men and 150 airplanes. For the Nationalists, the heavy Italo-German intervention supplied almost all their modern equipment, a substantial body of trained troops desperately needed, and a stream of highly competent, if not always welcome, advice. Franco, always prone to prudence even over pride, often preferred the slow, sure move rather than the innovations suggested by his allies. All agreed that they must maintain the initiative by renewing the attack, however. Another attack around Corunna Road seemed as pointless as renewing the war in University City. Franco decided to switch to the south.

Depending heavily on the Army of Africa, but with German support, Franco could cut across the Jarama River and break the Madrid–Valencia road link, achieving in the south what had escaped him in the north. The offensive would have five mobile brigades, supported by six 155-mm. batteries and a Condor Legion artillery group of the new 88-mm. guns.[24] Thrusting out along a north-to-south front against the Republican Army of the Center, the Nationalists hoped to achieve their major objectives before the Republicans under Pozas could respond. On February 6, the brigade under General García Escámez smashed into the newly formed Republican 18th Brigade, which, as expected, collapsed. The Republican "line" quickly proved as weak as the northern flank had been in December. To the north Ricardo de Rada's column advanced, taking the La Maranosa peak despite the resistance of two Republican battalions, which fought to the last man. On February 7, General Barrón's brigade reached the juncture of the Jarama and Manzanares rivers. His artillery began shelling the Madrid–Valencia road. One more heavy thrust across the Jarama and through the confused and disheartened Republican brigades would finish off Pozas.

In Madrid on February 8, Miaja was well aware that yet again the fate of Madrid hung in the balance. His staff began the hectic shuffling of troops to the south to new positions as yet unprepared. They sent the crack Brigades of Lister and *El Campesino,* committed the XI International Brigade, and then waited to see if they had moved in time. All during the following day, while the Nationalists ground closer to the Jarama River along the entire front, Pozas and his commanders hurriedly tried to reorganize their defense along the high ground east of the river. They finally managed to establish a reserve of sorts, including the XII International Brigade and the Garibaldi Battalion. This meant that (just as in the north) the Republicans had somehow managed to fill out the front in time. On the following day, February 10, the Nationalists failed to cross the Jarama River.

In the early hours of the morning of February 11, several Moors slipped along the Pindoque Bridge over the Jarama. They quietly knifed one sentry after another until the bridge was cleared. Then two regiments of Nationalist cavalry pounded down to the Pindoque and over the Jarama with hardly a shot being fired. The Republicans immediately detonated the explosive charges under the bridge. With the roar of the explosion the bridge rose in the air a few feet, paused, and then settled slowly back, damaged but quite passable. In the meantime, using similar tactics, Barrón crossed the river further north at the Arganda Bridge. By afternoon he had his brigade across despite the Republican air attacks and the stubborn resistance of the André Marty Battalion. At Pindoque, the Garibaldi Battalion moved up to the commanding high ground and pinned down the bridgehead. Asensio's column took all day to force its way over, but by dawn his men had taken the heights above the bridge. With Barrón over and linked up, the two could join in a new offensive wave. The situation was again growing ticklish for the Republicans. Despite Republican control of the air for the first time, the Nationalists had crossed the Jarama in strength.

On February 12, the XV International Brigade, including British and American battalions, was committed to battle for the first time. The British held up Asensio's and Sáenz de Buruaga's assaults for over seven hours, but in the process the battalion was all but destroyed. By dusk only 225 out of the original 600 members were still alive.[25] Sáenz de Buruaga tried to continue the advance but ran into the other International Brigades plus Russian tanks, and his attack stopped cold. The Nationalists had now committed all their reserves.[26] The Republican defenses had not broken; in fact, their pressure had increased all around the bridgeheads. On February 15, Miaja took personal command of the battle, integrating it with his Madrid command as the Second Army Corps under Colonel Ricardo Burillo. The final crisis point had been reached. Sáenz de Buruaga now attacked again and reached the first heights above the Jarama but could get no further.

On February 17, the new Republican Second Corps under Burillo counterattacked in force. One division drove Barrón well back across the Valencia road; another column crossed the Manzanares River and dug in. On February 23 and 27, the Republicans hit the Nationalists between the Pingarrón and San Martín, their strongest front. It was here that the 450-man American Abraham Lincoln Battalion saw action for the first time. For many of the men it was the only time. Their head-on attacks were smashed and the battalion almost destroyed. On the first day it lost 120 killed and 175 wounded. There was no second day—the shattered survivors were withdrawn. For his part, Orgaz, on February 23 and March 1, tried two heavy attacks. These were not so much part of the dying battle of Jarama as preparation for a new offensive elsewhere. They were extremely costly failures with 6,000 casualties and no ground gained.

The Battle of Jarama was all but over. The Nationalists had gained another thin slice of Republican territory 15 kilometers by 20 kilometers but at a cost of 20,000 men. The Republicans had held on to the Valencia road and protected Madrid's flank, but at a cost of 25,000 men. It was a stalemate again, another Corunna Road. Now, both north and south of Madrid, an intricate system of defenses had grown up, too strong to be breached without immense losses.

Franco's Italian allies had come up with a new plan as early as February 13 which opened up other possibilities. The Italians, encouraged by their easy conquest of Malaga early in February, now wanted another swift victory, or at least Mussolini did. General Mario Roatta commanded the Italian volunteers, organized into four divisions with exotic Fascist names—Black Shirts, Black Flames, Black Arrows, and more prosaically the Littorio Division. Roatta felt that his troops were well-equipped and sufficiently trained to face his "second-rate" opponents. They could easily give Mussolini the major victory he desired. Roatta's assessment of both his men and their equipment was in time to prove rather inaccurate. The Italian legionaries and their officers were not equipped for adversity. In preparing their attack plan, Roatta's staff made no provision for the possibility of bad weather, nor did they expect serious resistance. Fed for years on Fascist rhetoric and elaborate praise, the officers believed their own press clippings. The Republican troops around Madrid were far better disciplined and led than those who had collapsed in front of the Italians at Malaga and the new Russian equipment was in many cases superior to that of the Italians. The Italians chose to ignore the difficulties. Roatta felt that with the help of some Spanish troops on one flank and a diversionary attack by Orgaz on the Jarama front, his men could drive on Madrid from the northeast, down the Henares River valley to Guadalajara and from there on into Madrid. Franco accepted the proposal. It was a far more ambitious plan than he had supported at Corunna Road and Jarama, but the Italians were eager and the Spanish commitment small.

In Madrid there was a growing feeling that perhaps the worst was over. Miaja had twice prevented Varela and Orgaz from outflanking the city. The International Brigades had proved immensely effective, and regular reinforcements from the training camps kept them up to strength, despite appalling losses. The arrival of the Soviet fighter planes had for the first time given the Republic mastery of the air over Madrid. While this meant a great deal to the military commanders, it meant even more to the civilians, who during the fall and winter had had to suffer the Nationalist raids. Now, this momentary euphoria was about to be shattered.

On March 7, Roatta was ready to move. On his right the Soria Division under General Moscardó of the Alcazar was made up of 20,000 Legionnaires, Moors, and Carlists. His left, the main attack force, was to be all Italian, 30,000 men supported by 250 tanks and with 70 trucks attached to each battalion. There were 180 pieces of motorized artillery in close support of the mobile columns and 50 fighters and 12 reconnaissance aircraft. As usual, the Republican line in the quiet northern sector consisted of newly organized, poorly trained troops.

On March 8, General Giovanni Coppi's Black Flames Division

broke the two new Republican divisions with a motorized infantry and armored car attack, using the new German *blitzkrieg* tactics. To the west, Moscardó pushed aside the feeble Republican lines across the Soria Road. Once more the Republicans had been surprised. "All our battles had started in chaos. We were all amateurs, Russians, Spaniards and 'Internationals' alike."[27]

The great Italian offensive was away to a grand start, but within a few hours little problems began to appear. At noon the temperature began dropping; fog appeared, then sleet, and the roads iced over. Italian planes flying out of temporary fields far to the north had to be grounded. The Republicans, however, had a Russian squadron based at Barajas near Guadalajara. Although the weather was grim, the Russians were able to take off and harass the Italian advance. Despite the weather and the Russians, the Italian advance continued all the next day.

By midmorning Coppi had taken Almadrones and Masegasa, widening the great gap in the Republican front. General Nuvolari's Black Arrows moved up and took over the center of the line. General Moscardó continued his stolid drive, capturing Gogulludo. Roatta was not satisfied. Orgaz had not moved at Jarama. The Nationalist headquarters was not very encouraging about the date of the anticipated diversionary attack. After the two previous ventures and the loss of 6,000 men, Franco was apparently going to let the Italians do their own fighting. Roatta also did not like the Republican domination of the air and the miserable weather, but there was little he could do about either. At least his troops were moving ahead.

On the other side of the hill, the Republicans were going through their usual task of desperately rounding up troops and shipping them north to plug the hole in their line. A new Fourth Army Corps, under the command of Colonel Jurado, was shipped off. Other troops were moved to fill out a new front south of the Italian line of advance. The newly organized 11th Division under Lister, composed of the XI International Brigade, *El Campesino*'s men, a Basque unit, and an ex-Communist First Brigade, moved into the woods along the road from Trijueque to Torija. Cipriano Mera, with the XII International Brigade spearheaded by the Garibaldi Battalion, held the Brihuega–Torija Road. The little town of Brihuega now lay halfway between the newly constructed Republican line and the point of the Italian advance.

At dawn on March 10, the Black Flames of Coppi and the Black Arrows of Nuvolari moved into the town. The Littorio Division under Bergonzoli was still in reserve. Moscardó continued his steady, unopposed advance down the banks of the Henares River to Jadraque, but his deliberate movements had become secondary. The battle would be won or lost south of Brihuega, not on the flank. At noon the Garibaldi Battalion (Longo, Togliatti, Nenni and company) advanced north toward Brihuega, unaware that the Fascist Italians had already occupied the village. A mile or so short they ran into an Italian cyclist from Coppi's division who spoke and rode on. When Coppi learned that there were Italians south of Brihuega, he assumed that they belonged to Nuvolari's division and continued his own advance. When the commanders of the Garibaldi Battalion heard Italian spoken by the cyclist, they assumed Italian members of an International Brigade were to their north. The battalion pushed on until it made contact with the rest of the XI International Brigade, equally far advanced and unaware of the presence of the Fascists. Suddenly Coppi's light tanks appeared. The Garibaldi Italians recovered first and opened up with heavy machine-gun fire. The Black Flame infantry attacked. For a while both sides were thrown into considerable confusion, until they could figure out which Italians to shoot. Once this had been solved satisfactorily, they settled down to a private civil war centered on the Ibarra Palace. Some Communist leaders had great hopes that the misguided Fascist soldiers, workers and peasants all, would switch sides as soon as the issues had been made clear. A huge loudspeaker and propaganda team was rushed to the front.

This maneuver was regarded with a jaundiced eye by most of the Garibaldi Battalion, who feared they might lose their chance to kill Il Duce's Fascists. One Abyssinian volunteer was particularly horrified that after a journey from the heart of Africa all the way to the center of Spain he was going to lose his chance to revenge his country.[28] For the most part, the loudspeakers on both sides, Republican planes dropping leaflets, and the shouted pleas to desert were not too effective. A few Fascist Italian "volunteers" did surrender and a few were shot while trying to. After that, desertions trailed off, and the Italian civil war around the Ibarra Palace continued.

On March 11, the Black Arrows broke Lister's 11th Division front and captured Trijueque and drove on down the road toward Torija. The Republican position suddenly became critical. The Thaelmann Battalion had been badly mauled but its Chief-of-Staff, Ludwig Renn, managed to collect enough men to hold the road (Torija–Trijueque), while the Garibaldi Battalion continued its control of the Trijueque Road from Brihuega. On March 12, Republican bombers attacked the Italian mechanized column crawling along roads behind the front. Roatta's Chief-of-Staff, General Luizzi, was killed and morale among the Fascists was shaken. Then Lister attacked. His 11th Division, led by Pavlov's tanks, recaptured Trijueque. Many of the Italians surrendered to the Thaelmann Battalion and *El Campesino* Brigade. The Republicans continued along the road to Brihuega, and the Garibaldi Battalion finally captured the Ibarra Palace. The following day, Roatta fed in his other two divisions one at a time, General Rossi's Black Shirts and General Bergonzoli's Littorio Division. Both Fascist counterattacks were beaten off. On March 14, Pavlov's tanks rumbled unimpeded up the road toward Siguenza. Although the tanks captured a considerable amount of abandoned equipment, their foray had to be called off short of Siguenza, since there was no mobile Republican infantry to follow up the thrust.

As had been the case with the Nationalist offensive at Corunna Road and Jarama, an immediate success had bogged down so badly that the initiative had been lost. Obviously, the next step was an attack by the Republicans, but Jurado and Lister decided to wait until the troops had recovered and more reinforcements could be brought up. So there occurred a lengthy pause. Roatta left for Salamanca, to complain to the Nationalists about Orgaz's failure to attack on the Jarama front. In the interim the only preparations made to meet a Republican attack consisted of shooting "cowards" and explaining to the troops that "today we are victoriously resting after reaching our objective in order to take breath before continuing our advance."[29] Il Duce sent his greetings. The men were informed that the enemy was "a rabble of adventurers without faith."[30] Since special orders had to be sent out to watch for self-inflicted wounds and since executions for cowardice continued, some of the "volunteers" obviously were unimpressed with the victorious advance and even less interested in continuing it. Two more days passed with little activity.

On March 18, the entire Republican Fourth Army Corps went over to the offensive. At half-past one, eighty Republican bombers cratered the surroundings of Brihuega. Heavy artillery fire centered in the area. At two o'clock Lister and Mera, with seventy tanks, attacked from the west and east. The Italians, their positions shattered by the air bombardment and their movements restricted by the shelling, held on almost too long. Just before Mera and Lister had them encircled, they were ordered out. Within minutes their retreat turned into a rout. The Republicans continued the pursuit for several miles. On the west, Moscardó drew back. For the Republic it was the most successful day in a long while. The Italians had lost approximately 3,000 killed, 6,000 wounded, 2,500 prisoners, and, most important, a great deal of prestige. Under investigation, the Republicans found that the vaunted "volunteers" had never volunteered at all. The heaps of equipment, the piles of orders, documents, and letters all but destroyed the Italian Government's insistence that Roatta's men were in Spain unofficially. Almost at once, the highly effective international propaganda machine of the Republic ground out the news of victory in the battle renamed "Guadalajara." There fascism and democracy had met and the future had been won. Ernest Hemingway inspected the site and pronounced the victory one of history's most significant: "I can state flatly that Brihuega will take its place in military history with the other decisive battles of the world."[31] To Hemingway, this was to be the beginning of the end of Fascism.

Actually, of course, the Italian attack toward Guadalajara was much like the previous two attempts to flank Madrid. Despite their withdrawal, the Italians had still captured a slice of Republican territory. Despite heavy losses, they had probably inflicted approximately the same number of casualties on the Republicans as they had received. Finally, most of the units had fought well and stubbornly, but for the final day—certainly as well as the Republicans, who, despite the soundness of their political beliefs, often in the past had broken and withdrawn. The whole affair was, in fact, another stalemate. Another effort to take Madrid by the back door had failed.

Guadalajara ended the Nationalists' attempts to cut off Madrid. Although the idea was not entirely discarded, other offensives on other fronts always proved more attractive. Unlike the vast blundering attacks on the Western Front in 1914–1918, hopelessly seeking a breakthrough, the battles around Madrid had limited and quite reasonable goals. At Corunna Road in December and January and at Jarama in February, Franco had come very close to cutting the vital highways which supplied Madrid. The attack toward Guadalajara was farther from Madrid and, if successful, would have had a less immediate effect. Like many of Mussolini's maneuvers, it had been based more on pomp than planning. The end result, however, had been the same: a limited gain at the cost of a vast number of lives. Each of the three battles had ended as a stalemate. Each had been fought alone, isolated from the rest of the front. In this way they were set pieces, which usually proved the inability of the attacker to secure and hold even limited goals. Possibly at Guadalajara, an attack by Orgaz across the Jarama *might* have broken the deadlock or relieved the pressure against the Italians, but the Spaniards had been unable or unwilling to risk the destruction of their army. In the Madrid battles, Franco's greatest virtue, his sly caution, had often been apparent. A limited attack against a limited goal had been his most daring proposal. The general attack from the north had been an Italian affair. If Roatta succeeded, then the Nationalists would benefit; if he failed, then the Italians would suffer. Roatta had failed and the Fascist regime suffered a military humiliation, exaggerated by Republican propaganda, which remained a permanent blot on the Fascist military record despite later triumphs.

In Madrid, the tentative and uncertain optimism after Orgaz's failure at Jarama suddenly blossomed with the news of the victory at Guadalajara. They had not passed! Madrid would hold! With Madrid secure, the Fascist Italians shattered, the lifting of the envelopment and final victory was a matter of time. If this was the conversation of the crowd, Miaja recognized that only the stalemate persisted. Until one side or the other could assemble for an offensive nothing would change. The Nationalists were still in University City. The lines there seldom shifted; in fact, it became the only front in history where a front-line soldier could live at home and each morning take the trolley out to the trenches and each evening go back to his family. Even if Franco's four columns had failed to pierce the city's defenses from the outside, his Fifth Column, so christened by Mola, remained inside. There were stray shots, winking lights, and rumors.

Rumors of plots and rumors of coups and of sabotage. The thousands of civilians who wanted Franco to win, who plotted behind closed doors for the Republic's downfall, had become a vague menace, a great hidden pool of traitors. The countermeasures were often as mysterious: the police questions, the long black cars whirling through the night, the searches, the complaints about embassy spy nests, and the sudden unexpected arrests. Despite the enemy army entrenched on the edge of their city and a secret army in their midst, despite the erratic air raids, the lack of food, and the gutted and burned-out buildings, the Madrileños still preferred their city to evacuation. Correspondents still wrote, with admiration, of the city grown bleak and determined, but six months of war had taken away the edge of romanticism from much of their prose.

> *The unlighted houses are dark. Their windows stare blankly in the last light. A raw wind blows dust and newspapers among the crowds and flutters the edges of hastily putup posters. The city has a grim look as if stamped out of iron.*[32]

If this is how John Dos Passos saw the city in April, it was also how the civilians saw themselves. Yet, after all, it should now be the Republic's turn to attack. So that last refuge of the desperate Spaniard, the café, buzzed with rumors. The Communists wanted to attack at Brunete near the Corunna Road. The Valencia government did not. Miaja was in favor. Miaja was opposed. All of this was not pure gossip, because the Republic *was* preparing an offensive and the Communist choice of Brunete had won.

The offensive had been first suggested in the spring, not long after the battle of Guadalajara, by the chief Russian advisor of the moment, General Kulik. His proposal was for an attack in the form of a great hook from the Republican trenches along the Corunna Road, down through Brunete. This would cut off all the Nationalists in the Casa de Campo and University City. Largo Caballero and many Republican officers supported, instead, a broad attack in Estremadura toward Mérida. Although the Brunete proposal appeared more practical with its limited goals, the Communist argument was as much directed against their political enemy Largo Caballero as in favor of their own military tactics. When the Republicans still refused to take their advice and call off the Estremadura attack, the Russians announced they would be unable to supply air support. The Government got the point. The Estremadura offensive was canceled. For a variety of reasons, Largo Caballero resigned on May 18 to be replaced by Juan Negrín, a Socialist, but a man far more to the Communists' liking.

It was in fact miraculous that the Republic ever managed to come to a decision or to organize an offensive, in view of the continual political turmoil. While Franco had installed a cold brutal dictatorship, where any discussion of politics was prohibited and where the heavy hand of police security was ever present, the Republic had chosen chaos. Not even the threat of Nationalist armies could prevent the wrangling, bitterness, and unending suspicion. Unused to the forms and procedures of co-operative action, distrustful of all but the like-minded, often preferring intrigue and violence, the parties of the Republic carried on a ceaseless war for position and power. At times the struggle broke into the open, with actual street fighting and public purges, but always just below the surface seethed the threat of civil war.

Eventually, under Negrín, sufficient stability was introduced to allow serious planning for the new offensive. Directed by General Miaja, there would be 50,000 men in two army corps, the V Corps under the Communist Juan Modesto and the XVIII Corps under Colonel Jurado. The blow would be supported by a considerable build-up in equipment: 150 aircraft, 128 tanks, and 136 artillery pieces. On the night of July 5, wildly enthusiastic speeches were given by the Minister of War, Indalecio Prieto, and *La Pasionaria,* predicting confusion to the enemy. The crowds went home to bed confident of another holiday for Madrid.

At dawn the next day after heavy artillery bombardment and with close air support, Lister's 11th Division overran the Nationalist 71st Division without a hitch. Despite all the rumors and gossip, all the highly regarded effectiveness of the Fifth Column's intelligence apparatus, the Nationalists were surprised. What had been daily gossip in every café in Madrid, and the source of public comment the night before, had remained a mystery to Franco until too late. The Falangists and about 1,000 Moors broke. By midmorning, Lister had advanced ten miles and surrounded Brunete. While he closed in on the village, the Nationalists began running up reinforcements as fast as possible. Asensio's 12th Division, Barrón's 13th, and Sáenz de Buruaga's 150th were transferred from Guadalajara while the Condor Legion dispatched heavy artillery. General Varela took over control of the entire front and set up advanced headquarters at Boadilla. By noon Lister had taken Brunete. Some garrisons almost cut off held out against *El Campesino* and the XV International Brigade. By holding on to the edges of the gap cut in their line by Lister's dawn attack, the Nationalists forced the Republicans to advance through a relatively small gap. The Brigades became mingled, and the Russian tanks, attached to the infantry rather than concentrated into all-armor units, did not prove very effective. A large-scale tank attack was organized, but failed to clear out the Nationalists.[33] By midnight Varela could report to Franco that he had re-established a front. On the next day, July 7, the Republicans pushed across the dry, parched fields, through the blistering heat of midsummer. They had to fight for every step they took. The Nationalists had brought up thirty battalions and nine batteries. By July 8, *El Campesino* finally reached the tiny village of Quijorna. The Nationalists refused to evacuate under pressure. After twenty-four desperate hours, *Campesino* finally secured the stone ruins and two more little groups of ruined houses. The attack was reaching the point of diminishing returns. Asensio still had Boadilla and the cost of dislodging him seemed too great.

On July 13, the Republicans began to go over to the defensive. On July 15, after one more try at Boadilla, they began digging trenches. The offensive had gained an area twelve kilometers deep and fifteen wide, but it had not broken through and rolled up the Nationalist line. The Republicans now faced a counteroffensive. Three days later, in what was becoming as formal as the regularized moves in a chess game, the whole Nationalist front attacked: Sáenz de Buruaga on the left, Asensio on the right, and Barrón toward Brunete. The violent, bitter fighting over the same ground began again. Day after day in the dusty fields under the burning sun, the struggle went on. The violent resistance of the Republicans slowed down the Nationalist advance until July 24, when Asensio and Sáenz de Buruaga broke through on both flanks. Barrón at last reached Brunete. For another night, Lister held on to the Brunete cemetery, then, on July 25, he pulled his troops out. The Republicans had been badly mauled. Although they still held some of their gains, another thrust by Barrón might endanger even these small remnants of the great offensive. General Varela, satisfied with his progress, now prepared to renew the attack. Franco insisted, however, that he needed the troops released from Madrid so they could take part in the Santander campaign. The Nationalists, in any case, had begun to give up too much blood for increasingly limited pieces of real estate.

Franco's decision ended the Battle of Brunete. Miaja had lost 25,000 killed, failed to exploit Lister's breakthrough, and ended up with three villages and a strip of bloody ground five kilometers deep and fifteen kilometers wide. The Nationalists had been surprised, but had regained their posture and mounted a series of counterattacks which had driven the Republicans out of most of their gains. It was Corunna Road and Jarama and Guadalajara all over again. For the Republic it was once too often. The morale of the Republic's regular army had been badly shaken, that of the International Brigades almost shattered. The Brigades had been used as shock troops again and again to stem the monotonous counterattacks. The losses had been too heavy and the effort futile. Many of the survivors had lost much of their dedication. The Communists, having urged the offensive, now had to accept the blame for the failure. Their prestige had been damaged not only because of their military errors but also because of their arrogance, their political maneuvers, and, among the Spaniards, their subservience to Russia. No matter who was blamed, the impact on Republican hopes remained the same. If it still seemed impossible that the Nationalists could win, it also increasingly seemed difficult to find a firm hope of Republican victory. The carefully hoarded new equipment had been smashed and scattered in the fields outside Madrid. The International Brigades had failed and might never recover. The regular army's best had not been good enough. If Guadalajara had been the beginning of the end for fascism, the bloody weeks of July to the west of Madrid had reversed the Republic's certain belief in victory.

To many Spaniards the war now seemed hopelessly deadlocked. The battles would go on and on until nothing was left of Spain. Yet the people of Madrid were committed wholly to *non pasaron!* The stalemate had already lasted nine months; the fighting in the city and the four battles outside had not changed a thing. Any sacrifice, any indignity, even loss of faith, could be borne but not a Franco victory. The siege would continue, and so it did.

The Madrid front settled down into immobility and routine. Despite persistent demands for action from Rome and Berlin during 1937 and 1938, Franco proceeded to win his war with due deliberation. He was aware that the Italo-German commitment had become so public that neither Hitler nor Mussolini could withdraw aid until victory was assured. Their regimes were dependent on a steady diet of successes, real or contrived. As long as France and Britain gave no evidence of jettisoning non-intervention with its unofficial blockade of Republican arms purchases, time remained on Franco's side. The Republic was increasingly torn by faction and racked by quarrels which grew so violent as to lead to outright civil war in Barcelona. The vicious rivalries of the Left, the noticeable decline in Soviet aid, the increasing war weariness of the people of the Republic revealed the future to Franco. Thus he began nibbling the Republic to death, but not around Madrid. There the battlefields were too well marked; the possibilities, ploys, and alternatives too well known to both sides. There, only a massive attack which ultimately would include disastrous street fighting could be envisaged. That Madrid would surrender even after the Nationalists reached the city was unthinkable. Franco had made sure of that with his toleration, if not support, of mass executions. The policy of shooting all prisoners and all political opponents, real, potential and imaginary, had understandably lessened any latent interest in surrender. If Franco's police had your name on what appeared to be a very long list, there seemed to be no reason not to die in the trenches rather than in the courtyard of a Fascist prison. Thus Madrid would not surrender and could not be taken directly without massive losses. Renewed efforts to cut the city off from its supply lines did not appear promising. Madrid could wait. This was a very important decision and not at all what other generals less prudent and more emotional would have made. Madrid was the capital, the largest city, the center of Spain. As long as the Republic held Madrid, the Government would appear legitimate to much of the outside world. The international significance of Madrid was immense for the Republic. Yet Franco felt that the obvious fruits of victory might cost too much to snatch quickly. In time Madrid would fall into his hands at no cost.

In July 1938, the Republic made a violent effort to reverse the all too apparent course of the war by mounting an offensive across the Ebro River in Catalonia. In many ways, the result resembled the earlier battles outside Madrid: an initial success, a counterattack, a stalemate. The attack, if nothing more, proved the virility and persistence of the Republic to its defenders. To the faint of heart and to the realists, the failure of a major victory on the Ebro erased the last hope. During the fall of 1938, little occurred to encourage the Republic. The Russian troops and the International Brigades went home. Aid from all sources dwindled. Great Britain and France gave in with good grace to Hitler's demands at Munich. The international picture had become, if possible, even more bleak after Ebro. No sudden change advantageous to the Republic could be foreseen; rather, all the major powers seemed content to allow Franco to finish off the Republic. If, as it appeared, time was on the side of Franco, then the Republic's last, best hope was a negotiated peace before the Nationalists mounted the final offensive.

While the vituperative discussions over a peace feeler continued, the Nationalists with great care and deliberation undertook the preparations for the offensive to smash Republican power in Catalonia. Little interest in negotiation could be detected, for a successful attack would leave the Republic defeated in the field and denied its war industry, with really little more than a barren appendix of territory in central Spain. On December 23, 1938, the Nationalists attacked. In a month it was all over. On January 26, 1939, the victorious Nationalist army marched through the streets of Barcelona. Catalonia had fallen. Now it was apparently only a matter of a few days before Madrid collapsed.

Not all of the Republican Government took so dismal a view of the future. Prime Minister Negrín, strongly supported by the Communists, who still dominated the army, felt that further resistance was possible. In any case, for over a year Franco had shown no signs of clemency or moderation. Even feelers to insure the safety of purely military prisoners in case of a Nationalist victory had been spurned. Much of the army and all of the politicians had nothing to gain by surrender but a firing squad. There was the faint hope of a general war or a change of heart in Paris or of some unexpected international miracle. Other than Negrín and Foreign Minister Julio Alvarez del Vayo, however, most of the politicians not committed to the Communist cause could see little point in continuing. Colonel Segismundo Casado, the dominant non-Communist officer in Madrid, felt the end had come.

> *. . . it is necessary to wind up the war, because the people wish it, and because it would be a crime of* lèse patrie *to continue shedding blood uselessly, subjecting everyone to conditions of such horrible sacrifice. As for the heroic civil population of Madrid it is suffering from such ghastly hunger that the most terrible consequences cannot be long delayed.*[34]

In Valencia the Communists and Negrín would not give way. Returning to Madrid, Casado felt the people could not wait any longer without hope. On February 18, Franco demanded unconditional surrender from the Republic with no promises concerning possible reprisals. On February 26, Negrín met with the Republican military commanders near Valencia. Now, at its last moment, Republican Spain once more fell victim to internal passions. The deep fissures growing since the fall of Barcelona were clearly revealed during the discussions. Negrín, with no hope of negotiation, insisted there was no alternative but to continue. After the meeting he prepared to replace the defeatist commanders and fight on. The following day France and Britain recognized the Nationalist Government—there would be no *deus ex machina* in the form of last-minute Anglo-French intervention. The Republic had been firmly and formally abandoned to its fate. Casado returned to Madrid determined to seize power and end the war.

The situation in Madrid was very grim. Militarily there had been little change in a year filled with endless shortages and constant tension. The growing defeatism had long since eroded the bright spirit of resistance. Even Miaja, the hero of Madrid, who demanded continued resistance, had wavered at the Valencia conference to the extent of taking out a passport. Most of the civilians suffering through the last bleak winter now wanted only peace and at any price. Madrid had gradually become a vast neglected ruin with none of the necessities of a great urban area. Here the remaining civilians wandered about waiting for the end of the scant food rations or for the Nationalists and their reprisals. Both seemed certain to occur in the near future. The army was no more hopeful.

On his arrival in the city, Casado immediately began weaving the antiwar officers into his conspiracy. At best, he hoped for a broad-based *coup d'état* backed by President Azaña which would replace Negrín with a Government of Peace; at worst, he would simply take power. As always, when the rumors of his talks began to spread out, the secret became gossip. Negrín ordered him to fly to Valencia. Casado decided to wait no longer for total political support. On March 4, backed by most of the non-Communist military and political organizations, Casado's coup succeeded in Madrid. A government of sorts was created with Casado as President until Miaja somewhat reluctantly agreed to join the conspirators. Isolated in Valencia, Negrín could do little but let events proceed.

The remaining Russian advisors decided not to await the outcome of Negrín's deliberations or Casado's coup. They began packing. The Spanish Communists, for once outmaneuvered and now obviously being discarded by Stalin's agents, dithered for twenty-four hours, uncertain and unadvised. Finally, on March 5, Communist Major Ascanio, commander of the 8th Division, moved on Madrid; but the other corps commanders refused to lead the Republic into a pointless civil war. In reaction to Ascanio's move, Casado's troops began occupying key points in Madrid. The always uncertain communications in Republican Spain collapsed. No one could tell what was happening in either Madrid or Valencia. First gossip, then rumor and finally despair took charge. The Internationalists, Lister, Modesto, *La Pasionaria* and the rest followed the Russians. The fleet mutinied and sailed for exile in French North Africa. Negrín tried once more, futilely, for a last-minute compromise. No one was interested. On the afternoon of March 6, he, Alvarez del Vayo, and what was left of the cabinet of the Republic flew to exile in France. In the remaining Republican territory, civil order, never a strong point, disappeared. Local commanders cut off from orders or news became the only powers left; but only for a few days, then the Nationalists arrived. Republican Spain had simply disappeared into uncertainty and chaos.

In Madrid the departure of Negrín and his supporters went unnoted, for once more the city was torn by civil war. The Communist Major Luis Barceló had changed his mind about his loyalty to Casado. On the morning of March 7, he had taken over the center of Madrid for the Communists. That afternoon Cipriano Mera and the Fourth Army Corps arrived to crush the Communist counter-coup. All the next day heavy fighting went on in the center of the city. By dusk all efforts to dislodge Barceló, now supported by additional troops, had failed. Reports from the rest of Spain indicated that the Communist commanders still controlled what was left of the Republic's armies; but the same reports revealed that with Negrín had gone almost all of the Communist leadership. Abandoned and engaged in fighting their own allies, the Communist commanders in Madrid could see no point in continuing the struggle. They failed to consolidate their positions or to attack Mera's. The dry rot of futility had destroyed their interest in fighting. The next day Mera's troops advanced against uneven resistance. On the following day the pacification continued with lessening enthusiasm on both sides. Increasing numbers of officers began to consider the possibilities of flight more rewarding than shooting their former comrades. On March 11, a cease-fire began. On the same day a supposedly loyal Republican, Colonel Centaños, announced to Casado that he was General Franco's representative in Madrid. Casado, reluctantly discarding his immediate impulse to arrest the traitor, agreed to open negotiations through Centaños. The next day the Communist forces withdrew to their former positions, the last revolution was over, and Casado and Miaja could, they hoped, turn from war to diplomacy. It was too late for them as it had been for Negrín and for the others before him. Even the threat of continued resistance had grown hollow in view of the fleeing generals and politicians.

The Nationalists had obviously won, whether or not the Republicans in Madrid decided to resist. Franco thus had neither the need nor the inclination to discuss any terms. While watching the Republic collapse, he allowed one or two purely formal contacts concerning the method of surrender. On March 26, at one o'clock in the morning, Casado agreed to surrender the air force as the Nationalists had requested. Franco informed him that the Nationalist armies had begun their final advance and the Republicans could surrender by showing a white flag in front of their lines. By the time the Nationalists arrived at the former Republican lines, there was no one left to wave the white flag. Most of the army had demobilized themselves. The men were cutting across country trying to reach their homes or in some cases to get out of Spain. On March 27, the armies around Madrid also began to disintegrate. Members of Casado's council, Miaja and some senior army commanders, along with the remaining politicians in the city, began to filter south hoping to reach Valencia and the means to escape. Casado flew out to Valencia after ordering Colonel Prada to surrender the Republican Army of the Center. At eleven o'clock in the morning, Prada met with the Nationalist commander in the University City area and surrendered the army. At that moment not a single Republican soldier remained in the trenches of Madrid. At approximately the same time, the Nationalists moving north from Jarama at last met those moving south from Guadalajara. Madrid was surrounded, and the Nationalists closed in on the city. After thirty-two months Madrid had fallen. From out of hiding, from their refuge in the foreign embassies, from their obscure position or uncertain cover, the members of the long-hidden Fifth Column rushed into the streets, cheering hysterically. These pale and bitter people had waited years, living in dread and deceit for the day when the Nationalists would pass through the gates of Madrid. Now they had. *Hay Pasaran!* "They have passed."

In a very real sense the Nationalists did not so much pass into Madrid in victory as the Republicans fled in defeat. Two years before, in the wild and desperate days of November 1936, Franco had realized that a frontal assault would bleed his little army to death. Not even the prospects of a vast propaganda coup could persuade him to risk a continuation of the street fighting. At that moment the fate of Madrid shifted to the command of the flanks. Here, Franco chose the field, saw to the preparations, and watched while his troops had tried first to the north along the Corunna Road and then south on the Jarama River. Both battles had cost too much for too little return. The Italian offensive toward Guadalajara could be tolerated, win or lose. After these failures, although there were, of course, second thoughts and constant suggestions of new maneuvers before Madrid, Franco always seemed to find more pressing needs for his troops than another confrontation before Madrid. When another battle was forced on his commander at Brunete in July 1937, Franco had refused to allow General Varela to become involved in a counteroffensive which seemed to be evolving into an assault on the inner defenses of Madrid. Franco had then exercised caution, exceptional prudence, to deny the gleaming beacon of Madrid and total victory and chose rather to count the more bounded profits of a slow, careful war. Dependent not on politics or class, the army long remained Franco's single weapon to destroy Republican Spain, and he would not allow it to be ground down on the rock of Madrid.

On the other side of the hill, the Republicans had saved Madrid in November just as much as Franco had discarded it. The months from July to October, a period of defeat and disaster, had nevertheless been used by the Loyalists to create a military force sufficiently effective so that when it was cornered in Madrid it could force the Nationalists to draw back. The single great factor in the creation of the Republican militia army had been the revolutionary fervor of the untrained men who rushed to defend their long and dearly held ideological dreams from a massive assault out of the black past. That all the Republicans' goals were not the same would become clear in time. In the first months, however, revolutionary enthusiasm was sufficient. As military recruits the men crouching in Casa de Campo were raw, untrained, undisciplined. They should have broken and run once more as they had done all summer. That they did not was a combination of their total dedication to their revolutionary ideals fused with a military situation that allowed a battle. Around Madrid, the class loyalty, the passions of a century of suppressed politics, the utopian dreams and united front, all became one. At last the people could defend themselves. Naturally no one can say for certain, but the indications are that without Russian aid and without the arrival of the International Brigades the margin of safety would have been smaller and the depth of the Nationalist penetration greater. Given Franco's caution, the militia's enthusiasm, and the nature of street fighting, it is dubious that Franco could or would have taken Madrid in November or December 1936. That the International Brigades, during the key days of November, made a tremendous contribution is obvious, but it was at first mainly a contribution to the morale of Madrid rather than to its fighting capacity. The same can be said for the growing trickle of Soviet military supplies. In time, of course, the Brigades and Russian aid became vital for the continuation of the war just as the Italo-German volunteers and equipment were for Franco.

In November 1936, the key month, Madrid held out because of the fervor of its defenders and the caution of the besiegers. The wild crowds rushing through the streets waving tattered banners and crying "*no pasaron!*" believed in the justice of their cause. They died not for a nation or an army but for a belief in the nature of man. Later they carried their abstractions to the front lines at Jarama and Corunna Road and blunted the bleak forces of reaction. However dark and tortuous the political history of the Republic grew, stained with murder and conspiracy, it was the simple hopes of the Spanish militiamen that held

Madrid. That their hopes proved in vain, that the forces of reaction won, became one of the great tragedies of modern history for men in many lands. No matter how stained those Republican banners proved in reality, for a generation Spain remained the good cause, betrayed but not forgotten. For many the Fascists never did pass, and Madrid remains a symbol, encrusted with enthusiasms of an optimistic revolutionary epoch long dead.

More stolid observers, less given to utopian ideals or political analysis, had also come to Spain and to Madrid, wearing different uniforms or none at all, to seek practical answers to practical questions. They had come to find the most appropriate means of fighting a modern war, and the lessons they learned would influence the tactics, techniques and strategy of warfare for the next decade.[85] Generally they found what they sought, so that the Spanish War gave not so much revelation as vindication. Many Germans already committed to the methods of the *blitzkrieg* saw their theories become axioms despite the Italian failure to properly use motorized infantry at Guadalajara. Even there the Germans filed away the defeat of the Italian Army for future reference, for it had not been the tactics that failed but the

Italians. The French went home to assure their conservative colleagues that scattering tanks through the infantry had been successful, whatever young men like de Gaulle had suggested to the contrary. Strangely enough, the failure of the Russian tanks under Pavlov, organized into one armored formation, had far-reaching effects on Russian tactical methods; but the switch away from armor groups may have been as much a result of Stalin's suspicions of the relative independence achieved by the Russian Army in Spain as a balanced judgment of Pavlov's methods. In the endless quiet sessions following the war, where the lessons were mulled over and the campaigns refought, remarkably little attention seems to have been given to the struggle in University City. The lesson no one seems to have taken to heart was that, given the highly mobile nature of modern war, sieges are almost certain to occur. Franco's refusal to become further involved drew attention away from the fact that subsequent generals might not be so prudent or so placed as to turn elsewhere. Once more the siege was relegated to the past and the weapons of mobility and the tactics of movement honed for the next war. Spain did become a text, but the contents were enigmatic and the lessons of uncertain application.

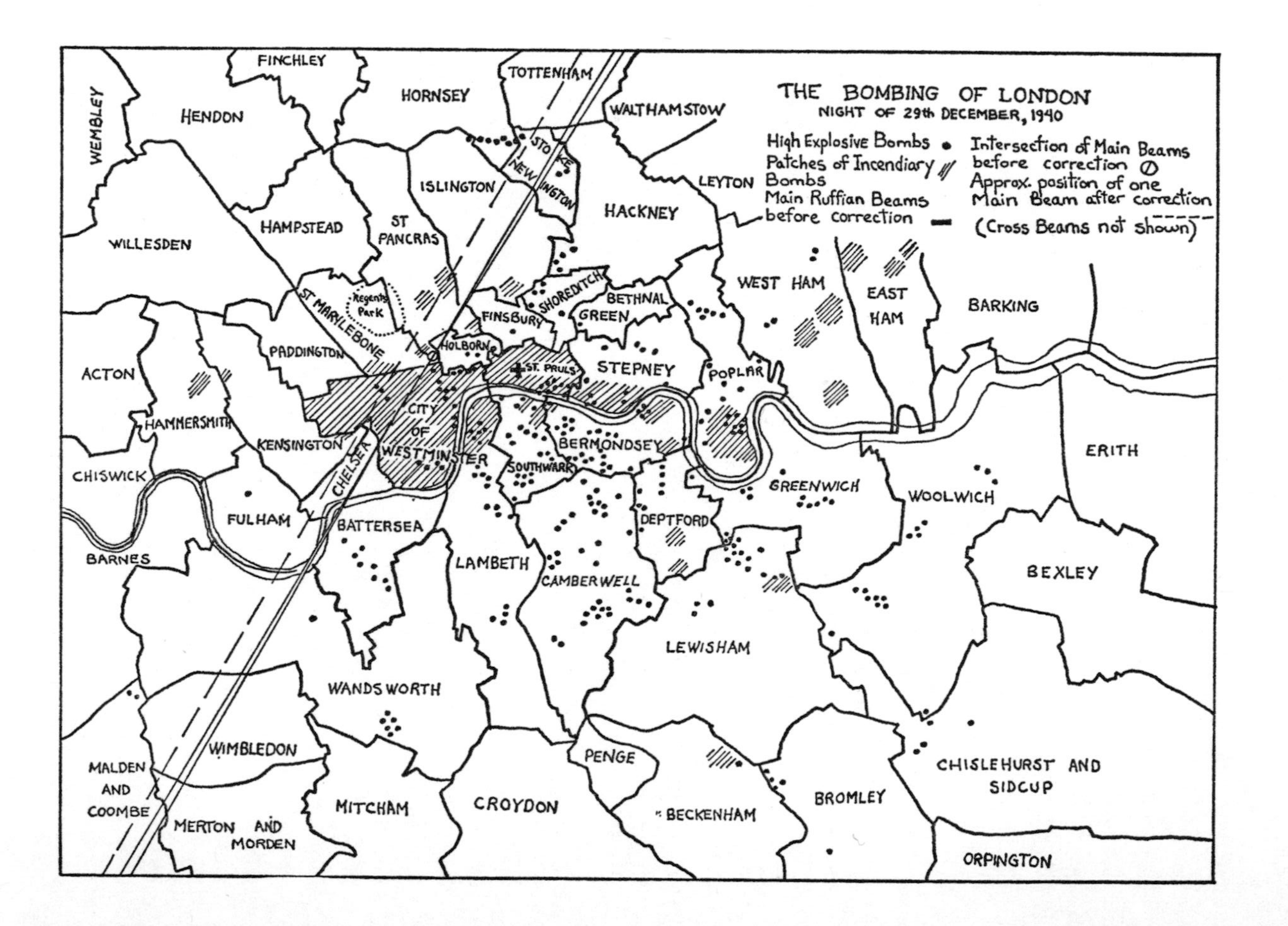
THE BOMBING OF LONDON
NIGHT OF 29th DECEMBER, 1940
High Explosive Bombs
Patches of Incendiary Bombs
Main Ruffian Beams before correction
Intersection of Main Beams before correction
Approx. position of one Main Beam after correction
(Cross Beams not shown)
WEMBLEY
FINCHLEY
HENDON
HORNSEY
TOTTENHAM
WALTHAMSTOW
LEYTON
STOKE NEWINGTON
ISLINGTON
HACKNEY
HAMPSTEAD
ST PANCRAS
WILLESDEN
Regents Park
ST MARYLEBONE
SHOREDITCH
BETHNAL GREEN
FINSBURY
WEST HAM
EAST HAM
BARKING
PADDINGTON
HOLBORN
ST. PAULS
STEPNEY
POPLAR
ACTON
CITY OF WESTMINSTER
HAMMERSMITH
KENSINGTON
BERMONDSEY
ERITH
CHISWICK
CHELSEA
SOUTHWARK
GREENWICH
WOOLWICH
FULHAM
BATTERSEA
DEPTFORD
BARNES
LAMBETH
CAMBERWELL
BEXLEY
LEWISHAM
WANDSWORTH
WIMBLEDON
PENGE
CHISLEHURST AND SIDCUP
MALDEN AND COOMBE
BECKENHAM
BROMLEY
MITCHAM
CROYDON
MERTON AND MORDEN
ORPINGTON

2 LONDON: 1940-1941

Siege by Air

> London was like some huge prehistoric animal, capable of enduring terrible injuries, mangled and bleeding from many wounds, and yet preserving its life and movement. —WINSTON CHURCHILL

WITH the advent of the long-expected European war in 1939, the exponents of mobility by means of massed air and armor seemed more than vindicated. The slashing attacks through Poland which brought victory in less than a month and the almost instantly victorious German campaigns elsewhere could, perhaps, be discounted in view of the primitive opposition, but the great and apparently total victory over the Anglo-French forces in Belgium and France could not. Here the success had been so swift and so complete as to stagger the imagination of even a Hitler. Once inaugurated, the war in the West had been won in six weeks by methods developed in theory during the twenties, applied in Spain, and enlarged in scale in Poland. There had been, except for the temporary resistance of Warsaw, no battle resembling a siege but only the rapid unfolding of the panzer attacks. The swift success in France required some while for Hitler to digest and by that time it had become apparent that, despite their humiliation, the British intended, pointlessly, to continue the war. With Germany's ultimate destiny still to be decided in the East, Hitler gave the orders to prepare an invasion plan for Britain—an invasion he had hoped, and for some time still hoped, would be unnecessary. If, as seemed likely, the British Fighter Command could be destroyed, the British might yet sue for peace without the necessity of a cross-Channel attack. Thus, in the summer of 1940, the German Luftwaffe began the Battle of Britain with the expectation of another swift victory. As the weeks passed and no decisive victory could be secured, there was increasing demand in Luftwaffe circles for a shift of emphasis to London. So it was that, almost imperceptibly, the Battle of Britain became the Battle of London, a siege by air.

ON the sunny fall afternoon of September 7, 1940, Reich Marshal Hermann Göring, surrounded by the glittering hierarchy of the German *Luftwaffe,* stood proudly on the cliffs above the English Channel at Cape Gris-Nez. Through his binoculars, he watched the massed planes of Field Marshal Albert Kesselring's *Luftflotte* drone overhead on their way to London and the long-delayed final victory over the British. In an hour, farther south at St. Cloud, the planes of Field Marshal Hugo Sperrle would take off, forming a dense second wave to finish the destruction of the docks and warehouses of London's East End.[1] This massive attack of over 300 bombers and 600 Messerschmitt 109 and 110 fighters would not only shatter the port of London but would also terrorize the civilians. Perhaps, as an added bonus, the raid would finally lure the outmatched Royal Air Force into a decisive battle with the massed German fighters. In any case, no nation could stand up under many of the monster raids Göring planned. The examples of Warsaw and Rotterdam had proved this to the *Luftwaffe* Command.

The theoretical genesis of the great raid of September 7 could be found in the closely studied works of the Italian General Giulio Douhet, who contended that 300 tons of bombs dropped on the principal cities of any nation would terminate resistance in a holocaust of destruction and panic.[2] Although Göring's *Luftwaffe* had generally ignored the possibilities of long-range strategic bombing, opting in favor of light bombers, often constructed to outrace fighters, the proximity of the world's largest target, London, and the number of planes available largely canceled out the built-in German weaknesses. Within twenty-four hours, the Germans would have dumped 330 tons of high explosives and 440 incendiary canisters onto the highly vulnerable dock areas along the Thames. Some hoped the blow would be so great that the German invasion, Operation *Sea Lion,*[3] would not be needed to finish off the British; but, in any case, the raid would assure the invasion's success. For the Germans the afternoon of September 7 was a halcyon time of untarnished optimism: British resistance, so hopeless and so unreasonable, would crumble at last, and the war won in June and pointlessly postponed throughout the summer would end in a German victory won by the *Luftwaffe.*

Göring was inclined to see the massive raid on London as a final battle, independent of the other services' needs and expectations. Two days before, he had even doubted if Operation *Sea Lion* would take place. In contrast the German Army and, particularly, Navy regarded the strategic bombing of London primarily as a maneuver to assure at least temporary air supremacy over southeastern England, a condition that—despite Göring's optimistic promises and despite the series of German victories in August and early September—had not yet been achieved.[4] On August 29, Kesselring's fighter command felt that "unlimited fighter superiority" was a fact[5]; but Sperrle and particularly Admiral Erich Raeder, although impressed with the success achieved, had some doubts. On August 30, Hitler and Colonel General Alfred Jodl, Chief of Staff of the High Command, had decided that because of the unexpected persistence of the RAF defense a final decision on Operation *Sea Lion* would not be made until September 10. During the first week of September, the *Luftwaffe* had felt the British strength had been badly eroded. German pilots reported, erroneously, that groups which once flew twelve to fifteen planes now met them with only five to seven. To some pilots British resistance had seemed more sporadic and disorganized, probably as a result of the successful attacks on the RAF sector stations. Apparently British reserves had been pulled back out of range of the ME-109s. Even the cautious Raeder had felt encouraged and had agreed on September 6 that if full command of the air could be secured by September 20, then the invasion could begin as planned.[6] Kesselring agreed. He felt only one final blow was needed. That would be on London.

The London target was obvious and had long been urged by many in the *Luftwaffe* Command who felt that a mass daylight raid would draw out the RAF instead of allowing the British to conserve planes and pilots by using piecemeal tactics. Hitler, however, had been reluctant to employ the terror attack on London not wanting to close the door finally on a negotiated surrender. On August 1, in Directive No. 17, although he announced his intention to intensify the air war, he also reserved "the right to decide on terror attacks as measures of reprisal."[7] By late August, he had shifted his position somewhat. During the day of August 24, as a result of a navigational error, a German plane had bombed central London. The next night, again by error, the Germans had dropped a few bombs on London. The RAF had swiftly retaliated with an 81-plane night raid on Berlin, followed up during the good-weather days of the next week with more raids. The British planes over Berlin had done little physical damage, but their presence had a decisive effect on Hitler. He ordered Göring to draw up plans for a reprisal raid on London. On August 31, the Command Staff of the *Luftwaffe* issued the preliminary orders for the raid. More detailed plans had been finished by the staffs of *Luftflotte* Two and Three on September 2. On the following day, Hitler had ordered the start of reprisal raids against London. A *Luftwaffe* conference at The Hague had discarded Sperrle's doubts and accepted Kesselring's contention that the RAF had been shattered. A mass attack against

London now seemed the obvious final solution to the Battle of Britain.[8] Hitler warned, "If they attack our cities, we will erase theirs."[9] On September 6, Göring had taken nominal command of an operation for the first time during the war. At last the task of the *Luftwaffe* seemed clear after months of conflicting objectives, doubts in high places, shifting emphasis, and the hampering demands of Operation *Sea Lion*.

Across the Channel, the British had no premonition that the Germans were about to switch their emphasis from the fighter sector fields which had been the prime targets during the first week of September. During most of the day on September 7, the central filter and control room for the Fighter Command at Bentley Priory had noted little of interest. Then, at four o'clock, the coastal radar stations began reporting formations of several over-twenty groups above Calais. Not for some time did Bentley Priory realize that this was not to be a repetition of the previous days. By then it was almost too late for the British fighter squadrons to respond. At 16,000 to 20,000 feet, the German planes crossed the Channel in stacked layers, passing up the Thames Estuary toward London's East End. An hour later the second wave came in over central London and on down over the burning dockyards. The unforeseen objective, the unusual heights, and a whole new set of German fighter tactics largely negated the RAF effort to intercept, despite hurried attempts to vector in on the German mass formations. Thus, except for the extremely inaccurate and very spotty antiaircraft fire and the barrage balloons, the Germans met almost no resistance. Kesselring's contention that the RAF had been cleared out of southeast England seemed well grounded as the German wave swept in over London untouched. From the ground it seemed like "a great wedge in the sky, it moved steadily on, black, menacing, apparently irresistible."[10] At a little after five o'clock, the first bombs began falling on Woolwich Arsenal and then on West Ham, Poplar, Stepney, and Bermondsey, all boroughs along the Thames. The major concentration was in the area of the Victoria and Albert Docks, the West India Docks, and the Surrey Commercial Docks. Although the raid was more or less in reprisal, Hitler and the Germans had selected military targets rather than scattering their bombs pointlessly over residential areas. The very size of the raid would ensure sufficient terror. For less than an hour, the black wedges droned over. "By six o'clock the skies were empty and all Thames-side blazed. As the sun began to sink, the vast expanse of red glow, to the west and southwest, sent a chill to the heart. It seemed that all London was burning."[11]

The East End docks were great boiling holocausts that turned whole districts to ashes, sucking up entire buildings in a single flame. A fire officer at the Surrey Commercial Docks desperately called Fire Service headquarters for help in the worst fire he had ever seen, "Send all the bloody pumps you've got; the whole bloody world's on fire." The fires produced heat so intense that the paint blistered on fireboats 300 yards away. On the West India Docks, the Rum Quay began to burn, cascading blazing rum and exploding barrels into the Thames. By morning one and a quarter million gallons had burned. Burning pepper filled the air with stinging particles, and burning paint produced a heavy varnish-filled smoke which coated everything with a permanent tarnish. A million and a half tons of soft wood flamed away unchecked. Rubber on the docks produced a dense black smoke, sugar turned to sweet, sticky flaming liquid. All the while the fires spread. The Fire Service was unprepared for fires of this magnitude. Ninety per cent of the firemen were volunteers. The Auxiliary Fire Service had never seen any fires, much less one like this. Strange fire brigades appeared in strange places. Water mains had been shattered. Telephone lines had been knocked out. Detail control of the entire area broke down and had to be abandoned. Many of the firemen simply had no experience in facing a holocaust, and the very enormity of the destruction hampered even the most professional crews. More and more pumps had to be called up to hold the fires. By prewar standards a fire requiring thirty pumps was a big fire; within hours there were nine fires with over 100 pumps and over 100 fires labeled "out of hand"—unsurrounded, uncontrolled, and spreading. There were 1,000 pumps at the L.C.C. docks and 500 in West Ham. The pumps trailed miles of hose through the shattered streets. The civil defense organizations, ill-prepared and untested, could do little amid the fires. Slowly stunned East Enders, often clinging to a handful of singed possessions, began to stumble out of the flaming ruins, moving mutely on, "dirty, disheveled and hurrying to get away." These thousands were homeless, shocked and uncertain; but there were also 306 dead and 1,337 seriously injured. By dawn many of the living had trickled away from the mass of flames and rubble and through to the alien elegance of West End where the full horror of the fires had not yet become clear. Even though all night one could read a newspaper by the light of the fires four or five miles away, those living in other parts of London could not fully comprehend the destruction in the dock area. The matter-of-fact official communiqué hardly dramatized what appeared to many Londoners as a catastrophe beyond bearing.[12]

> *Fires were caused among industrial targets. Damage was done to lighting and other public services, and some dislocation to communications was caused. Attacks have also been directed against the docks. Information as to casualties is not yet available.*[13]

To those who lived through the repeated raids from five in the afternoon until three in the morning, it seemed incredible that London could recover or that any of the East End, much less the docks and warehouses, still existed. Yet the official communiqué understatement proved more accurate than the impression left by the awesome fires, the civil chaos, and the casualties.

Although the raid of September 7 had come as a surprise to the British, the possibility of such raids had long been considered, and the most elaborate preparations had been made. What came as a series of surprises during the next weeks was the very considerable variance between the theory of air-raid defense developed over the previous twenty-five years and the actual practice learned under fire in twenty-five days. To begin with, the prime precautions had been taken against gas, then high explosives, and finally fire, a poor third. Suddenly fire had proven the most disastrous. Also, the Ministry of Health had prepared for massive casualties, anywhere from 20,000 to 30,000 killed the first night and a final total of 600,000 killed and 1,200,000 injured if the raids continued. In April 1939, the Ministry of Health had sent to local officials 1,000,000 burial forms to get the paperwork under way and 500,000 papier-mâché coffins were ready for the victims. Thousands of extra beds had been prepared in London's hospitals for the expected flood of maimed and wounded, and additional tents set up and lined with 10,000 beds for the anticipated overflow. Finally, elaborate preparations had been made to channel the expected panic of bomb-crazed civilians, for it was estimated that psychiatric cases would be three times the physical. Within the limits of the law and human ingenuity, everything had been done to lessen the wild exodus of the frantic population. The Government had, in fact, made preparations for a disaster of unprecedented proportions. The experts had viewed the 750 square miles of London as a giant unprotected target where nine million people, one-fifth of the population of the United Kingdom, waited to be massacred in a few terrible nights. Basing their estimates on British casualties during the Zeppelin raids of the First World War[14] and the reports of the population's response to the bombing of Barcelona during the Spanish Civil War, the civil defense planners foresaw a national catastrophe if London underwent a major air assault. Fearful of the unknown dangers of the air, expecting slaughter and chaos not so much from statistical evidence as from instinctive emotional dread, the British had anticipated the collapse of civilian morale and health, the breakdown of all utilities, services and transportation, and the decimation of the population on a scale which would make the great plague seem paltry.[15] As the flames swept over the docks, all their worst fears seemed justified; but with the first uncorrelated reports seeping in from the local organizations, the impact of the first great raid assumed a different proportion.

The first and most encouraging news was that the raid had produced far fewer casualties than anticipated. While over 300 dead had been reported, this was only a small percentage of the expected death toll. There had been no real panic, no sudden rush out of the city. The relief centers were swamped by the homeless, not by psychiatric cases. Instead of thousands of victims of bomb neurosis wandering the streets, there were thousands who needed shelter, relocation, clothing, advice or just a kind word.

There were not enough rest areas in the air-raid center, not enough soup kitchens or beds or blankets, nor sufficient preparations for a horde of living people. Often all the utilities—gas, electricity, and water—had been cut, the sewers broken, food supplies interrupted, and the limited resources of the civilian defense organizations strained by the presence of the living. Under the pressure some local government units faltered. The civilian defense organizations and the local as well as the national government faced an urgent complex of unexpected problems. As the raids continued, the lack of deep public shelters, long a source of official infighting, was to be solved unofficially through the purchase of a 1½d. ticket on the subway and the assumption of squatter's rights in the station. Within days the officials had to contend with tens of thousands of civilians huddled in the subway stations without sufficient toilet facilities, bedding or police protection. Others jammed into superficially safe zones, in reality often highly vulnerable but more reassuring than the fragile row houses. Instead of brief alerts the population found that the raids went on all night and sometimes all day, forcing many to remain for long hours below ground, losing sleep and totally disrupting the working day. Instead of the elaborate ritual of gas protection, the civil defense had to contend with an unexpected number of unexploded bombs, another unforeseen development, which cut off streets and utilities, hampered rescue operations, and added to the homeless. The homeless, growing in numbers daily, proved to be the most complex problem of all, for they required a wide range of services.

Even as the raids continued, the expanding social disorder, the lack of sleep, the privations of the homeless, the lack of post-raid services, the official confusion—all had to be straightened out in a hurried scramble to keep ahead of chaos. On the morning of September 8, the twenty-fifth anniversary of the first big Zeppelin raid on London, very little had been straightened out. As yet the authorities did not realize the limitations of their extensive preparations for doom. All they and London knew was that the East End had been struck a fearful, perhaps a mortal blow.

Across the Channel, the early German optimism seemed more than reasonable. Despite the loss of forty-one planes, there had been almost no opposition while flying over London. The pilots' reports of the size of the fires were fantastic and, more important, their impression was that the RAF Fighter Command was finished. Göring telephoned his wife that London was in flames and then announced publicly, "This is the historic hour, for the first time our air force delivered its thrust right into the enemy's heart."[16] The German newspapers reported that the damage to the dock areas had been so extensive that London could no longer be considered a seaport.

On September 8, Göring ordered the area bombed to be widened to include London's West End. Limiting its sorties during the day, the *Luftwaffe* reserved its main thrust for the evening, when over 200 bombers took off for the second night of attack. Even before the new German wave crossed the Channel, the effect of the September 7 raids became apparent. "Right from the French coast, on the way in, we could see the vast columns of smoke from the burning oil tanks bombed the previous day."[17] In a raid lasting nine hours, the Germans dumped an additional 207 tons of high explosives and 327 incendiary canisters into the smouldering dock areas. Twelve new conflagrations were started and 412 civilians were killed and 747 badly injured. All the railways to the south were cut and the reeling civilian defense organization further strained.

London proved to be almost completely defenseless at night. The city's antiaircraft batteries under General Pile were next to useless. The ninety-two heavy AA guns and the pointing devices were obsolete, built to vector on the planes of twenty years before. Doubling the number of guns within twenty-four hours added nothing to the defense of the city. The control system for firing proved so cumbersome that only a few guns could be fired and these inaccurately. The barrage balloons did keep the German bombers from point-blank range, but did little more. British searchlights could not hold German bombers nor penetrate clouds. They could not illuminate over 12,000 feet, not to mention their inaccurate tracking; in fact, they did little more than blind the few British night fighters and act as beacons for the Germans. The night fighters were as useless: a few *Blenheims* had air interception radar, and some *Beaufighters* had begun to trickle into service, but their early efforts proved futile, since the radar was too primitive and eye contacts too rare. In fact, the British "defense against night attack in September 1940, was entirely inadequate."[18]

On September 9, Göring decided to return to day attack since the British defensive seemed to have crumbled almost completely. During the afternoon of September 9, the British radar stations began picking up German formations in strength massing over the Calais–Boulogne area. The Germans were amazingly slow to realize the part that British radar played in alerting the Fighter Command and their efforts to destroy the radar towers had been, to be mild, cursory. This time the British reacted promptly. At five o'clock, the raiders began to come in over the coast. Göring and Kesselring anticipated only a few final spasms of fight from the RAF. Although hard-pressed, Air Chief Marshal Sir H. C. T. Dowding's Fighter Command was far from moribund. It had been cruelly extended by the unending defensive battles over Britain during the previous months, but there were still enough *Spitfires* and *Hurricanes*. The key factor had been the gradual and irreplaceable erosion of pilot strength. Replacements and refitted planes had kept up with the wastage, but experienced pilots had become rarer and rarer as the fighting had continued into September. During August, 260 new pilots had been turned out, but none, of course, had any combat experience, which meant they were exceptionally vulnerable. In the same month pilot losses came to just over 300. By September 1, a twenty-six pilot squadron had to get by with sixteen pilots. The German attacks on the forward airdromes and sector stations had been very effective: operations rooms destroyed, telephone communications broken, and over-all control of the squadrons, essential to an effective defense, threatened. With the pilots going and the physical facilities under attack, the British margin of safety had narrowed daily. As Prime Minister Churchill would later point out, between August 24 and September 6 the "scales had tilted against the Fighter Command."[19] The commander of Fighter Group 11, the key defensive organization based in a circle about London, Air Vice-Marshal K. R. Park, had feared that continued heavy German attacks on Fighter Command facilities coupled with heavy pilot losses might well cripple the air defense of southern Britain. Then, on September 7, the Germans had switched their targets. The sudden concentration on London had for a few days greatly eased the pressure on the sector stations, although the problem of the pilots remained. Dowding had been forced to put into operation a new system of classifying fighter squadrons. He also had to strip standing patrols from convoys and aircraft storage unit defense. Still, he had Park's Group up to strength and, with radar, the RAF would have ample warning to meet the *Luftwaffe*'s second monster daylight raid. The Germans would find that the RAF could not yet be counted out. This time there would be no milk run into London.

The major German difficulty all along had been the *Luftwaffe*'s intelligence reports, which grossly overestimated German kills and presented a glowing picture of the rapidly diminishing RAF. From the middle of August on into September, the *Luftwaffe* Command insisted all that was needed was a couple of days of good weather in order to finish off the RAF. Then, on September 9, the RAF hit the bombing waves solidly, forcing the German crews to break up their formations and jettison their bombs over a wide area. The bomber crews felt that their unexpected losses were the result of their Messerschmitt escorts' flying too far away, a common complaint of bomber crews. The *Luftwaffe* Command had been surprised at the RAF's ability to disrupt the daylight raid, but their built-in optimism remained. Neither commanders nor crews were dismayed. All agreed that the RAF must be nearly finished. Meanwhile, on the night of September 9, another heavy attack on London, lasting eight hours, had produced casualties of over 1,700 for the third night in a row. On the following night 148 bombers hit London again. One night's fires had scarcely been dampened before the next night's had been ignited.

Despite the undeniable damage being done to London, the *Luftwaffe* still had not secured the final collapse of the British Fighter Command. Operation *Sea Lion* could not be set under way as yet. Hitler had to postpone until September 14 the warning order he had scheduled for September 11. This meant that the earliest invasion date would be September 24, sufficiently far in the future to assure the air supremacy Göring continued to promise. The British, unaware of the German preconditions for Operation *Sea Lion*, grew increasingly uneasy as the invasion loomed closer and closer. From September 8 on, when the massive attacks on London seemed the final harbinger of attack, the British awaited the invasion daily. On September 10, Coastal Command aircraft reported twelve merchant ships, five destroyers and thirty E-boats off Dieppe. On September 11, Churchill broadcast to the country that German preparations for a large-scale invasion continued. In the meantime, the Germans renewed their daylight attacks on London and intensified their wide-spread activity over southern England. On September 11, the *Luftwaffe* shot down twenty-nine British aircraft with a loss of only twenty-five. That night 180 German airplanes were over London in the fifth straight night attack.[20]

The targets of the German bombers had widened beyond the docks. The West End had been hit by intention and the jettisoning of bombs had produced scattered hits all over the London area. The trivial as well as the vital were destroyed. On September 9, the brontosauruses at the Natural History Museum had been smashed. Some better known landmarks began to suffer as well: the Royal Courts of Justice and Somerset House.

On Wednesday night, September 11, for the first time Londoners felt that their defenses were up. The decision had been made to fire the antiaircraft guns even if they could not be trained. With twice as many guns, all firing at once, General Pile's command put on a heartening display. The Inner Artillery Zone alone fired 13,500 rounds. That the guns were untracked, unaimed and uncontrollable did absolutely nothing to reduce the delight of the civilian population, who felt they were getting their own back. Even the Germans were impressed with the massed fire: "Most dreaded were the AA guns, especially in the belt around London."[21]

On the following day the raids trickled off, but the regular nightly bombing continued. One of London's most cherished landmarks, St. Paul's Cathedral, was threatened when a huge bomb struck within a few yards of the north wall.[22] Instead of exploding, the bomb buried itself almost thirty feet deep. For three days, Lieutenant R. Davis and his chief assistant, Sapper Wyle, worked to remove it. For awhile it seemed as if all Londoners were more interested in the single bomb buried under the Cathedral than in the thousands falling elsewhere. Finally Davis got the bomb out and for the time being St. Paul's was secure. How long it and the other London landmarks would be secure grew increasingly problematical. On the morning of September 14, single German sorties dumped bombs all over the city: Whitehall, Trafalgar Square, Chelsea Hospital, and even Buckingham Palace, which was hit for the third time. That night 103 planes were over London again. Gradually the population realized that the bombing would neither cease nor even taper off. London had become a battlefield. "After the first few days of the Blitz on London we realized with indignation and resignation that this was a horror which had come to stay. . . ."[23] Whether the daily horror would increase still more depended on the RAF Fighter Command; if it faltered not only London but all of Britain would lie open, vulnerable to piecemeal destruction or instant invasion.

In Berlin on the following day, Hitler again pointed out that the lack of complete air superiority prevented a successful landing and final victory in the West; but he, like Göring, felt that four or five days of good weather would achieve decisive results. The Germans still had every reason for confidence. *Luftwaffe* intelligence reported the opposition of the RAF Fighter Command to be slackening and London obviously was being methodically battered to ruins. Still, without air superiority, Hitler at his Führer Conference on September 14 had to postpone the decision on Operation *Sea Lion* until three days later, September 17. The delay would give the *Luftwaffe* an opportunity for total victory, since all the pilots needed was a few days of clear weather. Hitler felt that the British had suffered severe losses and that the effect of the air offensive had been enormous, chiefly perhaps on the nerves; in fact, he still had hopes that an invasion might be unnecessary since "Britain might yet be seized by mass hysteria." Despite all the cheerful prospects, the fact remained that "enemy fighter forces have not yet been completely eliminated." Another heavy effort would be needed. The *Luftwaffe* Chief-of-Staff General Hans Jeschonneck suggested a bombing attack directed against the residential areas of London ought to do the trick. Hitler turned him down, for he still felt that "bombing calculated to create mass panic must be left to the last . . . the terrible threat of bombing population concentrations must be our last trump."[24] He was apparently still hesitant about waging total war against the English and obviously unaware of the already heavy loss of life and physical damage in London's "population concentrations." In any case, on September 14, Hitler felt he had more cards to play, in particular another monster raid against military targets within London. Göring's report that evening indicated a further lessening of RAF effort during the day. The end seemed approaching. With fine weather promised, a major and perhaps final effort could be made on the following day, September 15.

On Sunday, September 15, the German mass formations in the Calais–Boulogne area began to show up on the British radar screens. The Germans made no feints, allowing Park's No. 11 Group to concentrate eleven squadrons to intercept and Air Vice-Marshal Leigh-Mallory's No. 12 Group to send up five squadrons linked into a single great wing formation.[25] From the coast on toward London, the British squadrons hit the German wedges, first over Kent, then over the suburbs, and finally the huge five-squadron wing smashed into them over London itself. All told the British put up twenty-four squadrons, and twenty engaged the enemy. Standing in the underground Operations room of No. 11 Group at Uxbridge, the Prime Minister watched the squadrons committed one after another until there was no reserve left. Both the gravity of the German challenge and the calm response in the control room impressed him greatly. Simply watching the lights blink on and off, change color and position, would not reveal to him the direction of the battle above for hours. He went home to Checkers and took a nap while waiting for the results. Even before he left, it had become apparent there would be no other German attack. The *Luftwaffe,* too, was fully committed. The Germans put 300 bombers, protected by 700 fighters, over Britain, but the cost spiraled upward under the unremitting RAF attacks. Two hours later the second *Luftwaffe* wave met the same reception: heavy attacks all the way in and all the way out. Again formations broke and bombs were jettisoned at random. In the late afternoon the day's activities tapered off with a twenty-plane raid. Then, as always, the night bombers flew in over London, immune from attack. By the time the first bombs of the evening began to burst in London's streets, the air staffs of the RAF and the *Luftwaffe* had already reached some preliminary conclusions about the day's battle.

There could be little doubt the British had taken the honors. The public claim was 183 German planes downed with a loss of only twenty-six British planes. Although, as British intelligence soon became aware, the Germans had actually lost only sixty planes, the bag was still one of the war's most important. The unexpected reverse just at the door-step of final victory appalled the Germans. Unprepared for the heavy British resistance, the pilots and crews flew back to France sobered. Whatever they had believed or had been told, the RAF remained a formidable opponent. After two months and *Luftwaffe* losses of nearly 1,000 planes, Germany still seemed no nearer to securing air supremacy. The bomber pilots were particularly embittered at the seeming lack of fighter protection. They felt they had received, totally unprotected, the brunt of British attacks by fighter squadrons supposedly long ago destroyed. To appease them, Göring ordered the fighters to hug the bombers more closely, a tactic which added to the bomber crews' peace of mind but substantially reduced the fighters' protective value. More important than the change in fighter tactics, Göring, on the following day, decided to switch his main emphasis again to the Fighter Command. The bomber forces sent over London would be reduced in size and accompanied by huge masses of fighters. In "four or five days" the RAF Fighter Command would smash itself to pieces against the German fighters. Until that time arrived, however, Hitler was forced once again to postpone the initial date of Operation *Sea Lion*.

On his side of the Channel, Park, too, was changing his tactics, accepting to some degree the concept of wing formations, multi-squadron Groups long urged by Squadron Leader D. R. S. Bader and Leigh-Mallory of No. 12 Group. On September 16, there could be no immediate application of the new tactics of either the RAF or the *Luftwaffe* because of the weather. There was only the regular drone of 268 German bombers over London, dumping this night 334 tons of high explosives and 391 incendiary canisters. Whatever happened during the day, Londoners could be certain that at dusk the ubiquitous bombers would appear.

On September 18, the *Luftwaffe* Command, using the heavy fighter formations, put seventy bombers over London. Once more, RAF fighters broke up the formations and scattered the planes, although they bagged only nineteen for a day during which 1,165 sorties were flown. The Germans were still no closer to winning, new tactics not withstanding. Although Churchill had broadcast hopefully the results of September 15 and the general September returns in the air war had been good, all reports showed no lessening of German invasion preparations. If anything, the reverse was true. Despite the efforts of the British bombers, there was a growing concentration of German shipping in Channel harbors. Still, it was felt, the Bomber Command's regular night raids against German shipping must be having a substantial effect on the invasion flotilla. However effective the Fighter Command was by day and the Bomber Command at night, nothing could be done about the shuttle-service *Luftwaffe* bombers over London from dusk to dawn. London remained defenseless after dark, exposed to the steady, relentless pounding of the German attacks. On the night of September 18, 300 bombers, the largest number yet, dropped record tonnages of high explosives and incendiaries. The blitz had now lasted twelve days and nights.

As does a patient in severe pain, the civilians of London lost interest in the outside world, and concentrated only on their own agony.[26] Only gradually had the realization come that the Battle of London had been misnamed the blitz, for it was not to be a lightning encounter with a swift decision but a long and painful siege. By day and by night the Germans came, dumped their bombs and flew out. The shifting fortunes of the RAF, the change in *Luftwaffe* tactics, the rumor of the invasion had less and less relevance for Londoners. They had their own war all about them. On the way to work each morning, they could see the victims, the gaping craters, the burned-out churches, the flats with the fronts sheared off.

The day raids over London tapered off in late September, but the night raids went on and on. The total of German aircraft over the city varied from night to night, as did the number of tons of bombs dropped, but the differences seldom were apparent on the ground below. During October these regular, punishing raids night after night destroyed more and more of the city. The attacks seemed destined to go on until London had been reduced to a great, smoldering cinder heap. Even Churchill "saw no end but the demolition of the whole metropolis."[27]

The population had sorted themselves out after the first chaotic days and begun to find ways to live under the bombs. By the end of September, the various civil defense organizations, the voluntary groups, and the population in general had weathered the worst of the storm and adjusted to the unexpected. The all-night attacks had at first turned London into "a city without sleep,"[28] huddling in the shelters and the subway. Gradually the population adapted to the noise, accepting with delight the violent pounding of the antiaircraft guns after September 11, a night when it was estimated one-third of London's population got no sleep at all and almost another third less than four hours. By September 22, the figure for no-sleep had dropped to 9 per cent.

Even more than the need for rest, the problem of shelter strained the official organizations. At the end of the month there were approximately 30,000 homeless people and only the most skeletal organizations to rehouse them. Even those with undamaged homes had to have protective shelter available during the raids. The occupation of the subways, followed by the reluctant Government's acceptance of the public's solution, had gone a long way to providing the populace with a sense of security. Whether they actually used the subway or not, it was there and one could use it. At first, conditions in the subway stations had been appalling, but hurried efforts to provide minimum services, protection, and sanitation facilities proved decisive. All told, seventy-nine active subway stations were used, as well as disused stations, the entire Aldwych branch, and the uncompleted Liverpool Street branch, which created a super-shelter capable of housing 10,000. The total number of users, mostly from working-class neighborhoods, on September 27 was estimated at 177,000, probably the high-water mark, for the usual number hovered around 100,000. In time an elaborate underground life developed in the subways, with dancing instructors, a troupe of actors touring with Chekhov's *The Bear*, and the Swiss Cottage station even producing its own magazine. Although only 4 per cent of the population actually sheltered in the subway, its presence meant security for all, since neither poverty nor space limited its use. A very substantial portion of the population, whose number grew with time, about 60 per cent, simply slept at home. Others used communal or home shelters, but there was always a shelter for all when and if it was needed.

Other grave problems remained, for which the Government had simply been totally unprepared. Bluntly, too many people were still alive and demanding post-raid services. The inevitable red tape, the official evasions, the lack of direction, the incompetents, and the hopelessly inadequate formulas made even the dispensing of a little aid and comfort, if not impossible, at least difficult. In contrast, the Fire Service, the 200,000 air raid wardens, the Rescue Squads and the First Aid Service proved remarkably efficient, but to cope with the living and unwounded only a halting and uncertain collection of mainly voluntary organizations existed. In time this was to be rectified, but in the interim a growing bitterness could be discovered, particularly in the East End, over the Government's apparent indifference or inefficiency.[29]

The Government was, in fact, far from indifferent. The necessity of maintaining civilian morale pre-empted almost all other considerations. If London cracked, the war was lost. Aware of the lacks and gaps in civil defense planning, a variety of changes were instituted. The Londoner Herbert Morrison was appointed Home Secretary and Minister of Home Security, with Miss Ellen Wilkinson, equally popular in the city, as Under Secretary. A variety of special commissions and committees—on the subways, on the problem of the homeless, on shelters, on damages to roads, on public utilities, on the clearance of debris—began to produce results far sooner than expected, for they worked faster than the sluggish commissions of peacetime. Government officials on all levels hurriedly visited areas of stress and confusion. Churchill came to the East End with tears in his eyes and the people felt that he cared. Admiral Evans, chief of London's civil defense, toured the city nightly. Although there was no instant way through the tangle of administrative problems, gradually the homeless were temporarily resettled, the shelters equipped with food, blankets and lavatories. There was now aid and comfort with "determinedly cheerful helpers distributing eternal corned beef sandwiches and tea—the London County Council panacea for hunger, shock, loss, misery and illness. . . ."[30] Evacuation of the very old and very young was stepped up. Administrative machinery was created to contend with furniture and salvage removal, hostels and billeting, removal grants, cash compensations and all the problems of the unexpectedly living.

For the civilian defense groups, the greatest problem turned out to be the unexploded bombs rather than the never used gas. Reports from Spain had indicated that unexploded bombs (UXBs) had been no great problem, one more of the curious lessons of the Spanish Civil War to be unlearned. As a result, little had been done and responsibility for the problem had shifted across several desks. On September 7 only a very limited staff existed. By October, 7,000 persons were employed in bomb disposal and there were already 300 UXBs quarantined but unremoved. By late November the number of UXBs had risen to 3,000, and around each bomb for 600 yards everyone was evacuated from his as yet unbombed house, adding to the number of homeless. All that the bomb disposal units could do was to work at top speed, which they did with rapidly increasing efficiency.

Another difficulty for the civil defense had been the Germans' extensive use of incendiaries. From the middle of October on, the wardens had to man the roofs of London in a vast fire-watching scheme. The German incendiary could be readily extinguished if found in time, but a few hundred undiscovered incendiaries soon produced massive, uncontrolled fires. As the incendiaries were scattered out in the thousands from the large canisters, the only sure defense was to have a man on every roof. Often there were more roofs than men, particularly on weekends, and all the fire watchers could do was to look on as a warehouse was consumed in a fire that could have been snuffed out with a bucket of sand. Yet the civil defense somehow coped with this: fires were controlled, rubble searched, children evacuated, and the wounded treated.

For those who tried to live normal lives, everything had changed. Still, they were determined to maintain their usual routine, rigidly and unvaryingly, no matter what.[31] As many people found, the only possible way of dealing with death was to ignore it. To some extent the year of pointless alerts, the light raids, and then the repetitious attacks had worn out fear. Acclimatized by contact with destruction after passing the site of the night's carnage, everyone "came out on the street at daybreak now with the feeling that you personally had been helping to save the world."[32] All knew that as long as London could take it, Hitler would have failed. Just to go about one's business was a victory. Many would have liked to do more. "For most people there is too little and not too much to do in this war."[33] The least that could be done once the first September shock had passed was the scrupulous insistence, almost universal, upon continuing a normal life. One million people still moved into the city each day to work. The Conservative Members of Parliament still went to the Carlton Club, where on October 12, 200 of them miraculously escaped a direct hit. (According to the Labour Party, the devil had taken care of his own.) People still congregated in the Dorchester and Grosvenor Hotels, "the best places in a raid," or attended the Windmill Theatre's shows to see the "poses plastiques." Perhaps because the outside world seemed sufficiently mad, the number of mentally ill declined in the clinics. Perhaps because the outside world wobbled on its own, drunkenness was off 5 per cent, but whether from conviction or from lack of opportunity remained uncertain.

The hoarded pretense of normality gradually had to give way before the daily destruction of the city. London grew shabbier, patched and holed. The West End began to look derelict.

> *Gay and flashy Shaftsbury Avenue was very largely boarded up. Everywhere the dust of "incidents" lay thickly on top of the usual London grime. Windows were gaping black holes, and gave the houses a mournful and blind appearance.*[34]

The cinemas and theaters began to close. Out in West Ham only three of twenty-five cinemas remained open. Bombed shops, except for pharmacies and food stores, did not reopen. Little could be done to the bombed ruins except to clear them off the streets. Along with the houses and shops of the meek and the elegant, the physical presence of a thousand years of British history, the palaces and cathedrals, were turning to rubble. Each landmark became more precious as its life expectancy diminished. The great, heavy raids could almost be categorized by the number of Wren churches destroyed: a four-Wren-church-raid or an eight-Wren-church-raid. Even those who had had little previous interest or love for the fifty-two churches Wren had rebuilt after the Great Fire of 1666 came to mourn their regular passing.

> *. . . the smell of burning, the nude columns, the vacant window-frames, the sagging galleries and melted lead, the sodden piles of roofing, the elaborate doorway that led to the squalid gas-stove devastation of the vestry. I became an amateur in Wren ruins as I had never been an amateur in Wren.*[35]

What drove the Government to desperation, ruined their sleep, shadowed their lives was the knowledge that the night bombing could go on unhindered until London ceased to exist, until all fifty-two Wren churches and everything else had been battered down. Although Churchill knew first-hand of the determination of the population, he could not but doubt the ability of any people to go about their business until their turn came in a burning city.

> *How long would it go on? How much more would they have to bear? What were the limits of their vitality? What effects would their exhaustion have upon our productive warmaking powers?*[36]

Seemingly there was little more the military could do to lessen the pressure of the night raids. During the last week of September, Göring had once again tried to press the issue in a daylight battle. The *Luftwaffe* remained confident of the ultimate outcome: "Our forces feel greatly superior to the enemy as before, and there reigns complete confidence in the successful continuation of the air war."[37] On September 27, another heavy raid was launched. The *Luftwaffe* lost fifty-five aircraft. On September 30, the last great daylight battle was fought over England. The *Luftwaffe* lost forty-seven planes. Göring could not believe his losses. He could not understand the recuperative powers of the RAF Fighter Command. Once more he switched tactics, depending upon fighter bombers flying at great heights. For London this meant that October held only minor daylight raids, mainly hit-and-run affairs by fighter bombers.

By the beginning of October, the possibilities for a fall invasion daily grew fainter. Many quarters already discounted Operation *Sea Lion* even if Hitler had not canceled it as yet. The Italian Foreign Minister, Count Galeazzo Ciano, noted that on October 4, when Hitler and Mussolini met at the Brenner Pass there was "no longer any talk about a landing in the British Isles."[38] Still, officially, Hitler waited and the invasion hung fire while the air battles over England continued. As the Fighter Command concentrated on turning back the unending German sorties during the day, a variety of desperate improvisations were undertaken to find some answer to the night raids.

Anyone with an idea, however unlikely, was welcome. Planes with giant searchlights attached beneath them were developed and proved so dangerous to their crew and so useless against bombers that they were instantly discarded. Another quick failure was a weird "mutton" bomb, consisting of a parachute, a long wire, and a bomb, to be dropped in front of a German plane, which would then pull the bomb to it along the wire.[39] The hope of dropping a vast number of wires in front of the German bombers to tangle in their propellers resulted only in the scattering of south England with fine wire amid civilian confusion.

The only even vague hope remained the night fighter, almost useless when dependent on eye contact but still hopeful if air-interception radar could be developed. Despite the harried efforts of the radar technicians, progress during the fall of 1940 was very slow. The application of radar sighting for the antiaircraft guns went ahead at the same time; but for months the prime, in fact almost the only, virtue of London's antiaircraft guns was their effect on the nerves of the German crews and the civilian population, remarkably distressing in the former and soothing in the latter.

If British technology could not as yet devise weapons to get at the German bombers in the air, it could at least sow confusion. In one of the campaigns of what Churchill was aptly to call the Wizard War, British scientists first discovered the existence of the German navigational beams over London and then the means to bend them. The first German beam, the *X-Gerät* or X-ray, had become unreliable by November, and the newer *Y-Gerät,* introduced in 1941, would also become suspect by early spring. Beyond fouling German navigation, a considerable effort was made to mislead the Germans as to the nature and location of their targets. Colonel Turner devised a whole collection of decoy airdromes, flaming cities, and nonexistent targets for the Germans to waste their bombs on. British sources estimated that 5 per cent of German bombs were dumped on these ready-made targets.[40] All the false targets had little effect for London. Even when flying blind, an area of 750 square miles could hardly be missed, no matter how many false targets were scattered about. The determined civilians believed in the blackout, but their conviction was largely misplaced, for the searchlights—often visible from France—acted as beacons, and the fires of the first wave were sighting points for the next wave.

All during October, every night, the bombers came. Finally, on November 3, for the first time since the initial raid of September 7, fifty-eight days before, the German bombers did not fly over the city. On the next night 147 planes came over London to drop 184 tons of high explosive, the next night 119 planes dropped 139 tons. The night after, 192 planes dropped 233 tons, and the next night 193 planes dropped 242 tons. These regular, brutal raids night after night, uncontested and uncontained, which cost the Germans little more than maintenance and sleep, seemed to many British leaders an ideal way to break the will of the Londoners. No people could take it forever.

A shift, at first almost imperceptible, during late September and early October had been taking place in German circles which would result in a radical change in the nature of the air attack on London. The failure of the heavy daylight raids during the last week of September had caused considerable rethinking on the part of the Germans, not that as yet any real pessimism existed but rather a grimmer determination. On October 7, Göring put forth still another plan which proposed both the annihilation of London and the demoralization of the civil population.[41]

The new German tactics of hit-and-run fighter-bomber raids, usually at high altitudes, strained the RAF's capacity to react effectively, but in no way secured command of the air during the day or weakened the Fighter Command. During October, in fact, the position of the Fighter Command, particularly in the crucial matter of pilots, continued to improve. Efforts to intercept the German raiders proved exhausting and often futile, but the feeling of anxiety and crisis diminished daily. Only gradually did the realization come to the Germans that they were not going to achieve their original aims in the Battle of Britain. On October 12, unknown to the British, Hitler recognized the inability of the *Luftwaffe* to secure the necessary preconditions for invasion. He canceled Operation *Sea Lion*. The basic goal of the RAF Fighter Command had been secured.

The options still available to the Germans, however, were plentiful. In any case, the *Luftwaffe* Command could still not fully accept a stalemate over England. On October 18, Göring, the last optimist, insisted to his pilots that they had ". . . caused the British world-enemy disastrous losses by uninterrupted destructive blows . . . the losses which you have inflicted on the much vaunted Royal Air Force in determined fighter engagements are irreplaceable."[42] Still, the *Luftwaffe* had not won. Within the week the Germans turned their primary attention to night bombing, and the daylight sorties over England declined in number and intensity throughout the latter part of the month. The Battle of Britain was tapering off, but the Battle of London continued nightly with unabated fury.

The Germans still had high hopes for the raids on London. On October 24, Hitler felt that these attacks might force Britain to give in. Thus the monotonous pounding of London went on and on. Not until the middle of November had a serious change in the campaign been made. By then London had absorbed 13,651 tons of high explosives and 12,586 incendiary canisters. If nothing else, the blitz had proved Douhet and the far more practical *Luftwaffe* equally in error as to the effects of bomb tonnage on civilian morale. The physical damage to London had been impressive, and the casualties, while less than anticipated, were considerable; but the population's will to resist remained unshaken. Although there had been considerable dislocation and confusion, British war industry continued to function. So far the German air offensive could be regarded as punitive rather than productive.

In November the German decision to switch to multi-objectives was the result of many causes, not the least of which was faulty intelligence on the effect of the London raids. There had already been some criticism of repeated attacks on small areas: "Hard to see why same docks are being attacked over and over again. . . ."[43] More significant was the high number of readily accessible and extremely vulnerable targets elsewhere, going untouched while the *Luftwaffe* dumped bombs on London. Years later, in April 1946, Göring retrospectively contended that the courage of the British civilians had been a factor.

> *During the night air offensive I finally secured the Führer's permission to attack other objectives besides London, because it was always my contention that attacks on the British war industries would be more valuable. I argued that it was no use to have another hundred houses go up in flames. . . . I told the Führer again and again that inasmuch as I knew the British people as well as I did my own, we should never force them to their knees by bombing London.*[44]

In point of fact, the *Luftwaffe* held out hopes for another month that London would crack. The switch to provincial targets, the most renowned being the Coventry raid on November 14, seems to have been the result of the hasty periodic shifts of *Luftwaffe* policy combined with the obvious attractions of the advantages to be secured by broadening the night offensive. For London, after November 13, it meant a sporadic reprieve from the night attacks which had been going on since September. The German night losses had been only 81 planes, fifty-four by guns, eight lost to night fighters, four to balloons, and the rest from other causes. During the fall of 1940, German bomber production hovered around 300 a month, and, with 1,400 front-line bombers in service, the *Luftwaffe* could sustain night attacks indefinitely. There seemed no reason not to spread the effect around.

With the heavy attack on Coventry on the moonlit night of November 14, the next stage of the German air offensive began. That there was to be an occasional respite for London did not immediately become apparent, for on the next night 358 German planes were over the city. Then the raids tapered off until the end of the month, when two more heavy raids occurred. By then the *Luftwaffe* had attacked targets in Birmingham, Southampton, Bristol, Liverpool, and Plymouth.

For what comfort it could give the population, London no longer suffered alone. The nature of London's suffering had changed from the heroic days of September. Some kind of permanent individual adjustment to living under the bombs had been made by most, perhaps the most effective of all was simply to leave the city and avoid the bombs. To the Government's great surprise, after all its years of formal plans and detailed preparations for a panic-touched evacuation, some 2,000,000 Londoners quietly and on their own evacuated the city. They simply packed and shifted out into the provinces with neither official notice nor public panic. The others, by choice or necessity, remained. The civilians continued to function, if not normally at least effectively. The nighttime population of the shelters and the tubes declined. Newcomers were perpetually amazed at the seeming indifference of Londoners to the raids.

The civilian defense organizations had adapted to the actual conditions, repairing their weaknesses and shifting personnel and equipment where needed. The Auxiliary Fire Service, 30,000 strong, had matured from the amateur days of September. Directed from the underground centralized control station at Lambeth, completed just before the outbreak of the war in 1939, the Fire Service was capable of isolating and controlling most of the blazes. No amount of practice or experience, however, could prove sufficient to make the vast fires, the results of thousands of incendiaries fanned by high explosives, seem normal challenges. Still the Fire Service coped with them, as did the other services performing under the bombs. The rescue parties, the ambulance corps, the fire observers and the wardens refined and improved their skills through practice. The greatest weakness, the bomb disposal squad, had by the end of the year dealt with 8,000 of the 10,000 reported UXBs, while another 1,000 had detonated spontaneously and many of the remaining 1,000 were isolated in out-of-the-way places. The cost was heavy—123 officers and men killed and sixty-seven wounded—but the job, like so many others, would be done.[45] The post-raid services, if not perfected, were at least no longer totally make-do and haphazard. Red tape and confusion remained, but in three months whole new bureaus to handle rehousing, compensation, formal evacuation, and all the other social services, had been created. Thus, by late December, the British capital's population could feel that not only could they take it but that they were organized to endure.

An unenviable opportunity to test this endurance came on December 29 when a variety of circumstances produced a severe challenge to London's entire civil defense structure. The German raid on that night, while heavy, was by no means, at least according to London's standards, a major effort. Between seven and nine o'clock, the Germans had 136 planes over the city and dropped 127 tons of high explosives and 613 canisters of incendiaries, one-fifth as many as had been dropped on December 8 with far less effect. Although the pathfinder group, *Kampfgeschwader* 100, "the Fire-raisers," had followed the X-beam in over the intended target area at Piccadilly Circus, the planes actually unloaded their bombs two miles east near St. Paul's. The succeeding waves dumped their loads into the earlier fires. Because it was Christmas week and many of the office buildings and warehouses in the city had been stripped of fire watchers and locked up, the thousands of incendiaries fell unreported and unextinguished. Soon a vast number of fires had been started. The job of the Fire Service was immeasurably complicated by simultaneous breaks in several of London's major water mains. The fire control center at Lambeth was hit and burned out, but the prime difficulty was lack of water. The pressure for the pumps dropped, the static tanks ran dry, and the unchecked fires began to join and to spread. Efforts to use water from the Thames were frustrated by an abnormally low tide so that within two hours some 1,400 fires were burning, including two huge conflagrations, one around Fore Street and the other a half square-mile in size near St. Paul's. The Fire Service had 2,600 pumps in action and 300 more were brought in from outside the London area. Nothing seemed to help.

> *For miles around the sky was bright orange-red—the balloon barrage stood out as clearly as on a sunny day. St. Paul's Cathedral was the pivot of the main fire. All around it the flames were leaping up into the sky. And there the Cathedral stood, magnificently firm, untouched in the very centre of all this destruction.*[46]

Desperately, at times almost despairingly, the St. Paul's Cathedral Watch, organized by Dr. Allen and Mr. Linge, fought on through the night to save the Cathedral. Twenty-eight incendiaries landed on St. Paul's, some bouncing off the dome, where they left their scars next to the initials of the men who had built Wren's dome. Eight Wren churches were hit, as well as the Guildhall. All through the night the fires burned. As the flood tide came in, fireboats could be of some help. At dawn the worst of the second Great Fire of London began to die down. In the midst of the biggest area of war destruction in all Britain, acres and acres of smoldering ruins, one-fifth of the city, was St. Paul's, nicked and scarred but still standing. The Fire

Service lost two officers and fourteen firemen killed and over 200 injured. There were 163 civilian deaths and over 500 hospitalized. For a few days after the great fire, London had a respite; then, on January 9, the German bombers were over the city again. The winter of the bombs continued.

By 1941, London no longer lay totally defenseless below the *Luftwaffe,* for during the previous four months the desperate efforts to find some defensive weapons against the night blitz had begun to bear fruit. In the case of the antiaircraft guns, whose fire had been so chaotic and ineffectual in September, there had been a slow decline in the number of shells fired per aircraft shot down from 30,000 in September through 10,000 in October to 7,000 in November and December. By January the total was down to 4,000 with twelve German planes downed during the month. In the same month the still primitive night-fighter squadrons accounted for three more and would add only four more in February in contrast to the seventeen of the guns. After that the increasing effectiveness of the fighters' radar interception would begin to tell.[47] Despite these encouraging figures and the very real hopes for radar in the immediate future, the German wastage had hardly been more serious than normal accidental losses. The loss-per-sorties ratio was minuscule and no reason existed other than weather or will to prevent the German night campaign from being extended indefinitely.

The *Luftwaffe* Command, however, was far from satisfied with the winter campaign. On December 6, General Konrad, a liaison officer from Göring's headquarters, while admitting to the Army Chief-of-Staff, Franz Halder, the occasional signs of fatigue in the air crews, still insisted that one day the British would pass the limits of human endurance. On January 13, Jodl had directed that air attacks concentrate on ports, convoys, and aircraft and munitions industries, perhaps seeking more practical advantage from the air offensive but revealing that he was unaware of the targets of the past months. On February 6, Hitler reiterated Jodl's instructions. As some *Luftwaffe* personnel later recognized, there were too many targets. The raids lacked concentration. Although the British were unhappy about the low German losses, the *Luftwaffe* analysis was quite different: "Casualties, during these winter months, were out of proportion to the results achieved."[48] The doubts spread about continuing the raids which, even if the total losses were not impressive, wore out the crews and the machines. Many in the *Luftwaffe* began to feel they were being misused by leaders who did not know what they wanted. Outside the *Luftwaffe* the military value of the raids was increasingly discounted. Field Marshal Wilhelm Keitel, Chief of the German High Command, was dubious. Admiral

Raeder felt that they had crippled neither British production nor British morale and should be switched to shipping and ports. Because of this aura of uncertainty and the winter weather, there was a considerable reduction of *Luftwaffe* activity over Britain. London had only three raids in January, the last on the 29th, and then over five weeks passed without a serious attack. Even during the less notable raids, the attrition and destruction continued. On January 16, the Germans hit St. Brides, Fleet Street, Dr. Johnson's House, the Guildhall, and a bomb on Trinity House destroyed the extensive collection of old navigational instruments. There remained a lot of London left to destroy, but with the pause during February a few began to hope that the blitz might be over. The Germans, however—despite an increasing preoccupation on the higher levels with Hitler's plan for the invasion of Russia, Operation *Barbarossa*—were not yet finished with the air campaign over Britain.

On March 8, the *Luftwaffe* carried out a heavy raid. The Café de Paris, a West End night club, received a direct hit just above the bandstand. In an instant the dance floor was turned into a bloody shambles piled with the bodies of soldiers on leave and girls trying to forget the war. The next night the *Luftwaffe* hit again. Though the Germans had flown only two raids over Britain during February, in March there were eighteen major attacks. London was hit four times and once again landmarks disappeared in craters, fires swept the city, and the civilian casualty toll rose. On March 19, 479 German planes dropped 3,397 canisters of incendiaries, the largest number of the war so far, but the results, while awesome, did not equal the Great Fire of December. In April came two of the worst raids, "the Wednesday" on April 16 and "the Saturday" on April 19. Both were 700-plane raids, and on each raid over 4,000 incendiary canisters were dropped. On "the Wednesday" St. Paul's was hit with a high-explosive bomb and Chelsea Old Church smashed, as were twelve other churches and eighteen hospitals. For eight hours the raiders tumbled bombs on the city region, particularly south and central London, starting 1,500 fires, more than 400 of them serious enough to require ten or more pumps. Some 1,000 civilians were killed and 2,000 injured. On "the Saturday" the blow was repeated. For the seventieth time, the major fires were doused, the casualties rescued and hospitalized, the utilities repaired, the subways and trains rerouted, and the whole routine of recovery set under way. The ordeal of the city seemed endless, the Germans still determined to continue until everything had been destroyed. Even the rapid improvement in night-fighter performance and antiaircraft accuracy seemed of little avail. Although the March totals of twenty-two planes for the night fighters and seventeen for the guns had jumped in April to forty-eight planes for the fighters and thirty-nine for the guns, the German losses still remained very low in contrast to the number of sorties flown, not to mention the damage done. Although the British were no longer completely defenseless at night, the *Luftwaffe* was as capable of continuing the campaign as it had been in September. What London did not know was that Hitler's interest had switched elsewhere during the winter and that the *Luftwaffe* was already preparing for a new campaign.

The major raids during the early spring were more in the nature of a final effort to inflict "as much damage as possible in the short time remaining"[49] before the invasion of Russia. With only occasional breaks the German bombers were over Britain nightly, but London's turn did not come again until the night of May 10. Of all the raids on the city this, the last, was the most suspect militarily.[50] Only ten hours before the raid would begin, at two in the morning during a tea party in Hitler's headquarters in the Bavarian Alps, Martin Bormann suggested that Britain needed a lesson in view of the RAF attack on four German cities. For an hour a desultory argument continued over the merits of a major raid almost on the eve of Operation *Barbarossa*. Finally Hitler decided to initiate the attack. At eight in the morning, he called Jeschonneck and announced the reprisal raid. By nine o'clock the orders were out for a 500-plus raid. Targets were allotted in twenty minutes in contrast to the hours spent in September. Many of the *Luftwaffe* considered the whole affair a pointless and wasteful venture. At 5:10 P.M. on the evening of May 10, the main X-beam went on directly over West Ham. The British picked it up immediately. Within five minutes the London Fire Service learned the beam was on London. Fire Service central control began concentrating 1,000 pumps in the London area. Soon after ten o'clock that night, the radar had picked up the first German formation. By eleven o'clock the twenty bombers of the *Kampfgeschwader* Group 100 were over London. Two minutes later the first bombs began falling.

In twenty minutes the fire situation in West Ham was reported as dangerous. Already more than 100 bombers were over the target area stoking the fires begun by *Kampfgeschwader* Group 100. More were reported by the radar on their way in. London was obviously in for another bad night. Just before midnight an incendiary bomb landed on the roof of the British Museum. Out of reach of the firemen, the bomb burned untouched. In twenty minutes the rafters were hopelessly ablaze. The Roman Britain Room, the Prehistoric Room and the Greek Bronze Room caught. From above, the glare of the British Museum fire merged with scores of others. Once again London was burning. By midnight the German crews 160 miles away over Rouen could see the red skyline even before they had flown into formation.

At one o'clock in the morning the messages into the Home Security War Room for the London region began to stack up.

0055 WESTMINSTER H. E. approx. 0027. Westminster Cathedral. Further details not yet available.

0102 HOLBORN report fire at British Museum, Gt. Russell Street. No further details yet.

0116 CITY 0005 I.B.s on P.L.A.H.Q. Trinity Square. Fires extinguished. BETHNAL GREEN 2350. I.B.s. Fires. HAMMERSMITH 0018. 3 H.E. 20 casualties, including 18 trapped. WANDSWORTH 0015. 3 H.E. Wardens Post damaged. Casualties. LAMBETH 0005. H.E. 6 casualties. 0014 H.E. Westminster Bridge Road blocked. Bombing at CROYDON, BERMONDSEY, BARNET.

0145 WEST HAM 2350. No. 25–27 Sheds, Royal Albert Dock fired by incendiaries. Fairly extensive damage to export goods.

0158 SOUTHWARK. H.E. River wall bank, side near power station; river wall damaged. Tide now rising. Possibility of flooding.

2000 WESTMINSTER 0024 I.B. Children's Hospital, Vincent Sq. Fire.

2300 WESTMINSTER 0155. 3 H.E. Chambers of Houses of Parliament.[51]

By the time the report on the bombing of Parliament had sifted through, there were already 150 bomb incidents alone where people were trapped and over 2,000 fires, including nine giant conflagrations, the largest an unchecked monster at the Elephant and Castle. London was having one of its worst nights.

As usual the landmarks suffered along with the people. The flames spread through the House of Commons in minutes through the ancient heating system. When Churchill rushed to the scene, there was nothing for him or anyone else to do. The building had been gutted. He stood above the charred unrecognizable rubble and wept. That night there were scores of buildings to weep over. Fires got out of hand and swept the Inner Temple Library and Crown Office Row, including the Lamb House, the Wren Cloister, and the whole south side of Pump Court of Temple Church. All that could be done was watch history burn.

A high wind was blowing clouds of black smoke and burning debris. But when the wind abated, there was a continuous downpour of a golden rain of sparks. It was beautiful. Clearly something had gone seriously wrong. There was no water in most places, if the fires had spread like this. . . .[52]

St. Mary-le-Bow was battered but standing; however, Wren's bells, the Bow Bells, within whose sound a true Cockney must be born, the bells that called Dick Whittington back to London, were shattered into a pile of scruffy fragments. Wren's finest church, St. Stephen's Walbrook, went, as did London's oldest house at Ten Nevill's Court Road. Five ancient city halls were hit. There was the same strange variety of losses all over the great city, the treasured, the forgotten, the exotic, but all irreplaceable: 250,000 books in the British Museum and the skeletons of the kangaroos brought back by Captain Cook and St. Swithin's Bell. In City Road untold tons of Gordon's gin burned with a bright blue flame. Then at 5:37 A.M. the very last bomb smashed into the northwest turret of Scotland Yard, bringing down the massed index cards of a million criminals onto the desk of the Commissioner minutes before his arrival. In a quarter of an hour the all-clear sounded.

Not only gin and books had burned. The other losses might be less historic or exotic but they were more vital. One by one the railroad terminals had been knocked out, cutting off the routes in and out of the city, some until June. Twenty-nine miles of the subway had been made impassable, and above ground nearly a third of London had been cut off by 8,000 streets blocked by rubble and hoses. Fifty per cent of all telephone trunk circuits out of the Port of London had gone; 605 water mains had broken; gas and electric service over wide areas had been disrupted. Four large docks and twenty-four wharves had been hit. When the damage was toted up during the following week, 1,436 civilians had been killed, London's worst raid toll, and 800 others seriously injured. There had been 2,154 fires with 2,500 pumps engaged and an additional seventy brought in from the provinces. The fires had burned out 700 acres, one and a half times the area of the Great Fire of 1666 but not as concentrated. Approximately 5,500 homes had been demolished and a like number were beyond repair. Some 12,000 Londoners were homeless. All this on top of the disruption of services, the cut railroads, burned-out hospitals, and the damaged docks had cost the Germans only fourteen planes, a negligible ratio in view of the 507 sorties flown during the seven-hour raid.

With much of the city still smoldering on the following day, the service of evensong was held by candlelight and oil lamps on May 12 in the nave of the crypt of St. Paul's. There, in the only relatively safe part remaining, the Archbishop of Canterbury, a string orchestra and a choir gave a momentary sense of security. There was reason for thanksgiving in that while St. Paul's had been hit four more times with incendiaries, once again the old church had survived. Perhaps, somehow, its luck would hold. What no one at evensong or any place else in London could know was that the Battle of London was over. The last vindictive spasm of May 10–11 had been little more than a vicious afterthought on the part of Hitler. London had preserved its life and movement and with it the security of Great Britain.

The cost of survival had come high, but the price paid had been in a different coin than anticipated. The one million burial forms printed by the Ministry of Health had not been needed, although the battle had been far from bloodless. In London, during the last four months of 1940, 13,339 civilians had been killed, 18,378 hospitalized, and 33,756 slightly injured. For all of 1941, 6,487 had been killed, 7,641 hospitalized, and 13,236 slightly injured. The casualties of stress, particularly among the young and the elderly, the decline of medical care because of the concentration on the injured, and the reduction of services caused by the 687 hits on 326 hospitals do not show on official forms. These deaths and many over the next few years were as much a result of the blitz as a bomb casualty. The original estimates in 1937 of the Committee of Imperial Defence had been for a similar total for the first week alone and a grand total of 600,000 killed and 1,200,000 wounded. While the rounded figures of 20,000 killed and 75,000 wounded conceal immeasurable personal anguish and pain, they do not by any means represent catastrophic losses. The casualty rate for the Battle of London—in contrast to the mass slaughters of World War I and the civilian and military deaths to come during World War II—was relatively mild. The perfection of tactics and the development of larger bombs would later result in similar figures for single raids. Churchill recognized that if the conditions of 1943 had been applied to London in 1940 "we should have passed into conditions which might have pulverized all human organization."[53] In view of the later German experience, however, this may be an unduly pessimistic assumption. In any case, British losses, viewed coldly, were remarkably light. This is particularly true in view of the length of the campaign, September 7, 1940, to May 11, 1941, and the relative freedom of attack presented to the Germans by the inadequacies of British night defense. For nine months the *Luftwaffe,* with an all but free run over the British capital, could not drop sufficient bombs to inflict prohibitive casualties. It was the extensive physical destruction—about 80 per cent of which was caused by fire—a homeless population, anxiety and stress along with vast social disorganization which proved to be the main and unforeseen cost of the blitz.

From the very first the problem of shelter during and after the raids proved to be the greatest challenge for the British civil defense organizations. By May, one in six Londoners had been homeless at least once. In some areas in the County of London the figure was far higher, reaching 75 per cent with damaged homes. In Bermondsey only one house in ten survived undamaged. Of the 1,400,000 homeless in the London region alone, only one in seven had been accepted into the rest centers. The rest made their own way. In the nine months, 107,000 had been rehoused in the London region, 366,000 temporarily billeted, and 181,000 mothers and children evacuated. Other victims either had found housing without official assistance or had abandoned the city. This despite the over 10,000,000 repair operations, despite the 475,430 processed applications for advanced payment for losses, despite the best the Government could do under stress.[54] The turmoil and disorganization of a bombed-out family magnified a million times had by far the greatest impact on normal social and economic life in the city. What was, perhaps, the most amazing factor had been the ability of the Londoners to absorb the distress and maintain the vital services and war production. Only momentarily did some of the areas of the East End falter during the first few days. After that, although one area or another might be heavily hit, the official and voluntary organizations were capable of coping with disaster.

Yet a more single-minded concentration on the homes of the workers might have repaid the Germans more adequately than their efforts to destroy targets of military importance. Attacks on civilian housing would have, of course, been labeled purely terrorist; but such complaints had been ignored in the past by the Germans and would be in the future by all the belligerents. Almost any part of a great city is a "military" target if war production is to be crippled. One of the lessons of London was that the homes of the inhabitants were not only vulnerable but vital. Fortunately for the British war effort, the size of the German bomb loads and the nature of Greater London, with only 10 per cent built up and even in the center only 22 per cent built up—the rest being gardens, parks, and yards—prevented the destruction of sufficient homes to permanently damage the war effort.

For the Germans, the destruction of private homes had been a side effect of their main effort to crush the British war industry and in the process terrorize the civilians. Although at the time few in London would have credited Hitler with scruples about terror bombing, both he and most of the *Luftwaffe* Command felt that, if only for practical reasons, the bombers must concentrate solely on military targets, docks, warehouses, factories, and railways. At times "symbolic targets" such as Buckingham Palace or St. Paul's tempted the Germans, but the vast majority of strikes were intended to damage particular sectors of the war economy, not just kill civilians and burn Wren churches. The proximity of civilian housing and the certainty of error insured that nonmilitary targets would be bombed; but not, for whatever comfort it had for the civilians, with malice. The growing effectiveness of the RAF, the troubling presence of Pile's antiaircraft barrage, the tinkering with the German navigation system, had meant a far greater random bombing over the city and its surburbs than the Germans had intended. Whatever the Germans intended, the result had been the massive destruction of large areas of London. Acre after acre of the East End and the City were heaps of charred rubble. Hundreds of historic buildings and thousands of ordinary homes had gone or were only empty shells.

Amazingly, this enormous physical destruction seldom prevented the almost immediate resumption of vital services. Obviously the loss of a Wren church did little harm to the British war effort. Not only did the services necessary to London's functioning continue but the war industries continued as well. Despite the huge conflagrations, the loss of millions of pounds sterling in goods in the docks and warehouses, British war production suffered remarkably little. The German bombs were simply unable to destroy enough of London's factories and facilities to cripple the city. It is undoubtedly true that the war industry and the port would have functioned far more smoothly with tranquil and rested workers and without the need to rebuild, make-do and decentralize; but, nevertheless, the blitz cannot be said to have critically hampered Britain's warmaking power.

In view of the original aims of the attacks on London, the German efforts failed on all counts. The hope of forcing the British to commit their fading strength to a single great battle proved fruitless. From the uneasy first days of September the British Fighter Command surged back in ever-increasing strength. The four or five days Göring needed came and passed, again and again, without the final confrontation. The one or two mass daylight attacks which did draw British fighters in strength saw only exceptional German losses, not the end of the RAF. New tactics and greater effort proved only that air supremacy had not been won. The hope of terrorizing the citizens of London, cracking their morale and thus forcing the British Government to sue for peace without the need of invasion had to be abandoned. Some German circles kept hoping until December 1940 even in full knowledge that the raids were tapering off. Since the British Government held much the same basic assumptions as to the immediate effect of heavy air raids, such an anticipation on the part of the *Luftwaffe* Command should not be discounted as pointless optimism. Almost no one, in September 1940, could have been persuaded that millions of people could carry on under heavy air attack for nine months. The British were inclined to give the credit for such determination to certain heretofore undiscovered virtues in the British character. Consequently,

Allied leaders were later unprepared for the adaptability of the German population and of German industry under even heavier air raids. In any case, in 1940–1941, terror failed for the Germans. Not one of the objectives of the offensive had been achieved: destruction of the RAF Fighter Command and German air supremacy, collapse of British civilian morale, or even the curtailment of British industry.

All these had seemed within easy reach on September 8, when the reports that London was no longer a port soon proved premature as did each subsequent prediction of British collapse. Still, nine months of air attack had brought some rewards for the Germans, if not the full triumphs they had sought. The RAF Fighter Command had been gravely strained, many of its best pilots killed, and its ability to attack German-occupied Europe during early months of Operation *Barbarossa* badly hampered. The immense physical damage done to London, particularly to the docks and warehouses, coupled with the almost immeasurable property damage certainly curtailed the development of Britain's wartime economy. The military and industrial capacity of Britain had been severely strained. The Germans could, with good reason, ignore the British in the vital year to come when the war would be decided in the East. In view of the rosy dreams in September of total victory, mass destruction, nationwide panic and rapid collapse, the neutralization of Britain seemed little enough. The Germans had been guilty of hoping for too much, but neither they nor anyone else had known, nine months before, the limitations of strategic air attack. When the *Luftwaffe* did not prove to be an infallible weapon, the disappointment and disgust were the greater for the expectations having been so great.

Subsequently the Germans were to view the entire Battle of Britain and the Blitz of London through glasses of deepest black. Their prospects had been bleak, their leaders faulty, and their weapons unsuited for victory. They would contend that the British Fighter Command could not have been beaten in any case, that London was invulnerable to the available bomb tonnage, and that the *Luftwaffe* had been led down the garden path by the egomania of Göring and Hitler. "The German Air Force, lacking any clear objective laid down by the Supreme Command, was bled almost to death and suffered losses which could never be made good throughout the course of the war."[55] As is so often the case in retrospective German accounts, little attention is paid to the virtues of an opponent or his mistakes or to the errors of German operational commanders. On their side of the Channel, the British certainly felt that the *Lutfwaffe* had the capacity to defeat the RAF over southern England, perhaps even on a time schedule somewhat related to Göring's. The German failure to destroy the radar stations, so vulnerable and so obvious, is still inexplicable. Without them a basic

British asset would have been lost no matter what form the subsequent campaign took. The switch from the sector bases to London after the first week in September was the result of the over-optimism not only of Göring but also of the pilots and *Luftwaffe* staff as well. But even so, such a shift did not appear unwarranted. As General Baumbach would later point out, Germany had no established pattern of air warfare to follow[56] and the *Luftwaffe* made almost weekly shifts of emphasis, based on faulty intelligence work and as yet unproven theoretical considerations. The real failing was in reliable air intelligence to give a disinterested analysis of the British position. Without such a balanced survey, the Germans were led badly astray. Thus the decision to attack London rather than the sector stations, now so obviously a mistake, did not seem so at the time. Even with more accurate intelligence, the Germans might have made the same choice in view of the anticipated results. Both the Germans and the British foresaw the most far-reaching and devastating effects on the civilian population; furthermore, the German hope of luring the Fighter Command into massed combat was not an idle dream. Many in command in Britain wanted to meet the heavy German formations over London with massed British fighters just as Göring had anticipated. What *would* have happened if the British had switched entirely to heavy wing formations is obviously a moot question, but what *did* happen was that Park's tactics of conservation, determined more by technical considerations than by theory, worked. If he had used Bader and Leigh-Mallory's cherished big wings, there is no reason to assume that the Germans would not have reacted effectively. In theory, then, the German attack on London was valid in 1940 and, even in retrospect, could have proven decisive if the British had reacted differently. It is clear that the German decisions were not all foolish, their chances of victory not to be discounted, and the errors not all Göring's.

The Germans took a remarkably long time to react to their continued failures. To the *Luftwaffe* Command it seemed inconceivable that they could fail to achieve the desired results within four or five days or after a few more major raids. Even, by early October, when the time for success had passed if the air offensive was to be related to Operation *Sea Lion*, the *Luftwaffe* maintained its daylight campaign for several more weeks. As the emphasis shifted to night attacks, the extravagant expectations and uncertain planning which had hampered the Germans during the previous months continued. German intelligence never fully appreciated the weight of bombs necessary to deny the British a particular target. The tonnage dropped on London in 1940–1941 seemed immense by prewar standards. Thus the winter of the bombs was assumed at any given time to be more successful than the lack of concentration and the limited bomb loads warranted. When the British did not break, the Germans went to the other extreme and saw the night attacks as a sterile and pointless exercise in futility. The postwar German contention that the damage done was out of proportion to the heavy casualties hardly seems to be the case in view of the paltry success of the British night defenses and the havoc created in London and the provincial cities. While the damage to Britain proved to be neither fatal nor irreparable, the cost to the Germans amounted to little more than the strain and exhaustion involved, and material or personnel losses were not comparable to those suffered by the British. Few campaigns have so harmed an enemy with as little cost in blood and iron. Yet, since the Germans had expected victory not a successful campaign of attrition, the *Luftwaffe* felt the Battle of London had been a failure initiated by vague and incompetent commanders.

Once the population of London demonstrated that determination and dedication could surmount the most punishing attacks, the blitz had failed, if total victory remained the German aim. The German pilots, flying night after night over the cauldron of fires, the bursting antiaircraft shells, and the probing searchlights, were not at first aware of London's indestructibility. The population below, however, learned relatively quickly, certainly within a week, that they could maintain the vitality of London under massive air attack. For a very long time this knowledge did not seep through to the *Luftwaffe* Command. London seemed too vulnerable; the raid reports too glowing. The British would have to crack. Once the adjustment to the raids had been made, civilian morale improved so much that, if anything, repeated attacks only bolstered the population's determination. London was immensely vulnerable with its complex tangle of gas pipes, water mains, electric conduits, network of trains and subways, and miles of inflammable buildings and flimsy houses, but the city was so large that no single blow could disrupt all the services at one time. There was always time to adapt, to repair, to piece together temporarily. Even with a vastly greater and more concentrated weight of bombs, London could still have functioned once its population realized that they could live and work under the bombs or even that they preferred to die under the bombs rather than surrender. This realization was the vital factor in London's resistance. The people were willing to suffer to survive. By their very survival they denied Hitler and Göring a certain victory and won for Britain the siege of London.

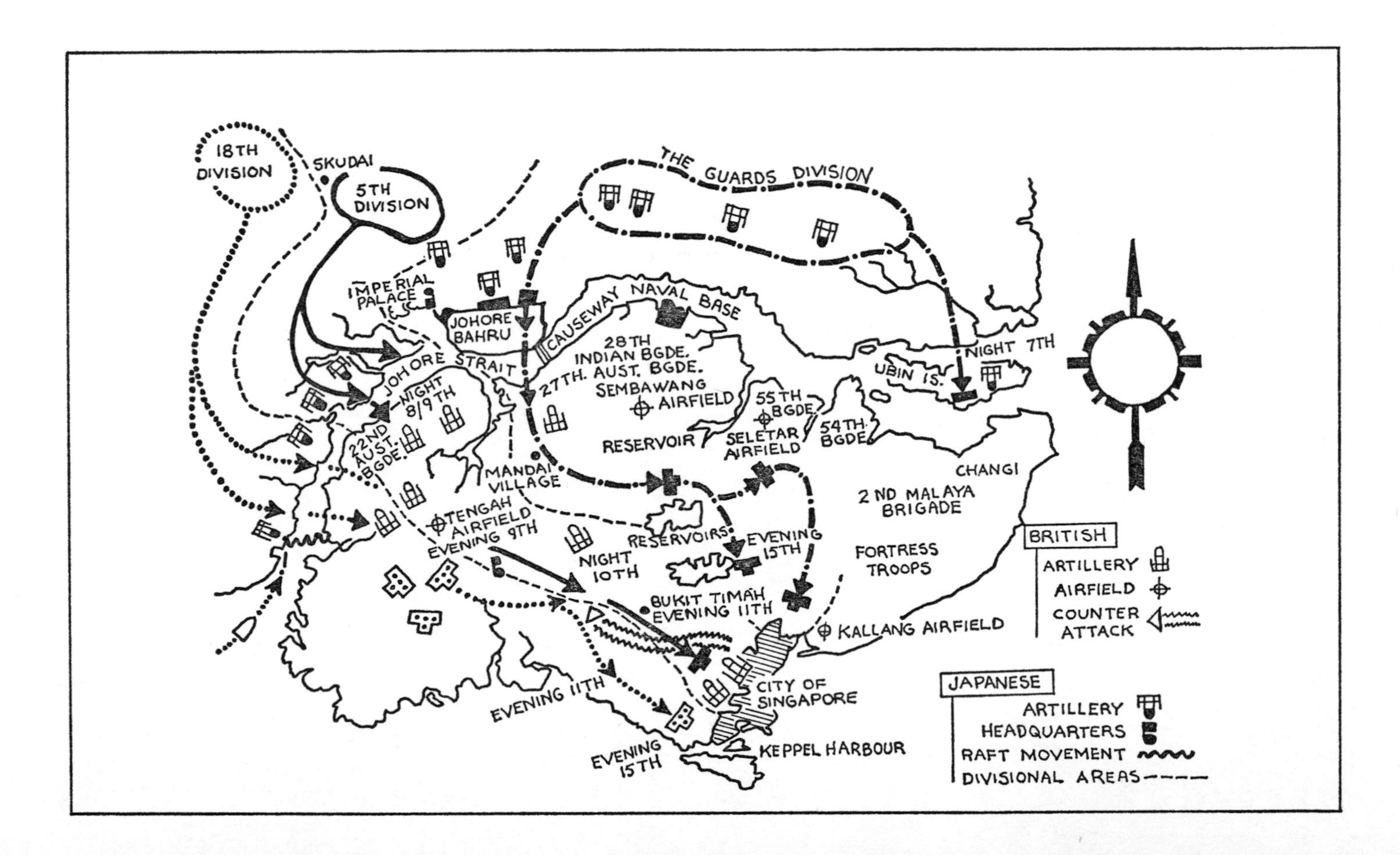
18TH DIVISION
SKUDAI
5TH DIVISION
THE GUARDS DIVISION
IMPERIAL PALACE
JOHORE BAHRU
CAUSEWAY
NAVAL BASE
JOHORE STRAIT
NIGHT 8/9TH
22ND AUST. BGDE.
28TH INDIAN BGDE.
27TH. AUST. BGDE.
SEMBAWANG AIRFIELD
RESERVOIR
55TH BGDE.
SELETAR AIRFIELD
54TH. BGDE.
UBIN IS.
NIGHT 7TH
CHANGI
2 ND MALAYA BRIGADE
MANDAI VILLAGE
TENGAH AIRFIELD
EVENING 9TH
RESERVOIRS
EVENING 15TH
NIGHT 10TH
FORTRESS TROOPS
BUKIT TIMAH EVENING 11TH
KALLANG AIRFIELD
EVENING 11TH
CITY OF SINGAPORE
EVENING 15TH
KEPPEL HARBOUR
BRITISH
ARTILLERY
AIRFIELD
COUNTER ATTACK
JAPANESE
ARTILLERY
HEADQUARTERS
RAFT MOVEMENT
DIVISIONAL AREAS

3 SINGAPORE: 1941-1942

The Illusion of a Fortress

. . . and I saw before me the hideous spectacle of the almost naked island and of the wearied, if not exhausted, troops retreating upon it.

—WINSTON CHURCHILL

WITH the German invasion of Russia in June 1941, the focus of the war shifted away from Britain and the West. As the year progressed with a series of major German victories on all fronts, it became increasingly possible that the Japanese intended to take the opportunity provided by the growing power vacuum in Asia to achieve long-held territorial ambitions. China had been neutralized, France eliminated, and Holland enfeebled. Soviet Russia stood on the threshold of complete defeat. The United States had not fully emerged from isolation and disarmament. The British presence in Asia was more a matter of form than fact. Seldom had so much been guarded by so few. Japan could never again expect to have such weakness to exploit. In six months a great Pacific empire could be a fact and the power of the West destroyed. The Japanese had, with traditional methods and contemporary technology, developed a highly skilled armed force, dedicated, determined, and ambitious, far surpassing in quality and quantity any potential Pacific opponent. Neither the British nor the Americans could comprehend the Japanese military accomplishment or credit their imperial ambitions. The British in Asia felt that no real threat could be mounted by a peasant army of Asiatics using second-rate imitations of Western weapons. As a result, the British, especially the civilians, felt particularly secure, the heirs to a tradition of military success and imperial stability. At no place was the confidence more apparent than in Singapore, a fortress to intimidate even the most audacious European power. Singapore was impregnable, a legendary fortress so strong as to make an attack unthinkable and a siege pointless.

THE fall of 1941 came to London, grim, cold, and unpleasant. There was too little fuel, too little food, too little hope. Day after day, the

British heard of defeats, of frustrated maneuvers, of failure. The heroic days of the blitz had petered away into shortages, strain, and anxiety. After two bleak years of war, the past remained a record of disaster and humiliation, while the future seemed to hold little encouragement. Every resource of the British Empire had been strained to hold Hitler in check; yet German panzer armies were driving deep into Russia, German submarines commanded the sea lanes, Axis troops occupied France and a dozen European nations. There had been some success in Africa, but elsewhere Britain had at best managed only a desperate stalemate. To compound British difficulties, intelligence reports indicated that Japan intended to expand the war in Asia. Japanese troops had landed in Indochina. Japanese diplomats seemed uninterested in a real compromise. In the blackened and bombed city of London, Prime Minister Winston Churchill, faced by insurmountable obstacles and irreducible shortages, could see few bright spots in the gloom. If the Japanese attacked in the Pacific, he had little on hand to oppose them unless the Americans came into the war. Until Japan moved, however, all that Churchill could do was to watch and wait while his commanders scraped the bottom of a nearly empty barrel to find some means of reinforcing the Far East.

Thousands of miles to the east, half a world away from the fighting war, the population of Britain's great Asian fortress city of Singapore remained calm, secure, confident. The streets of the city swarmed with troops from every corner of the Empire: Australians, Highlanders, Sikhs, Malayans, Gurkhas and Cockneys rubbed elbows with each other. Overhead flew American-built *Buffalo* fighters based at the vast Royal Air Force airdrome. At the naval base huge fifteen-inch guns, capable of sinking any ship afloat, thunderously fired practice rounds far out to sea. To the north, scattered through the seven hundred miles of jungle covering the Malayan peninsula were more airstrips, more troops, more defense lines. Even though the Japanese were in Indochina, Singapore rested easy. Tokyo would be mad indeed to challenge the might of the Royal Navy, the Imperial Army, and the Royal Air Force, all the forces of the Commonwealth, in a war which would surely involve the United States as well. Singapore was not only secure, it was impregnable—a fortress to intimidate even the foolhardy Japanese.

In point of fact there were three Singapores—an island, a city, and a naval base. The island of Singapore, a great low-lying oblong seventy-two miles around, is separated from the Malayan peninsula by the narrow Strait of Johore. Covered with rubber plantations and mangrove swamps, cut by winding tropical streams and modern highways, the island seemed an odd mixture of the South Seas and Suburbia. The west of the island still remained in the untouched grip of the jungle despite the golf clubs, factory buildings, and military installations to the east. Most of the population was concentrated to the southeast in the city of Singapore. The city held a polyglot mixture of all the races and religions of the world, attracted to the island by the wealth of Malaya. One of the world's newest cities, founded in 1819 by Sir Thomas Stamford Raffles, Singapore had grown into a symbol of British power in Asia. Here were fortunes to be made, jungles to be cleared, natives to be tutored. Here, in 1941, the Imperial ideal, refined and perfected, appeared untouched by the twentieth century. Each man seemed a stereotype from romantic fiction: the wealthy planter sipping gin, the hearty commissioner alternating cricket with malaria control, the rich and secretive Chinese entrepreneur. The arrogant and carping middle-class wives from Liverpool and Birmingham, the dedicated and stolid treasury official, the bitter Cambridge-trained "native" were much larger than life, as if imported by a Hollywood director to play parts in a film set in one of the most spectacular and beautiful of the world's tropical islands. Even the great naval base on the northeast shore was larger than life. Fronting twenty square miles of deep water with sufficient anchorage for the entire British Fleet, the base had cost over sixty million pounds sterling. Within the four square miles were machine shops, factories, repair areas, cranes, warehouses, and duplicated installations—two power stations, two water systems, and two reservoirs. There were two huge 50,000-ton dry docks, the George V Graving Dock, and a 50,000-ton floating dock which alone had cost 200,000 pounds to tow from Tyne to Singapore. To protect the base, heavily fortified, reinforced concrete gun emplacements had been installed, mounting not only the fifteen-inch monsters but smaller guns as well. The architects could feel confident that any naval assault would be doomed. Landward defenses had been thought unnecessary since such an attack would undoubtedly founder in the jungles of Malaya; in any case, if a hostile army did reach the tip of the peninsula, the base would be neutralized whether or not land defenses existed.[1] So Fortress Singapore was not a fortress at all but only a small island, a great commercial city, and a huge vulnerable naval base.

Despite the evidence before their eyes that Singapore was not surrounded by land defenses and not prepared with deep air-raid shelters, few of the population ever questioned the Fortress Myth. For years they had been told of the Fortress. For years the generals, the cabinet ministers, the press and radio had insisted that Singapore was a Fortress, that no enemy would dare attack, that no attack could succeed. In public and in private, the experts, the knowledgeable, the pundits, knew that the potential enemy, the Japanese, were second-rate, their troops uneducated peasants, their equipment shoddy copies of Western models. After the war began in 1939, the admirals and the generals reassured Singapore again and again. As late as December 3, 1941, the British Commander-in-Chief of the Far East, Air Chief-Marshal Sir Robert Brooke-Popham, told the press that the Japanese were not going to attack anyone and, in any case, the Royal Air Force was prepared. "We can get on all right with *Buffalos* out here, but they haven't the speed for England. Let England have the super-*Spitfires* and hyper-*Tornadoes*. *Buffalos* are quite good enough for Malaya."[2] Singapore believed him. Business went on as usual. The swimming pools, yacht clubs, squash courts, and movie theaters were jammed. Afternoon dances for the elegant went on daily at the famous mustard-colored Raffles Hotel, while the large Oriental dance halls—New World, Great World, and Happy World—did a land-office business at four cents a dance. Insulated from the real war, firm in their belief that Fortress Singapore was inviolable, the population watched the deepening crisis with Japan disinterestedly, dispassionately. The Japanese would never dare. "The greatest value of Singapore is the illusion of impregnability built up in the Japanese mind," Brooke-Popham explained.[3] A few, but only a few, did know that Singapore was vulnerable, that the Fortress was a myth, that the British military position in Southeast Asia was based on bluff, self-delusion and fond hopes.

Originally the major objective of the British Army in Malaya had been to hold off any invaders until the British Fleet could arrive. There had never been any serious consideration of defending a besieged island, which would have lost all value when the naval base came under fire. As the war continued to drain off British resources, the Malayan commanders suggested that the peninsula could be strengthened. Although the British Chiefs-of-Staff reduced the number of aircraft to be sent, they agreed to the proposal; by 1940, however, even these planes were unavailable. As an alternative the War Office decided to send men instead of planes. In August 1940, reinforcements in varying degrees of unreadiness began to arrive at Singapore. With an army of raw, untrained troops, with an airforce of 141 obsolete aircraft, with a navy lacking even one capital ship, the British commanders on the spot had to depend on bluff.[4] Unfortunately the population of Singapore and many of the troops were taken in by the soothing reassurances. The Japanese were not.

With the air filled with rumors of war, the arrival on December 4, 1941, of two huge battleships, the *Repulse* and the *Prince of Wales*, dispelled at once any possible uncertainty, any feeling of latent insecurity. A fleet had been promised in case of attack and now a fleet had arrived. Churchill, well aware of the value of Singapore, had decided to send the two ships "to exercise the kind of vague menace which capital ships of the highest quality whose whereabouts is unknown can impose on all hostile naval calculations."[5] To the civilian eye, the two battleships mounting fifteen-inch guns were, indeed, impressive. The deliberately obscure official communiqué—"The *Prince of Wales* and other heavy units have arrived in Singapore"[6]—reassured all but the experts who knew how vulnerable capital ships are without proper air and sea support. Vice-Admiral Tom Phillips had grave doubts about the strength of his fleet. The battleships were accompanied by only four destroyers, two of which were almost unserviceable. Aware of the lack of proper air support based at Singapore, he began to explore the possibilities of moving the ships to Port Darwin, Australia, safely distant from any Japanese airfields. With little protection from bombers or submarines, Phillips knew his force could hardly exercise a "vague menace" without risking disaster. Singapore, however, had no such doubts. The flag had been shown. The Japanese must know that the fleet had arrived. On December 4, these two great ships, paint gleaming, brass polished, were the capstone of confidence.

On the very same day, thousands of miles away off Hainan Island in the South China Sea, other men were equally confident and with far more reason. These were the soldiers of Lieutenant-General Tomoyuki Yamashita's Japanese Twenty-fifth Army who waited in twenty transports for dawn. Yamashita's objectives were first the capture of Malaya and then Singapore. In September of 1941, three months earlier, the Japanese had begun active preparations for military operations in Southeast Asia. Despite the haste with which the operation had been planned and organized, despite the lack of amphibious and jungle experience, Yamashita had few doubts. He had been given three strong divisions—the Imperial Guards, the 5th Division, and the 18th (Chrysanthemum) Division, with the 56th Division in reserve in Indochina. He knew that Tokyo was on the verge of "persuading" neutral Thailand to sign a treaty which would protect his rear and open an overland supply route. Most important, he could rely on the Japanese Air Force to support him with over 600 aircraft, giving him command of the air. Yamashita had little respect for the British troops and even less for the defenses of the vaunted Fortress Singapore. If the twenty transports carrying the 26,000-man invasion force could reach the target beaches near the Malayan-Thailand border without discovery, the conquest of the peninsula and the capture of Singapore would not only be possible but also probable. At seven o'clock on the morning of December 4, the transports weighed anchor and sailed south at nine knots an hour, escorted by two cruisers and ten destroyers, with five submarines protecting the flanks. If all went well, four days later, still undetected, they would be laying off the obscure beaches of Singora and Pattani in Thailand and Kota Bharu in Malaya.

General Yamashita would have felt considerably less confident if he had known that the British anticipated his battle plan. Years before, in 1937, a staff officer named Arthur Percival had drawn up a detailed report on the possibility of a Japanese invasion of Malaya. Percival had foreseen that the key to the peninsula would be the two small east coast towns of Kota Bharu and Singora, control of which would give the invaders access to the roads and railways leading south to the west coast. He had also pointed out that the Japanese would have to attack by the first week of December or risk a catastrophe when the monsoon season arrived. Then, in May 1941, the British War Office had ordered Arthur Percival, now a lieutenant-general, back to Malaya to take over command of the British Army. Month after month, through the summer of 1941, reports had reached Percival confirming his 1937 report. Japanese agents filled the key area, often staying at the same hotel with their British counterparts. Percival, therefore, readied Plan *Matador* to meet any Japanese thrust. At the first news of a Japanese invasion fleet, the 11th Indian Infantry Division, stationed in the north, would cross the Thailand boundary and take up defensive positions at Singora and Pattani twenty-four hours before the Japanese could land. The major drawback to *Matador* was that the British would have to invade neutral Thailand twenty-four hours before the Japanese hit the beaches. In London the Cabinet first decided that such a decision could not be made without their permission. Finally, in view of the growing threat of war in the Far East, the Cabinet gave the Commander-in-Chief in the Far East, Brooke-Popham, the power to set Plan *Matador* in motion without London's permission. With only a few days left before the monsoons, Percival and Brooke-Popham could only wait for the reports from their long-range reconnaissance planes, flying in continuous watch over the seas off Malaya and Indochina. *Matador* was set; the Kota Bharu defenses had been strengthened; all their forces were ready.

On paper at least, it would appear that Yamashita was sailing toward certain disaster. Percival had guessed when and where he would land. Percival commanded 86,895 men to Yamashita's 26,000. British airfields were within a few minutes of the beaches, while the Japanese airdromes were 700 miles away in Indochina. The *Repulse* and *Prince of Wales* were more than a match for anything the Japanese Navy had near Malaya. Battles, however, are seldom won on paper. The truth of the matter is that the two battleships had almost no air or naval support. The RAF's 141 ancient planes were to face 600 first-line Japanese aircraft, and Percival commanded a collection of poorly trained second-line troops, led by inexperienced officers. The veteran noncommissioned officers and battalion-level commanders had been siphoned off for active duty elsewhere. The Australians were eager but unprepared, while many of the Indian troops were something less than eager and equally unprepared. Only a few regular army units such as the jungle-trained

Argyll and Sutherland Highlanders, Second Battalion, were available to stiffen the raw troops. There were no tanks because the War Office, ignoring the Malayan highway network, had decided that armor could not be used in the jungle. Perhaps most dangerous, Percival was burdened with officers and men overconfident of their own ability, unprepared for jungle warfare, and unwilling to admit the excellence of the Japanese soldier. Many of his senior commanders were prepared to fight a gentleman's war with European field tactics against a second-rate Oriental army. General Percival himself was an unprepossessing man with a quiet charm and an analytical military mind, but he lacked the ability to project a dynamic image or to stir the enthusiasm of his troops. He could do little about his personality and even less about the desperate lack of trained men and first-line equipment which London could not or would not send to Malaya.[7] He could do little to create a sense of urgency in either his own officers or the civilian leaders of Singapore. He could only quietly make-do with the men and equipment he had and wait to see what the Japanese would do.

On the morning of December 6, the first firm word reached Singapore. Yamashita's hopes of a surprise attack went aglimmering when two *Hudson* reconnaissance planes reported the presence of the Japanese fleet 150 miles off the coast of Indochina. By two in the afternoon, the reports reached Brooke-Popham. In a little over an hour, Percival had put the 11th Indian Division in a state of first-degree readiness. The British were set in plenty of time to put Plan *Matador* into effect if the Japanese fleet moved toward Malaya. Then Brooke-Popham received a reconnaissance report that the Japanese had changed direction and were steaming toward Thailand. Yamashita's luck held. Brooke-Popham decided Malaya was safe. The heat was off. *Matador* was postponed. Even more important, on the eve of the monsoons, the weather worsened so that the British planes were unable to report the Japanese convoy's second alteration of course back toward Malaya. Finally one *Catalina* seaplane did break out of the clouds over the Japanese fleet; but before a report could be sent, the Japanese shot the plane down—the first British casualty of the Pacific War. At last, thirty hours later, on the evening of December 7, the *Hudsons* found the Japanese seventy miles off Singora. Brooke-Popham immediately gave the order for *Matador*, but it would take some time for the 11th Indian Division to get under way. At 2:15 on the morning of December 8, the green-line telephone rang in the Operations Room in Singapore. Kota Bharu reported ships off the coast. Then: "Someone's opened fire." The Operations officer asked if it were the British or the Japanese. "Us, I think. No it wasn't—it was the Japs."[8] By a combination of luck, audacity and careful timing, Yamashita had his surprise landing.

Standing on the deck of his transport offshore from the Singora beach, Yamashita remained confident of victory. His diary had a circle around January 26, 1942, the day he expected to launch his attack on Singapore. There was another ring around February 11, Japan's National Holiday. On that day, he expected to accept General Percival's surrender of the Singapore garrison. Between his troops and the city lay 700 miles of rugged mountains, dank mangrove swamps, unmapped jungles, and, of course, British defensive positions. Almost without exception his men had never seen a jungle and never fought in a tropical climate. They knew nothing of tropical warfare but what they had read in the slim pamphlet *Read This Alone and the War Can Be Won.* He still had no misgivings. The Japanese troops were hard, dedicated men, capable of improvisation, able to accept hunger and exhaustion in order to achieve victory. They were led by highly trained professional officers, backed by the planes of the Japanese Air Force and supported by the Imperial Navy. Even though the British had the advantages of numbers and good defensive positions, the Japanese Chief of Military Operations, Colonel Masanobu Tsuji, had advised Yamashita that the attack would succeed. "The reason for our ignoring the principle that in attack on a fortress the attackers require very substantial superiority of strength over the defenders was based on my estimate of the quality of the troops concerned rather than of their respective numbers."[9] Tsuji and Yamashita had decided that they would face second-rate troops. Once the Japanese thrust built up momentum, surprise, daring and unremitting pressure would destroy the fiber of British resistance. Yamashita expected the British, within forty-eight hours, to be scurrying back down the peninsula in a flight which would end with the surrender of Singapore and a victory for the Japanese Twenty-fifth Army.

Just after midnight the first Japanese landing barges hit the beach at Singora. The expected Japanese agent failed to appear, and the Thai troops refused to surrender. Fighting continued all night. Not until eleven o'clock in the morning did word reach the Thai colonel that a Japanese pact had been signed. At Kota Bharu the news from the landing reported heavy fighting and the loss of a transport. The British had pocked the beach with concrete pillboxes, laid out mines, and crisscrossed the sand with barbed wire. The Japanese suffered heavy casualties trying to creep close enough to knock out the pillboxes. For hours the assault remained pinned down while the men worked their way forward, digging attack trenches with their helmets. Finally one man leaped up and threw his body across the fire slit of a pillbox. Others tossed in hand grenades. The first breach had been made.[10]

Blind, confused and deadly, the fighting went on all night. British counterattacks bogged down in the swamps and in knee-deep mud. The

Japanese found that the high creeks and boggy ground made every advance slow and dangerous. The dead and wounded began to pile up. At dawn the Japanese were pushing on toward the airstrip despite their growing losses. Following orders from Singapore, the British planes and the ground staff suddenly evacuated Kota Bharu airdrome. In their haste they left the bomb dumps, runways, and gasoline supplies undestroyed. Although the Japanese were still a mile away, struggling through the mud, the Hyderabad infantry defending the airstrip became very uneasy. When the Japanese reached the defense perimeter, their first volleys killed the British commanding officer and his adjutant, and the battalion quickly disintegrated. The other British and Indian troops had to fall back. At two in the afternoon, the Japanese had Kota Bharu. At three o'clock Japanese planes began landing on the undamaged airstrip. Although the Japanese had lost 320 dead and 538 wounded, they had presented Yamashita with an airfield along with twenty-seven field guns, seventy-three heavy and light machine guns, seven planes, 157 cars and trucks, and thirty-three railway cars. It was a considerable haul for less than a day's fighting. The Japanese 5th and 18th Divisions now began driving south, building up momentum, while the British stumbled back, shocked and uncertain. The pattern on the ground had been set by Yamashita—advance at high speed, infiltrate, bypass, hook the flanks, ambush, advance again.

The war had at last come to Singapore. Just after four in the morning bombs began falling on the city. Prophetically one of the first bombs scored a direct hit on the Happy World dance hall. At the same time the Japanese hit the Seletar and Tengah airfields and the naval base. Only slight damage was done in the city; but, because of the lack of shelters and warning, about 140 civilians were killed. No one, then or later, was able to adequately estimate civilian casualties. There had been no blackout. Civilian defense organizations never did get under way. Antiaircraft fire had been sporadic and ineffective. Fighters had no time to get into the air. With the dawn came reassurance. Brooke-Popham announced, "We are confident. Our defenses are strong and efficient and our preparations are made and tested."[11] An official bulletin reported the withdrawal of the Japanese fleet. Everyone agreed the Japs had been foolish to risk the attack. News from Hawaii, the Philippines, and Hong Kong meant that Tokyo had bitten off more than it could chew. The raid had been a sneaky surprise, but Singapore and the RAF were now prepared. It would not happen again.

While the population of Singapore went about business as usual, the Japanese domination of the air came as swiftly as their successes on land. The RAF had 110 aircraft on the northern Malayan fields. On the first day, fifty were fit for operations while the Japanese already had 100 planes based at Singora and more at Kota Bharu. On December 9, only ten serviceable British planes remained. The field at Kota Bharu had been lost and the bases at Alor Star and Penang on the west coast had been heavily bombed. On December 10, all the British planes in northern Malaya were withdrawn. The British pilots, flying old planes, had been hopelessly outgunned by the 469 Japanese army planes and the 158 naval aircraft. Resistance had been useless. Command of the air, won almost by default, would remain a Japanese asset. Singapore was naked from the air.

Once the reports of the Japanese landings had been verified, the Royal Navy faced an impossible dilemma. If the presence of the *Repulse* and *Prince of Wales* had been intended only to create a "vague menace," then Admiral Phillips and his two captains, Leach of the *Prince of Wales* and Tennant of the *Repulse,* would be justified in moving the ships to a more protected port. Thousands of miles away, Churchill was mulling over the unlikely project of ordering the ships to cross the Pacific and join the American Fleet; but Phillips had to decide how to use his ships immediately. Withdrawal from Singapore would obviously have a disastrous effect on civilian and military morale. To remain inactive would not only invite constant air attack but also leave the Japanese free to continue their landings unhampered. The only remaining—in fact, the only possible—choice would be to sail out and attempt to smash the invasion fleet despite the lack of supporting units and the limited air cover available. A battleship is built to fight, and Phillips, whatever the odds, felt he had to fight. He decided to sail north, disguising his intentions until the last moment, and attack the beachheads. Speed, surprise, and a good deal of luck might bring the strike off. In any case, there was no other alternative.

At half-past six on the morning of December 9, Force Z, under the eyes of a waving and enthusiastic crowd, cleared the boom of the naval base. Air Vice-Marshal C. W. Pulford had promised to try to provide air reconnaissance ahead of the fleet. Then, after the ships had sailed, word came from Singapore: "Fighter protection on Wednesday, 10th, will not, repeat not, be possible." Phillips decided to "carry on without it."[12] So far luck was with him, for December 9 had dawned misty and cloudy. The poor visibility protected Force Z all during the day as the ships plowed north. Shortly before five the mist began to lift, and three unidentified aircraft were sighted trailing the fleet. After dark, with surprise lost, Phillips detached the destroyer *Tenedos* with instructions to radio Singapore the next morning that the strike had been canceled. During the night Phillips received word of a Japanese landing at Kuantan on the coast 140 miles north of Singapore. Since

Kuantan lay near his route back to Singapore and almost at a maximum distance from the Japanese airfields in Indochina, he decided to reap some benefits from the aborted attack by arriving off the beach at dawn. All the night of December 9–10, Force Z steamed south, hoping for action at last.

The previous twenty-four hours had been a period of frustration and confusion for Rear Admiral Sadaichi Matsunaga's Twenty-second Air Flotilla. Early on the morning of December 9, reconnaissance planes had reported the British battleships anchored in the naval base. During the day, preparations were made for a heavy attack on the anchored ships. At five in the afternoon a radio message, dispatched over an hour before from submarine I-56, patrolling east of Singapore, arrived in Saigon headquarters: "Two battleships proceeding northward."[13] The morning reconnaissance photographs were hurriedly developed. The "battleships" were revealed as large cargo vessels. The British had unwittingly been given nearly twenty-four hours of grace by the error and by the unexplained failure of the three Japanese planes to transmit their discovery of Force Z. The Japanese launched a strike force despite the darkness; but the attack had to be called off after one of the strike planes nearly bombed the heavy cruiser *Chokai,* flagship of Vice-Admiral Gisaburo Ozawa. Early the next morning, ten reconnaissance planes began taking off, and were immediately followed by ninety-six torpedo and bombing planes. The Japanese at Saigon waited for hours for word from this new strike. Once again no battleships could be found. It seemed incredible that the British could continue to elude them.

Admiral Phillips had discovered by eight on the morning of December 10 that no Japanese fleet of any kind was anchored off Kuantan. Force Z moved on toward Singapore. By then the Japanese reconnaissance planes were already on their way back to Saigon and the bombers were about to be recalled. At the very last minute, a Japanese bomber sighted the British ships. Fifteen minutes later, at ten-thirty, Saigon relayed the British position to the torpedo planes. At 11:18 the British opened fire on the first nine Mitsubishi "86" bombers flying in a tight formation at 10,000 feet. Almost immediately the Japanese bomb pattern hit all around the *Repulse.* The battleship almost disappeared in a huge tumbling cloud of water and black smoke, but only one bomb landed on the catapult deck. Immediately a Japanese torpedo attack was launched against the *Prince of Wales.* This also made only one hit but that proved deadly. The torpedo smashed into the stern, producing a great gout of water on the outside and a shambles on the inside. One propeller shaft bent and, whipped around by the force of the turbines, it tore out the bottom of the ship and devastated the engine room. Never under control again, listing and hardly under way, the *Prince of Wales* in less than a minute had become a sitting duck. The Japanese could sink her at their leisure.

The Japanese now began heavy low-level torpedo strikes against the *Repulse*. Twisting and turning at twenty-seven knots, Captain William Tennant combed the tracks in a beautifully timed maneuver. The Mitsubishi bombers began high-level bombing attacks, but they managed only a few near-misses. In a brief pause between the Japanese strikes, Tennant, unable to contact Leach or Phillips on the *Prince of Wales*, finally sent word to Singapore—"enemy aircraft bombing." Although the attack had been under way for nearly an hour, this was the first word to reach Singapore. It was much too late to summon help.

The Japanese were pushing their attacks again and again. Diving closer and closer, they scored three quick hits on the *Prince of Wales*. Badly mangled below the water line, the battleship began to go down slowly by the stern. The *Prince of Wales* would remain afloat for another hour, a great smouldering ruin covered by a pall of greasy black smoke. The Japanese turned their attention to the *Repulse*. Tennant again heeled his ship over and combed the torpedo tracks; but this time three Japanese came in from the side, dropped their torpedoes and swung away. The *Repulse* had to stay on course. Thirty seconds passed, a minute, a minute and a half, as the crew watched the three tracks streaking toward them. Two passed barely astern. The third hit solidly amidships. There was a tremendous explosion and the battleship shuddered. Tennant had dodged nineteen torpedoes before the twentieth hit, but even then, the *Repulse* still sailed on at twenty-seven knots on an even keel seemingly undamaged. Then torpedoes came from all sides. Lieutenant Haruki Iki's nine *Betty* torpedo planes came straight in at 125 feet until they were only 1,300 feet from the *Repulse*. The first three planes made two hits but two planes were lost. The second three got another hit. Iki's own torpedo streaked into the gunroom and jammed the rudder. The *Repulse* no longer answered her helm and veered off course. Although few but Tennant knew it, the *Repulse* was going down, hopelessly shattered below the water line. The guns continued firing until Tennant, unwilling to risk the lives of his crew, ordered the ship abandoned. There was no panic. The crew began to jump over the starboard side into the oily water. One man jumped from the main mast, missed and smashed into the side of the ship; twelve Royal Marines jumped too far back and disappeared under the propeller. More men leaped. Captain Tennant told his officers to leave the bridge. He would not budge. Finally they forced him through a narrow doorway and onto the deck. They had to throw him overboard. The list became 60 degrees to port, then 70 degrees. To Cecil

Brown, a CBS correspondent swimming fifty feet away, the bow of the *Repulse* stood straight up "into the air like a church steeple. Its red underplates stand out as stark and as gruesome as the blood on the faces of the men around me."[14] At 12:33 the *Repulse* rolled over and sank. Nearly an hour later, the *Prince of Wales* went under.

Just as the *Prince of Wales* disappeared, a squadron of *Buffalos,* based six air minutes away at Kallang, arrived. Not a single Japanese aircraft could be sighted. Below on the sunlit ocean lay two huge oil slicks, three destroyers, and the bobbing, oil-covered survivors. Choking in the fuel oil, they sang *Roll Out the Barrel* while they waited for the destroyers to pick them up. Flight-Lieutenant T. A. Vigors, commander of the *Buffalos,* took his plane down near the surface. The British crews, gagging and strangling in the oil, waved and gave him thumbs up. They were all that was left of the two great ships. In less than two hours the British had lost 845 officers and men, including Admiral Phillips and Captain Leach. More vital they had lost their only two capital ships in the Pacific and, with them, any hope of controlling the sea. Singapore was naked from the sea.

In three days the British Air Force had been reduced to a battered collection of ancient relics hiding out in bombed airdromes. The vaunted British Navy now consisted of a few destroyers. The British Army was on the run, surrendering in droves, abandoning mountains of equipment. On December 12, 500 men of the Japanese Saeki Detachment, backed by tanks, breached the Jitra defense line in fifteen hours, and 3,000 Indian troops surrendered. "We now understood the fighting capacity of the enemy. The only things we had to fear were the quantity of munitions he had and the thoroughness of his demolitions."[15] On December 15, the Gurun line broke. On December 17, the Muda River line dissolved. On December 20, the British abandoned the Krian River line. The defense could never get set. The officers could find no tactic to prevent the Japanese hooks around their flanks. They had no tanks with which to meet the Japanese armor. They had no experience in jungle fighting. Both officers and men began to doubt if the Japanese could be stopped. Harassed from the air, ambushed on the ground, ill-trained, poorly led, the men stumbled back mile after mile. The Japanese infantry, riding confiscated bikes, followed at their heels. Behind the lines Japanese engineers repaired the bridges almost as fast as the British demolished them. Captured British supplies and equipment, dubbed the "Churchill stores," moved up in captured British trucks over the undamaged British highway system. As the Japanese Twenty-fifth Army smashed down the peninsula, Yamashita's timetable appeared more and more realistic.

Far to the south in Singapore, untouched since the first day of the war, few were consciously aware of the growing disintegration of the British Army. The failure to halt the Japanese advance was hidden by the hopeful official reports, the distance, and the normality of everyday life. The lack of Japanese air activity over the island concealed the destruction of the RAF. The loss of the *Repulse* and the *Prince of Wales* had been a terrible shock. It seemed incredible that those two beautiful ships could be gone, but everyone retained his confidence in the reputation of the Royal Navy. In many ways the city remained a never-never land of rosy dreams and quiet assurance based on arrogance and ignorance. Although there were fewer parties, fewer dances, there was no real feeling of crisis. Insulated from violence for two years, the city still felt that the war was far away. In those two years almost nothing had been done to prepare Singapore either physically or emotionally for a war.

Tradition and indolence clogged all action. Proposals for effective air-raid shelters were lost in vague discussions of technicalities and finances. Suggestions for a civilian evacuation plan were pigeonholed as premature. Rationing was considered unnecessary, although the hotels did have two meatless days a week—chicken and game, however, were not considered meat. The most glaring failure was the almost total refusal to consider the Oriental population as more than a passive mass, open to panic and useless in defense. Pleas to allow the Chinese and Malays to form paramilitary units were regarded with deep hostility. Demands that mixed irregular guerrilla and commando units be set up by men who knew the jungle were turned down with regularity. Proposals to create British-Malay teams to remain behind Japanese lines were labeled defeatist. Even efforts to mobilize civilian labor fell afoul of rules, regulations, and interdepartmental squabbling. Reluctantly the police stopped arresting members of the Malayan Chinese Communist Party, the most highly organized anti-Japanese civilian force in Singapore. Reluctantly a skeleton commando force was authorized under the command of Major J. D. Dalley, who immediately began "illegally" enlisting men in Dalforce on a basis of enthusiasm and talent rather than race. Radio Singapore continued broadcasting plays and music "to build an audience." The censors chopped out any pessimistic reports. All criticism was suspect since it might endanger morale.

Certainly one of the most reassuring figures in Singapore was Governor Sir Shenton Thomas, a large, stolid administrator, bluff, likable, and totally unimaginative. Decades of uneventful service had closed his mind to inspiration or daring. He was as solid as a rock and about as flexible. At no time did he show any inclination to assume the position of a military governor with dictatorial powers; at no time did he deeply question the ponderous workings of the traditional system. Under him were capable, sincere men who worked hard and long. The men joined the Malayan Volunteers or with their wives spent their spare time as members of the various civilian defense organizations. Almost all "did their bit," followed instructions, went on about their business. There were a few who saw no reason to change the pleasant old ways at all. The secretary of a golf club refused to allow the army to build a strong point on the grounds until the proper club committees met to discuss the proposal. An ancient liverish empire builder complained bitterly because RAF officers were swimming in the hotel pool without first being introduced to him. Most of the British, however, tried to do their part; but they lacked the sense of urgency which a dynamic leader might have instilled.

Not until late in December did the British population begin to get an inkling of what war meant. Refugees began filtering onto the island with first-hand stories of bombing and terror. On December 15, the Japanese captured Penang Island, and within a few days a wave of refugees reached the city with the story of the rapid Japanese advance and the bungled evacuation. The news, despite confident official reports, grew worse. The list of branches of the Hong Kong and Shanghai Banking Corporation "closed until further notice" revealed the uninterrupted British retreat far more accurately than the news broadcasts. On December 29, the Japanese again bombed the city. After that, day after day, the exact, triangle formations of silver bombers came in over the island, dropped their bomb loads, and swung back north, seldom touched by the sparse antiaircraft guns or the few slow fighters. Although the Japanese concentrated on military targets, total accuracy was impossible. Civilian casualties mounted. There were still no air-raid shelters and no place to take cover but the concrete water drains. Work in the open became dangerous without any nearby shelters. The Asiatic labor force quietly evaporated. Rubble and bomb craters became more common. The hospitals filled with the maimed and dying. At night the Chinese air-raid wardens began firing at exposed lights. The war had at last come to Singapore.

By January even the most sanguine realized that the growing threat to the city could no longer be ignored. The Japanese bombers continued to fly over the island with impunity. The flood of refugees, with their tales of disaster, never ceased. The names of the battle sites crept south. On January 2, the Japanese took Kampar; on January 7, they broke the Slim River line. On January 11, the British gave up Kuala Lumpur and Port Swettenham. Two thirds of Malaya had been lost in a month. Slowly the civilians realized that the Japanese were not going to be pushed back, that Malaya might be lost. The same unpleasant conclusion had been reached by the generals. For over a month the army had been in retreat, bypassed, cut off, ambushed. Every line had been flanked by hooks through the supposedly impenetrable jungle, by surprise landings from the sea, by unexpected thrusts on rafts down unnavigable rivers. Many units had simply disintegrated, others had surrendered or lost the will to fight. Those still in the line were exhausted by the endless withdrawal. Despite an occasional, temporary success, by mid-January the British commanders began to accept a siege of the island as almost inevitable.[16]

In London a determined effort was finally made to reverse the relentless pattern of British defeats. For weeks the Prime Minister of Australia, John Curtin, had wrangled with Churchill over the conduct of the campaign. For Australia the loss of Malaya could well be a harbinger of invasion. Enmeshed as he was in a dozen crises, Churchill finally came to realize that unless he acted quickly a major disaster loomed in Malaya. He had already sent some reinforcements and now he agreed to send more, including the entire British 18th Division originally earmarked for Burma. On January 13, the first convoy arrived with infantry, antiaircraft, antitank troops, and fifty-one *Hurricane* fighters. During the last half of January, ship after ship ran the Japanese air gantlet. Thousands of troops disembarked, mountains of supplies piled up; but the sudden spate of help added little to Percival's fighting potential. The Indian troops were raw and unenthusiastic. The Australians were enthusiastic civilians in uniform; many had sailed only a few weeks after enlistment without having ever fired a rifle. The British 18th Division had spent most of the previous three months crammed aboard transports. The *Hurricanes* had been equipped for desert warfare and needed to be converted. An effort was also made to strengthen the command structure. On December 25, Brooke-Popham had been relieved, in what was announced as a long-planned change, and replaced as Commander-in-Chief by General Sir Henry Pownall, who, in turn, had been removed early in January. The new Commander-in-Chief in South East Asia, Sir Archibald Wavell, received a mixed bag of Australian, British, Dutch, and American units scattered over several thousand miles and facing a dozen Japanese threats. At the same time Churchill appointed Wavell, he recalled Duff Cooper, his personal Cabinet representative in Singapore, whose duties had remained vague. With unchallenged command Wavell still could do little to halt the deterioration of the military situation in Malaya. He decided to leave most of the decisions up to General Percival, his commander on the spot. On January 14, the command of the front itself was given to Australian General Gordon Bennett, who had loudly and publicly expressed his disgust at the continued withdrawals.

Although Bennett's Australians now put up a stiff fight, the withdrawals continued. The reinforcements were in no state to be tossed into the jungle, and Percival had to keep most of them in camps on the island. The *Hurricanes* proved very effective for a few days and then the Japanese numerical superiority wore them down. By the end of the month, the RAF again had only a handful of planes.

The British High Command in Singapore had been very slow indeed to react to the growing urgency of the military situation. Not until December 23 had General Percival ordered a "reconnaissance" of the north shore of the island. Weeks passed with no more positive activity than the drawing up of plans for proposed defense positions. Not until January 26 did a compulsory civilian labor plan become effective. Six weeks had passed and no one had made even a beginning on a defense line of the landward sides of the island. More appalling, only a very few responsible commanders even realized that the island had no defenses. Even Winston Churchill still believed in Fortress Singapore until too late. On January 19, his illusions were finally shattered after Wavell's report on the state of Singapore's "defenses."

> *Now, suddenly . . . I saw before me the hideous spectacle of the almost naked island and of the wearied, if not exhausted, troops retreating upon it.*
>
> *I do not write this in any way to excuse myself. I ought to have known. My advisers ought to have known and I ought to have been told, and I ought to have asked . . . the possibility of Singapore having no landward defences no more entered into my mind than that of a battleship being launched without a bottom.*[17]

Yet, there Singapore sat, wide open, with very little time left to throw up even a hasty barricade. When the troops began arriving from the north ready to take up positions in the defense line, they were stunned to find the beaches and jungles along the north and west shores untouched. Lieutenant-Colonel J. F. D. Steed of the 11th Indian Division checked with the Chief Engineer's Office to discover the progress of the fortifications his tired division would occupy. He found nothing.

> *I was dumbfounded . . . and learned that there was not a trench and not a bit of barbed wire on the whole north-east and north-west side of the island. We thought that during our time up country all these defences would have been installed.*[18]

Even the heavy guns protecting the naval base were going to be of little use. Either their trajectory was useless against a land foe or their only line of fire was out to sea. The unpalatable truth was that the Strait of Johore was not going to be much more of a barrier to the Japanese Twenty-fifth Army than the Slim River or the Muda River had been. Nothing had been done and time had run out. The Japanese advance had almost reached the tip of Malaya.

On the peninsula the British managed to pull back their front under steady Japanese pressure. They still held a ring around the only overland passage to the island, a massive concrete causeway across the Strait on the northwest coast. By the night of January 31, the bulk of the army had reached the island. At dawn on February 1, only a rear guard of tough Scots Highlanders remained on the far side. Shortly after seven o'clock, the weary troops watching from the Singapore side of the causeway heard the pipes playing *Blue Bonnets over the Border*. Then they saw the two battalion pipers, Steward and Maclean, walking slowly and alone to the tune of *A Hundred Pipers*. When they reached the island side of the causeway, they turned and began *Hielan' Laddie*. Then a battered handful of Argyll and Sutherland Highlanders started across. Only ninety ragged, dirty men were left out of the 900 who had gone upcountry. Their battalion had in another war on another battlefield earned the title "the thin red line." On the morning of February 1, 1942, they had renewed their claim. The little handful of men, the only jungle-trained troops in Malaya, marched smartly across to the pipes. Then their commander, Colonel Ian Stewart, walked across, the last British soldier to leave Malaya. The pipers stopped. To the disheartened and exhausted men who watched the few Argylls march across with their pipes, it was a fitting end to a desperate campaign. With more regiments like the Highlanders perhaps the story upcountry would have been different, but there had not been any more.

An hour later, an enormous explosion tore a huge seventy-foot chunk out of the causeway. The resounding roar of the demolition, clearly heard in Singapore, had been impressive; but the water in the gap at low tide would be only four feet deep. The same morning General Percival announced to the city that "the battle of Malaya has come to an end and the battle of Singapore has started."[19] He did not admit, probably even to himself, that Singapore was naked to assault.

On his side of the Strait of Johore, General Yamashita made his official report to Tokyo on the course of the campaign. There can hardly be any doubt that Tokyo must have been impressed. The Japanese Twenty-fifth Army had made an advance of 700 miles in fifty-five days, repairing 250 bridges along the way. The army had captured 8,000 prisoners, 330 guns, 550 machine guns, 3,600 vehicles, 800 locomotives and railroad cars, thirteen airplanes, and endless piles of still uncounted "Churchill stores." All the peninsula with its wealth of rubber and tin could be incorporated into the expanding East-Asian

Co-Prosperity Sphere. Yamashita could well be proud of his report. The Twenty-fifth Army was, of course, a little behind schedule, but there was still hope that he could take Singapore before his self-imposed February 11 deadline. The Japanese intelligence estimates of the inferior quality of the British troops had generally proved accurate. At times, however, resistance had been bitter; in fact, the Imperial Guards had become so enraged at their unexpected mauling at the hands of the Australians at the Muar River that they had taken time off from their attack to massacre their prisoners. Still, for the most part, all had gone as Yamashita had planned. Even when the General Staff had switched the air force's main strength to operations against the Dutch East Indies, he had felt no qualms. In fact, he had ordered his reserve division, the 56th, into the Burma campaign since the men were not needed in Malaya. Three divisions had proved sufficient. Malaya was now in Japanese hands.

General Yamashita intended to wait for a week while his troops regrouped and his engineers collected enough small craft for the landing on the island. Then, under a heavy barrage which would probably use up most of his limited store of artillery shells, the 5th and 18th Divisions would hit the swampy northwest coast. Later, the Imperial Guards would land slightly farther north. While there might be a bitter battle for a beachhead, once his divisions were landed in strength on the island the end would be in sight. If his landings were thrown back or even pinned down for too long, the Twenty-fifth Army would be in serious trouble. Yamashita had only about 30,000 men and he knew the British had more. He had received very little Japanese equipment during the past two months and could hardly continue a protracted fight on the island with captured supplies alone. The battle of Singapore would have to be quick. Yamashita remained satisfied with his battle plan, for he expected the British to break in front of his bluff.

> *My attack on Singapore was a bluff. . . . I knew that if I had to fight long for Singapore, I would be beaten. That is why the surrender had to be at once. I was very frightened all the time that the British would discover our numerical weakness and lack of supplies and force me into disastrous street fighting.*[20]

Risks or no, he really had no choice but to attack or else to wait to be attacked. Yamashita now set up Army Headquarters on the top floors of the Green Palace of the Sultan of Johore in full view of the British. His staff hurriedly began preparations for the final stage of the campaign—the assault across the Strait.

Everyone on the island knew the assault was coming. Once the last rumbling reverberations of the causeway blast had faded away, the civilians could only wait. Percival had no air force and no navy, but on paper at least he had a huge collection of troops, nearly 125,000. These had to be organized, sent to the beaches, and there made ready to throw back Yamashita's certain attack. Percival decided that the only hope of a successful defense depended on smashing the Japanese at the landing places—there simply was no room to fight a battle on the island. Rather than hold most of the troops in a mobile reserve, he decided on a static defense line all along the coast. Despite Wavell's suggestion that the danger spot would probably be the northwest coast, Percival felt the attack would come from the northeast. To this sector he sent his best men and his heaviest concentration of artillery. Despite the vast number of troops in Singapore, Percival could not organize a defense of the coast with the few trained men on hand nor could he set up a strong mobile reserve. Although he had over 100,000 men on the rolls, only a few first-rate units were dependable. His reinforcements, including even the British 18th Division, were either out of condition or without training; they could at best be used only for cannon fodder. Even more useless were the 15,000 rear-echelon troops—clerks, typists, cooks, servants and administrators, civilians in uniform. Percival was left with his veterans, men who in two months of retreat had reached the edge of physical exhaustion. Neither Percival nor his generals felt the situation was hopeless but it was obvious that no one, civilian or military, had ever envisioned a siege. In fact, the censors, still as rigid as ever, refused to allow the correspondents to refer to siege—they preferred "besiegement."[21]

The brutal fact remained that Singapore Island had been cut off, surrounded on land, sea and air. Yet, things could have been a lot worse. The army's food supplies were excellent: meat for three months, flour and tinned vegetables for four, and other items for five months. The ammunition situation was not quite so satisfactory, although there were enough artillery shells for three months and rifle ammunition, grenades, and mortar shells for six weeks. The major problem was that only twenty-three days of antitank ammunition and twelve days of pistol and submachine-gun ammunition could be found. There were 150 antiaircraft guns, a searchlight regiment, and still a few *Hurricanes* and *Buffalos* flying out of the Kallang airfield. With fields of fire set up and spotters on the top floor of the thirteen-story Cathay Building in downtown Singapore, the artillery setup was distinctly hopeful. The most critical situation was the water supply. A bad dry season in 1941 had lowered the level of the two large reservoirs and the demolition of the causeway had cut off about 50 per cent of the total water supply, which had been piped in from the mainland. Despite the wastage from the brittle pipe system, however, careful husbanding could supply the army and the population with water almost indefinitely. The civilians had a six months' supply of flour, and nine of meat. Even as late as January, there were over 100,000 pigs on the island. Thus, even with the refugees from the north, who had practically doubled the island's population, no one would starve and no one would go thirsty.

The population now lived on first-hand terms with a real war. The two-year vacation from violence had ended with a vengeance. The Japanese air attacks went on. With no shelters, no early warning, no fighter cover, each raid caused sudden and deadly havoc. The toll of civilian casualties grew. The hospital staffs struggled to treat the shattered bodies and then find some still unused corner for them. More and more fires seemed to burn out of control. Charred rubble and broken glass piled up uncollected. In the face of this piecemeal destruction, the city continued as best it could. The Auxiliary Fire Service, the Special Constabulary, the air raid wardens all stuck to their posts during raids and then went on with their daily activities when they could snatch a few hours. A revolutionary sign of the seriousness of the situation came late in January when the governor dispatched a circular letter to the Malayan Civil Service: "The day of minute papers has gone. There must be no more passing of files from one department to another. . . . Similarly, the day of letters and reports is over."[22] This was certainly a move in the right direction, but many felt that in January 1942 it was a couple of years too late. Elsewhere, signs of the normal old ways could be noted. The Indian laborers still trimmed the grass beside the highways. The brick factories turned out brick. The clubs served drinks. Milk was delivered. The shops were open, although both customers and proprietors deserted them when the planes came over—there was only one kind of plane, Japanese. There was mounting fear and desperation. So long nurtured on illusion, the civilians hated to grasp the fact of defeat.

> *In your heart you had no confidence in your own troops. There had been this retreat all the way down and nobody had stood up to the Japanese. You knew it was pretty well over. You couldn't see any chance of getting away from the Island.*[23]

As daily life grew more hazardous, this question of getting away became crucial.

Evacuation had become an increasing preoccupation as the fear of defeat and captivity grew stronger with each new bomb explosion among the crowded downtown blocks. Each raid meant more maimed and dead civilians. If the siege stretched out, the fate of the one million civilians would be grim. It was long past time to get out the women and children. A few had left early at the urging of the prudent, more had followed as the Japanese thrust down the peninsula. Even now the Government did not want to force anyone to go; but, on January 27, many heard Churchill's speech to the House of Commons broadcast over the Delhi Radio. He warned of more bad news from the Far East. He could only mean Singapore. The arrival of the 18th Division had done little to raise civilian spirits. Most of the British and many Orientals opted for escape in the face of any odds, and the odds were poor. The Japanese airstrips were within minutes of the burning docks and every transport was a target. The Japanese dive bombers set fire to the *Empress of Asia* when the captain tried to run the Sundra Straits into the city. The blackened hulk, aground near the Horsburgh Light, pointed clearly to the dangers facing any ship trying to make a run down "Bomb Alley" to safety. Even these risks did not seem too great in the face of the threat of years in internment camps. Twenty-four hours a day the Pacific and Orient clerks processed evacuees. When the women and children, the aged, the unneeded, poured onto the docks, they found wild confusion. Asiatic laborers had long since disappeared, refusing to work on the docks without shelter from the bombs. Following them had gone most of the harbor organization. Planned directions and governmental discipline had vanished. The refugees simply rushed on board without authorization, without passports. No one cared. Two transports, jammed with refugees, sailed on February 6. At noon the next day the *Duchess of Bedford* and the *Empress* sailed with 1,500 women and children. As expected, the Japanese carried out high-level bombing attacks until both ships were out of air range. Three more transports sailed the next week; but, by the end of the first week of February, the chance for any large-scale evacuation had gone. There were simply no more large ships in the port and no more available to risk the run to the port. More refugees would get out on smaller vessels, coastal steamers, and large motorboats, but the majority of the civilian population would have to suffer out the siege. Still, the British had managed at the last minute, in the face of heavy attack, to evacuate many of the women and children, including Chinese and Malayan civilians. Some of the vessels would not get through. All that would be known was that the transport left Singapore and never reached India or Java. No one would ever really know how many got out of Singapore. There were no longer any voluminous records in triplicate; in fact, there were no longer any records at all—a change as drastic as the air raids.

In contrast to the wild last-minute evacuation, the quiet on the northern perimeter was startling. The Japanese kept up a sporadic harassing mortar fire combined with an occasional air strike. The men crouching in shallow field works, hastily scraped down to the water level, waited morosely for the inevitable assault. Percival had too few troops, spread too thinly in positions not mutually supporting and with little depth. He continued to believe that Yamashita would hit the northeast coast near the naval base. On February 5, the Japanese began dropping shells into this area as well as on the southern end of the broken causeway. With shells falling on the northeast coast, Percival discounted intelligence reports that the Japanese were building up opposite the northwest coast. General Gordon Bennett sent out scout patrols to check these vague reports. Then, on the morning of February 8, Lieutenant-General Takumo Nishimura's Imperial Guards occupied Ubin Island off the northeast coast. Immediately the Japanese began to direct heavy fire on the Changi Fortress. Again Percival was reassured, despite more indications that the Japanese had concentrated on the northwest side of the Johore Strait. There, General Bennett grew increasingly concerned as the Japanese swiftly built up the heaviest barrage of the campaign. The rising noise of the Japanese artillery, the reports of his patrols from the mainland, and the sound of a hammering noise from across the Strait—all indicated an attack on the west, not the east. To stop the Japanese, Percival had given him only 2,500 men to hold twenty miles of swampy coastline covered with jungle. Listening to the heavy drumbeat of the Japanese shells, Bennett could not get to sleep that evening. At ten-thirty, he gave up and drove to his operations room.

At the same time Bennett reached his headquarters, the Australians along the coast sighted the first shadowy Japanese barges. Heavy mortar fire began dropping on their positions, smashing the telephone lines to the artillery positions in the rear. The emergency flares for searchlight and artillery support failed to function or if they did go off were not seen. Surprised, cut off from artillery support and rapid reinforcement, Bennett's 2,500 Australians would have to go it alone.

On their side of the Strait, the Japanese commanders were as anxious as Bennett. They expected real difficulties, and the first reports confirmed their fears. At ten-thirty the first barges had beached at the end of Lim Chu Krang Road directly in the plotted fields of fire of the Twenty-fourth Machine Gun Battalion. The Australians immediately opened up, spraying the boats and the first wave with heavy fire. All along the shore, the Japanese landings ran into bitter initial fire. Riddled collapsible boats and burning barges began drifting aimlessly with the current, but others pushed on to take their places. Under heavy fire Lance Corporal Yamamoto took his makeshift craft, three small boats lashed together, straight into shore. Shells smashed the two outside boats. A bullet knocked over his steersman and another tore open Yamamoto's chest, exposing his lungs. Somehow he managed to stay on his feet. Another shell hit the gunwale of one boat, showering splinters and killing two more soldiers. Just before he died Yamamoto managed to land the shattered and bloody wreck in front of the Australian positions. On either side were other beached barges, riddled and smoldering. Other men like Yamamoto continued bringing their barges into shore. An ammunition barge suddenly went up in a huge flash. Using the light to aim by, the Australians knocked off several more landing craft before the flaming barge sank and the blackness returned.

The Japanese still came on, swimming up creeks, crawling into the jungle. Some landed safely to the south in a mangrove swamp and began moving in behind the Australians, finding their way in the pitch dark with luminous wrist compasses. For two hours the Aussies held on. As they fought it out with the barges, they knew that a growing stream of Japanese was filtering around behind their position. Further back no one knew what was going on. The artillery sat silent, unaware of the landing. By midnight the Australian resistance began to dissolve in the face of the 4,000 Japanese already ashore. First one or two men began drifting back, then whole units. In the maze of the jungle, they wandered on, fearful of ambush and uncertain of direction. Ten minutes after midnight, the Japanese officers waiting on the mainland saw blue flares from the 5th Division's front. A few minutes later, more flares shot up over the 18th Division. The landing had been secured. Yamashita began pouring in his men as fast as the barges could shuttle back and forth. Soon strong tank-infantry teams were pushing eastward through the jungle on the heels of the Australians.

By dawn, Bennett's Australians had collapsed. Still unaware of the successful Japanese assault, the artillery troops suddenly saw the Australians moving past them toward the rear.

> *They came moving at a half-trot, panic stricken. I've never seen a thing like it. It was pouring with rain and most of them were clad only in shorts. Few were wearing boots, and some of the men's feet were cut to ribbons—they'd come across the rivers, through the mangrove swamps, through the bush, then out along the Jurong Road. They'd scrapped everything that could hold them back. They'd thrown aside their rifles and ammunition.*[24]

The battle to hold the Strait was over before most of the British commanders knew that it had begun. Even then the reaction was slow and uncertain. No one seemed to know what the real situation was except the Japanese. Yamashita's 10,000 troops were attacking up the jungle rivers. They expanded their early wedges in the Australian positions and forced their way toward the north-south Jurong Road, the obvious inland defense axis. The fighting grew increasingly chaotic. Back at British headquarters Percival and Bennett tried to create some sort of orderly defense line and mount a counterattack before time ran out.

On the other side of the Strait, Yamashita also had his troubles. His main strength still had not been shifted across the island. Only a few tanks had as yet been ferried across. Worse still, General Nishimura held up the Imperial Guards' landing in the swamps near the mouth of the Kranji River because of a report of blazing oil on the water. The Germans had long ago warned the Japanese that the British might wait until the invasion barges were off the coast and then ignite oil on the surface. Nishimura had postponed his landing and thrown the whole attack out of gear. Yamashita had to reorder the attack. Many of the Japanese were drowned by the rising tides or cremated by the flaming oil seeping down into the swamps from the burning oil storage tanks. Others died in front of the machine guns of the Twenty-seventh Australian Brigade. Nishimura pushed on, and by noon had a firm foothold for the Imperial Guards. This meant that despite the heavy initial casualties and Nishimura's initial procrastination, Yamashita's bridgehead was secure. Within twenty-four hours he moved his headquarters to the island and at the same time learned that the causeway had been repaired.

In the meantime, Bennett scraped together enough troops to launch a counterattack at eleven in the morning. With Nishimura's Guards pinned down in the flaming swamps near the causeway, Bennett hoped to turn the tide in the center and push the Japanese back into the swamps west of the Jurong Road. At zero hour, just before the attack jumped off, the Japanese hit the forward area in strength and forced the Australians to pull back toward the Tengah airfield. Despite the failure of the hastily planned counterattack, Percival still hoped to hold the Jurong line. He was reluctant to strip the other areas of the island to beef up the western front, although he did send reinforcements into the causeway area, the north flank of the Jurong line. He had not been able to create a mobile reserve and he was not yet sure that the force attacking Bennett was Yamashita's main effort. Fearful of a breakthrough or another landing, Percival prepared for the worst by drawing up a new defense line on paper. This line lay much closer to Singapore city and would reduce some of the difficulties of the long front. Still he had not given up hope for the Jurong line.

Despite the Japanese pressure in the center, the key position was the Kranji peninsula on the north where General Maxwell's Twenty-seventh Australian Brigade faced the Imperial Guards. Once Nishimura got his toehold in the swamps, he hung on. The bitter fighting continued all through the night as the Japanese hit the Australians again and again. All efforts to dislodge Maxwell failed. The Japanese casualties began to mount. Nishimura was having doubts about the wisdom of continuing, but Yamashita refused to call off the attack. Finally, just before dawn, the Australian defense suddenly melted. Neither Maxwell nor Bennett would accept responsibility for the withdrawal; but, whoever gave the order, the result was that the Jurong line was outflanked. The road to Singapore was wide open.

In the center Japanese pressure continued. When the Japanese point reached the Tengah airfield, the British gunners fired their fortress guns at point-blank range and withdrew. Sometime between nine and ten-thirty, Percival's secret plan for a new perimeter defense line nearer the city reached the commanders at the front. Many decided that withdrawal was now officially sanctioned. Others had grown increasingly uneasy as they watched the steady traffic of front-line troops toward the rear. No one was quite sure if his flanks were secure. No one knew where the Japanese were. No one knew what to do next. When one unit began to pull back, others followed. The defense troops began to retreat toward Singapore in growing confusion. Units became mixed, heavy equipment was abandoned intact, communication faltered. Absolute disaster seemed very close.

In the meantime, Commander-in-Chief Wavell flew in from Java to consult with Percival and Bennett. The three generals met at Bennett's headquarters on an estate on Bukit Timah, the highest hill on the island. It was also a prime target for the Japanese artillery. Almost as soon as Wavell arrived, the Japanese began to shell the hill. Much of the conference had to be carried on under a table while shells burst all around. A splinter smashed Percival's glasses. Others whistled through the conference room. The atmosphere was hardly conducive to logical thinking, much less enthusiastic plans. The shattered headquarters, his own position under the table, the expressions on the officers' faces revealed to Wavell, if he needed revelation, just how desperate Singapore's position had become. All the news was bad. There was still no reserve. Only Kallang airfield remained operative. Civilian casualties were incredibly high; no one seemed to know just how high. The city was in flames. Wavell urged an immediate counterattack. Before the attack could be mounted, the Japanese smashed down the Bukit Timah Road into the attack area. The counterattack swiftly turned into a withdrawal. All Wavell could do was to issue a brave bulletin.

> *It is certain that our troops on Singapore Island greatly outnumber any Japanese that have crossed the Straits. We must defeat them. Our whole fighting reputation is at stake and the honor of the British Empire. . . . It will be disgraceful if we yield our boasted fortress of Singapore to inferior enemy troops. There must be no thought of sparing troops or the civil population and no mercy must be shown to weakness in any shape or form.*[25]

Wavell flew out with a heavy heart and little hope. The Jurong line had been irrevocably lost. The Japanese had taken almost half the island in forty-eight hours. Many of the troops had behaved badly. Too many offcers had withdrawn without orders. Wavell knew, as did everyone else, that the fall of Singapore was now only a matter of time. Neither orders nor oratory was going to create a general reserve or a successful counter blow.

With defeat looming, the Governor gave the order on February 9 for the Civil Denial Scheme, the elaborate burned earth policy. Percival had already informed London that the army could not fight the Japanese and at the same time destroy the massive complex of military installations. Although demolition work had been going forward quietly at the naval base since January 27, the enormity of the task—the instructions for destruction of the base filled two volumes the size of telephone books—prevented all but the destruction of the most vital installations. The huge floating dock had been sunk, the machinery of the King George V Graving Dock destroyed; but still miles of warehouses, repair shops and depots stood untouched and abandoned. In the city demolition was hampered by the unscheduled evacuation of key personnel, the reluctance of owners to destroy their own property, and the growing panic and confusion as the Japanese columns thrust nearer. On February 10, an artillery team spiked the fifteen-inch guns of the Changi and Johore Battery. "It was sad for gunners to see those barrels fall open like peeled bananas."[26] Every morning for weeks the wife of the director of the Chartered Bank had climbed into a rickshaw loaded with five million pounds' worth of war bonds and carried them to the Treasury, where the bonds were destroyed.

By the time the Japanese landed on the island, the war bonds, at least, had been "denied," but many of the military installations had to be left untouched. Too little time, too few men, too much pressure resulted in a haphazard, superficial burnt-earth policy. At last the huge oil tanks went up, covering the city with a permanent black cloud of greasy smoke. As the Japanese moved in closer to the center of the island, they too had to decide on what to destroy. Their artillery targets and air strikes became more selective. There was no point in destroying today what would be captured tomorrow, for, if the pace of the advance continued, the entire island would be in Japanese hands within a few days.

Despite the swift success of his assault, Yamashita remained uncertain. From his side of the hill, the British resistance had been impressive. Worse, Percival seemed to be willing to continue fighting all the way back into the battered city itself. Yamashita lived every hour in dread of the days of street fighting. Japanese ammunition supplies, particularly rifle bullets, had just about been used up. Signs of British panic and the regular reports of further advances were both, of course, encouraging; but, if Percival held out much longer, the Japanese would have shot their bolt. Yamashita's runaway victory might very well be lost at the last moment if he ran out of bullets or if the attrition of street fighting began or if the British received reinforcements. Hopefully, on February 11, Japan's National Holiday and the date on which he had hoped to accept Percival's surrender, Yamashita ordered surrender pamphlets dropped over British lines. Twenty-nine wooden boxes about eighteen inches long, containing "A Message to the High Command of the British Army," fell over Singapore.

> *My sincere respect is due to your army which, true to the traditional spirit of Great Britain, is bravely defending Singapore which now stands isolated and unaided. . . . But the development of the general war situation has already sealed the fate of Singapore, and the continuation of futile resistance would only serve to inflict direct harm and injuries to thousands of noncombatants living in the city, throwing them into further miseries and horrors of war, but also would add nothing to the honor of your army.*[27]

Although it is likely that Percival agreed with Yamashita's analysis of the situation, he did not reply. Wavell's orders had been to "fight it out to the end and in close contact with the enemy."[28] Percival would hold on, waiting for new orders or total defeat. The Japanese continued to advance down the Bukit Timah Road near the Racecourse, seven minutes by car from the Raffles Hotel.

In Singapore, life inside the burning city became a daily hell. The huge mushrooms of oily black smoke covered the sun. The sound of guns and bombs seemed endless and unremitting. The civilian defense organizations gradually collapsed under the strain. There were too many buildings burning, too many dead and dying, too many enemy planes overhead. The streets were covered with tangled webs of telephone wires, the sidewalks piled with charred rubbish, the shop windows shattered, and the sound of falling glass constant. Every part of the city was choked with weary and disheartened troops. More and more deserters sifted into basement hide-outs. More and more men stumbled in from the front hoping to find safety. The situation in the hospitals grew worse. Thousands of wounded soldiers lay on the floors of corridors, in waiting rooms, on the stairs. There was not even room inside the buildings for the badly wounded. Stretchers were placed untended in tents, in dugouts, or simply on the shrapnel-flecked lawn. A mounting number of untended walking wounded huddled in flimsy sheds, in abandoned garages, in cellars and shell holes. Every hour, hundreds more of civilians were brought in. Dripping blood, the doctors worked twenty-four hours a day in the steaming heat, but they never caught up with the tide of shattered bodies. Gradually, organized treatment disappeared. The shells continued to fall. Low-flying planes shot past overhead, machine-gunning anyone who moved. With the military hospitals glutted, the civilians were taken to wait and to die in churches, in nearby buildings, in deserted stores. No one could imagine what worse could happen to the helpless, untreated patients. Then the Indian Military Hospital caught on fire. Long before all the patients could be evacuated nothing remained but a smouldering ruin filled with charred bodies. No one knew how many had been burned alive. There was no time to find out.

Everyone knew the end was very near. The Governor ordered the destruction of all the alcohol on the island in order to prevent drunken looting of the city by the Japanese. A million and a half bottles of spirits and sixty thousand gallons of Samsu Chinese whiskey went down the drains or up in flames. Within a few minutes the smell of spilled whiskey drifted over the city to join the cordite odor of bomb blasts and the stench of burning oil and rubber. The civilians still tried to carry on. Mr. Jack Bennett and two friends dropped in at the Singapore Club for their last drinks. Bennett signed his final bar chit. Four years later he received his club bill, including the final chit—"Someone was looking out after the books."[29] Many people went on looking after their normal business. The milk vans continued delivering milk bottles in the suburbs until the trucks were riddled with bullet holes. Some of the movie houses stayed open. Reller's Band at the Adelphia Hotel continued playing for the dancers. An exotic, dark-haired English girl in shorts and a light sweater exercised a pair of greyhounds to the delight of a couple of very surprised RAF pilots waiting to evacuate the last handful of planes. The Tamil laborers calmly continued sweeping the streets right up to the end. Many civilians went on working at their jobs even while the Japanese columns moved toward their homes. At nine-thirty on February 12, one woman left her cottage near the golf course for her office. During the morning an unknown officer telephoned her not to return home since there seemed to be some Japanese dug into her garden. On Wednesday, February 11, the last regular newspaper ended publication; but the Government Printing Office began running off 7,000 copies of a single sheet emergency newspaper. The Malayan Broadcasting Company evacuated the last employees to Java, where "Radio Singapore" continued broadcasting.

Friday, February 13, dawned bleakly through the clouds of black oil smoke. It was a grim, unlucky day. Percival had retreated within the final perimeter. The twenty-eight-mile front, in many places thinly held, barely included the last vital installations—the Alexandra Hospital, the main ammunition dumps, and the ordnance depots. The Japanese points were within a few minutes of the center of the city. Crowded inside the narrow pocket were over a hundred thousand troops and nearly a million civilians. Every inch of the ground became a desirable military target. Trucks, Bren carriers, military vehicles were parked hub to hub. Artillery pieces were everywhere. Deserters, untreated wounded, the lost and strayed, the useless staff officers, the generals without troops and troops without generals wandered vaguely through the rubble-piled streets. Water grew short as the broken mains spilled out five million gallons every day. The shops had finally closed, and food supplies became uncertain. With no civilian labor and only the remnants of the civil defense organization left, the fires burned unchecked, the wounded went untended, and the bodies unburied. All day the bombs and shells fell. No one could even guess the toll of dead and wounded. The sound of firing came closer.

Early in the evening, Percival gave the final official evacuation order. Some 3,000 nurses, service officers, technicians, women and children, and some civilian experts boarded the last small boats. That evening, one after another, crammed to the gunwales, the little fleet of tugs, tongkans, motorboats, sampans and launches moved out into the harbor lit by the flickering flames of the burning city. Every one of the 3,000 had a chance, however small, to escape. Looking back toward the ruin that had been Singapore, they knew they were very lucky indeed.

After dark the Japanese reached the Alexandra Hospital and ran amok. They shot many of the wounded and bayoneted others, including one man on the operating table. The next morning, they shot two hundred more. By dawn on Saturday, Wavell's demand that the fighting continue seemed only a death warrant for the million people crammed inside the perimeter. Twenty-four hours before, Percival's commanders had insisted that further resistance was hopeless. The 18th Division reported that ammunition was low and morale even lower. Wavell had insisted on continuing the fight. Now Percival learned that the collapse of the water supply was imminent. The water might last one or two days more. Percival decided to hold on as long as the water lasted. The First Malayan Brigade beat off a Japanese thrust from the southwest. Then, two hours after Percival had based his continuing resistance on the one or two days' water supply, the Japanese reached the reservoirs. For some reason, they did not immediately cut off the water. The confused fighting went on. The Alexandra ammunition magazine caught fire and began to explode in a chain of giant concussions. The entire port was ringed by the flaming oil and rubber stocks. Flames 600 feet high swept the timber sheds at Kallang. Warehouses burned on unchecked, hardly noticed. Japanese bombs continued to fall into the center of the city. Chinatown's narrow streets and fragile buildings were shattered and smashed. At last, Japanese pressure slackened. The exhausted British and Australian troops held on, waiting for dawn and renewed attacks. The advanced Japanese points had reached the Mount Pleasant residential area. One more hard thrust and the perimeter would collapse.

Wavell still insisted, "Your gallant stand is serving a purpose and must be continued to the limit of endurance."[30] Percival, however, felt that the limit had been reached. On the morning of February 15, he attended a Communion Service at Fort Canning and then called a conference of his area commanders. He explained to them that there would soon be no water, no gasoline, no artillery or antiaircraft ammunition. Unless a counterattack could secure the reservoirs, Singapore must surrender. One after another the senior officers told him that no such attack could be mounted. Their men were finished. Percival replied that he would, therefore, ask the Japanese to cease fire at four in the afternoon. At that moment official approval for the surrender arrived from Wavell. Percival sent a surrender party up the Bukit Timah Road toward the point of the Japanese 5th Division and at the same time cabled Wavell that he was unable to continue the fight any longer.

At one o'clock in the afternoon, the Japanese saw three British officers walking toward them waving a white flag. The Japanese were stunned. Yamashita's anxiety over the protracted siege had been growing. He and his Chief-of-Staff, Lieutenant-General Sosaku Suzuki, had been watching the battle from the heights near Bukit Timah. Suzuki had suggested that it would take several more days to capture Fort Canning and Fort Changi. The highly accurate British artillery fire, spotted from the top of the Cathay Building in the center of the city, had disheartened many of the Japanese senior officers. The Chief-of-Staff of the Takeda Division had urged Yamashita to pull back. This was the one course of action Yamashita could not follow. One step back and his whole bluff would be called. Thus Captain Sugita's signal from the front that the British wanted to surrender was not immediately taken at face value, although Yamashita agreed to set up a surrender meeting for six o'clock in the afternoon. The Japanese commander suspected that the British were stalling for time in hopes of reinforcements.

> *When the message came of the enemy surrender offer, I was very cautious about it. I was afraid it might be a trick. I ordered the British commander with his chief of staff and interpreter to meet me at 1,800 hours. I also ordered a guard of one thousand armed soldiers to protect us at the meeting place.*[31]

Percival arrived at the site suggested by Yamashita, a Ford factory just north of Bukit Timah, a half hour late. After some confusion he and Yamashita sat down at opposite ends of a narrow table at seven o'clock. At one end sat the Japanese general, determined to force immediate surrender before the British could discover just how few troops and how little ammunition he had. At the other end sat the British general, pale, his hands shaking, determined to surrender his shattered troops rather than continue a pointless slaughter. Discussion stumbled on for some time, hampered by inadequate interpreters and Percival's inability to put into words his willingness to surrender. Yamashita grew increasingly unhappy. The British general seemed to be stalling. He still could not believe that Percival was sincere.

> YAMASHITA: *You have agreed to the terms but you have not made yourself clear as to whether you have agreed to surrender or not.*
> PERCIVAL *nodded.*
> YAMASHITA: *If you've accepted our terms, we want to hear "yes."*
> PERCIVAL: *Yes, I agree.*[32]

At eight-thirty, forty minutes later, the roar of battle suddenly ended. A strange, heavy silence fell over the burning city. Only the crackle of flames, the tinkle of falling glass, and the muted cries of the wounded could be heard. Singapore had fallen. In seventy days Yamashita had driven down the long Malayan peninsula, across the Strait of Johore and into the city. He had lost just under 10,000 men. The British had lost 138,708, including 130,000 prisoners. They had also lost Southeast Asia.

The Japanese delegation returned in triumph to Army Headquarters. The staff officers cleared the table littered with maps and documents and placed a victory feast of dried cuttlefish, chestnuts and wine. It was a very happy group, and for good reason. The Twenty-fifth Army had imposed an unequaled defeat on the British Empire. At dawn Yamashita walked outside to the edge of the woods, faced the direction of the Emperor's Palace in Tokyo and began praying and bowing ceremoniously. His star was at its zenith: Singapore, The City of the Lion, The Fortress of the East, had become Shonan, Bright South, a Japanese bastion. The bronze statue of Raffles would be removed from Singapore, and outside the city a Shinto shrine would be built, a symbol of the new order in Asia.

While the Japanese celebrated their victory, a shaken Percival wrote his Order of the Day for February 16.

> *It has been necessary to give up the struggle, but I want the reasons explained to all ranks. The forward troops continued to hold their ground, but the essentials of war have run short. In a few days we shall have neither petrol nor food. Many types of ammunition are short, and the water supply, on which the vast civilian population and many of the troops are dependent, threatens to fail. This situation has been brought about partly by hostile air and artillery action. Without these sinews of war we cannot fight on. I thank all ranks for their efforts throughout this campaign.*[33]

For Percival it was the last act. The Union Jack had been hauled down and hidden somewhere. Thousands upon thousands of exhausted troops wandered through the rubble waiting for dawn and the arrival of the Japanese.

Not all the British waited hopelessly for the Japanese to march into the ruined city and put them into prison. All night long, small boats, dinghies, leaky sampans, and overlooked junks moved south away from the smouldering docks. General Gordon Bennett and two of his officers commandeered a tongkan and with twenty-one men on board sailed southwest. Eventually, on February 27, Bennett would reach Australia. Most of the men in the last desperate wave were not so lucky. The small boats struggling south toward the Dutch East Indies faced long odds. The Japanese planes swept the seas, and the slow-moving little boats were easy to spot and easy to sink. Even if they avoided the Japanese bombs and machine guns, many would come to grief on the scattered, bleak, uninhabited islands to the south. A little flotilla of three ancient Chinese river steamers converted to gunboats, loaded with 700 refugees including Air Vice-Marshal Pulford and Rear-Admiral Spooner, ran aground on the tiny malarial island of Pompong, little more than a barren rock, which the natives called the Island of Ghosts. Three months later the Japanese picked up the starving survivors. Pulford and Spooner had died weeks before. Even though an occasional boat reached the Dutch East Indies, the Japanese were sweeping through those islands in another runaway campaign. In a month or two the survivors often rejoined their comrades in the Changi prison back in Singapore if they were lucky, or were never heard from again if they were not. Despite all the hazards, a few like General Bennett managed to win through. Major Ivan Lyon of the Gordon Highlanders had set up a special organization in the islands to the south and managed to shepherd many escapees further south. Others somehow made it alone. One small handful of men sailed an open boat all the way to Australia through the Japanese-occupied islands. If the routes to the south were hazardous, escape to the north was even more dangerous. A few scattered men hid out hopelessly in the mountains or jungles. Most died swiftly in the alien jungles. A few did not. On their own, two privates of the Argyll Highlanders, Stewart and Bennet, managed to elude the Japanese for four years.

Organized units were rare. With Dalforce shattered at Singapore, the British resistance Force 136 in Malaya, undermanned and out of contact after Rangoon fell to the Japanese, let most partisan operations fall by default either to the Chinese Communists or to the bandits. Both of these groups viewed the presence of the British as an unwanted extra hazard. Except for the few daring or lucky ones, Percival's men marched off to Changi Fortress and years of captivity. All, that is, but the Argyll and Sutherland Highlanders. They brazenly commandeered their own trucks, and, while the Japanese watched uncertainly, they drove off to prison to the sound of their pipes. It was the last bright moment for many long years.

The very last act in the fall of Singapore would not come for four more years. On September 2, 1945, General Yamashita would again sit across a table from General Arthur Percival; but this time the Japanese general would be surrendering the Philippines to the Americans, while Percival, flown in from his prison camp in Manchuria, watched. Later General Yamashita, the Tiger of Malaya, after a hasty trial, would hang for war crimes. General Nishimura, former commander of the Imperial Guards Division, after spending the war in disgrace for his conduct during the landing on Singapore, would be executed for his part in the massacre of the Australian troops at the Muar River. Colonel Tsuji, Chief of Operations of the Twenty-fifth Army, would survive the war only to spend the postwar years wandering in disguise before finally returning to Japan to write *The Japanese Version of Singapore* in 1951. Few of the other Japanese officers and men, happy with victory in February 1942, would survive the war. Those who did returned to a homeland ravished by fire raids, crushed by two atomic bombs, unrecognizable in defeat. Although the Union Jack hauled down on February 15 and hidden during the years of captivity would once again fly over a British Singapore, all too few would live to see the city freed. In the Japanese prison camps, thousands died of starvation, of malaria, of untended wounds and multiple infections, of maltreatment. More thousands died in the valley of the Kwai building the Railroad of Death—two hundred and fifty miles long, with each mile costing the lives of sixty-four prisoners of war. Few prisoners who lived would ever be the same again. Some would take up the broken threads of their lives only to find that in the long years, the world had changed. Friends and relatives had died in battles they knew nothing about. Wives and children had been killed by a rocket weapon they had never known. Most of them gradually took up their old life; some, like Ronald Searle the cartoonist, who had begun by sketching the horrors of the prison camp, began a new one; but none would ever fully escape from the four searing years of despair.

On February 16, 1942, all this remained in the far and distant future. For the 130,000 British, Australians, and Indians, for the thousands of British civilians, there was only relief that the fighting had ended. The repeated shock of defeats, the steady roar of falling bombs, the random artillery explosions, and the burning buildings had dulled their senses and crushed their hopes. For the moment it was enough that quiet had come. Later there would be questions, but mainly and always the one great question: Why had Singapore fallen? Even after twenty years no one would ever give them an adequate answer. The cold fact remained that in seventy days Yamashita's small hard army of veterans had smashed down through Malaya and into Singapore. On February 15, 1942, Britain had suffered a massive, perhaps unequaled, defeat. In the darkening gloom as Percival rode back from the Ford factory, he little knew he had surrendered not only 130,000 men and the fortress city but also the myth of British invincibility and a way of life as well.

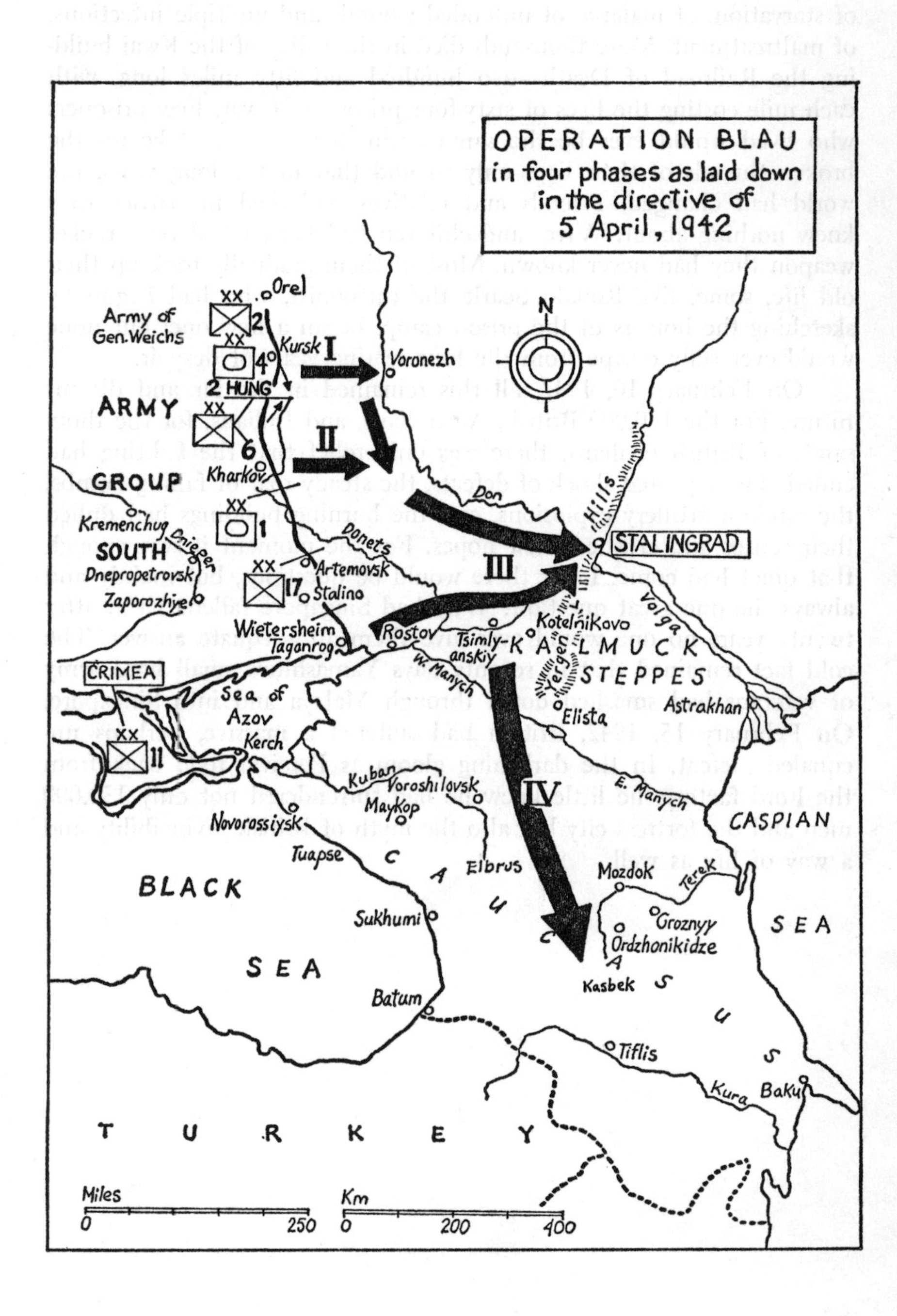
OPERATION BLAU
in four phases as laid down
in the directive of
5 April, 1942
N
Orel
Army of
Gen. Weichs
2
4
Kursk
I
Voronezh
2 HUNG
ARMY
GROUP
SOUTH
6
II
Kharkov
Don
Hills
1
Kremenchug
Dnieper
Donets
STALINGRAD
Dnepropetrovsk
Artemovsk
17
Stalino
III
Zaporozhye
Wietersheim
Taganrog
Rostov
Tsimly-
anskiy
Kotelnikovo
KALMUCK
STEPPES
Volga
W. Manych
CRIMEA
Sea of
Azov
11
Kerch
Elista
Astrakhan
Kuban
Voroshilovsk
E. Manych
IV
Maykop
Novorossiysk
CASPIAN
Tuapse
C A U C A S U S
Elbrus
Mozdok
Terek
BLACK
SEA
Sukhumi
Groznyy
Ordzhonikidze
SEA
Kasbek
Batum
Tiflis
Kura
Baku
T U R K E Y
Miles
0
250
Km
0
200
400

4 STALINGRAD: 1942-1943

The Strategy of a Siege

Remember . . . we must hold the city and strengthen our people's confidence in our Army's ability to defeat the enemy.

—KHRUSHCHEV in Stalingrad
on September 12, 1942

I stand and fight—those are my orders.

—GENERAL PAULUS in Stalingrad
on January 23, 1943

IF *Singapore had seemingly demonstrated that even the most fabled fortresses could not withstand a siege, the events of the next years of war would reverse such a judgment. In the Pacific island war, many of the campaigns were no more than classical assaults of besieged islands. In Asia, however, the land battles tended to be fought in jungles or in rugged terrain isolated from urban areas. Not until the Japanese defense of Manila did an army withdraw into a major city. In the European campaigns this was not the case. By 1942, the German Army, despite its lightning sorties or, perhaps, because of them, had been forced to invest two great cities, Leningrad and Sevastopol. The Russian resistance at Leningrad and the reduction of Sevastopol were not, however, considered by the Germans as typical of the Russian campaign. The siege remained a military anachronism. Although the resistance of Malta and Tobruk had indicated that envelopment by air or land did not necessarily lead directly to capitulation, these were considered peripheral events isolated from the main war in the East. The Germans, with Britain and America apparently neutralized in the West, felt that the war against Russia could be won during the summer of 1942 by a renewal of the panzer blitz. That their summer offensive would be decided by the besiegement of a major city or even by a static battle of attrition was inconceivable to the men who had brought the war of mobility and daring to perfection. The blitzkrieg, swift, elegant, invincible, contained within its very mobility the germs of disaster; for, once stalled, rapid strategical adaption would be necessary. Since the German offensive was on a grand scale, all the strategic decisions and reactions were vast, encompassing thousands of miles of territory and hundreds of thousands of men; but all these strategic decisions unexpectedly would culminate in the siege of Stalingrad, the central event of the war in the East.*

ON July 23, 1942, Adolf Hitler, Führer of the Third Reich, had won the war again. Twice before, his victory had proven to be ephemeral: once in 1940 because of the quixotic refusal of the British to recognize the obvious, and once the previous winter because the final thrust to Moscow came just too late to finish off the Russians. In the summer of 1942, however, seven months later, the Russians were at last finished and with them the war. Then from the Urals on the east to the Atlantic in the west, from Norway above the Arctic Circle to Egypt on the south, Hitler's Germany would face only the tattered remnants of the British and the distant Americans. The immediate basis of Hitler's quite justifiable optimism was the rapid progress of what had originally been labeled Operation *Blau*—the 1942 summer offensive to secure the Caucasus and crush the Red Army. As originally prepared on April 5, the operation would take place in four stages, moving from the center of the front to the south and east, securing the long bend of the Don as a flank anchored at Stalingrad on the Volga, to Rostov-on-Don, the jumping-off point for the final sweep south into the Caucasus.[1] By mid-July the operation, now designated Operation *Brunswick*, had been remarkably successful. The way to the Caucasus lay open before the panzer divisions, more often delayed by lack of gasoline than by Russian resistance. The northern armies, Army Group B, had reached the Don River within easy range of Stalingrad. As Hitler sat in his headquarters in East Prussia drawing up War Directive 45, he could not but have felt a justifiable glow of pride at his victory over not only the Russians but also the excessive caution of his own generals.

> *In a campaign which has lasted little more than three weeks, the broad objectives outlined by me for the southern flank of the Eastern front have been largely achieved. Only weak enemy forces from the Timoshenko Army Group have succeeded in avoiding encirclement and reaching the further bank of the Don. We must expect them to be reinforced from the Caucasus.*
>
> *A further concentration of enemy forces is taking place in the Stalingrad area, which the enemy will probably defend tenaciously.*[2]

In order to respond to the rapid collapse of Russian resistance to Army Group A in the south, Hitler, in Directive 45, rearranged Operation *Brunswick* into two new operations. Army Group A in Operation

Edelweiss would continue the drive toward the Caucasus. Although several units were to be switched from Army Group A, there seemed no reason to fear that the weak Soviet forces in the south could reconstruct their shattered front. The strengthened Army Group B on the Don Front in Operation *Heron* would now "thrust forward to Stalingrad, to smash the enemy forces concentrated there, to occupy the town, and to block the land communications between the Don and the Volga, as well as the Don itself."[3] The long flank, which steadily lengthened as the Germans moved east, would then be secured so that the occupation and absorption of the Caucasus could proceed apace. With winter approaching, the Russians would find their armies shattered, most of their country occupied, their option to continue to make war denied, and their will to resist broken. Almost as Hitler finished writing his Directive, word arrived that German units had seized Rostov-on-Don. There had been little resistance. The omens were bright indeed.

For Hitler the crowning triumph was very personal. The General Staff, the Army commanders, the whole galaxy of professional talent, had expressed doubts from the first. Even as the final preparations had been made doom had been predicted. On May 10, General Alfred Jodl, head of the Armed Forces Operational Staff and a man to whom independent thought was rare, expressed doubts. On May 12, General Franz Halder, Army Chief-of-Staff, had expressed doubts.[4] They were hardly alone in this, but Hitler ignored their reservations. No one had been able to offer any very plausible alternative. Suggestions for withdrawal or mobile defense in depth after three years of almost uninterrupted success did little to assuage Hitler's desire for final victory. Unconcerned with the art of the possible, almost unaware of it, uninterested in limited aims and consolidated gains, he sought total victory—a Russia dismembered, a Europe rearranged, a new world order. While no man is a total revolutionist, destroying all, creating everything anew, Hitler, almost alone among Germany's leaders, knew that this war was one of total victory or total defeat. Once the first step had been taken there was no turning back, no hedging. That he could often conceal his ultimate aims under a mask of sweet reasonableness made it possible for him to convince even the most reluctant generals of his own practicality and his own greater knowledge. His momentary rationality in no way had ever compromised his messianic view of the war.[5] Having expressed their doubts about the new offensive, having disagreed with the direction and scope of Hitler's proposals, having noted that secrecy had been lost by the Russian capture of an Army Corps order, having watched with dismay their memorandums and situation papers discarded, the reluctant generals swiftly turned to implement Hitler's directives.

The subsequent assertion by many of the German generals that a more modest offensive or even a holding action would have been more successful than Hitler's all-or-nothing approach must remain in the realm of speculation. Undoubtedly the Germans could not have lost at Stalingrad if they were not at Stalingrad, or in Russia for that matter, but this retrospective strategical insight is not too revealing.[6] In any case, by midsummer, most of the generals seemed content with the offensive, as well they might be. That it did fail is as much a reflection on the vaunted professionalism of the generals as it is on the strategy of Hitler. Their modest proposals of a fluid defense which would have worn out the Russians has since become the foundation stone of the generals' alternative strategy for the war in Russia. This military revisionism is as limited in its understanding of grand strategy as the generals themselves proved to be. The possibility of compromise or military stalemate with Russia, given the occupation policies of the Nazis, the nature of the Communist antagonism, and the growing Russian national purpose, had little relation to reality. The rapidly mushrooming power of the Western Allies and the almost ignored entry of America into the war meant that time was no longer on the side of Hitler. Even a war of attrition in the East could exploit little more than temporary Russian weakness while the Western Allies built up their forces and battered Germany from the air. Unless Russia could be destroyed, not just neutralized, the New Order was in danger. A "permanent" stalemate in the East would only mean defeat in the West. The time to destroy Russia was in the summer of 1942 before time ran out. The alternative was not, as the generals assumed, a limited professional war but total defeat; furthermore, by the summer of 1942, Hitler with good reason viewed all generals and all their options, technical or global, with a jaundiced eye.

The German Army generals, with few exceptions, had opposed everything—the Rhineland, Austria, Czechoslovakia, and Poland. Once the war began, they opposed the offensive in the West, Operation *Barbarossa* against Russia, and, even as late as the previous winter, they had opposed the stand before Moscow. Yet they had accepted everything, and, in accepting everything, they had achieved everything. They felt misunderstood, improperly used, and professionally limited. Their distaste for Hitler developed more from his interference in their province, more galling because he succeeded, than from the nature of his regime. His character was difficult, his associates odious, and his methods crude, but none of these were, the generals felt, their immediate concern. Unable to understand the nature of the man or of his regime, their whole frame of reference remained the narrow national aims of the historic German state and the traditional military means of Prussian experience. Somehow the generals did not truly comprehend the nature of Hitler's totalitarian regime in theory or in fact, with its mutual exclusiveness, its world view, and its primitive jungle politics enameled with theory. In their limited view, Hitler had evolved from a leader concerned with aiding the army to one determined to dominate it. All the more frustrating, Hitler had been right in his political and, worse still, military decisions. His military moves, from campaigns like Norway to the transfer of a single regiment in Poland, had been impeccable. His wildest ploys had proven possible. Now he wanted an offensive with excessive goals and limited means; of course, this had always been the case. Self-confessed specialists, supposedly unable or unwilling to understand economic or political arguments, the generals had been persuaded once more against their better professional judgment. Once more they would tolerate Hitler's amateur interference, accept his grandiose plans, plead for alterations and adjustments, and with all their skill go on obeying orders in which they did not believe, leading to a goal they neither understood nor any longer applauded.

Standing before the great war maps at his headquarters, watching the eastward flow of the little symbols representing corps and divisions, Hitler could not have cared less about his generals' likes and dislikes. Stretched on the map before him the war was a vast, complicated chess game. Here, far from the sweat and blood, the confusion and turmoil of the front, Hitler could watch his decisions translated into movements across incredible distances over almost impossible terrain. Only here, before the large-scale war map, could the nature of the vast battles thousands of miles to the south be fully understood. War is readily comprehensible at only two levels—that of the very small or the very large. Fiction often chooses the tiny field to reveal the nature of battle. The military mind prefers the intricate movement and balance of the whole army, the shifting of divisions, the massing of corps, the elegant and elaborate formations evolving out of scores of alternatives. It is this war on a grand scale, a game using divisions as pieces and nations as stakes, that has had such a persistent fascination. As Robert E. Lee noted, it is fortunate that war is so terrible or men would grow to love it. Hitler, a late arrival at the seat of grand strategy, had few qualms about the terror of war. He truly loved his vocation as warlord, for he had found in himself an innate talent for grand strategy combined with a prodigious memory for detail. By 1942 his skills had brought a string of victories unequaled in modern history. As the summer days drifted past in a flurry of victories and the little symbols moved ever eastward and southward, his absolute confidence in victory remained firm. Some of the generals, even though impressed with the present progress, were less sure. From July 17 on, the German Sixth Army under Colonel-General Friedrich Paulus had been fighting inside the great bend of the Don River. What disturbed Paulus had not been a defeat but the grudging victories. The Russians, obviously beaten, would not quit.

As Hitler continued to point out from East Prussia, the Russians were retreating day after day. The Sixth Army reported a never-ending streak of victories—towns captured, streams crossed, Russians slaughtered. Yet, unlike the previous year, the Russians had evaded a major encirclement. However weakened it might be, the Red Army remained in the field and continued to resist. In fact it was just this resistance that preyed on Paulus' mind. If the thrust to Stalingrad by the Sixth Army slowed down, Army Group A would be deep in the Caucasus with strong Russian forces still to the north. More immediate, the long flank to the north along the Don was very weakly held. Hitler was unimpressed but once again he had to turn from his grand strategy to listen to the carpings of his commanders. Gasoline supplies had run out and Army Group A was immobilized. Tanks were wearing out and being destroyed faster than they could be replaced. The summer caution, elevated to high criticism after the war, seemed to be based as much on a desire for more reinforcements as on an accurate appraisal of Russian potential. In the summer the long flank of the Sixth Army was relatively unimportant, since there were only negligible Soviet units opposite it. Hitler pointed out to the prudent that the German panzers had cut the last rail link into the Caucasus on July 29 and the Russian front south of Stalingrad had simply disappeared. On August 1, to help out Army Group B, he did, however, transfer a Panzer Army along with two German and one Rumanian divisions from Army Group A to the developing Stalingrad front. A sudden clutch of victories did not follow; in fact, for the first time, the opposite happened: the regular advance ended. During the first week in August, the Sixth Army could not push through a hastily organized Russian line on the Aksay River. When the Sixth Army finally broke through, it was unable to smash the Russian Army. By August 18, the country inside the Don Bend had almost been cleared of Russian units. Despite the battering they had taken, the Russians had managed to salvage their Sixty-second and Sixty-fourth Armies. Although reputedly a brilliant general, Paulus was not proving to be particularly imaginative. Perhaps he was just not lucky, a formidable military virtue, for he still faced a Russian front, however flimsy.

On the Russian side of the battle line, few would have taken seriously the proposition that the German generals had any doubts at all. Everyone from Stalin down recognized that the situation had become critical. On their wall maps, the whole southern front showed nothing but enormous gaps between scattered and disorganized armies. There was almost nothing to throw in front of German Army Group A to the south. As for stopping Paulus and the Sixth Army, few had any real hopes for the immediate future. The *Luftwaffe* commanded the sky, striking at the few roads and railways again and again, disorganizing the advance of the few ill-prepared reserve units. On the battleline, all the reports, even by the most optimistic, revealed the inevitable confusion of defeat: misunderstood orders, lost regiments, missing commanders, and always the retreat. For a losing army every mistake becomes costly, each error punitive.[7] There is no compensation of victory, no ignorant muddling through, only the cumulative burden of missed chances, exhausted resources, and disintegration. What had been remarkable, considering the vast open spaces of the Russian steppe and the daily defeats at the hands of the German armor, had been the ability, in some cases surely the luck, of the Russian commanders in holding together some kind of front without being cut off and annihilated. Subsequently much would be made of the fighting withdrawal, of the skill in evading the German pincers, and of the preparations for a counter-blow. In reality, during August, there were few bright spots for the Russians and little hope of a counter-blow. Over everyone hung the cloud of complete defeat.

On August 12, Winston Churchill arrived in Moscow to confer with Stalin. In the midst of the military crisis with the entire southern front collapsing, with the Caucasus open to occupation, bitterness and despair were very near the surface. Understandably, Churchill, an imperialist capitalist *par excellence*, met with a cold reception. There was no second front. Russia seemed to be fighting alone, slowly being ground to death, ignored and isolated. Even the cheerful news that British and American troops would invade Africa in the fall had no immediate effect. By autumn the very real possibility existed that Hitler's great gamble would have paid off. If, by a combination of miracles, the Germans could be held off until reinforcements and new equipment could be massed, there was a chance. While Churchill and Stalin talked, such an eventuality seemed slight. Defeat followed defeat. Little could be done by Stalin or even his front commanders, much less by Churchill, to improve the odds. The British Prime Minister left.[8] Moscow remained sunk in gloom and despair. Neither Stalin nor the Russian High Command, however, gave up hope. After all, the basis for a future battle remained: the Germans had failed to destroy the Red Army. In the Caucasus twenty German divisions, spread out over a 500-mile front and hampered by supply shortages, could advance but could not destroy the fleeing Russians. The Sixth Army ground to a stop again; this time for ten days because of a breakdown in gasoline supplies. Thus, because of one thing or another, the Red Army was still in the field, but the field was growing smaller and the day of reckoning drawing nearer.

The Sixth Army, despite its difficulties and shortages, now began to advance again even if more slowly. For Hitler every day the end of Red Russia drew nearer. The Russian bear was dead, moving solely by dying reflexes. On August 18, the Anglo-Canadian raid on Dieppe turned Hitler's attention to the long-ignored problems of the unguarded West. He shifted troops to protect Crete. He readily accepted the additional drain on the Eastern Front because of the obviously justified demands of General Rommel's highly successful Afrika Korps. By the end of August, his patience in the East appeared about to be rewarded. On August 21, German mountain troops raised their flag on top of Mount Elbrus, 18,481 feet above sea level, the highest point in the Caucasus.

On August 23, tanks of the 14th Panzer Corps reached the Volga at Rynok at the northern tip of Stalingrad. Even the prudent generals seemed hopeful despite the continued almost inexplicable Russian resiliency under the constant German pressure: "Something incomprehensible is, in fact, going on . . . the doomed divisions are continuing to resist bitterly. Fanaticism . . ."[9] That such fanaticism could have but one end now that the 14th Panzer Corps had reached the Volga seemed obvious to the Germans. During the day the 51st Corps also moved up to Rynok. On the night of August 23, the *Luftwaffe* put the final and traditional cap to the German attack. In the heaviest strike on the Eastern Front since June 22, 1941, Colonel-General F. W. von Richthofen's 4th Air Fleet, augmented by all other aircraft in range, hit the city in a massive raid. Some pilots flew as many as three sorties, dumping tons of high explosives and incendiaries into the city. Within minutes the flames flared up among the wooden buildings and within an hour the holocaust had grown so great that it was possible to read a newspaper by the light forty miles away.[10] Fanatics or not, Stalingrad, or what was left when the flames died down, seemed to be there for the taking.

South of the tanks of the 14th Panzer Corps at Rynok stretched Stalingrad, the final objective. The city itself had until then remained relatively unimportant, only a name on the map. Its capture would simply signify the clearing of the area between the Don and the Volga. With the five-mile wedge of bank seized north of Rynok, the usefulness of the Volga River as a lifeline to the south had already ended. Stalingrad itself meandered south for some thirty miles, an interlocking combination of giant factories, scattered residential areas and garden cities scattered along the west side of the Volga among a topography of low hills, ravines and narrow streams. Perhaps as much as any large city in Russia, Stalingrad represented the future, with its immense, raw, new factories, each designated by a revolutionary title, Red October or Barricades Plant. There was a city center of sorts, even a Red Square, but no real core other than the unifying Volga winding to the east of the city. With the low hills covered by walnut trees and Spanish chestnuts, and vineyards often planted near the river bank, the riverside city had a certain charm despite its concrete factories. Although as Tsaritsyn the city had gained some note as the site of a successful Red Army victory under the leadership of Stalin during the Russian Civil War, it was the concrete Tractor Factory which now gave the city its fame. On August 24, however, for the Germans it was nothing more than a smoking ruin that once occupied would end the summer's victorious campaign.

The population of Stalingrad had not seen themselves as the ultimate objective of the German offensive. All during the summer the life of the city had continued much as before. The tractor factories produced the T-34 tanks, the reinforcements had moved in from the railheads on the east and out to the front on the west. No fortifications had been built and even in late August none were being built.[11] The war had remained to the west. The reports and rumors had not been good, but something might turn up. Then the German panzers had jumped across the Don and probed toward the Volga. The sudden arrival of the front on August 23–24 changed everything. There were no more civilians: 50,000 volunteered for the People's Army and 75,000 were assigned to the Sixty-second Army. The girls became nurses or radio operators and the boys were organized by Komsomol, the Communist youth group, into fighting formations.[12] The very old and the very young, if they were still alive after the *Luftwaffe* raid, began trickling across the Volga and away to the east. The German air attacks intensified. Within days, the city had burnt out and even the concrete factories began to crumble. The entire city came under not only air attack but artillery fire as well. Because of the nature of the city, pressed like a long snake against the Volga, there remained no secure area, not even a relatively safe zone, as the Russian troops slowly retreated toward the river, exposing the entire city. The only security was across the Volga. The only food and medical care were across the Volga. There was no possibility of civilian life, for there was no haven for the useless, no food, and finally literally no space. Only those who fought remained.

Day by day the Germans narrowed the Russian hold on the west bank of the Volga and rapidly established a firm perimeter. On September 2, the Fourth Panzer Army and the Sixth Army made contact ten miles west of Stalingrad, completing the ring. Still the Russians evaded being rolled up or encircled. On September 10, German armor reached the Volga to the south of Stalingrad cutting between the Russian Sixty-second and Sixty-fourth Armies. Why the Russians continued to fight for the strategically unimportant pocket remained a mystery to the Germans. The Volga had been cut and Stalingrad neutralized. The Russians should have withdrawn to the east bank. Instead they insisted on holding out in a pocket which had to be supplied by river boats under constant German fire. Perhaps, more than any other reason, the Russians continued to hold on to the city because of the tentative realization by the commanders that they could. After a summer of defeats, the effectiveness of their resistance between the Don and the Volga had been a real tonic. The retreat was no victory, but the Germans had not been able to envelop their formations. It was obvious to the Russians that the advance toward the Volga must have cost the Germans both more time and men than they had expected to expend. Not the possibility but the reality of punishing the Germans, of chewing up their previously invincible crack troops, was reason enough to fight on the wrong side of the Volga. As the possibility revealed itself to the Russian High Command (*Stavka*), switches in command structure took place as the incompetent or defeatist were removed and the militant and determined sent in. The new men were Voronov, the artillery specialist, Novikov, for the air corps, A. I. Yeremenko for the Stalingrad Front area, and most important in the city, V. I. Chuikov and his political commissar Nikita Khrushchev. The over-all command was in the hands of Georgi Zhukov. Together these men were determined to hold out along the Volga so that a southern front could be re-established.

No one had foreseen a stand at Stalingrad. The city was totally unprepared for a siege. An abortive last-minute start had been made on fortifications, but nothing had been done about the evacuation of civilians or machinery. No supplies had been accumulated. More revealing, not only did the Russian Sixty-second and Sixty-fourth Armies have no idea of how to defend a modern city under siege, but the Red Army itself had no formal doctrine concerning the techniques of city fighting.

The experiences in the University City of Madrid had long been forgotten. If the city were to be held, everything would have to be improvised as the battle went along. That the defense continue was essential. The slower the rate of the German advance, the sooner would come winter and with it a breathing space, even a counteroffensive. Such a counterblow, which would reverse the tide of disaster, had remained a fantasy during much of August, with the whole southern front torn open and the panzers rumbling ahead. For the Russian grand strategists, nominally Stalin, but particularly his Commander-in-Chief, Georgi K. Zhukov, the success, however limited or temporary, between the Don and the Volga had given rise to more serious possibilities. With growing speed the Russian trans-Ural war industry was recouping the disastrous losses of 1941. New army divisions were being trained and armed. If Yeremenko's Front could hold a while longer, this reserve could be hoarded for a counterstroke. The Germans were now fully committed in the south. If Yeremenko held, then Hitler once more would be denied his final victory.

For the men of Chuikov's Sixty-second Army, however, pressed back by the tight German ring, grand strategy played little part. On September 12, Khrushchev told Chuikov that "we must hold the city and strengthen our people's confidence in our Army's ability to defeat the enemy."[13] By then, Communist encouragement was no longer necessary. The virtues of the Russian soldiers had finally found a proper battlefield. As they were being thrust back into the smoking ruin of the city, the soldiers found that persistence, stolid determination and fanaticism worked. Trapped in close combat, the Germans lacked the mystical aura of victory which had floated above the deadly panzers.

On September 13, the Germans attacked again. Depending more on momentum and less on a carefully prepared operation, Paulus hoped to crush the pocket and drive the Russians into the Volga before they could get set. As a result his own attack was hastily undertaken. Chuikov's Sixty-second Army held during the day. At night the 10,000 men of Rodimtsev's division began to be ferried across the Volga into the burning city. Rodimtsev, an old Spanish War veteran, could not present his division to Chuikov as a unit but by the boatload. So the men trickled forward a few at a time to the hastily prepared strong points in the basements of factories and in the shells of burned buildings. They did not have to move up far to find the front, for the Germans had already pushed very close to the center of the city. By the morning of September 14, German troops, many of them in a victory mood, had begun to push toward the inner core of the city. Crouched in their cellars, the Russians saw "Germans jumping down from their lorries, playing mouth-organs, shouting like mad and dancing on the pavements."[14] The Russians sprayed them with submachine-gun fire. The Germans scattered and brought up more troops, apparently without mouth organs. The fighting, still strategically inexplicable to the German commanders, continued, with the Russians clinging to their positions. Driven out they would filter back again in the dark. Gradually Rodimtsev's men moved up and stiffened the front line, if an unconnected collection of gutted ruins can be called a line. Despite their very fragile perimeter, the Russians counterattacked the following day in order to wear down the German mass. The attacks ran directly into heavy formations moving up to finish off the Russians. All that day and the next, the German blows continued nonstop. Paulus threw in a steady stream of reserves only to have them chewed up among the ruins. The *Luftwaffe* hit the Russian-held areas again and again. The roar and rumble of the German artillery never stopped. The entire city had become a seething cauldron. The weight of German firepower concentrated on the Russians was immense, but produced diminishing returns the closer it came to the front and their own troops. There, in an ill-defined zone of attack and counterattack, the bitterly bought gains narrowed down to bits and pieces—a floor of a factory, a heap of rubble, a grain elevator, even a vital room. Hour by hour the city had been reduced into a great slag heap, smouldering day and night by the side of the Volga.

On September 20, the Moscow press for the first time used the word "heroic" in reference to the defenders of Stalingrad. Perhaps some of the Sixty-second Army's determination—"There Is No Land Across the Volga"—had drifted north.[15] It was clear to all that Paulus' swift thrust into the city had been blunted. Tossing in more formations had not worked. Paulus, too, was aware of his failure. Of course, the Russian defense had been unexpected and his losses heavy, but as yet Paulus felt he had not unleashed the full massed force of the Sixth Army. He began preparations to do so. The Russians' attempts at counterattack to the north carried on by Gordov, Yeremenko's Deputy Front Commander, on September 19 were brushed back. The German buildup continued. Chuikov's Sixty-second Army dug into its shallow pocket, but could not hope to repeat the previous week's stalemate. All that was needed was one more heavy thrust.

On September 21, massed German formations again smashed into the center of the city. On September 24, after three days of constant attacks, the Germans broke through to the Volga, splitting the Sixty-second Army in two. With the end tantalizingly in sight, the Germans could not quite turn either flank to the Russians. Despite the breakthrough, Chuikov clung to the bank, penning in the German wedge. On September 28, a renewed German attack proved less effective. Losses on both sides had been heavy. All the front-line troops were exhausted. Switching their concentration, the Germans cut off the Russian Orlovka salient in the north on September 29. The Russians neither surrendered nor tried to break out. The Orlovka pocket became one more area to be stormed house by house, room by room. The beloved pincers maneuvers, the envelopment and sudden thrusts, became abstract and distant concepts in the ruins of Stalingrad. The great sweeping war of the Eastern Front had disappeared into gains measured in yards. The war had suddenly become very narrow, very bitter, and very costly.

> *The war moved into the jagged gullies of the Volga hills with their copses and ravines, into the factory area of Stalingrad, spread out over uneven, pitted, rugged country, covered with iron, concrete and stone buildings. The mile, as a measure of distance, was replaced by the yard. . . . For every house, workshop, water-tower, railway embankment, wall, cellar, and every pile of ruins, a bitter battle was waged, without equal even in the first world war with its vast expenditure of munitions.*[16]

Burrowed into their isolated wedges close to the bank of the Volga, Chuikov and his commanders had to develop brand-new techniques of warfare. In a school which allowed no failures, the Sixty-second Army learned to fight in a vast ruin of reinforced concrete and rubble-filled gullies. The whole idea of street fighting had to be jettisoned immediately. To move on the streets or in the open across parks or squares meant instant death. A new conception of city fighting began to be developed. Open spaces were avoided as deathtraps for the unwary. The real fighting took place inside or beneath the city among the hundreds of interconnected strong points, bunkers and cellars. Distance became deadly. Opposing positions were jammed as close to each other as possible. The battle lines merged to arm's length and then overlapped and mingled. Individual initiative, innovations, and painful failures developed a new and rapidly expanding tactical doctrine. New units, new means of co-operation and co-ordination, new methods appeared, were tested, and incorporated by Chuikov.

> *. . . I would like to emphasize the fact that it was the soldiers of the 62nd Army who understood more quickly than anyone else what city fighting means, and learned more quickly and better to make use of streets, buildings, basements, staircases, factory chimneys and the roofs of houses. Mastering the art of city battle, all organs of the Army—staffs, political sections and rear—continued to study it, acquired more information and drew more deeply on their experience. The art of street fighting did not spring into existence fully-formed, we perfected it; every soldier tried to devise, and devised, new and usually successful ways of fighting.*[17]

On their side, the Germans too had to learn or perish, but their future, with victory only a few thousand yards away, seemed less bleak. Command of the air, past superiority in technique, and a history of success tended to make the Germans more dependent on numbers and equipment than on newly learned skills. From Paulus down they tried to bludgeon their way ahead. The Germans felt that the continuing

Russian resistance must be a day-to-day affair held together by hope and fanaticism. It could not last. The Russians were split into small pockets, isolated, under constant air and artillery bombardment; in other words, they were defeated. Day and night the German perimeter squeezed them. Obviously the lifelines across the Volga were fragile. Obviously their casualties must be greater than the Germans'. Obviously the final end, even if the Sixty-second Army intended to fight to the last man, could not be far distant.

During the first week in October, the Germans again massed for heavy attacks. On October 5, the *Luftwaffe* flew 2,000 sorties over the city's factory districts alone. The Sixth Army struggled forward again. This time Paulus again secured more vital local gains, wiping out the encircled Orlovka salient. Again the cost was grim. His final thrust had once more ground to a halt in the face of the constant counterattacks and the resiliency of the interlocking Russian strong points. For the next four days, there was a lull in the fighting—at least, for those in the city, it seemed like a lull. The German sorties continued. The German guns fired. Increasingly, Russian artillery, brought up to the east bank of the Volga and dug in, answered the Germans. Local pressure continued, but there were no heavy attacks. For the first time the Germans appeared uncertain. By all previous experience, Russian resistance should have crumbled once the Sixty-second Army had been cornered and splintered into isolated pockets. That the Russians continued to resist was distressing. Discordant notes, indications of acute frustration and waxing pessimism, began to appear in captured German diaries. The Sixth Army's line was less than two miles from the Volga all along the front and yet, after two months, the city still held out.

Not only the front-line soldiers had misgivings. Uneasiness at the rate of German progress in clearing the west bank grew both at German Army Headquarters and at Supreme Headquarters. All the arguments for caution and restraint proposed in the spring and discarded in July returned to haunt the staffs. Only Hitler seemed immune, uninterested in forebodings, certain of victory. To the generals, however, victory seemed further away. The drive to Stalingrad had become so firmly wedged in the reeking heaps of concrete along the Volga that all mobility had been lost. The drive to the Caucasus, while impressive on paper, left much to be desired. Both thrusts could report progress day after day. In Stalingrad the attack had reached the point of diminishing returns; less and less cost more and more. In the Caucasus each step forward meant lengthened supply lines, dangling flanks and fewer fighting troops. Many generals began to fear that the great gamble so clearly secure in July had not come off. They did not so much sense defeat as feel disappointment. Some had begun to propose hedging the wild bets of the summer.

Three weeks before, Field-Marshal S. W. List, Commander of Army Group A, had advised Hitler to call off the offensive in the west Caucasus. Hitler had been shocked. Long annoyed by his Chief of Staff, Colonel-General Franz Halder, this new evidence of Prussian prudence and pessimism had seemed a betrayal. Worse, the usually servile Jodl, who had returned from inspecting the front, had agreed with List. This was one of the very few blemishes on his record of uncritical support of all his Führer's proposals and thus even more shocking. That the loyal Jodl had broken under the pressure had seemed the cruelest blow of all. Hitler dismissed List and for a while seemed determined to sack Jodl and perhaps even Keitel. Bitter and shaken at this disloyalty, he had withdrawn from contact with his generals. Jodl had been put in cold storage and his immediate assistant, General Walter Warlimont, sent off on a long leave. On September 24, Hitler called in Halder, told him that his nerves were worn out, and removed him.[18] Colonel-General Kurt Zeitzler, who might be more acquiescent, took over. Despite the changes, Hitler still felt no great enthusiasm for his generals. He brooded and, according to Zeitzler, cast a heavy pall over Headquarters.

> *He now led an entirely retired life, brooding upon his suspicions. He would shake hands with no general. No longer did he take his meals with the members of his personal headquarters and staff, but preferred to eat alone. When attending staff conferences he would enter, bow stiffly, and listen to his advisers' brief reports with a surly frown. Then he would once again give the assembled officers a stiff little bow and leave the room.*[19]

All the staff changes of September seemed to have no effect on the generals. As the struggle in Stalingrad continued during the first half of October, they persisted in pointing out the risks Hitler was taking: the weakness of the Sixth Army's flank or the extended position of Army Group A, or some other unpleasant fact. In October Hitler had agreed that a Russian winter offensive was a possibility, but winter was still far off. In the meantime he insisted on success not complaints.[20] Perhaps the German Army had grown tired or reinforcements were insufficient or the equipment wearing out. Yet, surely, if the Germans were tired the Russians must be exhausted. The Red Army was reeling. If the offensive could be pushed—a few more kilometers at Stalingrad, one more battle in the Caucasus—the end would be in sight. A victory now, in October, would prevent a Russian offensive in December. If he had ended the German advance, cutting his losses and admitting less than complete victory, the first long step backward would have been taken. Unwilling to take less than all, unwilling to rearrange his schedule of victory, perhaps ultimately uncertain that his guiding spirit would sustain defeat, Hitler closed his mind to his generals' carping. The generals, on their part, despite very considerable opportunity, could never learn how to persuade Hitler or deny him. In this they had much company, but they proved totally incapable of trying a new tack. The maneuverability and mobile defense in depth they so often urged on Hitler apparently had no place in their own war conferences. They still dragged out the military arguments, the professional axioms, the hard-won experience, only to see Hitler demolish their plans with a calculated tirade or a memorized table of economic data. By October, their alienation from the Supreme Commander had reached the stage where they could persuade him of nothing but their own timidity. Gradually they realized that a crucial hour was at hand, when flexibility would become essential, but they could not convince Hitler of the dangers faced by his daring because of their own unimaginative rigidity. They had cried wolf too often. Hitler insisted on victory. Paulus would again have to make an attempt to steam-roller the Russians.

The Russian counteroffensive within the city had been called off on the evening of October 13 when the solid German mass refused to budge more than a few hundred yards. At dawn three German infantry divisions and two panzer divisions moved forward along a three-mile front. The German steamroller was under way. Almost at once Russian communications collapsed in the roar of guns. Telephone wires were cut, runners killed, and radios battered. Strong points were flanked, isolated, and left behind, some to fight on, others to be only a pile of corpse-filled ruins. The Russians managed some cohesion by using radio relay across the Volga, but the battle remained a struggle of little groups against the German mass. By midnight, Chuikov finally sorted out what had happened. The Germans had advanced a mile and a quarter and had surrounded the famous Tractor Factory on three sides. They had left 3,000 dead outside the shell-pocked walls, but unless the Russians could hold, the price might have been worth paying. Both sides, in fact, were paying an impossibly high price: for example, the Russians managed under heavy German fire to take out across the Volga 3,500 wounded that night alone. The next morning the Germans attacked again. A few Germans broke through and reached the Volga. The Russians wiped them out. The tiny wedge to the river was pushed back. The Germans could not break through again. Although the fighting continued all the next day and the next, the Russians began to feel that at long last the worst was over; the defense would somehow hold.

> *It would be true to say that October 14 was our most critical day. After surviving it and the next three days we knew that the enemy would not be able to repeat an attack of this kind, that even though our Army had been split for a second time its regiments were, and would remain, on the right bank of the Volga.*[21]

Obviously Paulus did not at this point agree. More and more German reserves were funneled into the meat grinder. The endless, pounding hammer blows continued. Day after day the Germans moved up without guile, without elegance, and increasingly, without hope.

Russian reinforcements began to arrive regularly to fill up the heavily depleted ranks of the Sixty-second Army, but there were never enough reserves. Both Russian and German strength were running out. On October 24, the Germans gave up night attacks. On October 25, the Germans brought up their last reserves and attacked again. Chuikov knew he could hold. He could even predict with a fair degree of accuracy just how long it would take to maul the new German reserves after they reached his perimeter. The failures of the two months' battle began to erode the enthusiasm of the Sixth Army.

> *I saw the Volga for the first time today. Our attacks are having no success; we began our attack successfully, then retreated. . . . Heavy bombing at night. I thought our end had come. . . . Our next attack again unsuccessful. Bitter fighting. The enemy is firing from all sides, from every hole. You must not let yourself be seen. . . . At night there is no peace from Russian aircraft, artillery and "katyushi." Heavy losses.*[22]

The Russians too, despite their guarded optimism, had exhausted their formations. Yeremenko permitted some relief. Sokolov's new division began crossing the Volga on October 27, but the men only dribbled into the perimeter. For awhile there was some fear that Paulus might move in still more reserves from the quiet sections of the Sixth Army front, but the Germans had finished.

> *On the evening of October 29, the battle began to die down, and on October 30 there were only exchanges of fire: the enemy was utterly exhausted.*
>
> *We knew that the Soviet troops were winning the battle.*[23]

With the German Army increasingly forced to concentrate more and more of its strength on the narrowing Stalingrad front, the possibility, even the necessity, of a Russian counteroffensive became apparent. The Russians could hardly fail to see the over-all weakness of the German position with its long and lightly held flanks. This highly vulnerable line along the Don had been turned over to the Italians and Rumanians, whose equipment, leadership, and spirit often left much to be desired by German standards. If the Russians could puncture this line, the whole German position in southern Russia would collapse. During the summer this long flank had been quite secure, for it had faced no Russians. Since late August, however, there had been hope of a counterblow, but until the troops had been collected and a front stabilized, such hopes were vain. The stubborn defense of the Sixty-second and Sixty-fourth Armies, holding up the final German thrust, had allowed both men and equipment to be brought over the Urals. Zhukov had hoarded his reserves, dribbling a few into Stalingrad only when the battle reached a new crisis.

Just how closely Stalin became involved in the developing preparation for the counterblow remains a mystery, as does much in the Russian command structure. The major planning and organization was done in Zhukov's headquarters with Voronov and Novikov, in co-operation with the Front Commanders: Yeremenko, Stalingrad Front; Rokossovski, the Don Front; and Vatutin, Southwest Front. Subsequently, however, the Russian historians and even the actors have played a delicate and for them often dangerous game of carefully re-arranging the players and their parts depending upon the existing political climate. Khrushchev's significance as the Communist Party's representative has waxed and waned as often if not as regularly as the moon. The same might be said for Zhukov. If logic is applied, Zhukov would seem the likely candidate as the actual strategist. Since the strategy proved notably successful, this is an honor devoutly to be desired in Russian political life.[24] During the fall of 1942, however, the outcome of any offensive seemed uncertain.

The prime consideration had to be the continued resistance at Stalingrad. Not until the middle of September could anyone take this resistance very seriously. After that a delicate balance had to be maintained between reinforcing the Sixty-second Army in the city and accumulating a massive reserve for the counterstroke. Zhukov wanted to mass a heavy attack which at the point of penetration would have a substantial superiority over the defense. With the growing stream of reinforcements, particularly armor and artillery, he had great hopes if Stalingrad did not absorb too much. At times, particularly in the middle of October, it is likely that Yeremenko became a little too parsimonious with his reinforcements. Although the Sixty-second Army held on, no secondary counterattacks, no flanking maneuvers, no massive infusion of troops could take place. The Sixty-second Army held on alone and seldom aided. Although Chuikov said that he got all that he asked for as fast as possible, as an Army general he was not in a position to ask for more than replacements and artillery support. This he received. Everything else went into reserves.

These hoarded tanks and men still would give Zhukov only a small numerical superiority, but the key to his offensive was to be the secret massing of his men for two main blows. The two areas were almost self-evident: the two flank junctures in the north and south of the Sixth Army. On the northern flank, particularly, the quiet Don front held by the Rumanian IV Corps cried out for an attack. The attack in the south against the Fourth Panzer Army would be delayed for twenty-four hours to allow confusion to drift south. The Sixty-second Army inside Stalingrad would by its continued resistance furnish the auxiliary blow demanded by Soviet doctrine. Despite subsequent pretensions of Soviet writers, the counteroffensive was neither subtle nor particularly elegant. Zhukov could not help but note that all the German offensive power was buried in the ruins of Stalingrad and that, ignoring all else, the Germans had exposed their flanks. He simply built up a huge mass attack—a three-fold superiority in men, four- to six-fold in artillery. He had three hundred guns to the kilometer and forty tanks to the mile. Very few divisions could stand up to this kind of steamroller; and very few divisions were scattered along the Don front before it. The pincers, or double envelopment, used by Zhukov at Stalingrad could hardly be called strikingly original. Yet the Russian plan made use of just those virtues possessed by the average, newly trained soldier. Disciplined, enthusiastic and persistent, the men had little experience and limited training. They had to be used as a mass. The giant, awkward, clubbing blows of the masses would prove as damaging as a graceful rapier thrust. The most delicate area remained Stalingrad, where Zhukov and Yeremenko had to keep the Sixty-second Army intact. It was actually inside the ruined city that a real Soviet contribution to the military arts evolved. The skills of city-fighting were actually so limited that they might be called techniques rather than tactics. However restricted their application, the methods devised by Chuikov's army, unlike the remainder of the Red Army, depended on individual innovation rather than static doctrine. Most important was their effectiveness in holding off the Sixth Army long enough for the buildup in the areas of the main blow.[25]

The Germans, particularly Paulus, were well aware of the situation on the Don flank. Hitler, on October 20, had expressed some anxiety over an attack far to the south over the Don toward Rostov, but a week later he felt that Russian talk of an offensive was for propaganda purposes only. Paulus was not so sure. He tried to strengthen his flanks and hoped to beef up the Rumanian IV Corps by salting it with German units. The major overriding interest of the Sixth Army staff and, in fact, of the whole German Army on the Eastern Front remained Stalingrad. The city had cast a hypnotic spell on the Germans. Never before had it seemed more true that one last battalion tossed into the city would win the day. And for months the battalions had followed one another with the German emotional commitment steadily growing greater and the anxiety deeper. Everyone knew how weak the flanks were, but as long as the momentum continued in Stalingrad that did not count. The Russians, too, were thought to be as firmly wedged in the city as the Germans. The Russians, too, must have lost many times more dead and wounded than had the Sixth Army. The flanks were bad, but the battle was to be won in the city. The Russians could not hold out in November as they had in October.

For Hitler November of 1942 became the cruelest month. All during the indecisive days of the fall, there had been occasional hints, ignored omens, even specific evidence of disaster. Rommel's Cairo express had stalled. The dual offensive in the Caucasus and on the Volga could not quite manage the final step. Rumors of an Anglo-American landing continued. In the Pacific the Americans had taken the offensive at Guadalcanal. Then on November 2–3, Montgomery and the British broke through at El Alamein. Day-by-day reports of the rout accumulated. With good cause the Italians sank into gloom, even despair. On November 7 and 8, long before Hitler had expected, the United States and Great Britain launched Operation *Torch* against Vichy French North Africa. French resistance proved only symbolic, and within a few days Allied columns were probing eastward toward Tunisia. Suddenly Hitler, for almost the first time, had to react to his opponents' moves. Suddenly off balance, he had lost the initiative. He ordered the occupation of Vichy France and the build-up of a bridgehead in Tunisia to recoup his Mediterranean position. With the African front still very much in a state of flux, he spoke on November 8 at Munich in commemoration of his unsuccessful *putsch* in 1923. Faced by African reverses, he could still point with pride to the presence of German troops on the Volga—where they would remain. In light of his speech and in view of the apparent reluctance of Paulus to finish off the Russians, Hitler ordered one final effort to secure Stalingrad. The culminating disaster of Hitler's black November was about to begin.

For two weeks the pace of the battle among the Stalingrad ruins had slowed. The Russians had been laying in ammunition and supplies so as to be ready when their supply lines were severed by the ice floes building up in the Volga. Yeremenko had been shifting some of his massed artillery on the east bank away to the marshaling areas of the counteroffensive. On their part, the Germans showed considerably less interest in continuing the attack. The *Luftwaffe,* which had flown 3,000 sorties daily during October, flew only about 1,000.

This brief respite for the Sixth Army was short-lived. On Hitler's orders Paulus was to break the stalemate with one final thrust. On November 11, at six-thirty in the morning, the Sixth Army struck again. Five infantry and two panzer divisions plus parts of two other divisions ground into the Russian perimeter. At eleven-thirty the Germans committed their reserves. Their armor and infantry teams finally overran the Russian line on the right flank of Gorishnyi's division and once more reached the Volga. They cleared 600 yards. The Sixty-second Army was split once more, but as usual, Russian resistance continued. Efforts to expand the wedge failed. At noon the next day, the Germans tried again, but by evening the attack faded off in exhaustion. Paulus' new divisions lasted as viable units for only about four days. He was running out of reserves. Still the effort continued all along the front. On November 15, from Rynok on the north to Kuporosnoye on the south, Paulus had fifteen divisions fully committed. As usual the Russian position was critical. The Sixty-second Army was now in three parts. Communications and supply across the Volga had been cut off on November 11 by the huge ice floes. Red Army meteorologists' reports claimed the river would freeze solid by November 20, but all evidence on the river denied this. The wounded often piled up in riverbank dugouts. Gaps of two or three days in getting across the Volga became commonplace. There was less artillery support from across the Volga. Despite all their difficulties, two factors encouraged the Russian commanders in the city. First, no German attack, no matter how heavy, could intimidate them after the months of September and October. Second, although they did not know when or where, they did know that soon the long promised counterblow would begin. Thus, the more divisions the Sixth Army massed along their narrow perimeter, the more disastrous would be the German defeat. As Stalin had said in his Order of the Day on November 7, "There will be a holiday in our street too." After nearly two weeks of weathering the latest German threat, the word finally came. At midnight on November 18, Chuikov answered the telephone in his dugout to learn for the first time the details of the Russian offensive which would begin in a little over six hours.

November 19 dawned damp and foggy. At a little after six, the long-awaited Soviet offensive began with the rising roar of the huge artillery barrage. The juncture of the Rumanian IV Corps and the Sixth Army was literally shattered. By eight o'clock unopposed Soviet tanks were probing past the weak spots on the northern flank of the Sixth Army. Farther up the Don the Rumanian front had simply disappeared. The whole flank had been torn open. The Sixth Army fought back, but, as had long been predicted, the ill-armed and ill-prepared

Rumanians had fled. Within hours their former positions were overrun in depth. Soviet tanks bypassed the broken columns wandering to the rear and rapidly enlarged the depth of penetration to ten, then twenty, and by night, thirty miles. No one in Sixth Army headquarters could make out exactly what had happened. Desperately, Paulus began shifting his focus toward the west in order to prevent the Sixth Army, embedded in Stalingrad, from being overrun from the rear. On the dangling edge of the northern flank where the Russians had ripped a huge gap, Soviet armor began probing the empty areas to the Sixth Army's rear. The German 16th and 24th Panzer Divisions began to attack westward. Indeed, it was these responses on the flank which developed during the first twenty-four hours after the attack that saved the Sixth Army from immediate destruction. These German counterattacks, almost reflexive in character, had far-reaching consequences.

The key moment came sometime late on the night of November 19. Although confusion, uncertainty and contradictory reports poured into bewildered Sixth Army headquarters, there could have been little doubt that the long-expected, often-predicted Russian counterattack had begun. At the very least, the news from the northern flank revealed heavy breakthroughs—at worst, disaster. At this moment, Paulus faced a variety of alternatives. If his previous estimate of his own vulnerability, particularly on his brittle flanks unprotected by the Rumanians and Italians, were accurate, then the Sixth Army was in a very sticky position. Assuming that the Soviet commanders had even limited tactical intelligence, the worst had happened—the Sixth Army was burrowed into Stalingrad and its flanks were in the air. Right then the obvious move was to yank out the fifteen divisions committed on the city's perimeter as fast as possible and pull back, using a mobile defense until the huge rent in the line could be repaired. To sit in Stalingrad, whatever Hitler had said in his Munich speech, was obviously pointless if Paulus' estimation of the flank position had been accurate. Paulus, however, did not move. Clearly either he did not have the courage of his convictions in the face of Hitler's certain wrath or he made a mistake. True, yanking fifteen divisions out of the line is not a matter of a few orders. True, he did not know in detail the situation on the whole front or what a precipitous withdrawal might do, but still he had a pretty good idea. More to the point, he knew what would happen if he did not. Paulus, his subordinates, his colleagues, and his superiors had pointed out in detail the risks of the northern flank even while doubting the Russians' capacity to attack. Therefore Paulus must have considered the subsequent course of a massive Russian blow on the position of the Sixth Army in particular and the southern front in general. Yet he did not order a withdrawal. He did not even begin disengaging his fifteen divisions. Hitler had by implication ordered him not to retreat.

By retreating, he might disrupt the front and isolate Army Group A in the Caucasus. Similar situations before, with Russian tanks wandering about in the rear, had been rectified. Six divisions had even hedgehogged in an all-around defense and held out until rescued. He could always keep in instant radio contact with his immediate commander, Hitler, to request permission to disengage. There were scores of reasons not to panic, not to move too hastily. So Paulus waited. On the side of withdrawal, there were fewer rationalizations. It was simply and obviously the correct solution, but one which would require some military daring along with the personal courage to face a possible charge of disobedience. That Hitler would only after long and violent argument allow the Sixth Army to leave the Volga must have been clear. Waiting meant that Paulus would soon be ordered to wait. He had taken the safe course. He had not acted rashly. He had not risked the front. He had not moved the Sixth Army when there was a chance.

On the next morning, November 20, the second Russian main blow crashed into Colonel-General Hermann Hoth's 4th Panzer Army and the Rumanian 4th Corps south of Stalingrad. Hoth pulled back to the southwest, opening another vast gap on the Sixth Army's flank. Russian armor was reported plowing ahead in a great arc across the Don in some places seventy-five miles from the former front. The second breakthrough meant that a linkup with the northern pincers was not only inevitable but impending.

On November 21, Paulus suddenly realized that his options had become quite limited. Russian tanks were within a few miles of his headquarters. The rear of the Sixth Army had to be hastily protected by turning divisions around and pulling in the flanks as fast as possible. The Fourth Panzer Army and the Rumanian IV Corps, or what was left of them, were reported scattered and withdrawing rapidly. The whole Rumanian III Army Corps to the north had disintegrated. Even if Paulus received permission to abandon the siege of Stalingrad and disengage the Sixth Army, he would have his problems. Meanwhile, he had to prepare an all-around defense. The Russians had almost completed their encirclement. On the evening of November 21, Supreme Headquarters ordered the Stalingrad–Volga front maintained. The Sixth Army was to rectify the existing situation by counterattacking west of the Don. The next day the XI Army Corps and the XIV Panzer Corps were not only unable to counterattack westward but were forced to retreat across the Don. The Russian front was hardening to the west. On April 23, the two Russian attacks met at Kalach on the Don. The Sixth Army had been enveloped. For Paulus, fluidity and option had ended.

On the same day, in German headquarters, the situation had become somewhat clearer even if bleaker. The Sixth Army continued to hold most of Stalingrad while its flanks had wrapped back down to meet in a lightly held front facing west. Efforts to extend this front west across the Don had failed. Paulus and his staff moved to a new headquarters in the Gumrak railroad station and prepared their response to the demand from headquarters to stand firm. Paulus and his staff agreed that they needed to break out of their pocket. Although they had, in German terminology, hedgehogged, they had done so unintentionally and with absolutely no preparations for holding so vast a pocket; furthermore, the supply situation was critical. Every ounce of Sixth Army supplies had come in over the bridge at Kalach. Most of the food, gasoline, and ammunition had been used up in the ruins of Stalingrad, so that the Sixth Army had only very small reserve stocks. To stand firm was a sentence of doom. Later that evening, Hitler again specifically ordered Paulus to hold. On the following morning Paulus presented his plan to withdraw on the arc of the Don and Chir Rivers. He wanted permission by the next day, November 24, in order to launch the breakout on November 27.

Hitler, still in Germany when the Russians attacked, had traveled by special train to Leipzig and flown to his headquarters in East Prussia on November 23. He arrived at a critical moment. Paulus and his commanders in the pocket wanted out and right away. Army Chief of Staff Zeitzler, Hitler's choice, supported Paulus. All during the night of November 23 the usual struggle for Hitler's permission continued. He evaded. He avoided. He shouted, "I won't leave the Volga! I won't go back from the Volga!" Still Zeitzler did not give up. His position, however, was weakened by Hitler's attitude toward generals at large and pessimistic ones in particular. Hitler could point out that the same kind of advice had been given him before Moscow. He had been right, the generals wrong. He could point out that the situation had often been as uncertain, as fluid, and that envelopment of German troops was nothing new but that a retreat to which no one could foresee an end was new. In effect, he was denying defeat while the generals were proposing it. Then, providentially, there came a clinching argument for holding onto the Volga. Reich Marshal Hermann Göring absolutely guaranteed that the pocket could be completely supplied by the *Luftwaffe*. The *Luftwaffe*'s Chief of Staff, Jeschonneck, reported that Göring was confident of the *Luftwaffe*'s ability to put an airlift operation in action at once.[26] The generals were horrified but helpless. Zeitzler later gave the fabled account of the Göring promise, accurate in spirit if not in fact.

> HITLER: *Göring, can you keep the Sixth Army supplied by air?*
> GÖRING: *My Führer! I assure you the* Luftwaffe *can keep the Sixth Army supplied.*

ZEITZLER: *The* Luftwaffe *certainly cannot.*

GÖRING: *You are not in a position to give an opinion on that subject.*

ZEITZLER: *My Führer! May I ask the Reich Marshal a question?*

HITLER: *Yes, you may.*

ZEITZLER: *Herr Reich Marshal, do you know what tonnage has to be flown in every day?*

GÖRING: *I don't, but my staff officers do.*

ZEITZLER: *Allowing for all the stocks at present with the Sixth Army, allowing for absolute minimum needs and for the taking of all possible emergency measures, the Sixth Army will require delivery of three hundred tons per day. But since not every day is suitable for flying, as I myself learned at the front last winter, this means that about 500 tons will have to be carried to the Sixth Army on each and every flying day if the irreducible minimum is to be maintained.*

GÖRING: *I can do that.*

ZEITZLER: *My Führer! That is a lie.*

HITLER: *The Reich Marshal has made his report to me, which I have no choice but to believe. I therefore abide by my original decision.*[27]

Hitler must have suspected that Göring's promise relayed through the more reliable Jeschonneck was open to doubts, but it supplied the keystone to his arguments. It was a last, strong straw. Paulus would stay.

Inside the pocket, Paulus' corps and division commanders were urging action, even independent action. Paulus was in constant contact with Hitler, however, and did not see how he could consider direct disobedience of a specific order. To show him the way, on November 24, General Seydlitz, at considerable cost, withdrew his corps from its assigned position on the northwest edge of the pocket. Paulus ignored the lesson in disobedience. On the following day, Hitler, unaware of Seydlitz's move, placed him and his section of the front, out of which it was assumed a breakout would be made, directly under his personal command. Now Seydlitz would as a corps commander have the rare opportunity to disobey Hitler's direct orders. Seydlitz's new situation amused Paulus.

> *I handed this order personally to General v. Seydlitz at his Headquarters, which were close to my own, and asked him what he proposed to do about it? He replied that in the circumstances he had no option but to obey. This he did with soldierly devotion to duty to the very end, though that did not prevent him from urging me all the time to act on my own responsibility, regardless of orders from above.*[28]

The orders from above now included those of Field Marshal Erich von Manstein, Commander-in-Chief of the newly organized Army

Group Don. Manstein had the unenviable task of putting together the pieces of the southern front. His largest piece was the surrounded Sixth Army. On November 24, Manstein had arrived at his headquarters and reviewed the exchanges between Paulus and Supreme Headquarters. He agreed that Paulus should have been allowed to break out after November 19, but at the present the Sixth Army would remain in the pocket. In any case, even if Hitler had a change of heart, there was no possibility that the Sixth Army would be ready for a breakout before November 28. In the meantime the pocket—or, as the Germans called it, the cauldron—would be supplied by air while it tied down the Russian armies.

The Russians, once their pincers had met at Kalach, had to balance their forces between an inner perimeter facing Paulus and an exterior one pushing further out to prevent relief of the pocket. While Manstein had to worry about the whole southern front's collapsing and the hopeless position of Army Group A deep in the Caucasus, his opposite number, Zhukov, had only to concentrate on Stalingrad. The Russians had not prepared for a vast victory with huge advances. The Russians wanted to destroy the Sixth Army, nothing more, at least nothing more for the time being. Manstein sensed this, for he felt that he had a chance to re-create his shattered front while the Russians focused on the cauldron. In the next few days, the Soviets tried to increase the distance between the two perimeters by driving through the gaps left in the German lines. By November 24, the ring was often thirty to forty miles thick as the Germans pulled back to the southwest. Although the outer perimeter was often broken by roving mobile units, particularly armor, Zhukov wanted a continuous tactical front around the pocket. Thus within a week, with the outer perimeter sufficiently distant, Zhukov began to funnel troops into the perimeter around the Sixth Army. As yet the Russians did not squeeze too hard, rather they hardened the front, massed their artillery, and dug in. During the last week of November, the outer edge of the ring remained fluid. Manstein had not yet been able to stabilize his front. He still was not aware of Zhukov's limited aim: destruction of the Sixth Army. His major concern was to re-create his front.

On the Russian side, the major center of gravity remained Stalingrad. On November 27, Stalin telephoned directly to Vassilevsky, Chief of Staff in the Stalingrad area, and insisted on liquidation of the pocket. On December 3, the Russian Supreme Command adopted Plan *Saturn:* first objective would be to liquidate the Stalingrad pocket, second to capture the Don bend, and finally, if possible, to cut off the Germans in the Caucasus by an attack toward Rostov. First, however, would come the Sixth Army.[29]

Armed civilians patrol Madrid during the siege by Nationalist troops.
Wide World Photos

Prime Minister Winston Churchill (left), King George (pointing) and Queen Elizabeth (speaking to men in bomb crater) inspect German bombing damage to Buckingham Palace. *Wide World Photos*

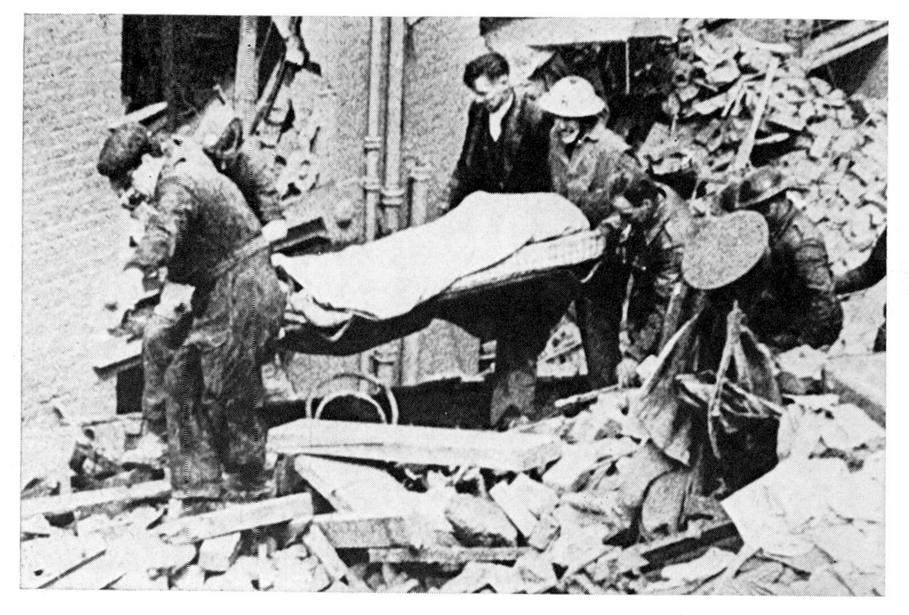

Rescue workers carry a body from a London building wrecked by Nazi air attack. *Wide World Photos*

London after the Great Blitz with Old Bailey in the background.
Wide World Photos

The last moments of the British battle cruiser *Repulse* (above) and the British battleship *Prince of Wales* sunk by enemy naval aircraft. *Australian War Memorial*

A stick of Japanese bombs bursting on Kalang Aerodrome, Singapore. *Australian War Memorial*

Amid the devastating wreckage of Stalingrad, the city's defenders stopped Hitler's war machine. *Sovfoto*

Field Marshal Paulus (front). *Sovfoto*

In Stalingrad each street, each house, was desperately defended. *Sovfoto*

Desolation in Stalingrad. *Sovfoto*

The Polish flag on the King Zygmunt III column at Castle Square in Warsaw.
Sovfoto

Jews leaping from burning buildings in Warsaw ghetto.
YIVO Institute for Jewish Research

Soviet machine gunners in Warsaw firing at the opposite bank of the Vistula, driving the Germans out of their entrenchments. *Sovfoto*

The David's Tower section of the Old City Wall of Jerusalem. Flares and fires set by mortar and artillery shells light the sky. *Wide World Photos*

War damage in the Jewish Quarter of the Old City, Jerusalem.
United Nations Photo, Department of Public Information

Two rabbis who carried the white flag of truce from Jerusalem's Old City Jewry to the Arab Legion lines await surrender negotiations.
Zionist Archives and Library

A cargo plane on the Berlin Airlift takes off from a new runway at Tempelhof Airport in Berlin while workmen finish construction of the runway. *Wide World Photos*

U.S. Air Force transport planes being unloaded in round-the-clock operations at Tempelhof Airport in Berlin. *Wide World Photos*

C-54 Skymaster approaching runway at Tempelhof. The children are waiting for candy bars which a U.S. airlift pilot floats down to them on handkerchief parachutes. *Wide World Photos*

The Germans had still not fully sorted out their over-all position. Manstein faced a variety of possible disasters, immediate and potential. Worst of all, his best troops were sealed in the cauldron. No one will ever know for sure just how many men were in the pocket. There were, however, elements of twenty German and two Rumanian divisions plus headquarter's troops, engineers, artillery, labor organization units, *Luftwaffe* staffs, and all the pieces and fragments of units driven in during the Russian breakthrough. Something over 220,000 seems probable. With this many men to be fed by an airlift, vast efforts would have to be made on the part of Göring and the *Luftwaffe*. Instead, the whole burden remained on General von Richthofen's Air Fleet. Richthofen soon complained of the strain.

> *All our JUs employed today in flying supplies . . . only thirty of them left. Of yesterday's forty-seven, twenty-two were lost, and today another nine . . . only seventy-five tons, instead of the 300 directed from above. We simply have not got the transport aircraft to do it.*[30]

With not enough planes, with limited gasoline supplies, and with bases far to the west, a regular effective airlift proved impossible. During the first twelve days of December, the tonnage delivered averaged 97.3 per day. Unless relieved or unless he could break out, Paulus felt that the entire Sixth Army would be eliminated. The danger to Rostov, key to the narrow corridor supplying Army Group A, remained equally urgent. During the last week of November, Manstein organized hastily-formed screens to cover the enormous gaps in his lines. If the Russians mounted any sort of attack toward Rostov, then not only would the Sixth Army be cut off but also the entire Army Group A. He had to make do with all sorts and conditions of units, for his promised reinforcements had not arrived. Fortunately, the Russian pressure was not too heavy and thus gave him a chance to turn from one losing game to another.

On November 28, Manstein sent Hitler his detailed appraisal of the Stalingrad situation. He felt that without waiting for all his promised reinforcements, an effort should be made to cut through to the cauldron. The Sixth Army could then be quickly replenished through the corridor, but "the army *must* be fetched straight out of the pocket, as it could not possibly survive the winter out in the open steppes."[31] On December 3, Hitler replied, seemingly agreeing with Manstein's conclusions. As planning for the relief attack continued, Hitler remained adamant that the Sixth Army continue to hold the line of the Volga. Manstein, however, felt that time was running out. His hope of a two-pronged attack had to be given up when the Russians mauled his formations.[32] Finally Manstein felt that the only practical approach was an attack north by a hastily assembled Army Group under General Hoth. Since Manstein envisioned a breakout operation, *Thunderclap,* by the Sixth Army toward the southwest to link up with Hoth moving north, Hitler's insistence that Paulus still hold the Volga would have to be ignored in practice. "In the event, undoubtedly, Hitler would have had no choice but to accept this fact, as he did on later occasions." Thus Manstein, ignoring Hitler's fixation about the Volga, decided to gamble on Hoth's reaching close enough to the edge of the pocket to allow Paulus to launch a breakout attack. Once contact had been made, the pocket would drain out through the corridor cut by Hoth. The real gamble was whether or not the scanty remaining German forces of Manstein's Army Group Don could hold off any Russian moves to rupture the front elsewhere.

On December 12, Operation *Winter Tempest* began with General Kirchner's 57th Panzer Corps spearheading Army Group Hoth. All went well for a while. From December 12 to December 15, Kirchner moved forward, pushing back the Soviet forces. The Russians had planned to begin the second stage of their offensive against Paulus to the north on December 16, and they now took several days to switch their emphasis from the inner perimeter to the outer. As soon as possible, they began throwing their reserves in front of Hoth's Army Group. On December 15, the Germans forced the Aksay River, but their progress on the other bank slowed down in the face of the stiff defense. The Russians committed Malinovsky's Second Guards Army and seemed willing to take heavy armor losses. The *Luftwaffe* had a field day against the Soviet tanks, but the Russians never seemed to run short. Their stolid straight-ahead attacks continued. With growing evidence elsewhere that his front was increasingly vulnerable, Manstein felt that the crucial hour in the relief of the Sixth Army was approaching. The time remaining for Army Group Hoth to reach the pocket was running out; in fact, it was quite unlikely that, given the nature of the Russian defense, Hoth could reach the perimeter at all. If the whole operation was to have a chance of succeeding, Paulus would have to help, scruples or not. Manstein sent his Intelligence officer, Major Eismann, into the pocket to persuade Paulus to break out and link up with Hoth. The Sixth Army's Chief-of-Staff, Major-General Arthur Schmidt, pointed out emphatically to Eismann that Hitler had specifically forbidden them to do so. Neither Schmidt nor Paulus would budge. Paulus insisted that surrender of the city was forbidden "by order of the Führer!" Eismann flew out of the pocket. Hoth would have to break in.

On the next day, Army Group Hoth reached and crossed the

Myshkova River. The Germans had reached a point where a breakout by the Sixth Army had become almost feasible. Elsewhere the German front was holding. In the rear, supplies had been accumulating for the Sixth Army. Hoth was even dragging behind his armor a long line of trucks loaded with food and ammunition. At noon on December 19, Manstein urgently appealed to the Supreme Command to let the Sixth Army disengage and break out toward Hoth. Hitler would agree only to the breakout, not to giving up Stalingrad. Manstein felt that this was impossible. It was also impossible for Army Group Hoth to get any closer to the pocket. The only hope was Paulus. Manstein ordered Paulus to break out to the southwest contrary to the directive from Hitler.[33] Paulus would not move. Double sets of orders were confusing, but in point of fact Paulus apparently had no intention of breaking out or even of making contact with Hoth. He claimed he would need six days to mount an attack. He claimed he had only enough fuel for a short armored thrust of twenty miles—and Hoth was thirty miles away. Both were patent excuses for inaction. Hour after hour, hectic conferences, radio messages, advice and appraisal took up the time of Paulus, Hoth and Manstein. They knew time was ticking away. The Russians had switched their strength to face Hoth, who now had no chance of advancing farther. Massive Russian reserves were moving up, indicating that his chances of even holding onto the Myshkova River bridgehead for more than a day or so were dubious. The few days were wasted in recrimination and confusion. Then the Russians struck the Italian Eighth Army front on the Don a massive blow. The Italians followed by the Rumanian Third Army collapsed in front of Vatutin's and Golikov's thrust. Within a few hours Russian armor was chasing the routed remains of the Italians and Rumanians toward Rostov. Manstein's whole delicate house of cards had been knocked down. Time had run out for Hoth. On December 24, in the face of heavy Russian armored attacks, the Germans withdrew across the Myshkova River to the line of the Aksay. The Sixth Army was on its own.

Manstein's Operation *Winter Tempest* by Army Group Hoth had been conceived in haste, mounted in confusion, and unrelated to either Paulus' professed possibilities or Hitler's orders. Its success had depended on deceiving the Supreme Commander as to its objective and on convincing Paulus to risk his honor and his army. Given the existing conditions on the key days of December 19 to 23, even if Paulus had been prepared to mount an effective thrust south, which he was not, the chances of success were limited. The Russians had jammed the front with armor and men. They had seven armies in the Stalingrad area. Even a temporary corridor through the ring could not have been maintained long unless the Sixth Army pulled out of the pocket and moved south. In this case the situation would have been fluid indeed. By December 20, the Sixth Army had a heavy percentage of exhausted, sick and frozen men, many of whom could maintain static defense positions, but few of whom could be expected in the Russian winter to fight their way on foot fifty or sixty miles without proper rations, ammunition or transport. Even to disengage from the pocket perimeter would have been difficult. On December 20, a very high proportion of Paulus' army was still pressed against Chuikov's Sixty-second Army along the Volga inside the city. If Paulus had tinkered with his perimeter, there was a possibility that the whole pocket would have collapsed; but, in any case, Paulus had not prepared the ram formation necessary to break through to Hoth. If he had, there might have been, as so many German generals have since pointed out, a real chance for a link-up with Hoth. The breakout was not, however, the last best chance of saving the army. Rather a breakout was an almost certain means of destroying most of the Sixth Army in the hope of saving something. For, whatever his reasons, Hitler's demand that Paulus remain on the Volga was responsible for maintaining the Sixth Army as a fighting formation for six more weeks. That it doomed the entire army can hardly be denied; but that it made more effective military use of their destruction than the desperate gamble proposed by Manstein seems equally apparent.

With the failure of Army Group Hoth to break through the ring, the Russians could turn their attention to annihilating the Sixth Army. Zhukov remained convinced that the elimination of the pocket was a better move than seeking in the shattered German front a wider and future victory. An army in the pocket was better than two in the Caucasus. So instead of concentrating everything on Manstein's front in hopes of closing the Rostov gap and cutting off Army Group A, the Russians massed around the Sixth Army. First things were to be put first. In the case of Stalingrad, the destruction of the pocket would produce a victory of almost unbelievable scope, another Cannae, and fitting revenge for the huge German envelopments at Kiev and Vyazma. The major blow would be made by the troops of the Don Front under Generals Rokossovski and Voronov driving the Germans to the east in an ever narrowing pocket. Yeremenko's Stalingrad Front would hold on, tying down a substantial portion of the Sixth Army along the Volga. In a limited way, Chuikov's Sixty-second Army had already taken the offensive within the city. At last, with the freezing of the Volga, a regular stream of supplies poured into the Russian pocket. As the slow massive preparations of the Red armies continued, piling up men and guns on the perimeter, the Germans and the Russians inside Stalingrad continued their bitter attacks and counterattacks. No matter who seemed to be winning in the outside world on the Don Front or in the Caucasus, Stalingrad remained the same, a private world of ruins, death and misery.

Along the Volga, six German divisions and five engineering battalions of the Sixth Army, almost a third of Paulus' strength, remained locked with Chuikov's men. The fighting went on and on with hourly counterattacks and swirling local battles. No prisoners were taken by either side because no one surrendered. Although the Sixty-second Army's position improved daily, the Germans continued to fight back bitterly. Their supply situation was very bad and growing worse: "The horses have already been eaten. I would eat a cat; they say its meat is also tasty."[34] The ammunition situation was critical. With dwindling gasoline stocks, mobility was impossible. With all these difficulties, the growing number of wounded and sick, many of whom could not be flown out, burdened the army. Many froze to death in unheated temporary hospitals. Hovering over the Sixth Army was the knowledge that as yet the Russians had been massing their troops to the west. Soon, however, the final steamroller blow would come. On January 8, the Russians formally requested the surrender of the hopelessly trapped Germans. If they refused, "the Red Army and Air Force will be compelled to wipe out the surrounded German troops." For a few brief hours an unofficial truce descended along the front while the Russians waited. Hitler, with Manstein's support, ordered Paulus to refuse the offer. The Sixth Army would fight on.

By the first week of January, the fate of the Sixth Army had become clear to all, generals and privates alike. The slow rot of fear and desperation in the face of death or surrender had begun to spread. Yet the lack of heavy Russian pressure on the perimeter and the relatively mild weather for a Russian January helped to disguise the hopelessness of the army. The gradual disintegration of the airlift meant that by January hunger had become a way of life and had begun to limit the military effectiveness of the troops.[35] The misery of the men became cumulative: exhaustion, frostbite and sickness—nothing was cured, relieved or repaired. Only a major wound meant a chance of being flown out if you could get to the field and on a plane. For the rest, they were doomed to huddle in their freezing, scratched-out burrows. For months the spirit of the army had been bludgeoned; for months, its physical capacity had been eroded. On January 8, the possibility of a long siege seemed slight. The Army was literally starving to death. Fed too long on hope and maintained by pride and habit, the men were no longer really capable, physically or mentally, of doing the impossible. The 195,000 men still in the pocket were too miserable, their suffering too great, their personal histories too bleak, to be considered in human terms by their commanders far away in Supreme Headquarters. To Hitler and to Manstein, the Sixth Army's symbol on their maps meant only that Paulus could tie up a certain number of Russian troops while the Germans tried to put a front together and get Army Group A out of the Caucasus. Just as Chuikov's resistance in September had been vital to the Russians, so was Paulus' defense in January. The agony of the army could not be considered. Even if the Germans did no more than allow themselves to be killed, the Sixth Army would have bought time with death. On January 10, the killing began.

At eight in the morning, the entire Don Front moved eastward in a giant lunge against the pocket. First came a vast artillery barrage, 7,000 guns and mortars with a density of 170 to the kilometer. The whole western edge of the pocket was cratered again and again by the moving curtain of fire. The German fortifications, often shallow and flimsy, disappeared in great gouts of smoke and snow. By the end of the first day, the Russians had advanced between three and five miles. Day by day, the Red Army squeezed the pocket. According to the Russians, the Germans continued to resist like "hounded wolves," stumbling back to scratch out new positions in the snow, holding on, folding backward again but seldom surrendering. Still the Russians came on. There were simply not enough German troops and those who did exist were little more than walking wounded. The lines of defense traced on staff maps existed only in the commander's head. Out in the fields, without cover, without food, without ammunition or even hope, the men plodded back through the snow, seeking a warm hole or a shred of horse meat. Then the mild January weather broke, and the bitter cold froze the weak, the wounded, the unwary. On January 13, the Red Army reached the Rossoshka River. The pocket was now fifteen miles long and nine miles deep. On January 15, the Pitomni air strip had fallen and with it the last hopes of escape. News from the outside world indicated that there was going to be no sudden shift in the front, no last-minute rescue. The Second Hungarian Army had disintegrated on January 15, and the German ring around Leningrad had been broken. The whole eastern front seemed to be trembling on the edge of an abyss.

On January 17, the Russians, having reduced the pocket by half again, sent Paulus a surrender offer. Generals Seydlitz and Schlömer favored accepting. They felt the misery of their men overbalanced the strategic time gained by resistance. Paulus had no authority to surrender; furthermore, the position of the Sixth Army was not hopeless. Despite every expectation the Germans had not collapsed under the

Russian blows. The western part of the cauldron was still, on January 17, a maze of pillboxes and dugouts. Inside the city, German units were still counterattacking. Most significant, very few Germans were surrendering. Between January 8 and January 17, the Russians had taken only 7,000 prisoners and most of these had been Rumanians. With two small airstrips near Gumrak, a much reduced airlift still could bring in vital supplies and take out a few wounded. Manstein insisted and Paulus agreed that the Sixth Army could for a limited time continue to hold off the Russians. Paulus refused the Russian offer. On January 22, the Soviet wave rolled forward again, driving the Germans eastward. On January 24, advanced Russian units began probing into the outer defenses of Stalingrad; the pocket had been whittled down to the suburbs. Obvious signs of disintegration now became apparent. Even Hitler seemed aware of the flickering will of the army. He made Paulus a Field Marshal. It had no tactical effect. On the same day, Hitler insisted to Zeitzler that "the army should fight to the last man."[36] The next day the Russian steamroller pushed on. The number of casualties from all causes had begun to mount rapidly. The army was dying. Paulus told Manstein that further resistance was pointless. Manstein agreed that the Sixth Army could no longer tie down sufficient forces. The Russians already had started to shift formations away from the shrunken cauldron. The time to surrender had come. Hitler refused: "Capitulation was futile since the Russians would never keep any agreement anyway."[37] Manstein was horrified at Hitler's callousness. He considered resigning in protest, but reconsidered.

> *. . . to throw up my task at this moment, however justifiable the human motives might be in the light of Hitler's attitude over the capitulation of the Sixth Army, struck me as a betrayal of those brave troops who were also involved in a life-and-death struggle outside the Stalingrad pocket.*[38]

Manstein would stay and carry out Hitler's orders. Paulus would stay and watch his army die.

The time had thus arrived for Paulus' next decision. Although Hitler insisted on continued resistance for military reasons, Paulus could see the desperate condition of his own men. From Manstein's attitude he could guess that there was considerable conflict over how much good the pocket was actually doing the German war effort. He did not need to guess about the Sixth Army. With plummeting temperatures, pounding Russian attacks, and no supplies, the army was dribbling away—frozen to death, starved to death, tired to death. Resistance was a brittle line of scarecrows wrapped in rags and reeking of infection. Wounds went untreated, frostbite unnoticed. There were no rations, even frozen horse meat and dried peas had gone. Typhus, the plague of defeat, had broken out. Paulus had to weigh the misery of his men, for whom he was responsible, with the direct orders of his commander, to whom he was responsible. Gradually his officers and his men had grown to believe their struggle was in vain, that they were being asked to suffer and to die for no reason or for no reason that they could understand. They felt they were betrayed, forgotten, discarded. They wanted an end to their agony. They wanted Paulus to surrender. Day followed day as he deliberated.

Paulus did not know, could not know, if Hitler's decision was militarily valid, but he did know that he had been ordered to continue to fight. In this case disobedience would not be an evasion or the seizure of an unexpected option; in this case it could be considered treason. A soldier's duty is to fight and if need be to die—capture, at least for most, was acceptable, but surrender came only when the situation was militarily hopeless. Hitler had insisted it was not. Paulus followed orders. That he refused to surrender could hardly come as a surprise. The misery and suffering of his men could be viewed with compassion but not allowed to compromise their military position. If generals refused to kill their men, there would be no wars. Trained for life as a military leader, Paulus' whole outlook and response was carefully nurtured by a professional code which defined his position in Stalingrad clearly and explicitly. Paulus had always obeyed orders, even when foolish or deadly. He had been trained as a soldier, not as a human being—the categories are often, if not usually, mutually exclusive. As Manstein had obeyed, so did Paulus; as did Paulus, so did everyone obey. The Sixth Army fought on in the ruins.

On January 23, the Russians overran the landing strip at Gumrak. One of the last planes out carried Paulus' final letter to his wife informing her of his intention to stand and fight. German headquarters was moved into the center of the city into the basement of the Univermag department store. On January 26, Russian troops broke into the city from the east and joined the units of Chuikov's Sixty-second Army. On the same day, the Red Army cut off a German pocket to the north of the main Sixth Army position. The Germans still would not surrender. On January 27 and January 28, the Russian ring narrowed; but bitter fighting continued. On January 29, the German positions were split again. Most of the Sixth Army, those still alive, had burrowed underground into basements, sewers, craters and unused ruins. In misery past understanding, most could only wait for death as the few active soldiers held up the Russian advance. Communications had disappeared. The little pockets knew nothing of the outside world where, on January 28, Hitler had announced the reconstruction of a new Sixth Army of Avengers without waiting out the final death throes of the old Sixth Army.

On January 30, Berlin reported that "the Russians are calling on the Sixth Army men to surrender but without exception they are continuing to stand and fight." Whatever Berlin thought, in the slag heap of Stalingrad after 180 days there was no more fighting to be done. On January 31, Lieutenant Fydor Mikhailovich Yelchenko reached the basement of the Univermag department store. The Germans announced that they would surrender. The lieutenant came out of the basement with fifteen generals and Field Marshal Paulus. Hitler was horrified, incredulous, at the surrender. He had fully expected the entire army to fight to the last man or to prevent capture by suicide. They should have gone out like Vikings on their shields. He took the surrender as a betrayal of him, of Germany, and of the army. "One had to assume that there would be a heroic ending." Paulus had bungled and lived. "I've no respect for a soldier who's afraid to do that but would rather be taken prisoner." He was particularly bitter that Paulus had not realized the implications of his last-minute promotion—"There will be no more field marshals in this war. We'll only promote them after the end of the war. I won't go on counting my chickens before they're hatched."[39] On January 31, German Headquarters reluctantly admitted that "a small number of German and allied soldiers have surrendered to the Soviet armies alive."

Even then, the battle inside the city had not finished. The tiny northern pocket held on. On February 2, the Russians brought in heavy artillery and moved it up to point-blank range. About noon, bayonets with white rags on the tips could be seen in the windows of the ruins. Eight more generals and the last of their men surrendered. The three-day total reached 40,000, the final remnants of the Sixth Army. Only one man escaped, a sergeant who somehow reached the distant German lines in March, only to die. The rest of the Sixth Army remained in Stalingrad. No one would ever be sure what the battle had cost the Germans. If the Sixth Army had a strength of about 220,000 on November 23, when the cauldron was created, then the Russian claim of 107,800 prisoners would leave 72,000 dead and about 42,000 flown out because of their wounds or their skills. Chuikov claimed 150,000 German dead were collected and buried. Whatever the figure, the five months at Stalingrad had changed the course of the war. Hitler's gamble for total victory had come to an end in the dark and bloody ruins of a city that at one time had been only a name on the map.

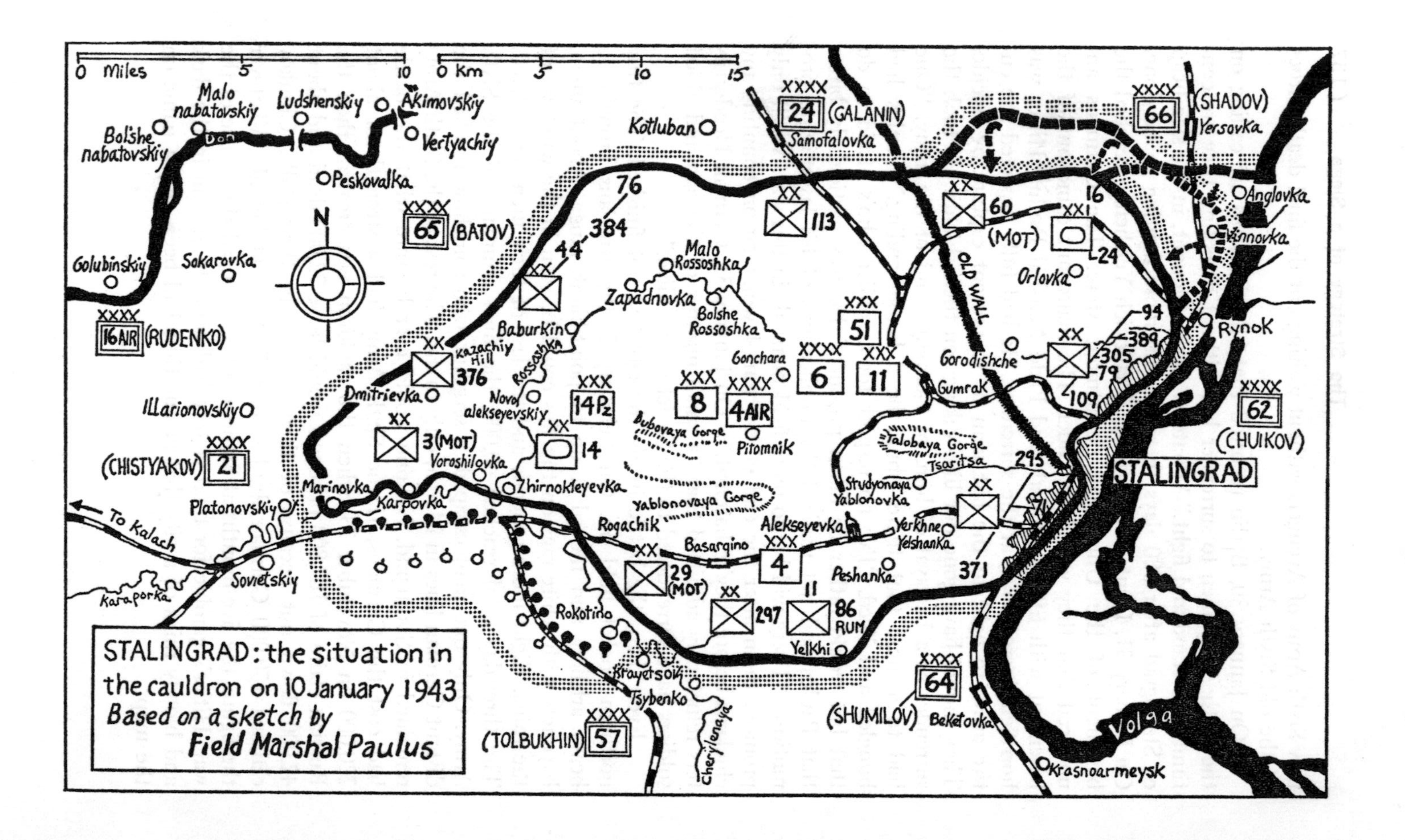

STALINGRAD: the situation in the cauldron on 10 January 1943
Based on a sketch by
Field Marshal Paulus

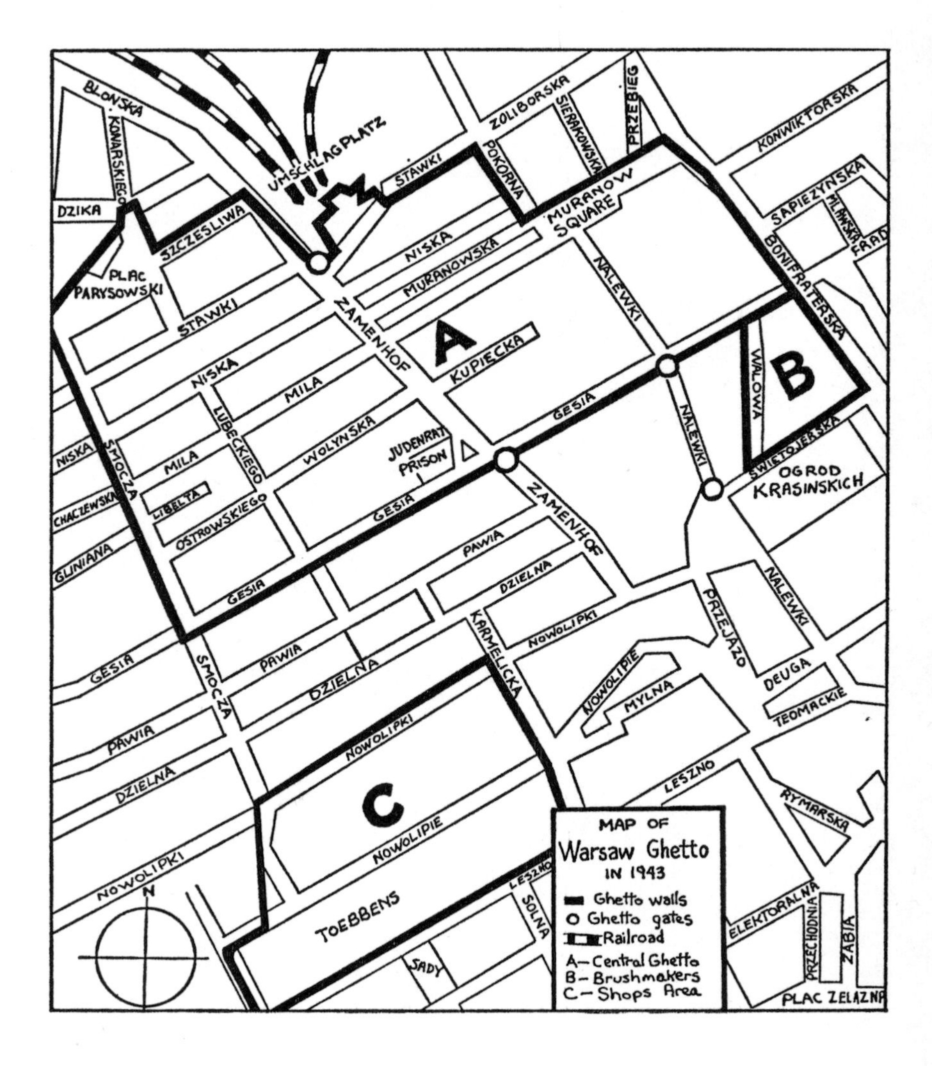
MAP OF
Warsaw Ghetto
IN 1943
Ghetto walls
Ghetto gates
Railroad
A—Central Ghetto
B—Brushmakers
C—Shops Area
A
B
C
UMSCHLAGPLATZ
MURANOW SQUARE
PLAC PARYSOWSKI
JUDENRAT PRISON
OGROD KRASINSKICH
TOEBBENS
PLAC ZELAZNA
ZAMENHOF
NALEWKI
GESIA
STAWKI
NISKA
MILA
MURANOWSKA
KUPIECKA
SMOCZA
PAWIA
DZIELNA
NOWOLIPKI
NOWOLIPIE
KARMELICKA
LESZNO
BONIFRATERSKA
WALOWA
SWIETOJERSKA
KONWIKTORSKA
SAPIEZYNSKA
ZOLIBORSKA
POKORNA
PRZEBIEG
SIERAKOWSKA
BLONSKA
KONARSKIEGO
DZIKA
SZCZESLIWA
LUBECKIEGO
WOLYNSKA
OSTROWSKIEGO
LIBELTA
CHACZEWSKA
GLINIANA
PRZEJAZD
MYLNA
DLUGA
TLOMACKIE
RYMARSKA
ELEKTORALNA
PRZECHODNIA
ZABIA
SOLNA
SADY
N

5 WARSAW: 1939, 1943, 1944

A Contrast in Sieges

Warsaw is a vanished city. It looks as though the city has been buried for years and only just dug up.
—CORRESPONDENT in 1945

AFTER the debacle at Stalingrad, the nature of the war changed for the Germans. Although for some time defense not defeat remained the watchword, the initiative had definitely passed from Hitler, who found his talents less adapted to conservation than to innovation. During the long, slow defeat of the German Army, the impact of Stalingrad grew from a local disaster to a national catastrophe, casting a long shadow over the army and the nation. Specifically, the question of the risks and advantages of defending cities was no longer considered as academic. The siege, usually as a denial of a port or a means of defense, became a considered possibility rather than a tactical accident, but within a year the Germans would find themselves as the besiegers.

During the latter part of the war, the German Army twice faced insurrection within a city already once besieged in 1939. Here the techniques of Stalingrad proved applicable. Of all Europe's devastated cities, few suffered repeated ruin as did Warsaw, nor did any other city undergo three separate sieges, each different, each disastrous. In 1939, the Polish Army and the Warsaw civilians, already defeated, held out in a campaign soon lost and forgotten in the clash of larger armies. Then in 1943 the Warsaw Jews rose in a hopeless gesture against German genocide, creating momentarily in the tiny Ghetto an isolated opposition to Nazi power, more a splendid gesture than a viable insurrection. A year later, in the waning hours of German power, the Polish underground army rose against the occupying army and seized most of the city. The two struggles within the same city, against the same foe, had little else in common, for one was doomed from the start and the other seemed destined for success. That the 1944 rising failed came as a great shock to the Poles as the limited success of the Ghetto rising did to the Jews. Both sieges by insurrection, however, not only underlined the validity of the techniques of Stalingrad but also the limitations of isolated insurrection in the face of the massed power of a determined state.

LESS than a week after the opening of the Second World War on September 1, 1939, with the invasion of Poland, the German Army had its first experience with siege warfare. In the heady atmosphere of lightning victory and massive envelopments on textbook timetables, the stubborn resistance of the Poles around Warsaw had subsequently been largely discounted as an omen of any particular import. Modern war was to be mobile, swift and fluid. Most observers in Poland wrote with awe, as well they might, of the splendid use of armor or the elegant relation of air, infantry and tanks—of all those aspects of the new wave in tactics, the *blitzkrieg*. Yet briefly, during the early fall of 1939, the Germans were given the opportunity to study the nature of modern siegecraft.

The Germans, of course, had the advantages of surprise, superior air power, mobility and mechanization, a massive manpower margin, and an opponent almost surrounded on three sides by German territory. As if these were not enough, the Germans also had a break in the weather, the best September in years. With the big battalions and the weight of metal, they hardly needed new tactics. Colonel-General Walther von Brauchitsch had 1,250,000 men in about sixty divisions, including four fully motorized divisions, five panzers, and four lightly armored divisions. There were two Air Fleets, each composed of from 500 to 1,000 planes.[1] Even against a prepared and competent opponent, the Germans would have had little difficulty. Against the antiquated and surprised Polish Army, victory was all but certain.

To face this massive, highly mobilized, and superbly equipped force, the Poles had only 280,000 men mobilized on September 1. Although the Polish strength supposedly lay in the size of their 2,500,000-man reserve, the speed of the campaign and the collapse of railway communications restricted the army in the field to some 600,000 men. Even worse, Polish equipment was an obsolete conglomeration of Russian, Austrian, German and French manufacture. In any case, the Poles intended to depend on horse cavalry instead of armor, peasant reserves instead of trained professionals, will instead of iron. Only in the air, with their 500 planes, did the Poles offer a threat to the Germans and even there they lacked early warning systems, protected airdromes and effective antiaircraft protection. With the country surrounded by modern German armies, mobilization not begun, and with distant allies, Marshal Smigly-Rydz must have realized how completely hopeless a task the Poles faced when the German attack began at 4:45 on that foggy morning of September 1, 1939.[2]

Within twenty-four hours, the *Luftwaffe* had command of the air, and the panzers were driving through and around the clumsy Polish formations. The *Luftwaffe* swiftly switched its attacks to the highways and railroads, preventing reinforcements and even withdrawal; meanwhile, the German armor pierced through to create sacks into which the advancing German infantry drove the Poles. Within three days Poland lay paralyzed; the Polish Army shattered. All real hope of resistance was gone. By September 4, the German Third Army, moving down from East Prussia, was nearing the Bug and Vistula Rivers north of Warsaw. On the following day, the President of Poland, Moscicki, along with Marshal Smigly-Rydz and most of the governmental and diplomatic personnel left Warsaw for Lublin. The Germans, however, were not primarily interested in the capital but rather in a great encircling movement which culminated in the Battle of Bzura east of Warsaw the following week.[3]

All this was not immediately apparent within Warsaw. The city, evacuated by the Government and the army, wavered uncertainly until Mayor Stefan Starzynski and local army units decided to resist. The possibility that Warsaw would be given an opportunity to hold out for long seemed slight. On September 8, the road into the city suddenly opened for General Hoepner's XVI Panzer Corps. Unable to resist the unexpectedly clear highway, Hoepner jumped at the chance for a coup. His panzers drove forward along the straight, unprotected highway right into the southwestern suburbs of the city. Facing his armor, the Poles had no organized defense at all and only a handful of troops, who had been throwing up barricades and digging tank traps mainly on their own initiative. Instead of surrendering, the soldiers and civilians rushed to stop the German advance. According to General Rudolf Gerd von Rundstedt, their unexpected resistance halted Hoepner cold. To their amazement, the Germans discovered just how vulnerable their armor could be when lightly armed civilians got too near.

> *The fortress of Warsaw was very stiffly defended, not only in the outer forts but also in the suburbs. At the very first time our panzers penetrated into the city, the inhabitants had shot from cellars and thrown bottles of gasoline onto the tanks from houses.*[4]

Although he tried to push on into the city the next day, Hoepner found his unsupported armor too weak. The Poles hung on. The Germans pulled back. On September 12, the German Third Army cut the railway lines leading to the northeast and turned in a great arc, completing the encirclement of Warsaw on September 14. Three days later the trapped Polish Army, 170,000 strong, in the east around Bzura, surrendered. Now almost the last island in a German sea, Warsaw was invested by four strong German armies. The Germans were not eager to smash into the city. Army Chief of Staff Halder urged prudence.

> *I am against an attack into the city. Must be starved into capitulation! We are in no hurry and don't need the forces now outside Warsaw anywhere else.*[5]

Rundstedt and Halder may have considered the city a fortress, but this was far from the case. Warsaw had no prepared defenses, no stockpiles of military supplies, no trained defenders or even a defense plan, and only makeshift preparations for protecting and maintaining the huge civilian population. Nevertheless, the Germans moved cautiously, depending on a gradual softening-up attack and heavy use of the *Luftwaffe.*

On September 17, heavy shelling began. The collapse of Polish resistance elsewhere allowed a greater and greater concentration of firepower on the city. The normality of the city's life, the open shops and cinemas, the café crowds and running trams of the first two weeks of the war, ended abruptly. Although the Poles, led by Mayor Starzynski and General Rommel, had every intention of holding out, they were increasingly horrified to see their city collapsing into flames around them. Starzynski spoke each night in a radio program prefaced by Chopin's "Polonaise," praising, urging, admonishing. Determination alone, however, soon proved fragile. The tempo of the German bombardment steadily increased. Actually the Germans seemed to be using relatively small-caliber shells set to burst in the air; for example, the fifteen-story Prudential Building, Warsaw's only skyscraper, took repeated hits without crumbling. The worst damage was caused by the unchecked fires and the high-explosive bombs. The Germans hit and set afire one after another of the showplaces of the city, seemingly out of malice rather than by mistake. With the broken water mains and the overworked, under-equipped fire department, little could be done to check the fires. By September 22, Warsaw was "burning like a torch."[6] On that day, the German Third and Eighth Armies launched a heavy and presumedly final attack. The Poles inflicted severe losses on the Germans and withdrew without breaking. The cost of tightening their perimeter apparently came as a shock to the Germans. They stepped up their air and artillery bombardment, hoping to force the Poles to surrender without excessive German losses.

> *The attack by the* Luftwaffe *and the great artillery concentration therefore were from our point of view an operation of war and not a woeful destruction of an open city.*[7]

To the Poles, however, the bombing of the Old Jewish Section on the Day of Atonement and the artillery shells landing with great precision on all the city's hospitals seemed more like a vindictive campaign of revenge than an operation of war.[8] The difficulties of defense mounted. Ammunition ran low. The fires burned on and on, producing a great coiling column of black smoke, visible for twenty miles. Food ran low. The horses had been eaten. Water supplies trickled out and ran dry. Essential services were breaking down. The capacity to resist was evaporating. On September 26, General Rommel asked for a twenty-four-hour truce to spare the population. The Germans refused and stepped up their shelling.[9] With the invasion of eastern Poland by Soviet Russia and the failure of the anticipated aid from Great Britain and France, there now seemed no purpose in resistance. On September 29, General Rommel formally surrendered.[10] The siege had ended.

When the Germans marched into smoldering Warsaw on the last day of September, everything changed. Poland itself disappeared in one more partition, divided this time between Soviet Russia and Nazi Germany. Even as the defeated Polish soldiers trudged home, the Germans began to reorganize their newly annexed territory. Temporarily the country had slipped into anarchy with only isolated pools of authority. The roads were jammed with refugees wandering in search of security or in fear of prison, moving back toward their old homes or forward to new ones. Wherever they went, they found burned buildings, shell craters, newly dug graves, and other refugees fleeing in a different direction. Of all the Polish cities, Warsaw, having been the gayest, now seemed the grimmest to the refugees stumbling into the bleak, shell-pocked streets.

> *Warsaw was a shocking ruin of its former self; the disaster that had befallen it exceeded in magnitude my direct anticipation. The gay metropolis had disappeared. The handsome buildings, the theaters, the cafés, the flowers, the cheerful, noisy, familiar Warsaw had vanished as utterly as if it had never existed. I passed through street after street heaped with rubble and debris. The pavements were black and grimy. The inhabitants were worn, tired, and disconsolate. Graves for the dead who could not be taken to a cemetery had been improvised everywhere in parks, public squares, and even on the streets.*[11]

The Germans were little interested in the atmosphere of despair and desperation which gripped the population or in the tumbled ruins and burned-out palaces, but they were very interested indeed in integrating Poland into the New German Empire. Orders, directives, instructions appeared in triplicate. The Poles were suddenly restricted and confined, hemmed about by a mountain of special regulations, unending demands, new permits and old prejudices. The Poles in Warsaw struggled from one day to the next on less food in confined and crowded quarters with little heat. Each day there seemed less of everything. To live through one more day became the limit of most Poles' hopes.

Others, even before the German occupation of the city, had begun planning for the future. Neither expecting war nor prepared for defeat, the Poles had made no plans for an occupation. Through the long, cold winter of 1939–1940, the time of stalemate in the West, the first steps were taken to form an effective underground organization. All the wiles and stratagems which would later become so familiar in the life of other occupied countries were developed, sometimes at great cost, but always with eventual success. While the Germans dismantled Polish factories, seized agriculture produce, shipped off laborers, confiscated property and carved out private empires, the Poles silently, secretly, began the arduous task of creating a clandestine state. In time, the Polish resistance built a vast, hidden organization with all the institutions of a modern nation: a government with ministries and territorial administrations, a parliament which met regularly, and, most important, a militia of 300,000 men organized into regiments. They contrived a secret educational system, underground courts, and even a radio station, SWIT, which supposedly broadcast regularly from within Poland.[12] In the face of an occupying army motivated by a philosophy which regarded Poles with undisguised contempt leavened with violence, this was an amazing feat. The creation of the Polish underground took place simultaneously with the German attempt to turn the nation into a collection of serfs. The Poles could daily expect wanton violence, public theft, and private terror at the hands of their Nazi overlords. Of all the Poles, the most vulnerable were the 3,500,000 Jews.

The history of the huge Jewish community in Poland stretches back into the early Middle Ages when a scattering of Jewish villages began to appear dotted through the Slavic areas along the Vistula and Oder Rivers. By the twentieth century there were more Jews in Poland than the entire population of Norway. In Lublin there were more synagogues than churches. Vilna was known as the Lithuanian Jerusalem. In Warsaw a third of the population was Jewish. All varieties of Jewish life were represented: the rational Maimonides, the socialist Bund, the romantic medieval Chassidim, the divided Zionists, and even the atheistic Communists. This huge population, rich in tradition, supported a network of religious, cultural and educational institutions which had made Hebrew and Yiddish the languages of millions. On October 1, 1939, this vast and divided community faced an uncertain challenge. In theory at least, Hitler and the Nazis intended, if not their destruction, at least their perpetual bondage. No one knew what the practice would be. Rumors and later personal reports from Germany gave little cause for hope and much for despair. Almost at once, the feared persecutions began.[13]

At first came "legal" anti-Jewish decrees: no Jew could work for the Government or in key industries or bake bread or ride on trains. Regularly the restrictions were extended, changed, reviewed. Jews over twelve had to wear an armband, had to have special permits, special licenses. The Germans managed to keep "the population ignorant of the way to live within the law from day to day."[14] The realization that Polish Jewry was, in fact, without the protection of the law came gradually. Robbery of Jews was encouraged; violence against them, particularly by Poles, was fostered, and murder of them condoned. On November 2, 1940, after a year of steadily increasing discrimination and terror, the Nazi Governor of the Warsaw District, Fischer, proclaimed the institution of the Ghetto. Here the Jews of the city and the surrounding country would be herded into a pen, isolated from Poland and the world. There they would suffer and die; their fate hidden by eight-foot walls.

The designated Ghetto area, one-twentieth of the city, suddenly absorbed a third of the population. More Jews fleeing from the violent persecution in the provinces arrived to seek Warsaw's limited security. Over 400,000 Jews crammed into the tiny Ghetto. By the spring of 1942, each room held an average of twelve occupants. The streets, the hallways, every corner was filled with constant movement, comings and goings. Hardly for a moment was privacy possible. All that most could do was to wait within the walls, surviving somehow in the crowd. The Germans had eliminated the chances of productive labor, so 60 per cent remained unemployed, hopelessly unable to earn a living. The soup kitchens soon served 130,000 people a day a meager, watery concoction. The German rations were carefully controlled in Warsaw so that the Jews received the least and paid the most. The legal ration level also assured the Germans that the Jews could not long subsist. If the Jews had depended solely on the official rations, the Ghetto would have been starved out within months as the Germans apparently intended. As it was, most of them suffered from hunger.

Idle, starving, desperate, the Jews attempted to create some sort of life within the narrow walls of the Ghetto. In order to evade the sudden German forays, the arbitrary arrests, the searches and seizures, the Jews gradually developed a complex system of hiding places: underground bunkers, sealed rooms, secret cupboards and safe corners. Many of these were linked up to form a vast hidden Ghetto. Without this network everyone would have been vulnerable at every moment. With its fragile security, life began anew. Newspapers were published, illegally, concerts given and classes taught, illegally; for all that was "legal" was to suffer, to starve, to die.

Somehow the Jews survived, although most had time for little else. Even to live was a major accomplishment. The hopelessly crowded conditions, the limited water, the overworked sewers meant disease. Typhus became rampant. With the plague and the growing malnutrition, the mortality rate mounted, particularly among the very young and the very old. In 1940, 8,891 died of "normal" causes; in 1941, the figure was 43,238, or ninety per 1,000 inhabitants; by the next year this rate had climbed to 140 per 1,000. In a way, the "normal" mortality of attrition was never so terrifying as the rarer death caused by the offhand violence of the Germans or their SS-trained Slavic police. Life in the Ghetto was always threatened by the sudden, irresponsible shot, the drunken invasion of soldiers on leave, the calculated provocation leading to instant execution or deportation. Every day Jews were beaten, insulted, humiliated. As if this were not enough, rumors began to seep into the Ghetto of worse to come, of the final solution. Few believed. Despite the sporadic violence, the typhus, the unclaimed bodies left on the streets, and the haunting rumors of extermination, most Jews still hoped. They struggled on, for seemingly things could get no worse.[15]

By July 1942, death by disease and starvation, plus arrests and occasional deportations had reduced the population of the Ghetto from the high of 430,000 in May 1941 to 380,000. Yet the reduction brought no relief from the crowding, the constant hunger, and the nagging uncertainty. On July 22, 1942, the Germans announced to the Jewish Council for Warsaw that "all Jews living in Warsaw, without regard to age or sex, are to be deported to the East" with certain exceptions for productive Jews.[16] While many still hoped that the deportation was no more than an additional step in the unending persecutions, others came to realize that the rumors of extermination might be true. Many had neither the strength nor interest to care. Starved into a state of numbness, some 20,000 Jews actually volunteered for deportation in exchange for food. In massive numbers the more cautious were driven out of the Ghetto and forced into the railway cars by threats and by force. Each day the trains moved out to the Treblinka Camp and death. Day after day the squads of Ukrainian irregulars or Polish police, or German troops, scoured the Ghetto, sweeping all the "unproductives" before them. Patrols ferreted out the hidden bunkers, combed and recombed the same buildings. Always the toll of deportations mounted. Although, since the beginning of 1942, Jewish organizations had been involved in underground activity, little could be done to resist the German deportations. There was as yet no effective Jewish military resistance in the Ghetto and very little liaison with the developing Polish underground. In the summer of 1942, with no arms and no possibility of acquiring them, with no physical security, with German patrols sweeping the Ghetto, there could be no practical action. Temporarily all that could be done was to hide from the Germans behind false documents, within buried dugouts, or in "safe" areas. Even to hide successfully required great skill and considerable luck.

In the forty days after July 22, about 250,000 Jews were shipped out of the Ghetto to be exterminated. The final terror came during the first week of September when all the remaining Jews were driven out into the streets. Probably some 20,000 had by this time hidden away in burrows or crannies. The remaining 120,000 were forced to wander the streets for two days and nights while the Germans chose who would receive a "life ticket" to be worn on the chest like a dog tag and who would be shipped on to Treblinka. On Monday, September 7, the final shipment of 80,000 Jews to Umschlagplatz and the death trains to Treblinka began. Within a few days, the last major "action" was over. On September 21, in one last vicious spasm another 2,196 Jews were seized and deported.

After this the Germans allowed the "productive" Jews license to live. There were about 33,400 Jews working for German employers and about 3,000 working for the Jewish Council; so that officially there were only about 37,000 Jews in the Warsaw Ghetto. In July there had been 380,000. In reality the Jewish population after the deportations was twice what the German census indicated. Thousands still lived in bunkers or secret rooms, but all lived on borrowed time, whether they knew it or not. With the population stripped to the "essentials" and the physical size of the Ghetto reduced by three-quarters, many felt the worst was over. "They continued living in their dream world of some kind of personal safety, some escape from reality."[17] Others, who accepted the reports from Treblinka, began plans for resistance in what they felt was simply a breathing space before the final solution.

On October 20, representatives of various organizations met to found a Co-ordinating Committee of Resistance. Efforts to create a single fighting organization were not wholly successful. The Irgun Zvi Leumi, long intolerant of half measures, could not be incorporated. Meetings between David Wdowinski of the Irgun and Zivia Lubtekin and Mordechai Anielewicz proved fruitless. The Irgun set up its own fighting group with Paul Frenkel as its military commander, and with the Betarim, the youth organization, as its base.[18] The remaining groups formed the Jewish Fighting Organization with Mordechai Anielewicz as military commander. During the fall, Anielewicz organized fifty fighting groups for resistance in case of another German "action." What he did not have and what proved almost impossible to get was arms of any sort. With vast ingenuity and great labor, secret "factories" were established to produce a few homemade grenades and bombs. Every corner of the Ghetto was searched for revolvers or rifles but with little result. The only possibility to arm the Jews was through contacts outside the Ghetto, with the so-called Aryan side. Liaison with the Polish underground was tenuous, and the Polish Home Army apparently was not overly keen to smuggle its own weapons into the Ghetto where in all likelihood they would simply go unused or be confiscated. In December, the Home Army did send in ten pistols; but this could hardly be considered more than a sop. In desperation, the Jews turned to bribery and blackmail. The money, jewels, and securities needed for purchases existed in hidden hoards throughout the Ghetto. Now wealthy Jews volunteered or were persuaded to contribute to the arms fund. Once a venal guard had sold his first pistol, pressure and threats were applied. This deadly underground trade in arms began to yield results, but so slowly and in such tiny quantities that any real resistance still seemed hopeless. When Jan Karski, on his way to the Polish Government in Exile in London, met with two of the Ghetto leaders, he carried out a message of just how fearful the situation had become.

> *We are organizing a defense of the ghetto . . . not because we think it can be defended, but to let the world see the hopelessness of our battle—as a demonstration and a reproach.*[19]

On January 9, 1943, the architect of doom visited the Ghetto in person. In a closed car Heinrich Himmler, the pale, grey director of efficient murder, was driven swiftly through the deserted streets between the four remaining Ghetto sections. Led by armored cars, protected on both sides by others, Himmler sat in his car surrounded by SS officers and peered at the high walls. Only a few Germans even knew he had passed through on the "final inspection." On January 11, two days later, Himmler, irritated by a partisan outbreak in Poland, ordered the arrest of all the "proletarian elements of outlawry and their deportation to the concentration camps of Lublin, Auschwitz and of the Reich."[20] Apparently at about the same time, the Nazi administrators in Warsaw felt that the time had come for the final liquidation of the Ghetto. Himmler's order was applied to the Jews. On January 18, the Germans suddenly began another action to round up the "illegal" Jews still in the Ghetto. A few of the fighting organizations received a warning through the secret Irgun telephone, but most of the groups were cut off from their weapons and from one another. Still, the

Jewish Fighting Organization under Anielewicz managed to get five groups armed and into action. The group under Anielewicz tried to meet the Germans in the streets at the corner of Mila and Zamenhofa Streets. Although the Germans were appalled at the effrontery of any kind of resistance, they recovered and wiped out the Jews facing them in the open street. Miraculously, Anielewicz managed to escape the slaughter. Elsewhere, scattered firing broke out. The other four groups had stayed inside apartment houses and fired on the startled Germans from there. The resistance soon degenerated into isolated sniping while the uneasy Germans rounded up between 6,500 and 8,000 Jews. After the Germans had withdrawn that night carrying their casualties, there were exaggerated claims of fifty Germans killed and 100 wounded. The numbers were not so exhilarating as was the fact of resistance: "It was hard to realize that we had really killed Germans, we had actually made them run."[21]

With morale high and their prospects improved, the Polish Home Army, apparently impressed with the skirmish, sent in forty-nine revolvers, fifty bombs and some dynamite. Polish underground instructors taught the Jews how to make and use Molotov cocktails (bottles filled with gasoline). The contact with the Polish underground did much to lessen the isolation, the constant loneliness, suffered by all the Jews cut off from the outside world by the walls of the Ghetto. Other changes were made in tactics. Anielewicz decided that he would have to mass the fighters behind cover. First, without covering fire or barricade, the streets were execution grounds, and secondly, his men scattered about through the apartment buildings had proved ineffectual, with some not firing at all. Massed in secure ambush, he felt he could defend, at least for a while, the center of the Ghetto. By this time the Ghetto he proposed to defend bore little resemblance to the Ghetto of 1940. The Germans had divided it into four separate sections: a workshop area, the brushmakers' area, a small Ghetto and a large Ghetto. The Jews had, however, in some areas tunneled under or through the divisions, linking up cellars and bunkers in a maze that so far had defied German searches. The Irgun had installed a 200-man bunker under a factory shop with German guards directing the work of "productive" Jews a few feet above them. Yet their bunkers and their little store of hidden revolvers were thin reeds in the face of the German Army and the security forces. Anielewicz and Frenkel had to ignore the real fact: that they were two tiny bands of poorly armed, half-starved men facing a real army. Instead they continued plans to punish the Germans by their unexpected resistance. Even to resist futilely was sufficient.

Despite the growing evidence of the Jews' determination to hold the Ghetto, the Polish Home Army remained reluctant to become too deeply involved in Ghetto affairs. The attitude of the "Aryan" underground remained the result of practicality, timidity, and certainly in the case of some, latent or even overt anti-Semitism—neither the advent of war nor the German occupation had been sufficient to eradicate this malignant predilection. Many Poles felt little sympathy for the Ghetto Jews, but racial prejudice could hardly be the major motivation of the leaders of the Polish Home Army. They were often men of good will, intellectuals, humanitarians by conviction, tolerant and humane. Yet they gave little help and what they did give "was negligible, insignificant."[22] Often no man is more cruelly practical than the previously isolated professional involved for the first time in politics—particularly illegal, conspiratorial politics. With little evidence that the Jews could or would defend themselves, the Polish Home Army held back its carefully hoarded arms on grounds of necessity. When the Jews fought back in January, another factor came under consideration. The leaders of the Home Army now feared that the Jews would set off a chain-reaction rebellion in Warsaw which would prematurely reveal their whole secret army. "An open fight at this time would mean complete extermination for all of us."[23] The Jews would have to face extermination alone and barely armed with obsolete revolvers, homemade bombs, and a few ancient rifles. The sweet reasonableness of the patriotic Poles' prudence left a bitter taste in Jewish mouths, but there was little left to do but prepare for the inevitable.

During March the situation in the Ghetto grew more explosive as the Fighting Organization became more daring. On Saturday, March 13, a full-scale fire fight suddenly developed with German SS troops and police near the corner of Mila and Zamenhof Streets. The Germans managed to kill 400 Jews while exchanging shots with the hidden snipers. Finally they grudgingly withdrew. The Jews had no idea of how many casualties they had inflicted, but the growing reluctance of the Germans to move freely about the Ghetto meant that their sporadic ambushes had been effective and probably provocative. Five days later, on March 18, Anielewicz sent a letter to the Polish underground. He noted that his men had killed two members of the German *Werkschutz* and wounded an SA man. He again asked for more arms and particularly ammunition since, out of the forty-nine revolvers sent in, only thirty-seven could be used because of the lack of ammunition. Anielewicz pointed out that his tactics had "definitely convinced the enemy he must adopt the methods of siege and force."[24] He expected the German final "action" to wipe out the Ghetto to begin any day. The Germans did not suffer defiance readily.

Nazi self-esteem had been shattered by the very limited and highly unsuccessful—in military terms—rebellion in January. That the Jews should resist was unthinkable, a violation of the Aryan ideals. During February and March, the Germans continued efforts to clean out the Ghetto but without taking great risks. Himmler continually insisted that his deputies, Krüger and Pohl, should finish off the Ghetto "because otherwise we shall never have any peace in Warsaw." Not only was it humiliating to have armed Jews lurking about inside the Ghetto shooting at Germans, but it was extremely dangerous to risk a general uprising in Warsaw and Poland by ignoring the situation. On February 16, Himmler had directed that "for security reasons I hereby order the Warsaw ghetto be destroyed." Efforts to trick the remaining Jews into resettlement had failed. Limited "actions" had been met with shooting. Finally the Germans decided on a three-day police action under the direction of the Police Chief of the Warsaw District, Colonel von Sammern. Himmler had serious doubts about Sammern's routine plans and at the last minute turned direction of the operation over to SS General Jürgen Stroop. On Stroop's arrival he would direct the available units of the Waffen SS, the Polish Blue Police trained by the SS, some dubious Ukrainian and Baltic units, and some regular engineer and artillery formations. This was a very considerable increase from the original fifty SS men aided by two sections of puppet police who had carried out the great deportations from July to September in the previous year, but the Germans were taking no chances; they wanted a swift, tidy operation.[25]

When Stroop, who had already directed several operations of liquidation, arrived in Warsaw on April 17, he decided not to change Sammern's plans at the last minute. He gave the final word to begin the "action" the following day. At two o'clock in the morning of April 19, German and Polish Blue Police began moving into position around the Ghetto walls at thirty-yard intervals. Almost at once the Jews' observers reported back that the final "action" was under way. Within fifteen minutes the Jewish Fighting Organization had moved its groups into position. From the scanty evidence available, apparently Anielewicz had prepared a series of ambushes at the various major arteries in the center of the main Ghetto. If all went well, the Germans would be lured into the inner Ghetto and in front of the prepared positions before they realized that the months of sniping and hiding were over. This time houses had been fortified, lines of fire prepared, and the fighting groups concentrated. Anielewicz did not want a repetition of the slaughter of January nor did he want his limited firepower scattered around the perimeter of the Ghetto, where it would prove ineffective. Concentrated in the center, his men could most quickly do the greatest damage. Once the rising had begun, Anielewicz had been promised some diversionary assistance around the edge of the Ghetto by dissident units of the Polish underground. That this help would be only peripheral was clear, but it should confuse the unsuspecting Germans for a while. The Jews did not expect the fighting to last very long.

At four o'clock in the morning, the Germans began stealthily moving into the Ghetto in small groups, hopeful of hiding the onset of the "action" until the last moment. Once within the Ghetto they smoothly combined into silent platoons to wait for dawn. For five hours a deadly silence hung over the Ghetto as the Germans maneuvered into position under watchful Jewish eyes. At seven o'clock the SS men moved up artillery outside the walls. Then in the gray dawn the harsh cough of tank engines turning over could be heard. The panzers, followed by armored cars, moved into the main streets of the Ghetto. Colonel von Sammern was ready, his infiltrated platoons commanded the streets, and the tanks could knock out any center of resistance. The Waffen SS troops marched in behind the armor, supremely confident that the prior planning would limit if not prevent another unfortunate incident.

At the intersection of Nalewki and Gesia Streets and also at Zamenhof and Mila, the Germans marched straight into Anielewicz's traps. The Jews opened fire, mowing down the surprised Germans. The rattle of small-arms fire and the crunching of Molotov bombs splashed across the Ghetto in a wave. The Germans pulled back in disorder. Some remained crumpled on the ground inside the Ghetto. Stumbling back, the Germans felt surrounded. Fire came from all sides. Along Muranowska Street, where the Irgun had set up headquarters at No. 7–9, the Jewish blue and white flag was flying. The whole neat "action" collapsed in chaos. A German attack on the brush factory district outside the central Ghetto broke down under a rain of grenades. When armor was brought up, a second shower of Molotov cocktails splashed around the tanks and began burning. The Germans pulled back. By afternoon they had evacuated the Ghetto entirely. Besides those Germans caught in the first ambushes—one ambush apparently turned into a six-hour struggle—many had been picked off while trying to storm the defended houses. Several Ukrainian police, standing rigidly before their "German" officers, had been machine-gunned by the Jews wearing the captured uniforms. The extent and planning of the resistance had come as a shock. Sammern had to report to Stroop that evening that he felt all was lost in the Ghetto—the Germans had been repulsed. Stroop took over personal command and began the construction of his "report" of the operation.

> *When we invaded the Ghetto for the first time, the Jews and Polish bandits succeeded in repelling the participating units, including tanks and armored cars by well-prepared concentration of fire . . .*

Already seeking excuses for even a limited failure, Stroop had to invent some "Polish bandits" to lessen the impact of the Jewish success and to fudge his casualty figures to show only twelve men lost. The simple police operation now appeared considerably more hazardous: the Jews were armed and ready but the Nazi hierarchy was unlikely to listen to excuses. If Stroop was having a bad night over his first report, the Jews were not so gloomy; in fact, they were wildly enthusiastic. The first day had gone far better than anyone could have expected. As Anielewicz wrote: "Armed resistance on the part of the Jews had been realized." Everything else would be a bonus, for the main gesture had been made. The Ghetto had risen.[26]

On the next day Stroop stepped up the number of men involved from 866 to 1,293, dividing them into two groups. The tanks moved in, followed by the Waffen SS and the Polish Blue Police. One of the main targets was the fortified brush factory. Stroop depended on mass rather than skill and sent in 300 men to overawe the Jews. The Germans moved up in formation, turned into Walowa Street and moved past the gates directly over a buried mine. The terrific detonation could be heard all over the Ghetto. The Jews reported seeing "bodies flying into the air, hands and feet separately. Eighty to a hundred dead can be counted."[27] The stunned Germans fled in considerable disorder. Elsewhere other Germans soon discovered that the entire Ghetto was crisscrossed with secret tunnels and honeycombed with bunkers. Many of the houses had, indeed, been turned into miniature fortresses armed with pistols rather than heavy weapons. The Germans called for artillery support, which proved ineffectual. German flame throwers could not get close enough to do any damage. All the while, heavy firing continued. Although behind the infantry the SS men managed to round up a few Jews for deportation, most of the Jews remained huddled in their bunkers waiting in an atmosphere of terror and delight for news. Late that day the Germans had begun to devise a method of clearing the Ghetto. The uninhabited parts of the Ghetto, the wild areas, were combed with great care. The SS men often sent the Letts or Poles in first. If, as was often the case, the house contained armed Jews, Stroop used a different technique. The house was shelled at close range, which would bring down the top stories; then the ruins were methodically set afire. In this way the Germans would not have to close with the Jews in house-fighting. They could wait in relative safety to round up Jews driven out of the rubble by the flames. Before the new technique could be extensively employed, Stroop had to pull his shaken men out of the Ghetto.

On the third day, the Germans began to set fires to burn out the Jews. Many of the blazes started by artillery and tank fire on the previous day continued to burn unchecked. All water, gas and electricity had been cut off, and the over 50,000 Jews in hiding had to depend upon their carefully hoarded rations. Holed up in this way, the civilians did not at first realize the menace of the fires. All during the day the Germans, still harassed by the Jews' strong points, set their fires. Soon the individual fires began to merge into a giant fire storm. Simultaneously with the fire technique, the Germans had moved to sever inner-Ghetto communication. The most impressive network, to the Germans' surprise, proved to be the sewers. Exits both in the Ghetto and in the surrounding neighborhood on the Aryan side were bunged shut, often after smoke candles had been lowered to gas any Jews in transit. For a time some of the main stretches of sewers were even patrolled by Germans until in the dark and fetid tunnels they met armed Jews. After that the Germans withdrew, sealing the last exits and with them the Jews' free movement under the Ghetto. The growing danger of the fires and the failure of their communications seriously hampered the Jewish resistance. Stroop could feel that after a sticky three days, things were looking up. He could now move fully over to the offensive. "I therefore decided to destroy the entire Jewish residential area by setting every block afire. . . ."[28] With the initiative firmly in the hands of the Germans, Anielewicz ordered his fighting groups, or those that he could reach amid the fires and confusion, to go over to partisan warfare, hiding out from the Germans and the flames during the day and shifting about at night. The first stage of the siege of the Ghetto had ended.

All during the fourth day, April 22, the Germans set more fires with their artillery and tanks. That night Heinkel 217 bombers flew in low and dumped their loads of bombs into the fires of the central Ghetto. In many places the fires had firmly joined, creating a giant conflagration. The sky over Warsaw turned red. The next day a single great plume of smoke swirled up over the Ghetto. The city was alive with rumors and uncertainty: "All Warsaw has come to life with the news of the fight between the Jews and Germans."[29] Yet life went on as before for most if not all Poles. The Jews exchanging fire with German patrols could hear the tinkling music of a merry-go-round just beyond the Ghetto walls. Polish crowds wandered down to the Ghetto area to watch the shelling and then on home to dinner. For other Poles the rising had been a chance to strike at the Germans more openly. The Polish underground hit a German artillery position just outside the Ghetto. Other unrelated incidents occurred around the city. The Germans were becoming uneasy. An insurrection in an occupied city held all kinds of risks. Eventually, by April 25, even the distant Joseph Goebbels felt that "in Warsaw conditions are chaotic not only in the Ghetto, but also among sections of the Polish population."[30] Worse, Stroop was finding that his destruction of the Ghetto was falling behind schedule. The Jews often refused to leave the burning buildings, preferring to die in the flames rather than surrender. Even Stroop was impressed.

> *Not until the flames reached their greatest intensity did screaming Jews make their appearance, and they were deported at once . . . entire families wreathed in flames—jumped from the windows or tried to let themselves down by means of sheets tied together. The necessary steps were taken to liquidate these Jews like the others.*

As a result of the fires, the Jewish noncombatant losses were enormous. Yet the little fighting groups managed to survive, slipping from one bunker to the next, and even achieved some results. The determination of the Jewish fighters to die in the Ghetto and the difficulty of getting at the civilians continually held up Stroop's operation. The Germans began to destroy the burned-out shells of buildings around the edge of the Ghetto with heavy mortar fire and mines, but they depended mainly on the flames to finish off the Jews deeper in the Ghetto.

By April 25, the entire Ghetto seemed in flames. The Germans had settled down to destroy the Ghetto piecemeal, burning building after building, mining the ruins, calling in artillery and mortar fire. It was a slow, relatively painless, and apparently effective method of turning the Ghetto into rubble. Yet, even in the burned and blasted ruins, some bunkers remained. The Germans brought in dogs and special sound detector devices. If there was any suspicion, a drilling machine was used. Nothing seemed to be foolproof. The Jews continued to resist, firing from sniper nests, even remaining in fortified strong points which flew the Jewish or Polish flag, flaunting the German failure to crush the Ghetto. Stroop felt it was a matter of time. The unchecked flames, the most effective weapon, would burn out the Jews. By the night of April 25–26, the holocaust reached a peak.

> *Whole streets were blocked by huge fires. Seas of flame engulfed houses and courtyards; wooden beams crackled noisily; walls collapsed. There was no air, only choking black smoke and burning heat, radiating from red-hot walls and the glowing stones of stairways.*[31]

The great fires burned out the chance of any effective united military resistance. Groups were out of touch, out of supplies. Many spent the days hiding in smoldering bunkers filled with air so foul that a candle would not burn. Always, however, they continued the sniping, the sudden ambush. Cohesion had been lost, but not the will to resist. To those listening outside the Ghetto with awe and sympathy, it seemed inconceivable that anyone could live in that inferno, much less fight back. Stroop's SS men continued rounding up increasing numbers of Jews driven into the streets by the fires or by hunger and thirst. During the first week of the rising, the Germans deported 14,000 Jews while 3,000 burned to death and 2,000 more were killed in their houses. This meant that approximately 20,000 Jews remained burrowed away, waiting. Few among them had either hope or arms. Yet the Fighting Organization was determined to continue the struggle. "We are firmly decided to fight to the end. We shall avenge all the injustices and crimes committed by the occupying power."[32] The fires were now burning over a fantastically large area. The cordon around the Ghetto drew tighter. New regulations were announced to prevent even an unlikely escape to the Aryan side by threatening "all who would bring aid to the Ghetto." The Germans remained uneasy about a general uprising, but no technique seemed available to speed the liquidation of the Ghetto.

The slow, agonizing destruction of the Ghetto continued day after day under the great, boiling cloud of funereal smoke. Each morning the Germans cautiously moved into the smoldering ruins with their tanks and artillery. Houses were cleared and shelled; then the fires were renewed. Patrols searched and searched again for the hidden bunkers. The captured Jews were dug out of their warrens and immediately murdered or deported to be murdered later. At dusk the Germans withdrew. At dawn they began again. The general fires were dying down. The listening Poles on the other side of the walls heard firing more rarely. The end seemed near. On May 8, the Germans stumbled onto the central headquarters of the Jewish Fighting Organization at 18 Mila Street. There Anielewicz had taken over a huge subterranean bunker, originally the private refuge of Shmuel Asher, the great fat leader of the Ghetto's thieves' guild. At first well-stocked and carefully prepared with electric lights, water, and even a kitchen, the bunker had soon lost its air of luxury. More and more fighters had arrived. The stocks of food soon disappeared. Within a week over 100 fighters were using the bunker during the day. By May 8, conditions had deteriorated even more. The air had become fetid and the temperature had risen as 200 people crowded into a space meant for 20. The agony and helpless terror of the civilians seemed to hang in the air as the German ring grew tighter. Then the Germans had finally come across the entrance. They ordered everyone out. The thieves and the civilians stumbled up. The fighters, including Mordechai Anielewicz, remained underground. The Germans, unwilling to risk their lives, finally released gas into the burrow and sealed the exit. The Jews began to strangle. Rather than face prolonged suffocation, many began to shoot themselves. Only a few in the rear discovered in time a hidden exit and escaped. The others, over a hundred, slowly suffocated. Yet even this disaster did not end the resistance.

With Anielewicz gone, the remaining fighting groups began to act independently. Some decided to break through to the Aryan side and reach the partisans in the forest. Despite the German efforts to close the sewers, it was still possible with considerable ingenuity and a great deal of luck to find a way through the secondary passages and around the German plugs. On May 10, a group made their way through to the Aryan side, but on their arrival the Polish contact failed to appear. For forty-eight hours they had to remain crouched in the sewer, twenty-eight inches high and half filled with thick, slimy water. They finally escaped, but a second group following them was wiped out with gas bombs by the alerted Germans. Other fighting groups simply continued their strange, nomadic existence, shifting hideouts, creeping past patrols, evading the flames and the Germans. "Only one aim was uppermost—to prolong this as long as possible, to inflict as much damage as possible upon the enemy."[33]

On May 12, it was reported that the struggles in the Ghetto were beginning to die out. Yet the glow of the fires, even after a month, still flickered on the clouds over the city. The only interruption in the methodical German operation came on the night of May 13 when a heavy Soviet airstrike against the city used the flaming Ghetto as a beacon. On the next day only one block of buildings remained intact in the Ghetto. The Germans finished that up and "in the evening the chapel, mortuary and all other buildings of the Jewish cemetery, were blown up or destroyed." The final solution had been achieved. Summing up, Stroop claimed 56,065 Jews captured and estimated 5,000 to 6,000 more had died in the flames. The grand total of arms captured came to fifteen rifles and fifty pistols, a rather small number in view of the Germans' difficulties. Still, the "action" had reduced the Ghetto to ruins. When Stroop had completed his elaborate report with its precise statistics of mass murder and careful descriptions of SS brutality, he had it neatly bound for his superiors. He entitled it proudly if inaccurately "Jewish Warsaw Has Ceased to Exist." In the fullness of time, it would help to hang him.

In the meanwhile, although Stroop had assured his superiors that "the ruins contain only enormous amounts of brick and sand," some Jews in the Ghetto continued an isolated resistance. The decimated fighter groups still evaded the Germans, ambushed their patrols, even at times flew their blue and white flag. The buildings might be gone but the Jews were not. During the last days of May, no one was more amazed at their survival in the midst of a smoldering ruin than the Jews themselves. "We hadn't imagined that after weeks of battle we would still be alive to discuss our end. We had been certain that the end would come earlier. . . ."[34] A few, a very few, managed to escape to the Aryan side and go underground. Most died in the barren hide-outs or ran into German patrols. Ammunition was gone, food was gone, even water could not be found. Armed resistance was no longer possible; even temporary survival seemed pointless. In June the Germans began the final destruction of the Ghetto. Protected by armed patrols, labor units began to demolish the remaining shattered buildings. Mines blasted the ruins into great heaps of rubble. The Germans now built two small narrow-gauge railroad lines to bring out the salvage. Under their heavy guard, the special slave labor teams of Jews from Greece, Rumania, France and Hungary worked to remove the blackened ruins. Finally the Germans ended their salvage operation. Only vast heaps of crumbled masonry remained. Hitler could at last be assured that the Ghetto had been erased from the earth.

Inside the Ghetto walls, still maintained by the Germans, nothing remained but the rejected ruins. Yet even there, in the huge block of black and broken rubble heaped two and three stories high like some wild lunar landscape, some Jews remained. These were the rubble men. Some were armed and continued a last nightmare struggle against the uneasy German patrols. That the Jews would dare to fight at all had seemed incredible in April; that they had fought not for a day or so but for six weeks had been inconceivable; but that they could still live in the Ghetto was truly unnatural. Dogs were used to smell out bunkers; sound detectors were again tried; power drills bored repeated holes. Still the patrols could not clear out the last starving survivors. The Jews again made tenuous contacts with the Aryan side. Poles, usually for a price, smuggled in food and ammunition. On August 16, smugglers reached a small group of forty with food, electric lamps, spirits and small arms. With these came a newspaper containing the report of Mussolini's fall. Elsewhere apparently the war moved on but in the Ghetto little moved. Hunger, thirst, disease, and always the Germans whittled away at the remaining Jews. By September the group of forty, for example, had shrunk to four. These four broke out by climbing the wall and scattering out into the Aryan side.[35] Yet they were not the last. Always someplace in the heaped ruins were Jews, hanging on, waiting. On December 3, 1943, the Jewish prisoners from Pawiak found a girl buried deep into a bunker. The Germans first resurrected her and then executed her, hopefully the last of the seemingly immortal rubble Jews. Still others lived on, however, maintained their contacts with the Aryan side, avoided the Germans and survived. When the Russians finally drove the Germans out of Warsaw a year later, there were still Jews burrowed into the Ghetto.[33] In this siege, a battle of extermination, there was no last man.

That the Warsaw rising should be considered a siege at all is open to question. More properly the rising in April 1943 was a protest in arms against genocide—in Christian terms, a witness to evil. Yet it *was* an insurrection, even if without hope of success or belief in survival. That the rising did not so much succeed in military terms as persist amazed not only the listening Poles and the humiliated Germans but also the Jews themselves. As other Germans had discovered at Stalingrad, the defenders in a modern city, if they are determined, resourceful and ingenious, have to be dislodged at great cost in time and blood. The task of rooting out and eliminating the well-armed, regularly supplied Russians had taken the Sixth Army months and had, of course, never been completed. It came as a terrible blow to the Germans that the same arduous procedure had been necessary with the half-starved, barely armed Jews. If anything, the Jews had been more fanatical in their resistance since they had nothing to lose, not even their lives which would be meaningless unless given dearly in the fighting. The destruction of the Ghetto had, however, finally been achieved despite the Jews' incredible persistence. Although Stroop had been trained, if that is the word, only in genocide and terror, he had responded to the new challenge of the Ghetto by stumbling on a solution. Unlike the Sixth Army he did not want to waste lives in close fighting within the buildings. Instead he developed a variety of techniques to use in an insurrectionist siege. The use of Slavic irregulars, the dependence upon armor and artillery, the withholding of Germans from house fighting, and, above all, the effectiveness of massive fires were means that the Germans would not forget. It was clear that an insurrection, however popular, however just its cause, however determined, could be smashed once it was isolated by the weight of iron and the help of fire. It took time but the method was sure.

For their part the leaders of the Polish Home Army would have concurred with the German estimate of the possibilities for popular risings. They would never risk their army or their cause while there remained a chance that the Germans could isolate them for destruction as they had the Jews in the Ghetto. Instead of attacking the Germans, the Poles decided to wait. With every report from the East, the time for waiting grew shorter. The Germans' last offensive effort at the Kursk salient collapsed. Then, in great spurts and starts, the unending Russian offensive began. Breaking out on one front and then another, flowing forward like a huge and unsteady lava stream, the Russian Army, despite immense losses, continued to move west during 1943 and 1944. Repeatedly punished by German quality and armor, the Red Army was like a great irresistible ocean difficult to sweep back and impossible to dike. Elsewhere the Germans were hard pressed. Italy had become a constant drain. On June 6, 1944, the long-awaited second front opened in Normandy. The German cities were gradually being battered into smoking ruins by the Anglo-American air offensive. Watching and waiting in Warsaw, the Poles could sense the decay of Hitler's empire. Week by week the German position crumbled away. Soon, but not too soon, the Poles felt that they must act. With the Red Army sweeping into eastern Poland, driving the broken Germans back, the Polish Government in Exile in London grew increasingly uneasy. Diplomatic relations with Moscow, always strained, had been broken off a year before over the discovery of the bodies of thousands of Polish officers in the Katyn Forest, apparently murdered by the Russians. With the Free Polish Army scattered under a dozen commands or totally incorporated into Allied units, with the unassailable position of Soviet Russia as a Western Ally, the London Poles had few assets. They could only foresee a Russian occupation of Poland and the installation of a puppet government. The Americans seemed totally uninterested, and the British were not overly concerned with the Poles' postwar worries. All the cards seemed to be in Stalin's hands.

On July 24, the Russians created the National Committee of Liberation in recently captured Lublin. The long-dreaded satellite government existed in embryo. With the Red Army almost to the Vistula, the fate of postwar Poland would be determined unless the Poles in Poland could take some immediate action. Only a last-minute coup could save Poland from once more being swallowed by an insatiable neighbor. The only possibility for the London Poles to salvage any vestige of independence was a carefully timed rising of the Home Army within Warsaw. If just at the right moment, when the Russians had reached the suburbs of the city, the Poles seized the city, then the ensuing prestige and the possession of the capital by the London Government in Exile might forestall the Communists. The London Government could then be flown into Warsaw before Stalin could install the Lublin puppets. Even with a hostile Soviet Army in the country, the London Government holding the capital by conquest would be in a strong bargaining position. Even Stalin would hardly depose his successful ally, the Western-recognized Polish Government securely ensconced in the national capital. Time, however, was running out. In Warsaw, where the leaders of the Home Army shared many of the apprehensions and ambitions of the London Government, the matter of timing had more than diplomatic overtones. The blackened ruins of the Ghetto stood as mute testimony to the fate of isolated insurrections. If the Home Army rose too soon, the Germans could even at this late date leisurely wipe out the entire Warsaw resistance movement. Yet, if it came too late, the Russians would already be in the city and the years of sacrifice and effort would be wasted.

> *. . . the Home Army cannot stand idle in the face of the German retreat and the Soviet advance, nor in the case of an internal collapse of the German forces and the threat of Soviet occupation.*[37]

During the last week of July 1944, the argument continued in Warsaw and in London. Many, particularly in Poland, advised caution, but events began removing the Poles' options. The long-standing rumors that the Russians were disarming and interning Home Army units as soon as the Red Army occupied eastern districts hardened into fact. It was amply clear that the failure to rise would be as politically disastrous as rising too soon would be militarily. The eager urged the commander of the Home Army, former Cavalry General Tadeusz Komorowski, known in the underground as Bor, to act. Bor held off. He also had advice from the timid, two colonels, Rawicz and Tarnawa, who sought to contact the exiled President Mikolajczyk, then in Moscow so that Bor could be ordered to hold off action. One of them, Rawicz, continued to insist the Russians would not arrive until August 15, and an immediate rising would lead to a massacre.[38]

Then suddenly the whole Thousand Year Reich seemed to shudder before collapse. On July 20, the army's attempt on Hitler's life failed but just barely. On the following day, Bor informed the London Government of the rapid, almost unimpeded, advance of the Soviet Army.

> *I foresee that the Soviet push to the west on this sector will be rapid, and that it will reach the Vistula without any great effective counter measures by the Germans and will cross the Vistula in a further push to the west.*[39]

In Warsaw the Germans began withdrawing administrative officials from the city. Fischer, the German governor, departed, as did German mayor Leist. Offices were quietly closed down and records shipped west. Tired, exhausted lines of bedraggled soldiers began to move through the city and on to the west. On July 22, the Poles intercepted German radio reports ordering the Fourth Panzer Army to withdraw across the Vistula.[40] On July 25, word arrived of the establishment of the Lublin Committee. Apparently the Russians anticipated an early arrival in

Warsaw. The final straw came on July 27 when Governor Fischer suddenly returned and almost as an afterthought ordered the drafting of 100,000 Poles "to build fortifications." This in translation probably meant that the Germans intended to seize and deport as many Poles as possible in the brief time remaining to them. If the Poles appeared as ordered, the Home Army's mobilization would be dislocated. Then, too, if past experience was any indication, the fate of the 100,000 Poles would be dim.[41] On July 29, the Soviet Radio Kosciuszko, broadcasting in Polish, began calling for the Poles to rise against the Germans.

> *The hour for action has arrived. Poles take to arms! There is no second to be lost!*[42]

To all but a few it seemed excellent advice, if from a strange source.

The roar of Russian artillery could be plainly heard off to the east of the Praga suburb. Within the counsels of the Home Army and the underground government, the clamor for action rose in unison. Still the fearful moderates urged caution. A new difficulty now faced Bor—the possibility of either a spontaneous revolt or one sparked by the dissident Communist underground which would trigger a full-scale but highly disorganized rebellion.[43] Bor might not have a chance to set the machinery of rebellion into motion if he waited. On July 30, the Russian Radio again urged "People of Warsaw, to arms!" Rumor said that the Russian troops were already in the outskirts of Praga across the Vistula. On July 31, the delegate of the London Government in Exile, Vice-Premier Jankowski, listened to the opinion of the leaders of the Home Army before making the final decision. In reality, Bor's analysis of the situation would be decisive and Bor had decided he could wait no longer. The revolt would take place immediately. Jankowski agreed. Operation *Tempest,* the seizure of Warsaw, would begin the following day, August 1, at five in the afternoon.[44] Even with his hand forced a bit, Bor's timing still looked very good. In three or four days the Russians would march into an already liberated Warsaw.

The Russians, too, were expecting to capture Warsaw. General Rokossovski's First Belorussian Front, including the First Polish Army, had pushed forward almost to the Vistula. On July 31, the Russian right flank clashed with the Germans near the approaches to Praga while the left flank drove on through to the Vistula south of Warsaw. Below Warsaw the Russians soon managed to establish two small bridgeheads, but heavy German counterattacks prevented their expansion. Even with this stiffening of German resistance, the capture of Warsaw appeared imminent. The momentum of the Soviet offensive, which had flowed forward so long like a great wave, now appeared to be ebbing. Still, with only shattered German units scattered about the front, one more last lunge should be sufficient to secure Warsaw. On August 2, *Pravda* printed a report from its correspondent "Outside Warsaw" beginning, "On to Warsaw! In an offensive there is a moment when the military operation reaches its culminating point and . . . goes ahead without any doubt as to what will happen next."[45]

On that day, the Russian offensive finally rumbled to a halt, its impetus gone. To the north, in East Prussia, the Germans mauled the Russian right flank. In the Warsaw area, Rokossovski's salient toward Warsaw was very narrow and very weak. Apparently Rokossovski still felt that the Germans were in worse shape than he and that a lunge to the city would succeed. He was mistaken. The Germans smashed into the First Polish Army in the bridgehead west of the Vistula. The number of *Luftwaffe* sorties jumped. German resistance stiffened all along the front. All Soviet forward motion ended. German General Heinz Guderian, who had taken over command of the front, had held the Russians at the last moment.

> *The German Ninth Army had the impression, on August 8th, that the Russian attempt to seize Warsaw by a coup de main (which in view of their hitherto uninterrupted success they might well have believed possible) had been defeated by our defense despite the Polish uprising, and that the latter, from the enemy's point of view, had been begun too soon.*[46]

That the Russians had expected the momentary fall of the city during the first week of August seems clear from the noncommittal comments and limited enthusiasm with which Molotov received the news of the impending uprising from Mikolajczyk on July 31. Mikolajczyk could not be too specific because he had begun his flight to Moscow before the final decision had been made. When he saw Stalin on August 3, he learned that the Russians expected to take Warsaw on August 5 or 6, but that there might be a delay. In any case, Stalin made it clear that his relations with the London Government in Exile could not be worse. "I cannot trust the Poles. They suspect me of wanting to occupy Poland again. They're making a lot of trouble." It is possible that Stalin still expected Rokossovski to capture Warsaw and eliminate the Polish question. In the meantime he promised Mikolajczyk to send in some communications officers.[47]

Soon, however, Stalin was to discover the changing situation on the First Belorussian Front. For the time being, at least, the Red Army could not alone solve the Polish problem. Stalin, to disguise his temporary military embarrassment, discounted the reports of the rising. He informed Churchill that "the information which had been communicated to you by the Poles is greatly exaggerated and does not inspire confidence." The British *Daily Worker* even denied the existence of a revolt within Warsaw.[48] But the problem of the Warsaw insurrection would not go away just that easily.

In Moscow, Mikolajczyk kept asking for Russian assistance. From London, Churchill urged Russian co-operation with the Poles. Gradually the realization grew that from Soviet Russia's point of view the Polish uprising had come at the ideal time. Almost from the moment of Paulus' surrender at Stalingrad, there had been a growing tendency on the part of Stalin to increase the political factor in strategic decisions. By the summer of 1944, the political motive had become dominant not only in strategic decisions but even in tactical ones. The anti-Russian motives of the Polish rising were obvious, but in view of Stalin's postwar plans, the attempt was futile. If the lunge across the Vistula had succeeded, the possession of Warsaw by the Home Army, even if the London Government in Exile had been flown into the city, would have been only a temporary irritation. In time, the Lublin Committee could be installed, the anti-Communists removed, and Poland incorporated into the Soviet empire. Even a successful rising would be no more than a momentary impediment, inconvenient but not irreversible. Now, with General Bor and the London Government in Exile fully and fatally committed, the Russians could afford to watch and wait; in fact, until they recovered from their long offensive, they could do little else. Rokossovski's salient had retracted, and it would be some weeks before the First Belorussian Front would be ready to move west—if moving west were desirable politically. In the meantime, Stalin had no intention of pulling his future enemy's chestnuts out of the fire, particularly when the fire was stoked by elements of at least four German tank divisions, including the elite Hermann Göring Division. Thus, at the same time, the Red Army got a needed respite, the Germans got a nasty mauling, and the opponents of the Lublin Government were liquidated.

By the evening of August 9, Stalin was no longer embarrassed by his military difficulties on the Vistula and could afford to be genial to Mikolajczyk. "Stalin showed much greater understanding of the problems concerning the fight for Warsaw."[49] Despite his reputation for cruelty and his long-range planning, the benefits of the Warsaw rising accrued to Stalin not as a result of his omnipotence or guile but because of his adaptability.[50]

Obviously the Poles in Warsaw had not foreseen any of these developments of the first week of August. Instead, from General Bor down to the lowliest woman auxiliary, they had expected only to "hold out for a few days"[51] while waiting for the Russians to arrive. Bor had an army of 40,000, including 4,200 women in auxiliary work. His force was organized into three infantry divisions: Colonel Niedzielski's 8th, Colonel Rokicki's 10th, and Colonel Edward Pfeiffer's 28th.[52] Bolstering them came the last-minute volunteers. Civilians rushed unasked to build barricades. Escaped prisoners of war crept out of captivity; slave laborers escaped; all the exotic dispossessed hurried to revenge themselves on the Nazis. The Polish Home Army soon contained English, French, Czechs, Ukrainians, Russians, Georgians, even Armenians and Azerbaijani. As might be expected, a newly appointed correspondent for the *Times* of London appeared and even sent dispatches to London over the underground radio. Although he had no tanks or artillery, Bor felt that surprise and enthusiasm would ensure the capture of the city. Then, with light weapons, homemade antitank bombs, and barricaded streets, they would hold off the Germans for several days. He intended to strike everywhere at once, wiping out all the Germans within the city and the suburbs before they could get away. After that it would be a matter of holding and waiting.[53]

Fighting broke out in one or two places prematurely, but the Germans reacted slowly. Then at five o'clock in the afternoon, the zero hour, firing spread rapidly throughout the city. "In fifteen minutes, an entire city of a million inhabitants was engulfed in the fight."[54] Startled by the unexpected hail of bullets, the Germans in the streets tried to find shelter. Once dug in, the better armed and better trained Germans could punish the enthusiastic Home Army, but at first few Germans managed to reach shelter or dig in. As the hours passed, the individual struggles continued over the city. The Poles wiped out isolated Germans and seized public buildings. For both the Poles and Germans, liaison between the various sections of the city became very difficult. No one knew quite how the fighting was going, but from all directions the bursting of hand grenades and the rattle of small arms could be heard. By the next morning the situation seemed slightly clearer. The Poles still held the initiative and were clearing one lightly held sector after another. Most of the major buildings had fallen to the Home Army. The red and white Polish flag could be seen flying over the Prudential Building and the Town Hall. The Germans, however, had not been wiped out, nor had they fled the city. Various units had managed to hole up in several major buildings. They repulsed four heavy Polish attacks on the telephone building and hung on waiting for help. Still, the Poles had occupied the Old Town near the Jewish Ghetto, the general post office, the power station, the gas works and the Prudential Building, as well as large residential areas. Although heavy fighting continued in the central and western districts, other sections of the city had apparently been swept clear. By the evening of August 3, the Home Army had extended its control in the south and in the center. The western part of the central district was almost entirely occupied by the Home Army. General Bor had come very close to seizing the entire city as planned. Scattered German pockets, isolated and under heavy fire, continued to hold out, but after five years Warsaw was again in Polish hands.

On August 4, the majority of the Poles suddenly realized that they had become a real part of the Allied war effort. For the first time they listened openly to the BBC Polish-language broadcast. They read the fifteen underground newspapers, which could now be sold on the streets. They could even mail letters stamped with Free Polish postage stamps. Poland was in the war again. Most important, specific help arrived from the Allies. Flying from their base in Foggia, Italy, Allied planes, some with Polish pilots, made a 1,700-mile round trip to drop military supplies into Warsaw. On the first attempt only two planes could get through the bad weather and heavy antiaircraft fire, but the announcement of their arrival was greeted with great enthusiasm.[55]

The only worry was a lack of a similar effort by the Russians. Instead of aid there had suddenly been a diminishing of artillery fire from the east. The growing stillness on the east bank of the Vistula gradually began to worry many. For those in authority, the very heavy expenditure of the limited stocks of ammunition had been irksome. No contact could be established with the Russians, and the London Government in Exile seemed reluctant to send in the Polish Parachute Brigade. A few began to worry about another desertion of Poland by alien and distant allies. Thus the airdrop was a great morale booster. More specifically the British antitank bazookas, PIATs, were extremely welcome, for the Germans had recovered their balance and begun moving heavy tanks up along some of the main east-west arteries.

On the following day, August 5, the Polish Home Army continued to consolidate its hold on the city, but reports began drifting back that German resistance was far stiffer. Ammunition was growing short. The first feelings of elation began to drift away as some began to ask the unanswerable, "When will help from the East come?"[56] The arrival of Soviet Captain Konstanty Kalugin in the city quieted much of the growing uneasiness. With contact at last made with the Russians, surely it was just a matter time before the Red Army arrived.

On August 6, the initiative began to shift to the Germans. They brought up armored cars and artillery. The *Luftwaffe* began hitting Polish positions. The tactics of the Ghetto were to be applied all over the city. Flame-thrower units moved up to the edges of the Polish perimeters and the fires began. German armor began to feel out the Polish street barricades, thrown together out of tipped over tramcars and heaped pavement stones. Hourly the Germans increased their pressure. The variety of civilian services so carefully prepared began to show signs of wear. Hospital supplies proved insufficient; firefighting equipment broke down. The siege had already gone on a day or two longer than most Poles had anticipated, and the strain was showing.

During the next two days, the German air raids were stepped up and the infantry continued to set fires. The Poles, now on the defensive around the edges of the city, continued their attacks on isolated German-held buildings. As German strength around the city built up, tank-supported infantry attacks hit the Polish perimeter. The volume of artillery fire increased. Two armored trains arrived and began firing into the city. The rising air and artillery bombardment spread the fires despite the efforts of the Polish fire service. Even the most optimistic realized that something had gone wrong. The Russians should have reached the city. On August 7, Captain Kalugin had broadcast an appeal to Stalin by way of London. On August 8, he left to report to Rokossovski. On the same day, General Bor pleaded with London for the Polish Parachute Brigade. The Germans had cut off the suburb of Praga.

On August 9, the Germans drove their first wedge through to the Vistula by blasting through buildings. The salient was protected by bricking up the lateral walls so that a straight walled highway, patrolled by twenty heavy tanks, had been driven through the center of the city. The Poles had to give up the district of Wola to the west.[57] As the bitter fighting went on, a feeling of uncertainty and isolation grew. The people of Warsaw seemed to have been abandoned once again. Instead of a swift coup and a Free Warsaw, they had doomed themselves to a battle they could not win.[58] They could hardly know that the Germans were equally as gloomy.

The Warsaw uprising had badly frightened the Germans. Suddenly, unexpectedly, the hated Poles had put an estimated 100,000 armed men into the field in a vital spot. Many foresaw a gaping hole torn in the already weak Eastern Front with the Russian Army pouring across the Vistula and driving on toward Germany. For the first few days everyone was haunted by the specter of complete defeat.[59] The Poles' rapid success had, of course, been achieved against General Stahl's garrison troops, transients, and the various "occupation" forces more at home with liquidation and terror than with real fighting. Fearful and uncertain, various SS units had sought to crush the rebellion by their usual means: the murder of all Polish prisoners, the destruction of hospitals, and attacks on civilians. Women and children were driven in front of advancing tanks. The prison population was liquidated. None of these methods worked. On August 8, SS Gruppenführer Eric von dem Bach-Zelewski, an expert in partisan warfare, had arrived to suppress the Poles. The growing success of the German Ninth Army in holding up Rokossovski's advance meant that Bach-Zelewski would have the necessary time to apply the appropriate remedies. Some of the German gloom began to lift. If the front held, Bach-Zelewski would be able to turn Warsaw into a second Ghetto operation. He could not depend on regular army units tied down on the front, so Himmler suggested two special formations, the dregs of the German manpower barrel. One, the Kaminski Brigade, was composed of anti-Communist Russians and a variety of SS-trained Slavic Nazis. The other, the Dirlewanger SS Brigade, was composed of German convicts on probation and led by Oskar Dirlewanger, an expert in extermination and a devotee of sadism and necrophilia. In the close and bitter house-to-house fighting, with its problem of recognizing Polish civilians, German tactics from the first had been brutal. With the arrival of Dirlewanger and Kaminski, the situation, if possible, got worse. Prisoners were burned alive and babies spitted on bayonets. Himmler informed Goebbels that violence and terror would smash the revolt "in a very few days." When Polish resistance continued in the face of the growing German brutality, four police battalions were moved in to stiffen Dirlewanger's convicts. Finally some units, particularly armor, were detached from the regular divisions on the Vistula. The 73rd Infantry Division was committed. The Hermann Göring Division moved in from Italy, the Totenkopf from Rumania, the SS Viking Division from the Lublin sector. Pure terror would now be backed by the weight of metal and men.[60]

With the initiative firmly in his hands, Bach-Zelewski applied the tactics of the Ghetto with a vengeance. Rather than risk SS men's lives, he depended on flames and firepower. If possible he sent in the men of Kaminski and Dirlewanger rather than German troops as had been done in the Ghetto. If possible he preferred to use the flames rather than risk close contact with the Poles as had been done in the Ghetto. The crushing of the Warsaw rising would be a slow, brutal process just as had been the destruction of the Ghetto; but as long as the regular German Army held the front, Bach-Zelewski had all the time he needed. The Germans combined increasing air strikes with a blanket artillery bombardment to spread the fires. They moved up rocket launchers, firing six incendiary shells, which created such a piercing racket that the Poles called them "shrieking cows." Heavy Thor mortars, similar to those used in the Sevastopol siege, were brought into action. To shatter the Polish barricades and open up whole streets to destruction, regular armor was used but also the "Goliaths," remote control tanks each filled with 500 kilos of explosives. By August 11, the Poles seldom tried to man their barricades but protected them from overlooking buildings. On their part, the Germans pulled back their tanks out of range of the PIATs and shelled the Polish buildings hour after hour. Heavy siege guns (including one of the caliber used to lob shells across the English Channel) were moved close to the perimeter. Depending on their tanks and the two armored trains, the Germans drove three wedges along the major east-west highways directly through the Poles' position. The Poles continued to hold their divided sectors. The city was an inferno of sound, the roar of tank and plane engines, the constant crunch of artillery shells, and the rumble of falling walls. The Poles' position seemed desperate. Their ammunition was running out and most felt that "the fight will collapse in a few days" without aid.[61] Bor pleaded with the Allies and the London Polish government to do something. The fate of the Ghetto did not seem far away for the whole city.

On August 12, after having split the Poles' position, the Germans moved first against the most vulnerable and historic, the Old City. In the setting of narrow streets and frail houses, the Poles settled down to a violent and determined defense. Daily the massive German blows slightly contracted the perimeter. The Germans bombed and shelled the entire area on a twenty-four-hour schedule. Individual fires quickly spread and joined in the now familiar fire storm. Observers, creeping through the sewers or watching from the central sector, were appalled.

> *A sea of fire and bombs had swallowed up a square kilometer of ancient, dry rotted buildings, packed with tens of thousands of people. Now I know the nature of that gigantic pall of smoke which had been hanging over the Old City for weeks.*[62]

Despite the fires, the Poles hung on. The 40,000 Germans committed to the Old City had to smash down the blackened, burning ruins one by one. In just one attack, on August 19, the Germans massed ten infantry and two engineer battalions and a platoon of mine throwers and flame throwers, supported by a company of Tiger tanks and fifty remote-control "Goliaths," backed by twenty self-propelled 75-mm. guns, six 75-mm. guns, two 38-cm. guns, along with three heavy mortars and an armored train. The *Stuka* dive bombers usually hit the Old City five to twelve times a day. Under this kind of pressure, it seemed remarkable that the 5,000 poorly armed defenders could have any chance at all. The Germans rediscovered the almost insurmountable problems of occupying heaps of shattered, burned-out concrete. The Poles' real enemy became the flames and their own growing exhaustion, but they stuck it out all through August. The fires spread and burned on long after it seemed possible that anything could be left to burn. The fighting fell into a routine of German bombardment followed by massive attacks on the smoking ruins. On August 23, out of the 1,100 houses in the quarter, 300 had burned and 400 more had been destroyed. In a few more days, little remained of the others but heaps of ruins.

Fighting began to concentrate around the one sure escape hatch—the manhole over the sewer which led toward the Polish-held center of the city. When General Bor arrived on his last inspection of the Old City position, he found "the skeletons of burnt-out houses standing in a sea of rubble, with an occasional chimney looking like some fantastic amputated limb."[63] On August 29, he gave the order to abandon the Old City. Seventy men managed to fight their way across the German lines, even breaking through the strongly held east-west artery. The rest, both soldiers and civilians, had to risk the sewers. After a terrifying dark journey through the reeking, fetid tunnel, the first of the long line began to emerge in the Polish sector: filthy gasping children, a mad woman wrapped in a lace curtain, the wounded, the shell-shocked. It was as if Hell had vomited up the Devil's rejects: "an endless procession of bloody ghosts, armless, legless, faceless, went on and on, their wounds caked with the filth of the sewers."[64] The following day the Germans occupied the rubble. Demolition teams began systematically blowing up the debris to eradicate forever any vestige of the Old City.

The German concentration on the Old City had given the remaining Polish-held quarters of the city a rest. Even while the Old City was disappearing into the flames, the Poles had snuffed out several of the isolated strong points in the central sector. Communications with the other sections had been laboriously established by exploring and exploiting the sewers. In the midst of this grim defensive action, the news of the relief of the Paris insurrection came in a BBC broadcast. Although the Poles had expected a similar swift victory, some kind of "normal" life had been devised and hope had not yet been abandoned. Food supplies, as to be expected, were limited; but both the individual larders and the consumers' co-operative stores' supplies had been confiscated so that no one starved as yet. The water supply remained stable for quite some time, but eventually the city had to depend on the new wells dug by German prisoners. Still there was never enough water. Long lines of people with buckets snaking back from the wells produced a regular crop of bomb casualties, but there was no alternative except thirst. Beginning in September, however, the problems of food and water grew more acute. The rare airdrops did little to alleviate the situation. Surprisingly the sanitary facilities proved adequate; despite the lack of water or soap, the open latrines, and the growing number of shallow graves, no serious epidemic occurred. The Polish doctors and nurses in the hastily fitted-out emergency hospitals did a magnificent job, but time and German attacks whittled away at their supplies and their staff. The seizure of the Riverside Power Station assured the Poles of normal service in one area. After several weeks the German shells finally smashed the power station and thereafter the Poles had to depend on batteries for electric power. The batteries, recharged with automobile engines, were used to produce light for surgical operations and to power the bulbs in the underground tunnels. The civilian defense organizations, like all the basic services, began well, but soon the strain of the long siege lowered their efficiency. The fire service was simply unable to cope with the fire-storm tactics of the Germans; the constant heavy shelling, the dive-bomber raids, the flaming perimeter regularly relit, finally took the heart out of them. At last the "people became resigned to the destruction of the city."[65] As the weeks passed, most of the civilians huddling starved, frightened and bitter in the cellars of the city began to lose hope. The Home Army, however, would not accept defeat. They could not feel their effort and blood had gone to waste. They could not fully accept what the civilians saw as obvious: that the rising had been abandoned to liquidation.

As the Poles had known all along, Warsaw was doomed without Russian assistance. Even if the Anglo-American airlift had been able to function far more effectively than it did, it would only have prolonged the reduction of the city. All depended on the Russians, and all the news relayed from London was bad. The Russians had continued their truculent attitude toward Churchill's pleas for aid for the Home Army. On August 16, they had even refused to allow British and American planes to land on Russian airstrips after making their airdrops over Warsaw. All during the latter part of August, Roosevelt and particularly Churchill continued to urge some sort of Russian action.[66] Stalin remained evasive. By early September the military situation along the Vistula had changed. Rokossovski had recouped his losses and regrouped his forces. A short advance to a more natural geographical front, the Vistula, was possible and even desirable. An offensive which envisaged crossing the Vistula in the face of stiffening German opposition was probably out of the question militarily, and politically it was pointless.[67]

During the previous month, it is likely that Stalin had begun to consider more specifically when and where he wanted all his armies to move. Clearly, a hastily prepared thrust through central Poland into the heart of the German defense of the Reich was undesirable before far larger areas of Eastern Europe had at least been occupied by the

Red Army. Thus Rokossovski could move to the Vistula, which would mean the occupation of the suburb of Praga, but not risk a crossing. The presence of idle Russian troops just across the river from Warsaw would certainly cause a worsening of Stalin's uneasy diplomatic relations with the West. Then, too, among even the Poles of the Lublin Committee, there was a growing uneasiness at the apparent Russian indifference toward the Warsaw rising. Perhaps Stalin felt that a conciliatory gesture, which would cost little and change nothing, could be made toward the Poles. On September 9, at long last, Warsaw learned "that to-day Marshal Stalin promised help for Warsaw."[68] On September 10, Soviet fighters were again seen over Warsaw. To the desperate Poles in their battered city, hope again stirred.

Bor had already spent the previous two days in tentative armistice negotiations, more to gain time than to prepare for surrender. The nature of the German terror tactics had persuaded the Poles that continued resistance had its virtues. Once these early discussions fell through, the Germans intensified their attacks. For their purposes Warsaw was taking too long, particularly with signs of Soviet movement to the east. The Germans hoped to pinch off the center of the city from the Vistula River, which would eliminate any possibility of help trickling in from the east and persuade the Poles of the hopelessness of further resistance. By mid-September only the Czerniakow sector, the last opening to the east, remained. Once again the regular drum-roll bombardment, the screaming *Stukas,* the fires, and, finally, the massive clockwork attacks proved effective. Not only along the Vistula sector but elsewhere, the Polish perimeter contracted under German pressure. The Poles would not give in. Russian planes flying at rooftop height began airdrops over the shrinking Polish sector, but the drops were made without parachutes, so that much of the material was damaged and the supplies lost. Efforts to contact Rokossovski failed. The Russians did not reply to radio calls. Bor grew desperate as his situation deteriorated and yet he knew that the Russians were moving closer, even if he could find no way to reach them.

On September 12, the Russians began to attack the outskirts of Praga. Inside Warsaw, the Poles noticed no slackening of German pressure; in fact, on September 14, heavy German attacks resulted in grave Polish losses. Many of the civilians were quite literally starving. Everything had given out: food, water, medical supplies. The city seemed to be a mass of flames and explosions. Yet the Russians had nearly reached the Vistula. Deliverance might be at hand.

The Russians would later complain that Bor continued to act independently of them, failed to inform them of his plans and generally treated their overtures with suspicion.[69] Certainly to establish close contact in the given situation along the Praga front in the middle of September would have been difficult enough; but when the Russians were apparently uncertain as to just how effective they wanted such liaison, making contact proved impossible. On September 14, the Lublin Radio promised that victory was near and urged the Poles to keep fighting. Bor still could not reach the Russians, who were now fighting inside Praga. His messengers finally made contact, but effective liaison could not be established.[70]

On September 16, for uncertain motives, Rokossovski permitted an attack across the Vistula by a unit of the First Polish Army under General Berling. Relatively few of the Poles managed to get across; probably about two battalions totaling 500 men reached the west bank, although the Russians reported that six battalions had begun the assault. The Home Army men hanging on in the Czerniakow district found that many of the men who had struggled across the river were peasants who had been drafted from the Lublin district only a few weeks before. Still, most important after the agony of waiting, contact had been made. Soviet planes were continuing their strange drops. The Red Army was consolidating its position in Praga. Yet the Home Army leaders could not completely discount previous Russian conduct nor the unexplained radio silence. The Home Army commander in the Czerniakow district reported through the sewers that no Soviet reinforcements had moved into the bridgehead. In fact, the whole situation, with the apparently quiescent Red Army separated from the city more by the Vistula River than by the Germans, caused increasing uneasiness.

On September 18, after one postponement, help came from a more distant source. Stalin had finally relented and agreed that the Americans could shuttle into Warsaw. As a result, 104 *Liberator* bombers, filled with 1,800 supply capsules, were on the way. Protected by 200 fighters most of them got through. The sudden arrival of the American planes made a deep impression on the Poles, who rushed from their cellars and dugouts to watch "the gigantic, shining, silvery planes, and from them hundreds of multicolored parachutes floated down . . . most of them on the other side of the insurgent lines."[71] The flight over flaming Warsaw made a different and perhaps deeper impression on the American crews, who had picked out their target from forty miles away by the huge cloud of smoke and fire hanging over the city.

> *After seven weeks of fighting not much remained of the Polish capital. Of large districts of the town which had covered areas of several square miles nothing remained but heaps of rubble which looked impressive even from the great height.*[72]

Down in that rubble the Poles still held 20 per cent of the city. The airdrop temporarily gave them new hope, but the situation had reached the critical point. The Home Army losses had been enormous, and, as the days passed, the killed and wounded totals among the civilians grew past counting. Yet, for many, it would all have been worth the sacrifice if the Russians could have expanded the bridgehead across the Vistula in time. Only that would save Warsaw, not a few hundred parachutes. On the night of September 18, the Russian Captain Kalugin crossed the Vistula to act as liaison man for Bor. He was not heard from again. The intentions of the Red Army remained enigmatic.

The commander of the Soviet 5th Division opposite the bridgehead of the First Polish Army had promised a landing but reported only delays. The Polish General Berling promised help but none came. On September 19, the Germans stepped up their pressure on the remaining Polish fragment of the Czerniakow district. Radoslaw decided to get his exhausted, beaten men out before the Germans cut him off entirely. That night the Home Army evacuated the district, very probably without being able to contact the Polish forces in the bridgehead. On September 21, a German tank-infantry attack split the bridgehead and shattered the Poles' defense. A handful of the men who had crossed the Vistula managed to reach safety on the Russian bank of the river. No further contact could be established with the First Polish Army; in fact, Berling apparently completely disappeared at this time.

Even with the collapse of physical contact with the Red Army, all hope was not abandoned. Twice, Soviet parachutists dropped into the Polish areas. Finally, on September 24, for the first time, the Soviet radio replied to the Home Army. By then sufficient liaison had been established to allow the Poles to act as artillery spotters for the Russian guns. While this encouraged some, the general situation in the three Polish sectors had deteriorated so badly as to overshadow even Russian co-operation. Even with the most stringent rationing, the food was almost gone, would be gone within a day or so. The horses, dogs and cats had long ago been eaten. The wells were drying up and no one had the strength to dig more. Most civilians remained in their cellars, stunned, exhausted beyond terror, waiting for death. Dysentery was rife. Scarlet fever had broken out. It seemed miraculous that worse plagues had not yet occurred, but the great killer remained the flames and shells. Warsaw burned on and on in front of the bloodshot eyes of the Home Army. The buildings continued to collapse under the artillery and tank fire. The Germans' heavy attacks smashed against the perimeter somewhere in the city each day. Still the Poles held on to their burning barricades, their rubble, their ruined streets. Contact continued through the sewers, where grim battles were fought with the Germans in the bowels of the city. Courage, endurance and determination would not, however, be sufficient. For Warsaw to be saved, the Russians would have to cross the Vistula.[73]

On September 27, the Polish perimeter in the Mokotów area had been reduced to a few streets. Heavy German fire blanketed the area all day. Finally there was no one left to hold the barricades. Out of the sewers word came to Bor that Mokotów had been lost. No word came from Rokossovski that day or the next or the next. The German pressure continued. The city burned and the civilians starved. A last envoy was sent across the Vistula to Rokossovski. On September 29, the Germans launched a massive attack on the Zoliborz area. The next day, with still no word from the Russians, Bor gave up hope. Even if the Red Army came, which it would not, it was too late. On October 1, Bor prepared for the final act.

Recognizing that Warsaw could no longer defend itself, he decided to enter into negotiations for surrender, "with full combatant rights, which the Germans fully recognize." His intention was to arrange for the safety of the civilian population in conjunction with the question of surrender, which he predicted would take place on October 3.[74]

Bor and Bach-Zelewski opened discussions which proceeded at a formal, almost leisurely, pace. The Germans, or at least SS Gruppenführer Bach-Zelewski, had decided to be most considerate toward their brave opponents. The realization that Germany was not going to win the war—in fact, the knowledge that defeat was certain—had spread in certain SS circles. Some efforts began to be made to build a record or to prepare a way out. Bach-Zelewski obviously realized that his methods in Warsaw could lead directly to a war-crimes trial. Rumors of the vile conduct of his men had resulted in a protest from Guderian reaching Hitler, who naturally ignored it. If even the sturdy German military conscience had been appalled, Bach-Zelewski could look forward to little mercy from tomorrow's victors. He removed Kaminski and had him shot, removing at one stroke a witness and a villain.[75] Now he confided to Bor that because of the Poles' brave fight the men of the Home Army would be treated as prisoners of war rather than as brigands or bandits. Translated from Nazi jargon this meant that they would not all be shot. On October 2, Bor agreed to the terms. After sixty-three days the struggle had been lost. The Poles once again had been left to fight alone.

This is the stark truth. We were treated worse than Hitler's satellites, worse than Italy, Rumania, Finland. May God, Who is just, pass judgment on the terrible injustice suffered by the Polish nation . . .[76]

The Germans demanded that all the Poles leave Warsaw by October 6. As the long lines of stunned and spent Poles snaked their way out of the city and toward the German detention camp at Pruszkow, they left behind only the seared hulk of a city, great blocks of rubble separated by littered and crater-pocked streets. In every clear space among the grimy rubble could be found the thousands and thousands of fresh graves scratched out beside the twisted tramcars, the burnt-out tank hulls, and the overlapping bomb craters. No one would ever know for sure how many Poles died in Warsaw during the sixty-three days, but at least 25 per cent of the population was dead—over 200,000 men, women and children, including most of the Home Army.[77] The Germans lost 10,000 killed, 7,000 missing, and 9,000 wounded.

Even after the fighting ended on October 2, the Polish deaths continued. While Bach-Zelewski might have been interested in building up a postwar record of good intentions, Hitler, Himmler and a substantial portion of the SS men were not. Germans threw hand grenades into the crowds of stumbling civilians and shot men suspected of being "bandits." For most of the Poles the future held deportation for slave labor, liquidation, or a slow death from exposure, disease or malnutrition. At the Pruszkow Camp, where 500,000 people were "processed" in three months, conditions were little better than they had been in Warsaw.

> *The people are in a state of utter exhaustion; among them are many sick and wounded. There are no drugs or medical aid. People who are seriously ill are lying by the roadside in the cold. Hundreds of thousands camp in the open field without food or shelters. Families are being separated.*[78]

On the city itself, Hitler vented his spleen. As early as October 3, teams of slave laborers had begun a systematic looting of the ruins. They emptied the National Library, sent off the undamaged paintings, dismantled and shipped anything within the city their German directors thought useful. On October 11, Hitler sent the order "to raze Warsaw to the ground." In the Thousand Year Reich, Warsaw would be a small pastoral village on the Vistula surrounded by green fields and grazing herds. Now, there was little left to raze. Few buildings remained untouched and most were in ruins. The Germans, however, began to tear down the blackened skeletons and detonate explosives under the shattered hulks.

As the dark days of winter came, the Germans turned their attention once more to the ominous Russian threat from across the Vistula. Apparently Stalin had no intention of driving through Poland into

Germany until he had made sure of the Balkans. The Soviet drive into Rumania had already begun on August 20, but the Polish front remained static. Finally, in January, the Red Army was ready. Along the front the Russians had a huge superiority estimated at eleven to one in infantry, seven to one in tanks, and twenty to one in both artillery and aircraft. This was despite the fact that German war production during the last half of 1944 had not declined under the heavy Allied strategic bombing but had actually increased. The fact was that too much equipment had been expended in the Ardennes offensive or frittered away. Even with more equipment the German Army itself had been bled white. No longer was it the splendid polished weapon that had slashed into Russia. Now it was a ragged collection of old men, young boys, and wiry professionals, honed too thin by years of wear. On January 12, Koniev's First Ukrainian Front broke out of its bridgehead over the Vistula. Zhukov, the new commander of the Russian Front opposite Warsaw, opened his attack next. By January 14, Zhukov, Koniev and then Rokossovski had forced Guderian to commit every Panzer division in Poland. The German XLVI Panzer Corps tried to pen Zhukov in his two bridgeheads across the Vistula south of Warsaw, but the German force simply did not have sufficient weight. Irresistibly, Zhukov swept it back. The way to Warsaw swung open.

At the same time, Rokossovski's armor swept in an arc from the north. Some of the German troops in the Warsaw area simply packed up and left. Even at the last moment, however, with the Russian armor ready to pinch off the city, certain units took time to dynamite as many of the remaining buildings as possible.[79] On January 17, after linking up with Rokossovski's armor, Zhukov occupied the Warsaw area against erratic resistance. It was difficult to call liberated Warsaw a city. Rather it was the greatest, single man-made ruin in the world, square mile on square mile of rubble, arduously created piecemeal by conventional weapons over a long period of time. An Allied correspondent attached to the Red Army sent out the first description: "Warsaw is a vanished city."[80] Hitler, as was so often the case, had not had the time to build the small town in the green meadows beside the Vistula, but he could feel satisfied in knowing that his orders had destroyed one of Europe's greatest cities. Sprawling alongside the river lay a ruin as final as Babylon or Nineveh, a weird geological curiosity rather than a city.

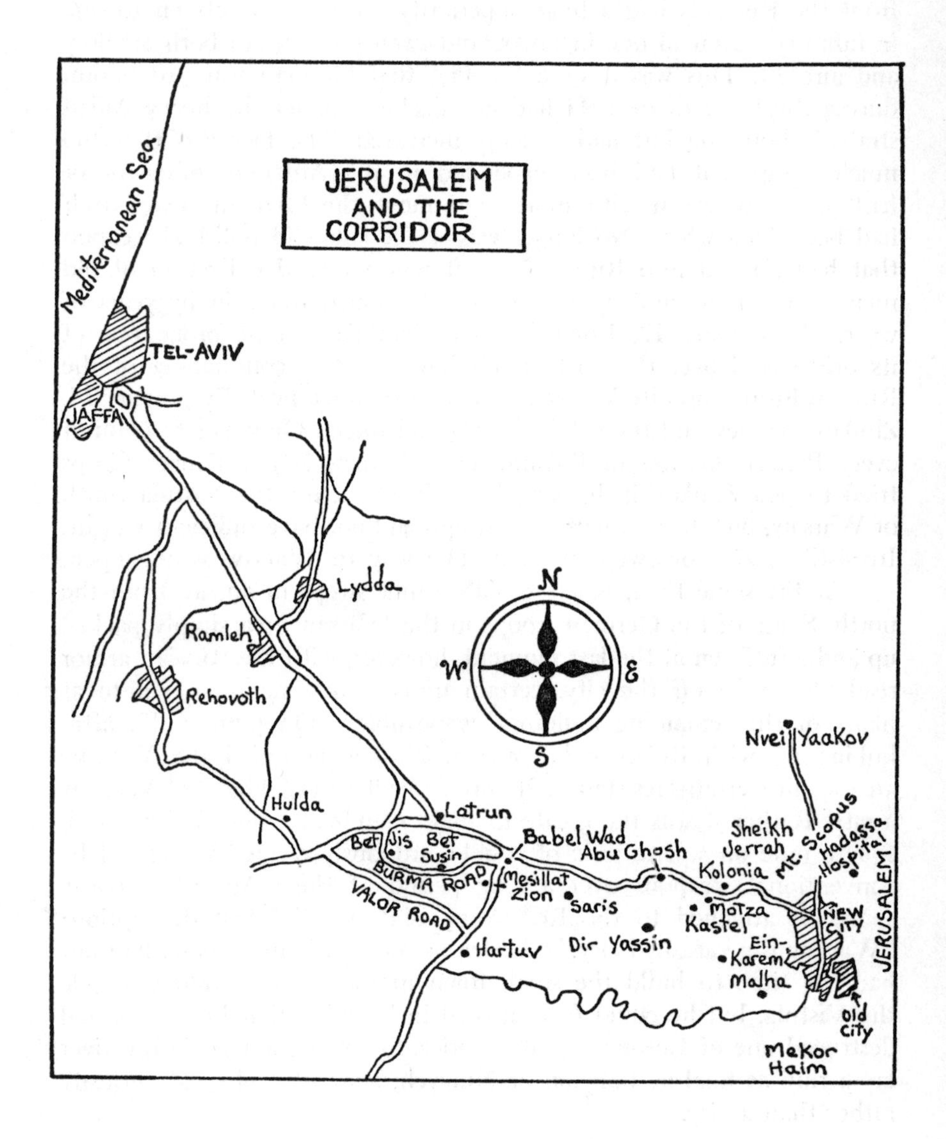
JERUSALEM
AND THE
CORRIDOR
Mediterranean Sea
TEL-AVIV
JAFFA
Lydda
Ramleh
Rehovoth
N
W
E
S
Nvei Yaakov
Hulda
Latrun
Bet Jis
Bet Susin
Babel Wad
Abu Ghosh
Sheikh Jerrah
Mt. Scopus
Hadassa Hospital
Kolonia
BURMA ROAD
VALOR ROAD
Mesillat Zion
Saris
Motza
Kastel
NEW CITY
JERUSALEM
Hartuv
Dir Yassin
Ein-Karem
Malha
Old City
Mekor Haim

6 JERUSALEM: 1947-1949

A Clash of Destinies

. . . and all the people returned to Jerusalem. And it came to pass after this, that there arose war . . . —I *Chronicles* 20:3–4

WHEN the Second World War came to an end in the blinding nuclear flashes over the Japanese home islands, not even the most optimistic observers foresaw a trouble-free postwar world. Some did feel that the atomic bomb had made war obsolete, but within a year the possibilities for military action grew. Small wars, even by great powers, could be undertaken to settle the clash of interests not sufficiently vital to endanger the security of the major powers. Soon the Moslems and Hindus were alternately slaughtering each other in India, and the Chinese engaged in a vast and irresolvable civil war. Elsewhere, while the great powers maneuvered into the Cold War, the colonial peoples of Asia and the Middle East grasped the changed power structure to seek independence, some by diplomacy and others by force.

Of all the arenas of conflict, none seemed less open to solution by peaceful means than the British Palestine Mandate. In twenty years no one had been able to suggest a peaceful solution to the clash of Jewish and Arab aspirations. As British power waned in the Middle East and the new Labour Government seemed determined to dismantle the British Empire, a Jewish-Arab war of some sort appeared inevitable. As was the case with all the little wars, it would have to be fought with left-over weapons and old tactics. The Arab states, if not the Palestine Arabs, had at least conventional forces, but the Jews had to depend on a poorly armed secret army. Thus, on paper at least, the prospects of the Jews were so poor that few, particularly in Britain, could imagine a lengthy conventional war. The best the Jews could expect was the rapid intervention of an outside force to forestall total destruction. The Jews might hold on to a few fragments of Palestine, but more likely the real armies of the forty million Arabs would sweep through Palestine in a single great wave. A siege in one or two places might be possible, but the Jews simply did not have the men or the equipment to hold out very long. Only a few like David Ben Gurion and King

Abdullah of Transjordan had a clear idea of the strengths and weaknesses of both sides.

STEEPED in history, Jerusalem, Holy City for three great religions, spreads out haphazardly across the rolling foothills east of the Judean Mountains. During thousands of years of history, Jerusalem had been many cities to many peoples, capital of David's kingdom, fortress for the Crusaders, administrative headquarters for the Turks, seat of rebellion to the Romans. In 1946 Jerusalem was actually three cities: the medieval Old City, the mushrooming Jewish New City, and the scattered surrounding suburbs. The population was, perhaps, the least homogeneous of any major metropolis; for Arabs, Jews and Christians were present in a profusion of sects and orthodoxies and a variety of races and nationalities. There were national colonies—Abyssinian, Greek, Armenian, German. There were British Mandate bureaucrats, Jewish Marxian Socialists, French Catholics, Arab ultranationalists, capitalist entrepreneurs, and effendis; all were united only in their common residence in the Holy City. In each area of the city, the mosaic of races, religions and nationalities mingled and overlapped.

The Old City, filled with historical and religious memories, was divided into four major quarters—Arab, Jewish, Christian, and Armenian. The twisting stone streets, the narrow passageways, the numerous shrines, mosques, churches, and temples abutted against one another among the maze of alleys. Here, crowded together, are the Via Dolorosa, the Church of the Holy Sepulchre, the Mosque of Omar, the Wailing Wall. Here the Romans, the Crusades, the Bible and the Koran seemed very close. Outside the thick walls to the west of the Jaffa Gate was another Jerusalem, the New City where the modern commercial and governmental quarters were built. This world of shopping centers, hotels and British administrative buildings was a far different world, centuries removed from the Old City. Spread out beyond the center of the city were the suburbs, mainly Jewish but pockmarked by Arab areas, particularly to the north and east, and dotted with the national colonies. In some areas Jewish districts formed enclaves in the midst of predominantly Arab sectors; for example, the Hadassah Hospital and the Hebrew University on Mount Scopus were completely surrounded by Arab districts. In other cases, old Arab villages remained isolated in the new Jewish suburban developments. Beyond the suburbs, spread the Arab rural land, unchanged except for the intrusion of a few Jewish agricultural colonies. Until 1946 the intermingling of Jews and Arabs, the isolated settlements and quarters, had meant little to Jerusalem's citizens; but, after the end of the Second World War, the city had day by day become the center of conflicting ambitions. Isolation had become dangerous, as the threat of violence, even of war, had become first a possibility and then, by 1947, a reality.

During the two years after the surrender of Germany, the Arabs and Jews in Palestine had stepped up their demands that the British Government give up its Mandate, granted in 1922 by the League of Nations.[1] The difficulty was that the Arabs and the Jews had very different ideas as to what should replace British authority in Palestine. The British, who had governed for a generation, had in the past been unable to find an acceptable compromise between the Jewish demands for a state and the Arabs' insistence that all Palestine should become an independent Arab nation. Despite seemingly endless proposals, investigations and suggestions, the British diplomats could not find sufficient common ground between the two to allow a peaceful political solution. By 1947, the British Labour cabinet had lost patience with both sides, neither of which appeared to be impressed with Britain's propositions. Unable to find a compromise, unwilling to force a solution on the population, and incapable of continuing to support the expense of maintaining their hold on the Mandate, the Labour cabinet had finally turned the fate of Palestine over to the United Nations. Despite assurances to the contrary, the decision was made with ill-will and very real bitterness. Harassed by Jewish terrorists, distrusted by their Arab allies, and freely criticized by those who did not have the responsibility of maintaining order or seeking a solution, the British Government felt misunderstood. Neither the Jewish Agency, the shadow government of the Palestine Jews, nor its Arab counterpart, the Arab Higher Committee, had any great faith in the British appeal to the United Nations. That London would withdraw voluntarily from a vital bridgehead in the Middle East seemed unlikely. Actually the Labour cabinet, faced with mounting domestic and international crises, had given little time to Britain's real interests and intentions in Palestine. There was sentiment in favor of holding on to the Mandate, in favor of forcing a solution on one side or the other, in favor of getting out of the whole dilemma. With no real policy of its own, United Nations' action had seemed the best alternative to the Attlee government.[2]

After considerable discussion, the United Nations sent an investigating committee, which examined the issues in detail and later debated solutions at length. In September 1947, the General Assembly met to consider the committee's proposals. Momentarily the growing disorders in the Mandate slackened as thousands of miles away at Lake Success, the delegates prepared to decide Palestine's future. The entire apparatus of world Zionism concentrated on securing a two thirds' vote in favor of partitioning Palestine into a Jewish and an Arab state. To the Arabs the proposal to divide the Mandate into two nations was anathema. Both in Palestine and in the capitals of the independent Arab states, spokesmen iterated their determination to prevent partition by force if necessary. For them Palestine was an Arab state with a Jewish minority. Partition, carving an alien enclave in the Arab world, was theft. So, from September to November, the British, the Jews and the Arabs focused their attention on the deliberations of the United Nations. On November 29, 1947, the General Assembly finally voted to partition Palestine, thirty-three in favor, thirteen opposed and ten abstentions. According to the diplomats, within a year there would be a Jewish state, an Arab state, and an international zone around Jerusalem. To the Jews, the vote seemed to be the culmination of a two-thousand-year dream. To the Arabs the vote was a bitter act of international treachery with no validity. The British response was ambiguous, revealing little of London's intentions except a growing unwillingness to co-operate with the United Nations. The remainder of international opinion hoped that at last the Palestine problem had found a diplomatic solution. In Palestine, however, it became increasingly obvious that the future of the Mandate would not be determined by the ballots of the United Nations delegates.

On the day after the vote at Lake Success, Sunday, November 30, Arabs attacked two Jewish buses on their way into Jerusalem. They ambushed an ambulance driving through the Arab suburbs north of the Old City. On the following day rifle fire and explosions could be heard all over Jerusalem. On December 2, an Arab mob rushed out of the Jaffa Gate into a Jewish shopping district in the New City and looted stores. The British police failed to intervene. The looting continued until members of the still-outlawed Jewish army, the Haganah, arrived. Having promised to prevent partition by force, the Arabs had acted. Having correctly predicted violence in the wake of the United Nations vote, the British seemed reluctant to prevent it. London announced that Britain would make no effort to implement partition and allow no United Nations officials into Palestine. The Mandate Government, backed up by the British Army, would maintain order until the day of the formal evacuation, still undetermined. To the Jews of Jerusalem, who saw the British police stand by while the Arabs looted, who saw the British Army confiscate the arms of the "illegal" Haganah, who knew the British Navy seized shiploads of "illegal" Jewish immigrants and interned them in camps on Cyprus, the kind of order which the British were maintaining appeared curious. Day by day the impartiality of the British appeared more compromised, their sponsorship of Arab ambitions more open. For some time Britain would remain *the* enemy for most Jews, who could not believe that after thirty years Great Britain was going to give up Palestine merely because of an international vote thousands of miles away.

During December, the façade of British law and order could not conceal the fact that the Mandate was slipping into anarchy. Reports of snipings, burnings, and bombings increased. In Jerusalem convoys had to be formed to supply the outlying settlements, increasingly isolated by armed Arab bands. In the city no Jew was safe when passing through an Arab area. On December 4, the Arabs ignored the British-imposed curfew, seemingly with impunity, and attacked the Jewish quarter of the Old City. The roll of fatalities grew steadily. During the second week of December, seventy-one Arabs, seventy-four Jews, and nine British were killed. The British authorities continued to insist that they were maintaining order. To the Jews their efforts appeared increasingly partisan: they continued their blockade against Jewish immigrants; they stepped up their extensive search for illegal Jewish arms; and they grew more tolerant of Arab violence. More serious for the 100,000 Jews in Jerusalem than British policy were the Arab attacks on Jewish vehicles. These incidents threatened to cut off the New City's food supplies. Months before the British proposed to evacuate, months before the Haganah could come out into the open without fear of search and seizure, months before a state could be established and arms and reinforcements legally secured, Jewish Jerusalem faced an Arab siege.[3]

In 1947, the only direct highway from Tel Aviv on the Mediterranean to Jerusalem ran southeast from the sea through the coastal plain and then twisted east in the Judean Mountains through narrow passes and along the sides of ravines below the Arab villages on the hilltops until it came within a few miles of Jerusalem, where the craggy mountains then gave way to the rolling hills of the western suburbs. For the Jews of Jerusalem, the sixty-five kilometers of the Tel Aviv road became an increasingly vital preoccupation during December when Arab irregulars began interrupting traffic. This slender link with the coast overnight became the major artery through which flowed their food and supplies. Although the railway to the coast still remained open, the line was obviously highly vulnerable—open to British interference and Arab attack. As the supplies coming into the city from the outlying Arab agricultural areas dribbled to a halt, the Tel Aviv road became the only major means of supplying the city. The Arabs were soon aware of this. During the last two weeks of

December, the sporadic firing on Jewish road traffic gave way to organized attacks and permanent roadblocks. Reluctantly, the Jerusalem Jews had to recognize the tightening noose of the Arab blockade and the increasing unwillingness of the British Army to protect Jewish transport. In January 1948, the Arab attacks along the Tel Aviv road quickened. Communication with the Jewish settlements to the north and south of Jerusalem grew increasingly difficult. Even the most optimistic had to admit that the United Nations' partition plan now depended on Jewish endurance. Whatever the British had told the world about the situation in the Mandate, Jerusalem was turning into a battlefield. As the days passed and the casualties mounted, Jerusalem became a city divided as Arabs and Jews "illegally" sniped at each other while the British Army stood aside, avoiding casualties. Neither the Arab fire nor the British indifference to it posed a deadly threat to the Jews. What could not be tolerated was the Arab stranglehold on the Tel Aviv road. Without food, fuel and water, Jerusalem would be starved out in a matter of weeks. Without a hold on Jerusalem, the Jewish position in Palestine would collapse. Partition would be unworkable. The British would have been proven correct.

The British authorities in Palestine were not as cold-bloodedly Machiavellian as the Jews assumed. They had been placed in a difficult situation by the Labour cabinet whose over-all policy and intentions remained vague. Local officials and military commanders had to carry out the day-to-day response to the growing crisis by interpreting vague policy statements with hurried improvisations to meet each new distraction. With orders not to implement partition, the Mandate government had informed the Jewish Agency that they could not supply escorts for Jewish convoys since "this might be interpreted as British implementation of partition."[4] Foreseeably the Arab attacks multiplied. Since the Jews were not allowed to use armored cars or armed guards, the Tel Aviv road had become all but impassable. The Hebrew University and the Hadassah Hospital on Mount Scopus became almost totally isolated from the New City. The settlements of Neveh Yaakov and Atarot to the north and the four Etzion bloc colonies to the south remained beleaguered in the midst of hostile local Arabs. On January 17, a unit of thirty-five Haganah troops, mostly Hebrew University students, tried to reach Kfar Etzion. Hundreds of local Arabs attacked and killed them all. The Jews understandably blamed the British for the expanding violence.

Delighted with the local Arabs' early success, the Arab League called for volunteers to bolster up the irregular bands tightening the Jerusalem blockade. By the middle of January, the volunteers began crossing the borders of Syria and Transjordan to join the Palestine

Arab forces. By the end of the month, over 2,000 armed men had moved into the Mandate. Unwilling to risk an open clash, the British ignored the border violations. Unwilling to lose men uselessly, British commanders increasingly avoided interfering in the fighting. In an effort to open up the Tel Aviv road, the Haganah went into action near the Arab village of Kastel where the highway from Jerusalem enters the Judean Mountains. Forty Arabs and eight Jews were killed in the bitter fighting before the British Army finally intervened. British fire killed two more Jews. By January the Jews felt that British policy seemed to allow, if not to encourage, the Arabs to thwart partition by the use of force. They assumed that London intended to make a deal with the Arabs after the unarmed, unprepared Jews had been defeated either by the volunteer bands or by the promised invasion of the Arab states. Obviously civil order, except directly under British guns, had dissolved. The Mandate had declined into a state of anarchy which the British appeared unwilling to correct. The Jews had no sympathy for the British problems in evacuating a country in the midst of a secret hit-and-run war. By the end of January, the Jews in Jerusalem felt that they had been left at the mercy of British whim and Arab attack.

The sense of isolation in Jewish Jerusalem grew daily as the civilians began to realize what their leaders had known for some time. Very little food, fuel or military supplies were coming in over the Tel Aviv road. In February only two convoys broke through the Arab roadblocks at Bab el Wad and Kastel. Food became difficult to buy. Few liked to consider what would happen if the Arabs cut the only water pipeline into the city. While the situation inside the city was indeed precarious, the prospects of the outlying settlements were perilous. The massacre of the Hebrew University students on January 17 and the total isolation of the Etzion bloc had been a severe shock to the population. The isolation of the nearly 2,000 Jews trapped inside the Old City remained a constant concern to all. Worse, no one in the Jewish Agency headquarters in Tel Aviv on the coast seemed to be taking positive steps to help.

Actually the fate of Jerusalem remained foremost in the minds of the members of the Jewish Agency. The Chairman, David Ben Gurion, was determined that the new Jewish state should have the Holy City as its capital—whatever the United Nations or the Arabs thought. Far from ignored or neglected, Jerusalem was, in Ben Gurion's mind, the ultimate prize. If the Arabs had accepted the partition plan, he might have allowed an international administration; but, since the Arabs had resorted to force, he was unwavering in his intention to save the city. As early as December, he had ordered Dov Joseph and

Golda Meyerson to head a Jerusalem Emergency Committee and to prepare for a siege;[5] no one had then, however, foreseen how rapidly the siege would develop. As yet the increasing preparations for the siege had made little impression on the civilians, who could only watch helplessly as normal life ground to a halt, as the Arab attacks continued, as one unpleasant rumor followed another.

On the other side of the city, the Arabs, too, realized the precarious Jewish position. For them all the news since the partition vote had been good. They now accepted as proven the sweeping promises of their more fanatical orators. The Jews would be swept into the sea in a week. Jerusalem would fall like a ripe plum. Believing implicitly in the grim fate of the hapless Jews, the Arabs either went home contentedly to wait for the new exodus of the Jews or else sought to hasten the day by random shooting into the New City. They casually discounted the existence of the Haganah, a Zionist gang, or the determination of the Jewish population. Their leaders, however, both in Jerusalem and in the capitals of the Arab states, felt far less sanguine; for they accepted the estimates of their intelligence experts that the Haganah and the elite Palmach commando units had at least 60,000 men, possibly 100,000. They believed the Jews were in possession of a vast array of modern equipment. More discouraging, they knew their own weakness. Only the first preliminary steps had been taken to invade Palestine and prevent partition by force. National conflicts, personal jealousies, and historic suspicions had prevented a joint Arab policy. Publicly their proclamations of undying unity and unceasing opposition to partition continued, but privately they feared that their military weakness and political divisions would allow a Jewish victory. The news from Palestine had been good, but if the local Arabs aided by the volunteers failed, then the Arab states would have to intervene. If they did not, they would face revolt from their own citizens fed for years on rosy propaganda.

Six Arab states eventually decided on armed intervention formally in the name of Arab unity but actually for peculiarly national reasons. Lebanon committed token units to give nominal support to the principle of Arab unity. Syria secretly hoped to secure boundary adjustments. Iraq wanted a dominant role in Arab affairs while it sought to divert attention from the Government's domestic difficulties. King Farouk wanted Egypt to keep the leadership of any pan-Arab movement, and, nearly as important, he wanted to restrict the ambitions of King Abdullah of Transjordan. Neither Yemen nor Saudi Arabia was willing to do more than allow its citizens to volunteer.

The only Arab leader who had a truly positive policy, unclouded by rhetoric or pretense, was King Abdullah. He felt that an Arab

Palestine, either as the jigsaw country proposed by the United Nations or as a state made up of the entire Mandate, was an idle dream. The only realistic policy was for him to incorporate the Arab areas on the west bank of the Jordan River into a new Hashemite Kingdom of Jordan with Jerusalem as the capital. He doubted if the Jews could be completely crushed. He doubted if the Arab League battle plan, drawn up by an Iraqi general, would prove effective. He knew that any All-Palestine government under the Grand Mufti of Jerusalem would be only an Egyptian puppet. Paying lip service to unity, Abdullah was prepared to absorb as much of Palestine as he could. He alone of all the Arab leaders felt that he possessed the military strength and diplomatic skill to achieve his ambition in the face of what he expected to be massive Jewish resistance.

King Abdullah's confidence was based in the main on the existence of the Arab Legion, trained by the British and commanded by officers seconded from the British Army. The Legion, under John Bagot Glubb and by far the most effective Arab military force, should be able to occupy and hold central Palestine. Once Jerusalem and the west bank of the Jordan were secure, his interest in continuing a holy war against the Jews was minimal. In fact, Abdullah had already carried out secret negotiations with representatives of the Jewish Agency seeking a diplomatic solution so that he would not have to risk the Legion against the Haganah. What he wanted, however, was just what Ben Gurion and the Jewish Agency wanted—Jerusalem. Since a compromise with the Jews was impossible, Abdullah would commit the Legion, secure in his knowledge that the British Government would probably accept his annexation of the west bank. In the meantime he could afford to wait while Jewish strength in the Jerusalem area was whittled away by the attacks of the local and volunteer Arab units.

In Tel Aviv and Jerusalem the impending invasion of the Arab Legion remained a distant threat. The months of January and February had shown the Jews that the Arab hold on road communications in Palestine might very well prevent the establishment of a Jewish state. Unless the situation could be reversed and the isolated settlements, particularly Jerusalem, be supplied, then Abdullah might never have the opportunity to test the Arab Legion against the Haganah. During March, efforts to double the daily number of trucks coming into Jerusalem over the Tel Aviv road collapsed in the face of continued Arab ambushes. On some days six trucks managed to run the corridor, but increasingly there were days when not a single vehicle could get through. On March 27, the Arabs wiped out a small convoy. During the following week the road remained sealed tight. The one major attempt to break through occurred on March 31, but the Arabs shot up several trucks and the rest had to fight their way back to the Jewish base at Hulda.

By April 1, Jerusalem knew the worst. The city remained cut off from the coast. The convoy system had broken down. The British still refused to protect the trucks or to allow the Jews to protect them. Unless the still illegal Haganah came out into the open to take Bab el Wad and Kastel, the city would starve. If the Haganah did risk a full-scale operation, the British might well intervene in force in an attempt to disarm and intern the only mobile forces available to the Jews. Ten weeks before the formal establishment of a Jewish state, ten weeks before the regular Arab armies proposed to invade Palestine, the fate of Jerusalem and the Haganah hung in the balance.

Although the Jewish Agency had not expected the climactic moment for Jerusalem to come so swiftly as it had, Dov Joseph's preparations for a siege had been going forward for months. The British authorities had complicated the preparations, and the British army and police in the maintenance of order had narrowly restricted Jewish activities. They had prevented the movement of arms and ammunition into the city, prevented the training of a local militia, forbade the construction of fortifications, and continued arms searches and seizures. Not only had the British been adamant in their refusal to allow Jewish defensive measures but they had also been reluctant to allow the stockpiling of food, water and fuel, reticent in protecting Jewish hospital and supply convoys, and insistent that the Jewish Quarter of the Old City should be supplied only with sufficient food to maintain the population from day to day. Since the Mandate government seemed unwilling to limit the Arabs in a similar manner, the Jewish authorities, already badly disillusioned, grew increasingly bitter. Not only did they have to prepare for the siege but they had to do so "illegally" and secretly.

To further add to the burdens of the Jewish authorities, they had to set up a shadow city administration to take over the functions of the decaying Mandate government. This, too, was a secret and unauthorized undertaking. In January 1948, the British delegate at Lake Success, Sir Alexander Cadogan, had announced that Great Britain would relinquish authority in the Mandate on May 15 and complete evacuation of the army by August 1. Until May 15, British forces would be fully responsible for order in Palestine. No governmental powers would be turned over either to the local population, Arab or Jewish, or to the United Nations.

In the climate of violence after the partition vote, the agencies of the Mandate government had gradually dissolved. Arab and Jewish officials, one by one, failed to appear at their offices. Many of the

British civil servants were sent home. The Jewish Agency called this administrative collapse Operation *Chaos* and mocked the British pretension that business was proceeding as usual. They felt the British were making a conscious attempt to allow the Mandate to collapse so as to prevent the establishment of a Jewish state, prevent the United Nations from taking any constructive actions, and, more important, prevent their own withdrawal. The Jewish Agency and its representatives determined to forestall Operation *Chaos* by filling the vacuum created by the British with their own authority. As one after another the British administrative organizations—the courts, the tax collectors, the police—withered, Jewish shadow organizations sprang up and took over their functions. Each week the Jewish Agency assumed more authority as it hectically sought to create a parallel administration.

The immediacy of the crisis was so apparent to the population of Jerusalem that the take-over progressed relatively smoothly. With few exceptions, the Jewish civilian population did all it could to cooperate in preparing the city for siege. The major problem facing the Jerusalem authorities was not setting up a city government but simply attempting to keep the population alive in the face of imminent starvation. The major considerations were food, water and fuel. Without even one of these, any siege would be brief and disastrous. Yet even to collect and store a minimum supply seemed an insurmountable undertaking. Shipments on the railroad were limited and would stop altogether as soon as the Arabs felt that they could cut the line with impunity. The water pipeline was equally vulnerable. The Tel Aviv road was closed. But under the leadership of Dov Joseph, exercising the powers of a military governor, efforts to secure stockpiles of food, fuel and water achieved some measure of success. The water supply was augmented by the secret filling of all the cisterns in Jewish Jerusalem. New cisterns were constructed and old ones repaired. Along with the water in the Romena reservoir, Joseph created a supply sufficient for about ten quarts a day per person for 115 days or seven quarts for 164 days. At worst, Joseph estimated there would be five quarts for 250 days. While hardly sufficient for washing, cooking, and drinking, the secret cisterns would supply enough water to prevent the fall of the city because of thirst.

The problem of food was even more critical. Stockpiling was limited because of the regular needs of a city of 100,000. There was hardly any food left over. Even when a meager surplus could be collected, warehouses and cold-storage facilities were limited. Finally, all the paraphernalia and organization for rationing and distributing had to be created from scratch. Truly Herculean efforts and considerable ingenuity coupled with the strictest rationing kept starvation at bay—

but just barely. By the beginning of March, 1948, there was no meat, eggs, milk, vegetables or butter, except for children, pregnant women, and hospital patients. Gardens hastily planted in backyards and edible weeds gathered at the risk of land mines and snipers failed to supply more than a small percentage of the needed vegetables. Central bakeries produced only enough bread to allow a minimum caloric standard. The difficulty of feeding the population while maintaining the last food reserves remained a constant and dangerous problem. From March on, the possibility that the iron ration would give out before new supplies could be acquired remained an ever-present threat. Even the civilians, forced to eat Spartan diets, never fully realized the narrow margin between the city and starvation.

If possible the fuel situation threatened to be worse. Actually, until the end of February, 80 per cent of the normal fuel supply arrived. Not until April, when the British refused to continue their convoys, did matters become critical. The basic problem was that no reserve existed. There was simply no reserve supply of fuel. On March 3, if the railroad had stopped running for five days, there would have been no gasoline in Jerusalem. Without fuel there would have been no heat, electricity, bread ovens, vehicles, private cooking or refrigeration. Essential hospital, communication and military services would have ended. Massive restrictions, which cleared the streets of all but a few vital vehicles and all but eliminated private use of fuel, helped some. Yet even when a little extra gasoline or fuel oil was collected, there were no storage facilities, no tanks, and even very few jerry cans or gallon tins. Thus, despite all efforts, the limited stocks of water, food and fuel continued to endanger the future of Jerusalem.

Though the supply problem demanded their major efforts, Dov Joseph and his associates sought to improvise other services. The Home Guard, *Mishmar Ha'am,* with a "uniform" made up of a raincoat, beret, baton and armband, had been set up in November, 1947 to carry out a host of nonmilitary functions. Although they were given limited training with small arms, their major task was to organize and supervise the activities necessary to turn the city into an armed camp. For beleaguered Jerusalem, the *Mishmar Ha'am* became the backbone of civilian resistance. It supervised food distribution, built fortifications, maintained order, protected the wounded, and collected fuel oil. Besides the *Mishmar Ha'am,* a new legal and administrative structure was created to replace the collapsing British authority. A Health Council sought to prepare the available hospitals for the expected wave of casualties. With the Hadassah Hospital cut off and useless, the Health Council had a vastly difficult job. On December 17, a blood bank was created and within two months, 1,200 bottles of plasma were on hand. *Kol Hamagen,* a secret radio station, began operation to keep Jews informed of the news without the restrictions of British censorship. Yet despite the incredible efforts, the secret arrangements, the hidden cisterns, and the self-imposed rationing, Jerusalem could not hold out alone until May 15. Unless the two roadblocks at Bab el Wad and Kastel could be knocked out and food supplies brought into the city, the end would be a matter of a week or two.

Ben Gurion and the Jewish Agency had long since decided that Jerusalem could not be abandoned whatever the risks or sacrifices. On April 1, the Haganah High Command agreed to risk British intervention by bringing their troops into the open and, if necessary, to resist British interference with force. The Haganah would undertake the opening of the Jerusalem corridor, Operation *Nahshon*, during the first week of April. The time had come to wage war, six weeks before a Jewish state could be legally established. Operation *Nahshon*, named after the Biblical figure who first jumped into the Red Sea on Moses' orders, was not to be a raid but rather a full-scale attack of over 1,500 troops to take the Arab strong points above the highway and hold them. Ben Gurion realized that Operation *Nahshon* would be a gamble. In order to shorten the odds against the Haganah, he ordered the Jewish secret agents in Prague, who had secretly been purchasing war material, to load as many rifles and machine guns as possible on a *Dakota* transport plane and fly them immediately into Palestine. The *Dakota* landed at a secret airfield on the night of April 1. The arms were unloaded and the plane took off before the British could intervene. Another cargo of illegal weapons arrived on a disguised arms ship. Still in their original packing the guns were rushed to the troops about to attack the hill villages. With their new arms, the Haganah planned a two-pronged attack; from Jerusalem toward Kastel and from Hulda in the west to clear the positions around Bab el Wad. As soon as these two positions were neutralized, several huge convoys were to be rammed through the open corridor to Jerusalem. Even if the road could be opened only briefly, these convoys would stave off the day when Jerusalem's resources would be exhausted. If the Arab positions could not be taken or the British interfered, that day would be very near, indeed.

On April 4, the first Haganah attack captured the village of Kastel, perched on a 2,500-foot mountain and dominating three vital miles of highway curving around below the height. The Arabs hurriedly launched a heavy counterattack and dislodged the Palmach unit holding the village. The local Arab area commander, Abdul Kader el Husseini, hurried back from Damascus to take personal control of operations. Before he arrived, the Jews once more gained possession of Kastel. Reinforcements moved in to hold the village against the expected counterattacks. As yet the British had not intervened. For the moment the eastern end of the highway was open. For several days Kader directed counterattacks against the Palmach's positions. One after another the Arabs seized the outlying positions, but the Palmach obstinately held on to Kastel itself, keeping the road below open. By April 9, the Arabs had forced the Jews back inside the narrow streets of the village. With no relief in sight, the Jews decided to withdraw. A few minutes before the final retreat, a Palmach machine gunner mistook three Arabs walking casually down the middle of the main street for Jewish reinforcements. At the last minute he realized his mistake and opened fire, killing all three instantly. One of the three was Kader, the only competent Arab military leader in the Jerusalem area. Apparently Kader had been under the impression that Kastel had been recaptured. His optimism cost him his life. Unaware of Kader's death, the Palmach withdrew; but, without their leader, the Arab troops quarreled among themselves and they, too, withdrew from Kastel twenty-four hours later. The Jews quickly reoccupied the heights and once more the highway was open in the east. On April 6, three days before, a confused Israeli offensive to the west had finally succeeded in clearing the hills dominating Bab el Wad despite some British interference. Although the village of Bab el Wad could not be taken, the Haganah positions about it neutralized the Arab roadblock.

At one minute past midnight on April 6, the first convoy left for Jerusalem. The trucks took nine hours and forty minutes to cover less than forty miles, but they did get through. On April 12 and 17, major convoys moved slowly over the road into Jerusalem. On April 20, Ben Gurion rode into the city on the lead truck of the third convoy, symbolizing his solidarity with the Jerusalem Jews. The Arabs had come down out of the hills and mauled many of the 294 vehicles. Many of the trucks joined the ranks of the burned-out hulks scattered along the roadside. At the same time, the Arab irregulars retook the heights above Bab el Wad. The corridor was closed. The forces to reopen the road existed, but rising demands in other parts of Palestine for the troops concentrated in the Jerusalem area forced the Haganah to call off plans for a counterattack. Jerusalem would have to make do with the supplies brought in by the April convoys. Despite the renewal of the siege, the atmosphere in the city had changed. No longer did the Jews feel alone. No longer did the threat of starvation loom so large. Perhaps equally important, no longer did the Jerusalem Arabs have an effective military leader or an unblemished record of success. For the first time the average Arab felt tinges of uncertainty. Since the defense of Jerusalem depended to a large extent on the stamina and endurance of the Jewish civilians, Operation *Nahshon*'s success, even if temporary, was vital. Jerusalem was besieged but no longer forgotten, beleaguered but not defenseless.

The decision to risk Operation *Nahshon* had touched off an undeclared war throughout the Mandate between the still illegal Haganah and the Arab irregulars and volunteers. Few stranger wars have been fought; for, under the eyes of a neutral referee, military operations on an increasingly broader scale and with rapidly mounting casualties were undertaken by both sides. Occasionally the British referee intervened, usually to the benefit of the Arabs, but on occasion to prevent the massacre of Jewish units. Neither side trusted the British, who were gradually evacuating the Mandate, but both were willing to seize the opportunity to wage open war. It was to be a savage, bitter war, expanding almost daily in scope and intensity; and yet the fighting was hedged about by political considerations, confined by unwritten rules, and restricted by unadmitted conventions. For the 100,000 Jews in Jerusalem, the six weeks of war before the state could be established were used to consolidate their position in the city. In the remainder of the Mandate, the Haganah went over to the offensive despite their lack of any real reserve or the weapons of modern warfare. Ben Gurion's "Zionist decision" that there should be no retreat from any settlement, no matter how hopeless the situation, proved sounder than his military advisors had expected. With one or two exceptions, the tenacity and bravery of the poorly armed defenders prevented the Arabs from overrunning the isolated settlements and the Jewish quarters of mixed cities. Without the need of frittering away their limited strength in dozens of small defensive actions, the Haganah occupied the mixed cities of Safed, Haifa, and Tiberias, and dominated the Arab cities of Jaffa and Acre.

The Arab Liberation Army, a multinational collection of individualistic volunteers, found that enthusiasm and a just cause were not sufficient assets in meeting the Haganah's attacks. The Arabs were unable to secure even one clear victory for prestige purposes until the last day of the Mandate. While the news of the Haganah's success encouraged the Jerusalem Jews, the situation in and around the city gradually deteriorated. Neveh Yaakov and Atarot to the north and the Etzion bloc to the south remained cut off without hope of relief. For these settlements the "Zionist decision" seemed a sentence to death. The position of the 1,700 Jews still in the Old City appeared equally hopeless, with the British still limiting their supplies and the Arab attacks growing bolder. In the New City the supply situation, temporarily alleviated by the April convoys, grew worse and then desperate. If the Jewish Agency could be guardedly optimistic about the situation in the rest of Palestine, it could only regard Jerusalem with uncertainty and concern.

April was the crucial month. On April 10, the Arab Liberation

Army began bombarding the city with its French 75s. On April 12, Jewish prestige was badly damaged by an Irgun attack on the village of Deir Yassin which ended in a bloody and unprovoked massacre of the Arab civilians. On April 14, the Arabs ambushed a large convoy on the way to the Hadassah Hospital on Mount Scopus, killing seventy-seven doctors, nurses and teachers. On April 20, the Arabs recaptured the heights around Bab el Wad, closing the Tel Aviv road.

Inside Jerusalem the increasing tempo of the undeclared war persuaded the civilian and military authorities that immediate steps had to be taken to prepare the city for attack by the regular Arab armies, particularly the Arab Legion. Day by day it became clear that the local Arabs and the volunteers had failed to "drive the Jews into the sea." Soon the regular Arab armies would move and Jerusalem had to be ready. The major problem was that all the Jewish areas had still not been consolidated. Although individuals and families had moved out of predominantly Arab quarters, some Jewish districts remained separated from the Jewish New City by intervening Arab areas or villages. The Haganah prepared a new operation, *Jebusi*, the original name of Jerusalem, to link up the scattered Jewish districts by the capture of strategically placed Arab sectors.

The Haganah's operational plan had three major objectives: to open a route to Neveh Yaakov, to break through to Mount Scopus, and to link up with the Mekor Hayim area to the south. In order to reach Neveh Yaakov to the north, several well-defended Arab villages would have to be stormed. To reach Mount Scopus, the Haganah would have to occupy the Arab quarter of Sheik Jarrah. To the south the Arab quarter of Katamon would have to be overrun. It was an ambitious project.

On April 26, after some early gains the attack toward Neveh Yaakov ground to a halt. The operation turned into a disaster. The Arabs killed thirty-three men and most of the assault commanders. The Haganah did, however, capture the other objective in the north, Sheik Jarrah; but the British intervened, insisting that the area was on their evacuation route and could not become the scene of fighting. After the British brought up tanks and a battalion of infantry, the Haganah withdrew, unhappily accepting a British promise to turn the sector over to the Jews after their evacuation. Only the attack on the Katamon quarter succeeded. The Haganah not only captured Katamon but also the Greek Quarter and additional districts outside the original scope of the attack.

Although only one of the objectives of *Jebusi* had been secured, the morale of the Jews had greatly improved. The Jerusalem Haganah had proved it could not only defend them but could also attack the Arabs. The basic situation, however, remained unchanged. The outlying settlements in the north and south were still isolated. The Jews in the Old City were still cut off. The Tel Aviv road remained closed. In preparing the next operation, the Haganah commanders had to choose whether to commit their slender resources in an effort to reach the outlying settlements and to relieve the Old City or once again to break the Arab hold on the Tel Aviv road. As always the demands of the 100,000 Jews in the city for food and fuel restricted the Haganah's freedom of action. The isolated Jews would have to wait while a new offensive, Operation *Maccabee,* reopened the corridor.

On the night of May 7–8, the Haganah's Harel Brigade opened operations with an attack on Bet Mahsir, an Arab village on the commanding heights in the Judean Mountains to the west of Jerusalem. The Arabs resisted fiercely. Not until May 11 did the Haganah gain command of the highway from Bab el Wad to Jerusalem. Even then the road could not be used because of new Arab positions farther west at Deir Ayub and Latrun. When the Jews tried to push a convoy through, the Arab Liberation Army, using new artillery and supported by additional reinforcements, smashed the attempt. Not until May 15, after the Givati Brigade had badly mauled the Arabs, did the Haganah reopen the highway. Only one hastily organized convoy of forty vehicles could be rushed through the gap before the Haganah had to withdraw on May 16 to meet the threat of the Arab invasion. After two weeks of fighting, Jerusalem still had no free line of communication.

While the fighting continued to the west in the Judean Mountains, Haganah forces inside Jerusalem used the last days before the end of the Mandate to prepare Operation *Pitchfork*—the seizure of all the security zones in the city as the British Army moved out. During the first four months of 1948, Jerusalem had become divided into thirds, each third completely sealed off from the others by barbed-wire entanglements, concrete guard posts, "illegal" armies and self-appointed soldiers. Through the center of the city ran the British security zones, isolated by high fences, pillboxes, patrolling tanks and machine guns. Here the remaining British troops and officials lived securely isolated from the conflict between Arab Jerusalem and Jewish Jerusalem. Once the British withdrew from their security zones, the Arabs and Jews would race each other to fill the vacuum. For the Haganah commanders time was essential, since they expected the Arab Legion to arrive in Jerusalem within twenty-four hours. What they could not win and hold during that time would in all probability be lost to the Legion. It was the arrival of the Arab Legion which gave the Haganah nightmares; for however bitterly the local Arabs fought, they were amateurs. The Legion troops were highly trained, well-armed professionals.

While the Haganah completed preparations for Operation *Pitch-*

fork and for the defense against the Legion, the civilian population could do little but wait for May 15, when their state would be established and when the Arab armies would invade Palestine. They tried to keep up the pretense of normality. It was a feeble pretense. Firing was almost continuous along the edges of the Jewish-Arab sectors. Erratic artillery fire from Arab positions in the hills took a steady toll of the Jewish civilian population. There were no mails, no courts, no buses, no banks, and no railroads. Business remained at a standstill. Many factories and offices had been isolated by Arab sniper fire for months. Others had no supplies or no workers. The last vestiges of the Mandate's authority and personnel had dribbled away. Only occasional British Army patrols and the sight of the security zones reminded the people that the date of evacuation had not yet arrived. For most persons there was little water and less food. Mealtime became a social obligation to keep up morale rather than a time to eat; for, by the middle of May, the daily ration was hardly enough for one unsatisfactory snack. There was not even a chance that somehow the war would bypass the Holy City. All the efforts to achieve an effective armistice or to turn Jerusalem into an open city had failed. The United Nations, the neutral consuls, the Mandate government, and the British Army had failed in every attempt to persuade both sides that a truce in the city would be to their advantage. So Jerusalem sat out the last dark days before the Arab invasion listening to rifle and artillery fire. The make-believe world of the "undeclared war" was about to be replaced by a real war. The new state would be attacked at birth.

Then, just before the official end of the Mandate, on May 14, came the worst news of the undeclared war—the Arabs had taken the Etzion bloc of settlements. That morning the last message arrived soon after the International Red Cross had negotiated the surrender of the remaining defenders: "Men and women are sent toward Hebron. The wounded are transferred to Bethlehem. Greeting from the men of Massout. This is the end of the Etzion bloc. Tonight we shall not be here any more."[6] The Arab Legion, still in Palestine to aid the British in maintaining order, had used the sporadic Jewish interruption of its road communications as an excuse to wipe out the bloc. Strategically the loss of Kfar Etzion was unpleasant but by no means decisive. The depth of the shock to the Jews in Jerusalem was of far more concern to Ben Gurion. He knew that the Jews in the city would have to maintain their spirits under desperate conditions in the face of a series of defeats. He urged them not to despair at the very moment that the state was coming into being.

At exactly eight o'clock on the morning of May 14, 1948, the British High Commissioner of the Palestine Mandate, Sir Alan Cunningham, came out of the Government House in Jerusalem, reviewed the honor guard, spoke briefly and stepped into his official black, bullet-proof Daimler to the sound of the Highland Light Infantry's bagpipes playing a Scotch funeral dirge. As the armed convoy with the Daimler in the middle wound its way toward the Kalandia airport in the northern suburbs, heavy firing began throughout the city. Operation *Pitchfork* was under way. Soon the last British battalion had withdrawn from the city and the last Union Jack had been lowered. After thirty years the British were gone. Neither the Jews nor the Arabs had the time or the interest to note the occasion—the open struggle for the city had already begun. At four o'clock on the same afternoon, the ceremonies to establish the new state of Israel began eight hours before the official termination of the Mandate, since the rabbis would allow no official business to be transacted on the next day, Saturday, *Shabbat,* which began at sundown. In Tel Aviv at the Museum on Rothschild Boulevard, David Ben Gurion rose and quietly began reading the Declaration of Independence, the Scroll of the Establishment of the State. Within a few minutes the ceremony was over. After 1,887 years, the State of Israel was reborn. In Tel Aviv, in Jerusalem, in the isolated desert settlements, there was a moment of almost unbelieving joy. At last Israel was a fact and not a dream. In Cairo, in Damascus and in Bagdad, there was only bitterness and renewed determination to erase that "fact" with force. However unsure and divided they were privately, the leaders of Egypt, Syria, Transjordan, Iraq and Lebanon had already ordered the invasion of Palestine. As they had feared, the local Arabs and the volunteers had not been able to prevent partition. Now they would have to commit their armies. At five o'clock on the morning of May 15, twelve hours after the creation of Israel, Egyptian *Spitfires* bombed and strafed the Israeli airfield outside Tel Aviv. The official war had begun.

Although the joy of Jerusalem's Jews at the establishment of Israel had been as deep as that of the Jews in Tel Aviv or in New York, that joy had been tempered by the situation in the city. No one could forget the fate of the Etzion bloc. No one could forget the Arab Legion. No one could forget the rising din of Operation *Pitchfork.* For sixty hours after the British Army withdrew, fighting around the old security zones was general. The Arab artillery barrage increased. Despite bitter Arab resistance in some places, the Etzioni Brigade managed to secure most of its objectives. Etzioni seized the King David Hotel, the General Post Office, the railroad station, and the strategic Monastery of Notre Dame. Generally the Haganah proved quicker in occupying the "vacuum areas" and proved more adept in defending its gains than did the local Arabs.

By Sunday night, May 16, Operation *Pitchfork* was all but over. The Haganah was forced to turn its attention to the expected arrival of the Arab Legion, which had momentarily withdrawn into Transjordan so that its invasion would be "legal." Besides the Legion, units of the Egyptian Army accompanied by more volunteers were hurriedly moving north through Hebron toward Bethlehem and the southern suburbs. On the surface, the possibility of a successful Jewish defense of the city in the face of regular army attacks appeared remote. British military experts freely predicted that the Arab Legion would sweep through Jerusalem in a matter of days. The Jews had no aircraft except Piper *Cubs,* no artillery in the city except for a few homemade heavy mortars, *Davidkas,* which made a reassuringly loud noise but did very little damage, and no armor except for homemade armored cars. The major hospital complex on Mount Scopus was useless and had been replaced by makeshift quarters. Munitions and military supplies were low. The huge civilian population on limited rations might prove open to panic. Yet the Haganah commanders were not unduly disheartened. Operation *Pitchfork* had been a success, securing both strategic territory and vitally needed arms and supplies. The local Arabs had proved to be undisciplined soldiers and the Arabs in the regular armies might be no better.

In their estimation of the difficulties faced by the Arabs in storming the city, the Haganah commanders would have found themselves in agreement with General John Glubb, the British commander of the Arab Legion. King Abdullah had only recently informed Glubb that the war plans of the Arab League had been jettisoned and that the Legion instead would move on Jerusalem. Abdullah, back in Amman, felt that the situation around Jerusalem was most favorable. The Tel Aviv corridor was still cut; the Jewish Quarter in the Old City was on the point of surrender; and the Jewish settlements still holding out to the north were ripe for the taking. In fact the Jews were already drawing back. By May 17, Neveh Yaakov and Atarot had been evacuated; and the Jewish outposts far to the east, Bet Haarava and the Potash Works at the northern tip of the Dead Sea, had been evacuated without a fight. King Abdullah's enthusiastic analysis of the Jerusalem situation was not shared by Glubb, who realized that the Legion would be least effective in the confined, house-to-house fighting necessary to take Jerusalem. He expected little effective help from the unruly crowds of volunteers, whose enthusiasm could not make up for their lack of training and discipline. He feared that the hastily mounted invasions by the other Arab states would not draw off the Jewish troops in the Jerusalem area. Most important, Glubb expected to meet a Jewish army several times the size of his own. Abdullah, however, was not to be denied: the Legion would be used in Jerusalem.

Early on the morning of May 19, the Arab Legion finally opened the attack on Jerusalem by moving against the Sheik Jarrah Quarter, occupied by the Irgun during Operation *Pitchfork*. Glubb felt that his force was dangerously small to force a way into the city from the north, but he did not want to delay his attack longer. The Irgun defenders of Sheik Jarrah had eased Glubb's problems considerably by waiting until the last moment to prepare their defensive positions. By half past seven in the morning, the Legion had taken over the entire quarter and again cut off Mount Scopus. By two o'clock in the afternoon, the Legion reached the Damascus Gate and moved into the Jewish New City. One Arab spearhead attacked the Jewish quarter in the north and a second tried to force its way past the Mandlebaum Houses up the Street of the Prophet toward the center of the city. Unlike the swift advance of the morning, however, the Legion soon found itself engaged in heavy fighting. For several days the Arabs sought to pound a way into the city from the north with little success. Glubb finally broke off the attempt because his casualties were piling up too rapidly. Without any decently trained reserves, he was unwilling to see the Legion decimated in sterile house-to-house fighting.

To the south, the Arab drive into the city proved for a time more successful. The settlers in the key village of Ramat Rahel withdrew under Arab attack after a heavy artillery bombardment smashed the outlying positions and interrupted communications with Jerusalem. The Egyptian troops, augmented by volunteers who had swept into Ramat Rahel as the demoralized defenders retreated, proved something less than adequate as a defense force. If the Arabs could have held Ramat Rahel as an advance base, the way into the New City from the south would have been open; but looting seemed more important to the poorly disciplined "troops" than preparing for a counterattack.

> *The Egyptian flag was waving over Ramat Rahel by eleven o'clock. We found cows—beautiful, fat cows. We found chickens —thousands of nice, fat, plump chickens. Every man grabbed two, ripped off the heads, and roasted them in the fires of the burning buildings. We ate chickens all day. . . . I was still eating chicken when the cowardly Jews attacked. They caught us by surprise by sneaking up on us at midnight. The Jews never show themselves in battle until they are on top of you. They never fight so that you can see them. Cowards! I took one last bite and ordered my men to retreat. But we will capture the village back again.*[7]

Ramat Rahel did fall again to the Arabs but the Harel Brigade retook the settlement once more. It was to change hands three more times before the Haganah finally succeeded in seizing and holding it.

The way into Jerusalem from the south was proving as difficult for the Egyptians as the northern entry had been for Glubb.

With the Egyptians bogged down at Ramat Rahel and his own troops tied down around the Mandlebaum Houses, Glubb shifted his attack to the center. His objective was the Convent of Notre Dame de France, which overlooked much of the Old City and was only a half mile from the center of the New City. At noon on May 23, his artillery zeroed in on Notre Dame. From the Damascus Gate Legion troops, led by armored cars, moved slowly through the narrow streets parallel with the walls of the Old City. The column's slow advance toward Notre Dame was suddenly halted by a well-placed Molotov cocktail thrown by a boy who was reputed to have fought with the Maquis in France. The remaining armored cars could not find a way around the burning wreck and had to withdraw. The Legion infantry continued the attack all afternoon and evening. At one time they reached a point within fifteen yards of the main building. Firing continued all night. At seven o'clock on the morning of May 24, the Arabs finally broke into the grounds of Notre Dame. All during the day they clung to their position despite heavy Jewish fire. At one time, ten Arabs momentarily got inside one of the buildings. The breakthrough was not followed up, however, and they had to withdraw. By five o'clock in the afternoon, Glubb felt his men had absorbed enough punishment.

> *Of the 200 infantry who had set out to attack Notre Dame on May 23, nearly half were either killed or were stretcher cases—the walking wounded as usual remained in the line. 4 Company had lost all its officers and N.C.O.s except one. At five o'clock on the afternoon of May 24th, the attack was abandoned.*[8]

Glubb's worst fears were being realized. The Legion he had spent years training to fight fluid actions in the open desert was being eaten up in house-to-house fighting. The Jerusalem Haganah had blunted the pincers from the north and south and repulsed the frontal assault on Notre Dame. Tied down in the city, the Legion could not come to grips with the Haganah's main forces out in the plains and hills where the Arab superiority of armor and artillery might win the war. If the stalemate continued, the city might turn into a deathtrap. Abdullah's hopes for an easy, early victory in Jerusalem had proven ill-founded.

For their part, the Jews had no reason for glee. The Haganah had inflated ideas about the strength of the Arab Legion and no real idea of Glubb's limited reserves and ammunition supplies. The Jews also knew how severely their own defenses had been stretched. The reports reaching Jerusalem during the first week of the invasion were vague but still far from reassuring. The Egyptian troops had moved almost unchecked north toward Tel Aviv. The Syrians and Iraqis had moved into central Palestine and attacked several kibbutzim. The Egyptians had attacked Tel Aviv from the air. Troops of the Lebanese Army had moved south. Worse, the Jews' own limited success in holding off the Arab Legion had been clouded over by news from the Old City. There the situation in the Jewish Quarter that had first grown desperate during the undeclared war was now apparently hopeless.

On May 15, there were still 1,700 Jews left in the Quarter out of the 2,500 who had originally lived there. Since December 1947, the Quarter had been almost isolated, cut off from the Jewish areas of New Jerusalem by the intervening Arab districts inhabited by some of the most fanatical Moslem sects. The British had prevented all but a trickle of war material from reaching the Quarter. Food supplies had arrived on a day-to-day basis. There was no backlog of medical supplies, fuel or ammunition. In March the British had expelled the one outstanding Haganah officer, Avraham Halperin, and there was no leader of sufficient stature to replace him. The constant sniping, the occasional Arab forays, and the sense of total isolation in the midst of a hostile city had all chipped away at civilian morale. In any case little could be expected of the civilians. Many were elderly and a substantial percentage belonged to the "old Yishuv," Jews who had been living in Jerusalem for generations, dedicating their life to the study of the *Torah*. The ultra-orthodox Yeshiva student, the member of the Neturie Karta sect who opposed national independence as blasphemy, the secretarian mystic—all proved poor material for a civilian militia. The defense depended on 120 Haganah men, sixty-five young volunteers, and some Irgun units, whose efforts in the Quarter were not always co-ordinated with the Haganah. When the British had pulled out on May 14, the Arabs assumed with some justification that the Old Quarter—isolated for six months, inhabited by elderly rabbis and frightened students, defended by badly armed civilians—would fall in a matter of hours, or at the most in a day or so. British officers freely predicted that if the local Arabs did not massacre the 1,700 Jews, then the Legion would move in and capture them. In either case the Jews' position would be hopeless.

The moment the British withdrew from the Old City, the Haganah hurriedly occupied many of their positions around the perimeter of the Quarter. At the same time, the Arabs struck at the Jewish positions at the Zion Gate, the probable route of any relief column from the New City. The Arabs took the Gate and began increasing their pressure around the edge of the Quarter, taking one house after another. Within twenty-four hours some of the defenders of the Quarter began to feel their position was hopeless: "Help us immediately. Otherwise we will not be able to hold out."[9] The commander of the Jerusalem Haganah, David Shaltiel, a former member of the French Foreign Legion, replied, "You are to hold out at all cost." By the following day, May 17, under continued heavy pressure only a few hundred square yards of the Quarter remained in Jewish hands. Much of what remained was merely rubble. No place was more than a few yards from the front lines. To the frightened civilians huddled in cellars the sounds of dynamite explosions and rifle fire seemed continuous and ever closer. In the New City the sight of the black pall of smoke over the Quarter and the unending sound of firing increased the growing concern of both the civilians and the Haganah commanders.

Realizing that time must be growing short, Shaltiel hurriedly put together an operation to break through to the defenders and either bring in reinforcements or take out the survivors. The operation would be a two-pronged effort. One section of the Harel Brigade was to capture Mount Zion in order to enter the Old City by way of the Zion Gate. The other, made up of four platoons of the Etzioni Brigade, would concentrate at the old Commercial Center and attempt to storm the Jaffa Gate. The Etzioni platoons, hampered by administrative difficulties and a lack of proper liaison with the Harel Brigade, did not reach the Commercial Center until daylight. When they made their assault on the Jaffa Gate on the evening of May 18, the Arabs, who had observed their arrival at the Commercial Center, were fully prepared. Heavy Arab fire killed or wounded all the Jewish sappers before they could reach the Gate. The entire operation collapsed into efforts to remove the wounded from the open square in front of the Jaffa Gate. At least the Harel operation benefited from the diversion created by Etzioni's unsuccessful attack. On the same evening they captured Mount Zion in a surprise attack. Early on the morning of May 19, the Harel force reached the Zion Gate. Despite heavy Arab machine-gun fire from the walls above, the sappers set the charges and withdrew safely. At 3:25 A.M., the explosion of the charges tore a narrow breach in the gate. Taking advantage of the thunderous explosion, the assault platoon, led by a sixteen-year-old runner, rushed through the gate. The siege of the Jewish Quarter was lifted. "We have carried out the great task and reached the Jews of the Old City . . . 1,700 souls have been saved."[10] A temporary supply line was immediately put into operation. For the first time rifles, Sten guns, and ammunition passed freely into the Quarter. Suddenly the Arab position, so hopeful a few hours before, had become endangered. With a Jewish bridgehead in the Old Quarter, all Jerusalem might fall before the Legion could arrive in strength and counterattack.

Jewish command problems, however, came to the aid of the Arabs,

The two-pronged assault had been hastily planned and badly organized. Reinforcements to hold the Zion Gate either did not exist or did not arrive. The assault force had neither the resources nor the defensive positions to withstand the Arabs when daylight came. Just before dawn the gate had to be given up. The Quarter was once again isolated. Left behind were eighty-seven Palmach troops and an additional supply of arms and ammunition, but these were scant compensation for the renewal of the siege. Civilian morale, momentarily sky high, began to decline. There was still no leader inside the Quarter capable of organizing and inspiring the defenders. Trapped in their ruins, even the soldiers began to feel that Shaltiel did not fully understand their danger. He, in turn, felt that he had given the order to hold out and broken through once with reinforcements. Now the defenders should be able to hold on without constant reassurance.

Fighting in the Quarter continued and took an even more ominous turn for the remaining Jews. All the Arab irregulars were withdrawn and replaced by crack troops of the Arab Legion. Pressure on the defenders grew hour by hour. Communication between strong points became difficult, depending almost entirely on small boys dashing from one post to the next. Repeated attempts to break through to the Quarter through the Zion Gate failed. The Arabs would wait until the Haganah assault forces entered the gate and then spray them from above with machine-gun fire, turning the narrow entrance into a deathtrap. Inside the ruins, panic mounted among the helpless civilians who had little to do but crouch in basements waiting for the Arabs to break in and massacre them.

Outside the Quarter, in the New City, Shaltiel assumed that the defenders would be able to hold on until another attack could be mounted or even until the United Nations could impose a truce. He tended to discount the increasing anxiety of the defenders, who had often been promised relief which never seemed to come.

Despite their desperate situation and their growing fears, the remaining defenders hung on. The ferocity of their defense, their refusal to give up an inch of the Quarter without violent resistance, persuaded the Arab Legion that the entire area was a heavily held, almost impenetrable fortress. The casual optimism of the local Arabs had long ago evaporated. The Legion had to force its way ahead yard by yard. Unknown to the Arabs, organized Jewish resistance degenerated into individual defense operations. Outposts would hold out long after they were isolated from the other defenders. No one knew what the situation was in the Quarter except in his own few yards of flaming ruins. Ammunition and hand grenades were running out. Unwounded defenders were rare. The terror of the civilians increased.

By dawn on May 28, the defended area was little more than a

burning ruin filled with frightened survivors protected by a handful of battered and exhausted men. Although continued defense for twenty-four hours more was possible, the Haganah men feared that if relief did not come then, the Arabs would smash into the cellars and murder the civilians. On the day before, the Arabs had taken the Bethel section and all of the Street of the Jews, killing four Jews and wounding thirty-eight others. If they crossed the street, only six feet wide, they would be in the Yohanan ben Zakkai Synagogue, which sheltered 800 civilians. No firm promise of relief within twenty-four hours came from the New City, so at last the remaining Haganah commanders and the rabbis decided the time had come to surrender.

On this morning of May 28, Rabbi Ben Zion Hazan Ireq, a tall, bearded, black-robed man of seventy-two, came hobbling out of the ruins with a cane in one hand and a sheet on a pole in the other. He was accompanied by eighty-six-year-old Israel Ze'ev Mintzberg, who was draped from head to foot in a long, black cape. They emerged from the devastated shambles to begin negotiations with Captain Abdullah el Tel of the Arab Legion. Although the Arabs wanted unconditional surrender, Abdullah el Tel agreed to discuss terms. Rabbi Hazan went back into the ruins. After three hours a formal Jewish delegation returned. After confused discussions, interrupted at one point by the capture of the Jews returning to the Quarter, the Legion agreed on the terms. The old men, women, and children would be allowed through to the New City and all others would be treated as prisoners of war. At 3:25 P.M., the Jews accepted the terms.

The Arabs had taken the Quarter, but their prize was a smoking heap of smashed buildings, charred wood and ruined temples. When the Jews stumbled out into the open, the officers of the Arab Legion were shocked to see only a handful of defenders and a pitiful collection of arms. One Legion officer told his new captives, "If we had known that this is what you fought with, we would have beaten you with sticks. In fact, you cheated us into granting terms of surrender after you had been defeated completely."[11]

The end of Jewish resistance in the Old City on May 28 was also the signal for the end of any major fighting in Jerusalem. Although both the Arabs and the Jews carried out a few limited operations to straighten defense lines or seize minor strong points, the major area of battle shifted to the corridor. In Jerusalem the Haganah did not have the resources to mount a serious offensive, and Glubb did not have the reserves to continue the street fighting and also meet a new Jewish challenge to his positions overlooking the Tel Aviv road. The city would have to wait on the result of the fighting in the Judean Mountains to discover its fate. In the New City the problem of supplies had again grown critical. Meat, cheese, and eggs were almost nonexistent. Even bread, the main staple, was scarce. The daily caloric ration hovered near 900, a starvation diet. On June 9, the stock of bread was only 42,600 loaves for the entire city—six ounces a person for three days. The water ration had dwindled to six quarts a day distributed by official trucks. All fuel had been commandeered for military and hospital use, leaving the public without transportation, cooking facilities and, usually, electricity. By June 3, the fuel remaining was only three tons of fuel oil, 600 gallons of gasoline, and thirty-seven tins of kerosene. Life in the city had to come to a halt. Only the official food shops were open and then only for a few hours a day. The population waited at home, hungry, uncertain and bored.

Despite their hardships, most of the civilians managed to maintain their spirits. Although Jerusalem's Jewish population was a strange mixture—ultra-orthodox sects, recent arrivals from displaced persons camps, socialist reformers, native-born *Sabras,* illiterate Oriental immigrants—they all felt a unity of purpose, a conviction that they must stay in the city or die. Ben Gurion's decision that there was to be no retreat, however great the military necessity, meshed with the conviction of the Jerusalem civilians that no retreat was possible. Jews had been running for too many centuries; now they would stay in their own land. For most, the siege was a time of passive suffering, for they could contribute little to the defense of the city. They could only wait for news of relatives, wait for the broadcast of the Voice of Jerusalem to give them news of the war. They had to suffer the Arab artillery bombardment in silence with only the occasional sound of a *Davidka* mortar to encourage them. They had to listen to the sound of firing all around them without being able to help the Haganah. Every week 10,000 artillery shells dropped into the city. Every week the toll of fatalities rose. The endurance of the civilians was not, however, sufficient of itself to prolong the siege. All their stoic bravery would be wasted if the food supplies gave out. A tiny erratic airlift, using small one-engined planes, was of little help. Dov Joseph regularly informed Ben Gurion of the worsening food supply. If the corridor could not be opened, Jerusalem was going to starve. On the other side of the hill, Glubb and Abdullah, too, knew that despite their failure to take the city by storm, success was still possible if the Legion's hold on the heights above the Tel Aviv road could be maintained.

Ben Gurion ordered an attack on the Arab position at Latrun, where the Legion's Fourth Regiment was holding a mountain spur over the coastal plain which dominated traffic on the western stretch of the highway. The Haganah High Command pointed out that there were no troops and no time to prepare such an operation. Ben Gurion insisted. There were to be no excuses, no delays. If there were no troops, then they must be found. The Haganah's Chief of Operations, Yigael Yadin, knew that a hasty piecemeal attack was almost hopeless, but Ben Gurion would accept no alternative—the need was too great. Within forty-eight hours Yadin organized the new Seventh Brigade out of new immigrants, equipped it at the last minute with recently arrived equipment, and, on May 25, sent it into action against the Legion at Latrun. The attack, made by poorly armed civilians in broad daylight under accurate Arab fire, of course failed. The corridor remained closed. Encouraged by its success, the Legion captured a strategic height near the eastern end of the road. It held the hill against Haganah counter-attacks but could not advance farther to close another stretch of road. Still its position at Latrun kept the corridor sealed. Ben Gurion demanded another attack on Latrun.

Additional reinforcements and equipment were scraped together. Ben Gurion also appointed a single commander for the Jerusalem front, Colonel David "Mickey" Marcus, an American volunteer, who had already led a series of successful commando raids against the Egyptians. Marcus, a graduate of West Point who had served on General Eisenhower's staff in Europe, was one of the men Ben Gurion hoped would turn the Haganah into a regular army. Because of the threat to Jerusalem, there was no time for anything but another hurried attack with untrained troops. Even with Marcus and additional men, the second assault on Latrun was also a makeshift operation. Heavy Arab fire disheartened the green infantry troops, who failed to follow up the success of the armor. Marcus cabled Yadin: "I was there, saw battle. Plan good. Artillery good. Armor excellent. Infantry disgraceful."[12] The second battle of Latrun was over and the road to Jerusalem remained closed. The newly created Seventh Brigade had been badly battered, with 137 men killed between May 24 and May 31.

Although the Haganah commanders were justly discouraged, Ben Gurion felt that the two attacks had eroded the offensive capacity of the Legion. In this he was probably right, for King Abdullah could not afford to have the major prop of his regime enfeebled by huge losses. The Legion was more important than victories or even, in the last analysis, Jerusalem. Without the Legion, Abdullah's entire position in the Arab world would be undermined. Although both Abdullah and Glubb continued to worry about the heavy losses of the Legion, they were encouraged by the two battles of Latrun. Despite these major Israeli efforts, the corridor to the coast remained closed. If the Legion could hang on, Jerusalem would be starved out. The Arabs would probably have been less confident of Jerusalem's fate if they had known of the discovery made by three young Israeli soldiers.

Late in May, three men of the Harel Brigade, who had been granted leave in Jerusalem, attempted to make their way on foot to their homes on the coast. They found that they could walk through the Judean Mountains down to the coastal plain along a fairly satisfactory trail. On June 1, a company from the Harel Brigade followed the same path and later a jeep was sent over the route to see if it could be used for vehicular traffic. Engineers felt that eventually only a few hundred yards of the path just east of Bet Susin, where there was a four-hundred-foot rise, would still be impassable, so the Israeli High Command decided to turn the dirt path into a secret road. For twenty-four hours a day, 500 workers labored, often under artillery fire, to transform the trail into Israel's Burma Road. Almost from the first day, troops and then mule trains began moving supplies into Jerusalem. Later, trucks from Jerusalem arrived at the edge of the remaining three impassable miles. From the other direction convoys drove until the road disappeared and then their supplies were transferred to a forty-mule train. The mules moved up the final three miles. Here a human conveyor belt of 200 men carried forty-five pound sacks twice a night to the Jerusalem trucks. Eventually all the road was opened to trucks, except that in one direction, at the steep rise, the vehicles had to be pulled up by a bulldozer. Despite the limitations of this Burma Road, supplies moving into Jerusalem soon averaged 100 tons a night. The fear of starvation vanished. What the Seventh Brigade had failed to accomplish in front of Latrun had been managed by the construction of the secret road. Although the corridor remained sealed at Latrun, Jerusalem was no longer cut off.

Even with the Burma Road operational, Ben Gurion remained anxious to seize Latrun and open up normal highway traffic into Jerusalem before the United Nations efforts to secure a truce were successful. After three weeks of disappointments and setbacks, the Arab states were showing an increasing willingness to consider the truce which the diplomats back at Lake Success hoped would put an end to the Palestine war. Neither the Arabs nor the Jews considered the proposed truce as more than a pause to prepare for another round of fighting, but both felt the need for such a breathing space in order to regroup. Realizing that the cease-fire was imminent, Ben Gurion prodded his commanders to make one more effort to take Latrun. On June 9, the Israelis attacked from the rear, but had to withdraw from their advance positions. On June 10, the Legion successfully counterattacked, seizing the important Jewish settlement of Gezer. On the last day before the truce, the Israelis recaptured Gezer, but were unable to organize another full-scale attack on Latrun. Time had run out.

Just a few hours before the truce deadline, the last man was killed on the Jerusalem front. An Israeli sentry, who spoke little Hebrew and less English, challenged a white-sheeted figure in front of brigade headquarters. The man's reply was inaudible. The sentry challenged again. When the man did not give the password, the sentry fired. Mickey Marcus fell dead just a little over six hours before the cease-fire became effective, a tragic end to the four weeks of war. Yet, despite Marcus' death, despite the continued Legion stranglehold on Latrun, despite the fall of the Jewish Quarter of the Old City, Israel had carried out a series of successful defensive actions and then an increasing number of offensive operations.

In the south, the Egyptian Army, uncertain as to the strength of the Haganah, had moved slowly up the coast to Isdud, twenty miles south of Tel Aviv. Here the advance halted while the Egyptians sought to consolidate their position in the Negev desert and southern Palestine. Although they did gain control of several vital arterial highways, the stubborn defense of the individual settlements prevented the Egyptians from securing more than a deadlock.

In the north, attacks by the Lebanese, Syrians, and Iraqis had failed to smash through the Israeli defenses, and, by the first week of June, the Arab armies had been forced back. The Haganah occupied the entire coast from Isdud to the Lebanese border and much of central Galilee. The Arab forces holding the central triangle, Jenin–Tulkarem–Nablus, had been hard pressed to maintain their positions, much less drive on to Haifa and the sea. In the center, the Arab Legion had been unable to force the Jewish positions in Jerusalem, unable to prevent the construction of the Burma Road, and barely able to hang on to Latrun. By the first week of June, each Arab commander felt his position to be precarious. Each demanded vast additions in men and material. For their part, the Jewish brigades were decimated and their supplies depleted. Both sides determined to use the truce to make good their deficiencies and prepare for the next round.

The twenty-eight days of peace which began on June 11 were the result of the intensive efforts by the United Nations to end the Arab-Israel war. Early efforts to force the belligerents to agree to a truce had failed when the British delegate, Sir Alexander Cadogan, showed considerable reluctance to admit the existence of a breach of the peace. After all, every competent British observer had assured London that its Arab allies would give the Jews a bad buffeting. One positive step had been taken on May 21. Count Folke Bernadotte, President of the Swedish Red Cross, accepted a United Nations appointment as Mediator. His opportunities to mediate would be limited until either the United Nations could agree on a line of action or the Jews and Arabs showed evidence of moderation. Days went by at Lake Success without any sign that the Arabs intended to agree to a truce or that the British were willing to support sanctions to enforce such a truce. Bernadotte arrived in Cairo on May 29 to urge a truce, but the Arabs still showed little interest in a cease-fire. Finally, on June 1, the Arabs agreed to a truce on June 3; but when the deadline came, they continued fighting. At last, in view of the increasing United Nations pressure and their own worsening military position, the Arabs agreed to a cease-fire effective at six o'clock on the morning of June 11. After four weeks, peace had come to the Holy Land. Bernadotte hoped to freeze the war for four weeks while he discovered a peaceful solution. Neither the Arabs nor the Jews believed in the possibility of such a solution. The Arabs remained convinced that somehow they could destroy Israel and create an Arab Palestine by military means. The Jews remained determined to defend their state until the Arabs accepted the fact of Israel. As a result the peace that came to Palestine was a façade that cloaked hectic preparations for renewing the war.

For Israel the truce had come like "dew from Heaven,"[13] giving the troops time to rest and regroup. The Jewish world-wide secret supply network now had an opportunity to ship in additional heavy equipment and material. The civilian population had a few weeks to recuperate from the anxieties and dangers of war. At army headquarters in Tel Aviv, Ben Gurion pushed through his plans to reorganize the Haganah and Palmach along regular army lines despite the objections of many of his officers. The new Israeli army, the Zahal, officially created on May 28, gradually evolved into a modern military machine instead of a collection of independent brigades. Despite bitter dissension and several unaccepted resignations from his commanders, Ben Gurion got his way. On June 21, Ben Gurion forced a showdown with the dissident Irgun over the distribution of arms from the Irgun ship *Altalena*. Fighting broke out between the Zahal and the Irgun. For a few hours the possibility of civil war loomed before the Irgun gave in. Whatever the cost in bitterness, Ben Gurion felt that by smashing the Irgun he had assured the continuation of the war "under a single authority and with an Army united."[14]

By July 9, the Zahal had been united under a single command and the capacity of the Irgun for independent action had been broken. The most striking change in Israel, however, was the vastly increased personnel and equipment of the armed forces. An air force, including four-engined bombers, had come into existence. Heavy artillery and tanks were available. The number of troops had been increased from around 25,000 on May 15 to nearly 60,000 on July 9. Although the army was not yet as well equipped as several of the Arab armies, the disparity was no longer so appalling; moreover, the Zahal now had a three-to-two ratio in the number of troops in Palestine. With a united, reorganized army, vastly increased in size and adequately equipped, Ben Gurion could look to the future with confidence.

The rapid and encouraging changes in the army were not as noticeable to the Jews in Jerusalem nor was the respite in the siege as tranquil as had been hoped. The ravages of the long bombardment were visible on all sides—smashed houses, rubble in the streets, dangling wires. With the former frontlines twisting between houses and across streets, a total cease-fire was almost impossible. Sniping became a city-wide sport. Bursts of firing were regular. By June 24, Dov Joseph reported thirty-six breaches of the peace to the United Nations Truce Commission composed of the consular officials of the United States, France and Belgium. The Truce Commission had its share of complaints from the Arabs as well. With its ambiguous position and limited personnel, the Commission could do little about the truce violations except keep score as the incidents continued. The Israeli authorities had difficulties with the Commission's interpretation of what could and what could not be brought in over the Tel Aviv highway. Within a few days, the Jewish authorities had been almost permanently alienated by the Commission's actions.

> *The Truce Commission, determined that no stocks of food should be built up, had apparently decided that if Jewish Jerusalem was in a state of near starvation at the beginning of the truce, that is how they would have to be at the end of it. . . . In the last analysis it boiled down to the point of view of the Truce Commission, and one regrettably had to recognize the fact that this body in practice showed partiality toward the Arab side and allowed them in effect to dictate the course the Commission should follow.*[15]

However distasteful the United Nations Commission's interpretation of its duty might have been to the Jews, they paid as little attention to the restrictions as possible. Despite the Commission's efforts to freeze the food situation by limiting the number of convoys using the Tel Aviv road, the food crisis gradually lessened. While the "legal" convoys under strict supervision moved over the regular highway, additional supplies arrived by way of the Burma Road. Although food was not plentiful, the population did have a more normal diet. Elsewhere there was a relative return to peacetime. Limited bus service resumed. The blackout was lifted. The Ohel Theater Company arrived and gave two performances. Electricity, as well as mail and telegraph service, was again available. There was, however, no great influx of soldiers and equipment. The Israeli High Command intended to use its new forces in a major offensive action elsewhere rather than commit them to street fighting in Jerusalem. Although Zahal headquarters expected the Jerusalem commander to mount local attacks, its attention was focused elsewhere. The major task of Jerusalem would again be to hold on while the army defeated the Arabs outside the city. For the civilian population, holding on appeared much less a challenge than it had on May 15. They were quietly confident of the outcome of the next round.

> *Well, I held out in spite of all that they could do to me when we were cut off, unprepared and almost without weapons. Now we have the Burma Road, our armies are stronger, we know the worst they can do and it is not enough to subdue us.*[16]

Although Israel felt that the opportunities opened to the Zahal by a renewal of the war would be considerable, the leaders at Tel Aviv, for diplomatic reasons, agreed to continue the truce. The Arab leaders, however, felt that their prestige would be fatally compromised without a renewal of the war. No longer did even the most enthusiastic hope to drive the Jews into the sea. Now their ambitions were limited to securing some advantage, some tactical gain, on which to base a claim of victory. Syria hoped for a foothold in eastern Galilee. Egypt counted on holding on to the Negev. Iraq and the Arab Liberation Army wanted one victory. Abdullah depended on the Legion to retain "his" half of Jerusalem and a slice of central Palestine. To secure their "victories" the Arabs reinforced their armies, bringing the number of troops up to about 40,000. New equipment was moved in despite the restrictions of the truce. As usual, however, efforts to form a united command or agree on a joint plan of attack failed. Once more the Arab armies would fight as independent units. Once more each army would be committed to battle for narrow national interest. This time, however, few Arab commanders hoped for more than a successful defensive campaign.

The Zahal High Command felt confident that within a few weeks the Arab armies could be driven back, perhaps entirely out of Palestine. The Arabs simply had failed to put enough troops in the field to stop the Zahal. At best they would have to sue for peace to keep a toehold in Palestine. The one factor the Zahal commanders tended to overlook was time. They felt that once the Arabs renewed the war, the United Nations would not be able to impose a truce in time to prevent them from defeating the Arabs. Their belief was encouraged by the endless rounds of discussions and delays at Lake Success when the fighting resumed.

Now, in the north, bitter fighting around the Syrian bridgehead failed to dislodge the Arabs, but it sharply limited the Syrians to a small wedge. In central Galilee, the revived Arab Liberation Army was defeated and the area around Nazareth occupied. In the south, the Zahal prevented the Egyptians from consolidating their grip on the Negev by a bitter defense of key settlements. It was in the center, however, that the main Israeli blow fell. A heavy attack north of the corridor quickly overran the Arab cities of Latrun and Ramleh and moved into the surrounding hills by July 12. The entire Arab position on the central front was badly shaken. By the next evening, however, the Israeli High Command realized that a serious error had been committed in ignoring the deliberations of the United Nations. Once the news of the fall of Latrun and Ramleh reached British ears, demands for an immediate truce began. Instead of having unlimited time to carry out their operation in the center in careful, well-prepared steps, the Zahal was forced to accomplish as much as possible before the inevitable truce. Operations both on the central front and in the Jerusalem area became a race against the United Nations clock as the Arabs scrambled to accept a truce and stave off total disaster.

In Jerusalem, Colonel Shaltiel had been given three objectives: first, the villages of Malha and Ein Karem as a base for a joint action with Harel Brigade in the west to seize the railway to the coast; second, the Old City; and third, the Sheik Jarrah Quarter, which would reopen a way to Mount Scopus. Because of Jerusalem's isolated position, the reorganization and resupplying of the available troops had gone forward slowly. Shaltiel, assuming he would have plenty of time, had not been in any particular hurry; in any case, the early results of his attack had been encouraging. On July 13, a youth unit of Zahal captured Malha. Four days later, Israeli units occupied Ein Karem. Coupled with the gains made in the capture of Latrun and Ramleh, the result was a broad corridor, including the railroad line. By the time Shaltiel had secured his first objective, however, the chances of taking the other two had faded. By July 14, it was obvious that a truce was in prospect and might be enforced in Jerusalem earlier than in other parts of Palestine. Shaltiel decided to undertake immediate operations to capture Sheik Jarrah Quarter and the Old City. Simultaneously the local commander of the Arab Legion decided to reopen hostilities in the Jerusalem area despite Glubb's contention that the battle around Latrun was the key to the center. On July 18, the Legion attacked from the north, seizing the Mandlebaum buildings and some houses south of the Damascus Gate. Determined Israeli counterattacks succeeded only in reoccupying some of the houses. The Legion attacks around the Damascus Gate succeeded not only in some local Arab gains but, more important, in throwing out of gear Shaltiel's offensive plans.

On July 16, Ben Gurion informed Shaltiel that the truce would be imposed in Jerusalem at 5:45 the following morning. The Israeli Chief of Operations, Yadin, immediately ordered Shaltiel to carry out both the attack on Sheik Jarrah Quarter and on the Old City; but if there were not time for both, he should limit his offensive to the Sheik Jarrah area. Shaltiel decided instead to attempt Operation *Kedem,* the capture of the Old City by frontal attack. Some Irgun units managed to advance a few yards into the Old City through the New Gate but could not capture the Collège des Frères, which dominated their wedge, before dawn and had to withdraw. Despite a heavy preparatory artillery barrage joined by *Davidka* mortars and machine guns, Hish military units attacking the Zion Gate were equally unsuccessful. The explosive charge laid beside the four-foot-thick outer wall of the Old City failed to make more than a dent. Thus, Operation *Kedem,* hastily attempted at the last minute, was a failure. Although bitter fighting continued for two more days around the Mandlebaum Houses despite the new cease-fire, the second truce stabilized the front line to the east of Jerusalem where it had been on July 9, before the ten days of fighting had begun. Jerusalem remained divided; but, with the broadening of the corridor, the clearing of the railroad, and the rapid construction of alternative highways, the city was no longer cut off from the coast.

In fact, the Arabs could feel fortunate that they still held on to the eastern quarters of the city. The Israeli offensive against the Arab Legion had threatened to drive on through Latrun and toward the Jordan River, cutting Arab Palestine in half and leaving Jerusalem to be mopped up at leisure. Given time, Shaltiel's attacks within the city had an excellent chance of driving out the Arabs through repeated frontal assaults. The Legion had been stretched very thin and only its determined resistance at Latrun and Shaltiel's late start had prevented Israel from securing a military solution to the Palestine problem during the ten days.

Even after the two abortive attempts to secure a solution by force had been called off by the United Nations, neither the Arabs nor the Jews could foresee any possible diplomatic compromise. Despite their military failures, the Arabs remained convinced that somehow they could reverse their fortunes. Each state sought to find the cause of failure among its allies. Transjordan had withdrawn from Latrun and Ramleh. Lebanon had avoided battle. Egypt had refused to co-operate. Treason was suspected and duplicity assumed. As a result, the Arab leaders could not bring themselves to believe that the initiative had passed to Israel despite the gloomy reports of their military commanders. Their armies were again reinforced and partially re-equipped; once again, however, the unending recriminations and the age-old mistrust prevented a united military command. Divided and uncertain, the Arabs waited.

On the other side of the truce line, the Zahal redoubled preparations until, by October, there were nearly 80,000 well-equipped troops under arms. These were supported by an effective air force and a small navy. Arms shipments were now limited only by the ability of the state to pay for them. The country was united and confident. Nation after nation extended diplomatic recognition. Immigrants flowed into Israel in ever-increasing numbers. Normal administrative services and commercial activities resumed. Yet there was no peace. Though Ben Gurion had a modern army, he could not force the Arabs to make peace so long as the truce continued. More frustrating, the truce had not brought a solution any nearer or even lessened tensions. The Arabs, fearful of renewing the war but reluctant to admit defeat, would not consider further negotiations. Week after week, the truce dragged on. The Arab armies remained in Palestine. The Arab leaders refused to withdraw or to attack. In the exposed settlements, particularly in the Negev, the truce was merely hiding a limited war, a war of sniping and raids in which Israel's heavy offensive potential was useless.

In Jerusalem, cut down the center by the cease-fire line, the United Nations appeared unable to prevent this border fighting. General Glubb later noted that during the cease-fire "the situation was not unlike that on a quiet sector in France in 1916 or 1917. On neither side did the troops come out of their positions to attack, but both sides fired periodically."[17] At times fire from rifles or mortars along the truce line would be local and sporadic; at other times firing would spread rapidly along the entire line and continue for hours before dying down. Occasionally, one side or the other would begin an artillery or mortar bombardment in retaliation for a previous bombardment. Soon it was impossible to determine the "guilty" party since both sides pursued an aggressive cease-fire. The regular Tel Aviv road remained blocked by the Arab Legion despite the truce conditions. Israeli units occupied a height overlooking the Arab-held road into Latrun and harassed traffic despite the truce. The water pipeline into Jerusalem was cut when the Arabs blew up the pumping station at Latrun. The Israelis attacked an Arab-held ridge overlooking Government House. The Legion attacked a Jewish outpost on Mount Scopus. Difficulties arose over supposedly demilitarized areas, over Jewish access to the Holy Places in the Old City, and over the water supply. Both sides, with ample justification, accused the other of bad faith, of constant violations, of aggression. On August 18, Bernadotte reported that "not only has firing practically never ceased but the situation is gradually getting out of hand."[18]

When the Arabs blew up the Latrun pumping station on August 12, Ben Gurion had felt that he had the excuse needed to end the phony truce and renew the war. The High Command prepared operational plans for a new offensive; however, the majority of the members of the Government, fearing international repercussions, preferred to wait. The offensive was postponed. Tension all along the Legion front grew as the situation in Jerusalem became explosive. Rumors of a proposed Arab attack on September 15 were released to foreign correspondents by "informed Israelis." On September 15, observers "learned" that the Arab attack was postponed until September 21. The long-predicted next round seemed only days away.

On September 17, Bernadotte flew into Jerusalem from Damascus to seek a lessening of the tension. The commanders of the Arab Legion felt that the situation in Jerusalem was so dangerous that the Mediator should either postpone visiting the city or else accept an armored escort. Bernadotte refused and drove into Jerusalem, crossing over to the Jewish New City for lunch with United Nations observers at the YMCA. After lunch, the Mediator's convoy of three cars drove to the old Government House, which was being considered as the location for the United Nations headquarters in Palestine. There were no incidents. The truce line was quiet.

After the inspection the United Nations party drove back through the Katamon quarter. An Israeli Army jeep, parked across the road, forced the convoy to halt. Since the four men in the jeep appeared to be wearing the uniform of the Zahal, the United Nations drivers assumed that they had reached an official Israeli checkpoint. Three of the men got out of the jeep and began walking down the row of cars, one on one side and two on the other. They reached Bernadotte's car, the last in line. The officials in the car thought that the Israelis were about to ask for their passes; instead, when the men reached the Mediator's car, one opened fire at Bernadotte with an automatic pistol held at point-blank range. The other two riddled the tires and radiators of the three cars to prevent pursuit. All three assassins then leaped back into the jeep, which disappeared around a corner. French Colonel Serot, sitting next to the Mediator, was killed instantly, hit seventeen times. Count Bernadotte, hit six times, died a few minutes after he was brought into the hospital.

The next day the members of the Stern Group appeared to be involved. There was also evidence that the murder was an individual act of terror. An unknown group called the Fatherland Front claimed that they had killed Bernadotte because he was a British agent. Whoever had been specifically guilty, few doubted that Israel would be held responsible. World opinion was horrified at the assassination of Bernadotte. Opinion in Israel, however, glutted on terror and immune to violence, was less sensitive. Many had thought the Mediator was a tool of the British, an enemy to Israel. His proposal of June 27 would have turned Jerusalem over to the Arabs despite the fact that the Legion had been unable to take the city by force. To many others his plans and suggestions had seemed to be mainly motivated by a desire to please Great Britain. By September 1948, the prestige of the United Nations and Bernadotte had reached an all-time low in Israel. While there was little nation-wide outcry that the assassination was a criminal act, there was very deep concern over the possible consequences. Fear of international retaliation rather than horror at the murder was the prevailing emotion. In the midst of war, all had grown hardened to sudden death. Officially, however, the response of the Israeli Government was immediate and proper. Ben Gurion arrested hundreds of suspects and outlawed the Stern Group. The assassins were never found despite Ben Gurion's efforts. Public interest faded as it became clear that the United Nations did not intend to take punitive action. An American, Dr. Ralph Bunche, took over as Acting Mediator and the truce continued as before.

Ben Gurion's determination to achieve a solution by battle was intensified by the publication of Bernadotte's final proposals. The Bernadotte Report, completed at his headquarters on the island of Rhodes before his fatal trip to Jerusalem, gave the Negev to the Arabs, Galilee to Israel, and made Jerusalem an international zone. The only alternative Ben Gurion could see to accepting a United Nations compromise along the lines of Bernadotte's last will and testament was to change the existing situation by renewing hostilities. All Bernadotte's suggested boundaries were closely based on the military frontiers. If the United Nations delegates were suddenly presented with the *fait accompli* of new military frontiers, advantageous to Israel, there was a good chance they would have to recognize them. Thus Ben Gurion felt that the truce would have to be broken before Israel lost Jerusalem and the Negev when the cease-fire lines were frozen into international boundaries. Although he continued to believe that the war would be decided on the central front—the security of the corridor and of Jerusalem remained his *idée fixe*—the High Command persuaded him to attack the Egyptians and ease the desperate situation of the isolated Negev settlements. In the south the Egyptians' hold on the major highways and their continued attacks on the settlements threatened to undermine Israel's position. Since the situation in Jerusalem and the corridor appeared stabilized despite the uneasy truce, Ben Gurion agreed on Operation *Ten Plagues* to open a way into the Negev and damage the offensive potential of the Egyptian Army.

On October 16, after a carefully prepared incident—the Egyptians, as was their custom, fired on a "legal" convoy—had taken place under the eyes of United Nations observers, the operation began. By October 22, despite complications, unforeseen difficulties, and at times determined Egyptian resistance, Operation *Ten Plagues* had broken the Egyptian hold on the Negev in one of the most brilliant battles of the war. The Egyptians were left in Palestine with only two truncated fingers of territory, one along the coast and the other terminating in the small desert village of Auja. Worse for the Egyptians, 2,500 of their men were cut off and surrounded in the Faluja pocket. Farther north the collapse of the Egyptian front had opened up the area around Hebron and Bethlehem to Israeli occupation. Only the prompt arrival of the still "neutral" troops of the Arab Legion prevented Israel from occupying all Palestine south of Jerusalem. Ben Gurion did not want to risk broadening the war by firing on the Legion, since rumors had already reached him that King Abdullah was considering beginning armistice negotiations. The Legion was allowed to keep what it could occupy before the Israelis arrived. Again uneasy truce settled down in the south where the Zahal in bitter fighting mopped up the loose ends of the *Ten Plagues*.

In a masterpiece of mistiming, the Arab Liberation Army renewed offensive operations in Galilee on the very day, October 22, the truce was renewed in the Negev. The Zahal High Command seized the opportunity and hurriedly prepared Operation *Hiram*, the occupation of all Galilee. In view of the reluctance of the other Arab states to aid the Egyptians during Operation *Ten Plagues*, Ben Gurion felt relatively confident that the Arab Liberation Army could be finished off without the other Arab armies intervening. He proved an excellent prophet. The Zahal opened operations on October 28. The Arabs watched from the sidelines. In sixty hours, the Jews had occupied all Galilee except for the tiny Syrian wedge. The Arab Liberation Army had been reduced to scattered groups of fleeing refugees. The war in the north was over.

Once again the scene shifted to the diplomats as the British attempted to win back at the bargaining table what the Arabs had lost on the battlefield. On November 4, the British persuaded a majority of the Security Council to vote for the withdrawal of the aggressive Israeli forces, but Acting Mediator Bunche managed to arrange a compromise at the last minute which allowed Israel to keep its garrisons in the occupied territory although its mobile forces had to be withdrawn. Despite considerable British displeasure, the compromise, which in effect recognized the Israeli gains as legal, stood.

Closer to home, Israel could watch with equal pleasure the rapidly deteriorating relations between its Arab enemies. On October 1, the Mufti had become president of an All-Palestine Government in an open Egyptian move to thwart King Abdullah's ambition to annex central Palestine. The Mufti's phantom government, isolated in Egyptian-held Gaza, in no way limited Abdullah's plans. The splits in the Arab world, previously hidden, were now revealed to all.

Yet despite the Arabs' problems and the British diplomatic failure in the United Nations, despite the success of *Ten Plagues* and *Hiram*, a final solution seemed as far away as ever. No Arab leader felt sufficiently secure to explain the hopeless military situation to the Arab populations. No one dared to treat with the Jews or to withdraw from Palestine. The United Nations had imposed a cease-fire, but found that it could not impose a solution. Once more the truce dragged on. Bitter fighting took place in the Negev. The endless incidents continued in Jerusalem.

During November, Transjordan took the first tentative step toward disengagement by allowing Lieutenant-Colonel Abdullah el Tel of the Arab Legion, who had arranged the surrender of the Jewish Quarter of the Old City, to conclude a "sincere cease-fire" for Jerusalem with Colonel Moshe Dayan. On December 1 this bilateral truce became effective. For the first time in almost exactly a year the firing in Jerusalem tapered off and stopped. The city at last was quiet. Abdullah, however, felt that he could not make the first move in any armistice negotiations with Israel. He had already strained the bounds of Arab "unity" too far for many of his subjects. The hundreds of thousands of Arab refugees crowded into Legion-occupied territory were too inflammable for him to risk antagonizing them. Someone else would have to take the next step. The other Arab states, however, saw no need to seek negotiations. Lebanon was too small and no longer had troops in Palestine. Syria wanted to keep its small wedge of Israeli territory. Iraq had no common boundary with Palestine. Egypt, the largest and most powerful of the Arab states, with its army intact and still occupying part of Palestine, informed Bunche that Cairo would not consider negotiation. Israel again decided to force the issue by beginning a new offensive in the south against Egypt which would give King Farouk in Cairo the dubious alternative of accepting total military defeat or of beginning armistice talks.

On the afternoon of December 22, the new offensive, Operation *Ayin*, began with a heavy artillery barrage, followed by a series of probing attacks. Within a week the Egyptian Army was stumbling back, battered and disorganized. Cairo learned that the entire army was on the verge of being surrounded inside Egypt at El 'Arîsh. On the evening of December 29, the commander of Operation *Ayin*,

Yigael Alon, stood on a sand dune three miles south of El 'Arîsh, secure in the knowledge that within twenty-four hours the entire Egyptian Army would be in the bag. Once more diplomatic considerations prevented an outright Israeli victory. The United Nations Security Council passed a resolution ordering an immediate cease-fire. Great Britain unilaterally demanded that Israel get out of Egypt or face British intervention. Although Alon was forced to withdraw, Ben Gurion permitted him to mount a frontal assault against the Egyptians at Rafah on the Palestine border.

By January 6, once again all Alon needed was twenty-four hours to push his wedge through to the sea and capture the Egyptians. In Cairo the Egyptian Government was in a state of near panic. King Farouk's personal airplane stood by to fly him to the Suez Canal Zone. The British Army prepared to occupy Cairo and Alexandria in case of civil war. No one knew what the mobs would do when they found out that the Jews had won. Time had run out at last for the Arab cause. Cairo announced that Egypt was willing to enter armistice discussions at the Mediator's headquarters on Rhodes. Despite one last incident, when five British fighters were shot down over Israel, the war was over. Operation *Ayin* had cleared the Negev and forced the Egyptians to make peace. The other Arab states would follow, publicly reluctant but secretly relieved.

In Jerusalem the "sincere cease-fire" and the news from the Negev brought hope that peace might return to the Holy City. The population realized that their future had gradually fallen into the hands of the diplomats rather than the soldiers. It became increasingly clear that King Abdullah, knowing he would have to fight alone, had no intention of allowing the Arab Legion to face the full might of the Zahal. When he felt the diplomatic situation opportune, he would undoubtedly sign an armistice. Such an armistice, however, would be little more than a permanent cease-fire. Without a final treaty, the ultimate fate of the city would remain ambiguous. For nearly a year the United Nations had insisted that the final decision on Jerusalem would be made at Lake Success and not in Palestine. One proposal after another had been suggested, quickly modified in view of events in Palestine, and then discarded. Bernadotte had first suggested that the city be turned over to the Arabs and then later urged internationalization. Many Roman Catholics as well as influential Protestant and Orthodox institutions remained gravely concerned as to the future status of a city filled with shrines, churches and sanctuaries. All efforts to find an "international solution" so far had foundered on the determination of both Israel and Transjordan to keep what they occupied.

On December 5, 1948, Ben Gurion had publicly announced that

Israel would not give up Jerusalem willingly. King Abdullah, still secretly determined to annex the west bank of the Jordan and Arab Jerusalem, had been equally reluctant to consider internationalization. On February 14, 1949, the Israeli parliament, the Knesset, met for the first time in Jerusalem, underlining Israel's determination to incorporate Jerusalem as an integral part of the state. For his part Abdullah could not move as openly, for he still had not negotiated an armistice with Israel or calmed the anxiety of the Palestine Arabs on the west bank who still dreamed of an Arab state. On April 3, 1949, Transjordan finally signed an armistice after Abdullah had been prodded first by Israel's bloodless seizure of the southern tip of the Negev and then by the threat of one more Israeli offensive. Although the agreement was limited mainly to cease-fire conditions and military boundaries, the *de facto* division of Jerusalem was in effect recognized by both sides.

The armistice was an anticlimax. Despite the presence of Arab troops a few blocks away, the war in Jerusalem had long been over. The siege did not suddenly lift. There was no dramatic moment when the citizens were freed by the arrival of a long-awaited relief force. There had been no day of deliverance, but rather an almost imperceptible relaxation of tension, a day-by-day easing of the siege. By December 1, the first day of the "sincere cease-fire," Jewish Jerusalem had long been secure. The months of the troubled truce, the limited frontier war, had not been a siege, but rather a harrowing and distracting way of life. Even before the second truce, the fighting during the ten days had been an effort to extend the front lines, not to defend the city before an overwhelming attack. Even during the four weeks' truce, life had gradually returned to something resembling normal. Everyone had a feeling that the worst was over. By the spring of 1949, the memories of the siege, the public water trucks, the desperate food shortage, the unending artillery barrage, had faded into the daily routine of normal life. The Knesset had met. New immigrants arrived and were absorbed. New factories and apartments sprang up around the city. The Valour Road replaced the old Burma Road. Yet Jerusalem did not become just another city; for now there were two Jerusalems, separated by a barrier patrolled by hostile sentries and watched over by international observers. The barbed-wire entanglements of the cease-fire line, created by the armistice and accepted by both Arabs and Jews, remained as a constant reminder of the siege.

After the final armistice agreement had been signed with Syria on July 20, 1949, both the Arabs and the Jews had expected further negotiations under the auspices of the United Nations to lead to final treaties. This did not prove to be the case. The Arabs soon discovered that the United Nations could not force them to recognize Israel and so they preferred the status quo, a permanent armistice—no war, no peace. All the outstanding issues—the Arab refugees, alteration of boundaries, compensation, diplomatic recognition—remained unsolved. Only the status of Jerusalem, divided down the middle by a no man's land of control posts and pillboxes, was determined. On January 23, 1950, the Knesset proclaimed Jerusalem as the capital of Israel. On April 24, 1950, Transjordan formally annexed Arab Palestine west of the Jordan River, including the Arab sector of Jerusalem. Jerusalem officially became two cities. There would be no free access across the boundary. The Jewish Quarter of the Old City, the Wailing Wall and the temples, was closed to the Jews. The Hadassah Hospital-Hebrew University enclave on Mount Scopus gradually decayed into unused, dilapidated ruins. The Arabs who had fled from the Jews could not return to Israel. Jerusalem had become two closed compartments, a twin city divided not only by an international boundary but also by the fading memory of the long siege.

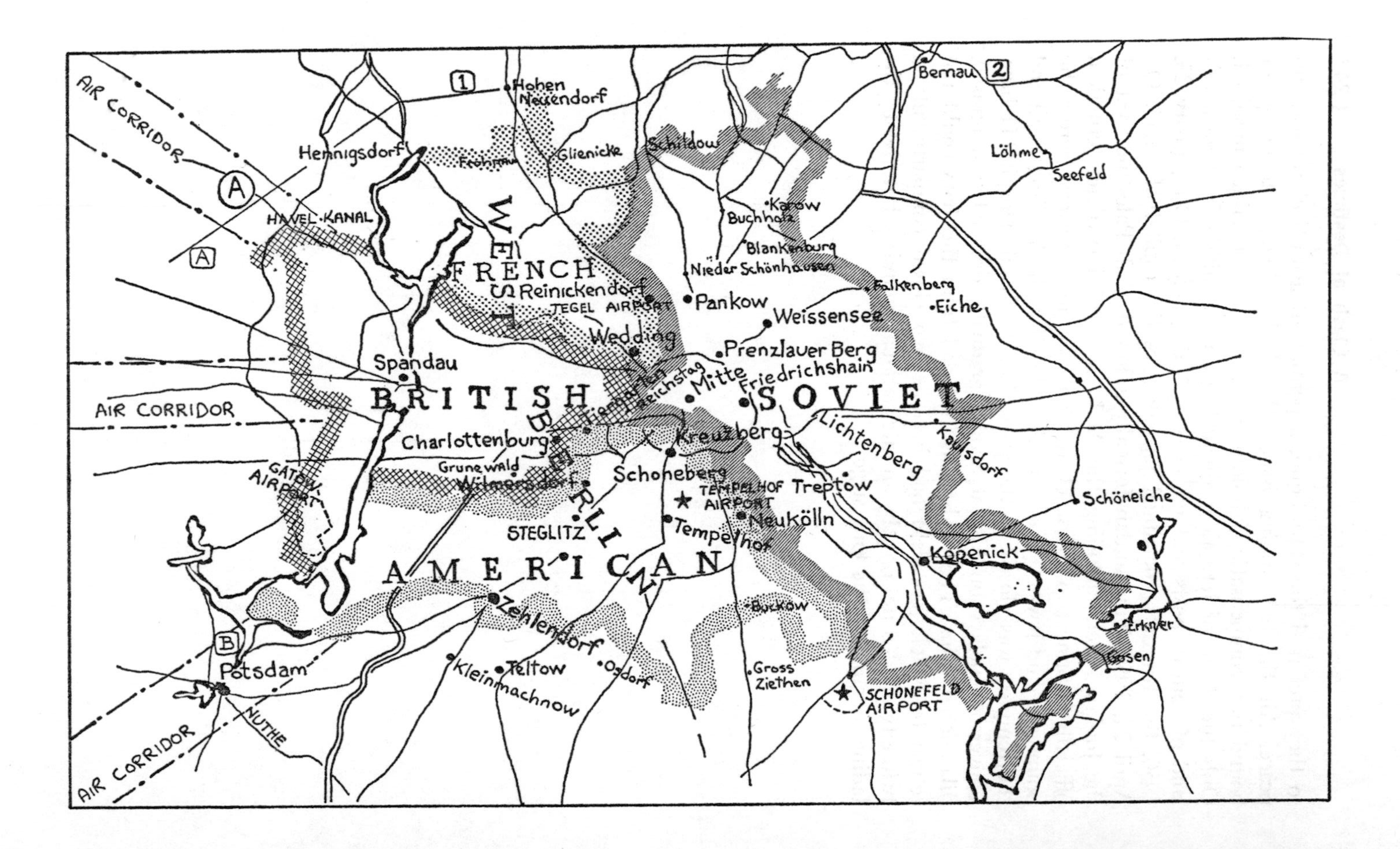
AIR CORRIDOR
A
A
HAVEL·KANAL
Hennigsdorf
1
Hohen Neuendorf
Frohnau
Glienicke
Schildow
Bernau
2
Löhme
Seefeld
Karow
Buchholz
Blankenburg
Nieder Schönhausen
Falkenberg
Eiche
WEST
FRENCH
Reinickendorf
TEGEL AIRPORT
Pankow
Weissensee
Wedding
Prenzlauer Berg
Friedrichshain
Spandau
Tiergarten
Reichstag
Mitte
BRITISH
SOVIET
AIR CORRIDOR
BERLIN
Charlottenburg
Kreuzberg
Lichtenberg
Kaulsdorf
Grunewald
Wilmersdorf
Schoneberg
TEMPELHOF AIRPORT
Treptow
Schöneiche
GATOW AIRPORT
Neukölln
Tempelhof
STEGLITZ
Kopenick
AMERICAN
Zehlendorf
Buckow
Erkner
B
Potsdam
Teltow
Osdorf
Gross Ziethen
Gosen
Kleinmachnow
SCHONEFELD AIRPORT
NUTHE
AIR CORRIDOR

7 BERLIN: 1945-1949

Siege by Diplomacy

If we withdraw, our position in Europe is threatened. If America does not understand this now, does not know that the issue is cast, then it never will and communism will run rampant. I believe the future of democracy requires us to stay . . .

—Lucius D. Clay

TO the great powers the Arab-Israel war remained a peripheral event of serious concern only because of the dangers of setting off a world conflict. Almost from the moment of victory over Germany, relations between the Western Allies and Soviet Russia had deteriorated into what journalists called the cold war, a confrontation without open battles. The most optimistic prophets had foreseen an era of peace after the bomb at Hiroshima, for war could no longer be profitable but only totally destructive. The less hopeful had, on the other hand, proposed a variety of new techniques and tactics for the armies of the future in an atomic war. Few had seen any open ground between a nuclear cataclysm and a sullen peace. Small nations and distant peoples might, like the Arabs and Jews, use conventional weapons in traditional battles, but the great powers had only a choice of total war or total peace. With the passing of time, the nature of the postwar challenges gradually became clearer to the new leaders of the Western world in Washington. Reluctantly and often haphazardly, the Truman Administration began to define America's interests and responsibilities.

The first harsh break with the Soviet Union came over the blockade of Berlin. There, for months, the West seemingly faced the alternatives of evacuation and humiliation or a war which could only be waged successfully with atomic means. More than any other event, the peaceful siege by blockade went far to disclose the nature of the Soviet threat and to define the means of Western defense. Out of Berlin would come the maxims and methods of cold-war policies, the military pacts, the economic programs, the diplomatic alignments, which would dominate world events for over a decade. For the West, the rules of a war without open battle, a struggle with limited means for narrow ends were first learned in Berlin.

IN August of 1945, after three months of peace, Berlin remained a vast and dismal ruin in which huddled three million stunned and apathetic Germans. The city had in its turn become, as had so many others in Europe, a lunar landscape of craters and caves, serried ruins, twisted cables and pipes, heaps of broken glass and mounds of crumbled bricks, pocked over with shallow graves. Only among the Allies, the occupying powers, could there be found activity or interest as they hammered out the formulas to govern the remains of the former Nazi capital. On August 15, news arrived from the other side of the world that the war with Japan had ended; after six years, peace had come to the entire world. The news of the Japanese surrender seemed to the British and Americans sufficient reason for a joint Allied victory parade down the Unter den Linden. The new Russian Supreme Commander in Germany, Marshal Georgi Zhukov, agreed enthusiastically and invited himself to give the appropriate speech. After some maneuvering all the ground rules were accepted, and the first Allied victory parade took place through the ruins of Berlin. Marshal Zhukov had draped himself in his most dazzlingly elaborate uniform, bespeckled with decorations and crisscrossed with stripes and sashes. General George Patton, representing General Eisenhower, wore, in contrast, simple battle dress. Almost at once Zhukov began maneuvering for the high ground—the dead center of the reviewing platform and one step ahead of Patton. For several minutes the two shifted about uneasily. From a distance, of course, it was difficult to tell just what was the object of Zhukov's shuffle, but there was no doubt that the American general and the Russian marshal were out of step.[1]

In August these little differences between the Allied occupation forces in Germany were hardly novel nor did the Western Allies consider them particularly ominous. The West could not understand why the Russians felt them necessary nor why their Eastern colleagues were so often truculent and suspicious. A victory parade hardly seemed the place for petty problems of prestige. Then, suddenly, violating the agreed ground rules, 100 giant, new Stalin tanks clanked down the empty Unter den Linden past the bombed and burned-out ruins of Berlin and back into the Eastern Zone.[2] The Zhukov shuffle, the huge tanks, the crude Soviet tactics fell into place with their habitual distrust of the West. Despite the difficulties discovered in keeping in step with the Russians, the West felt that close Allied co-operation in Occupied Germany would be possible. After all, for the Allies, the Germans remained the enemy, not one another.

The wartime plans for dealing with a defeated Germany had been worked out in general terms among the Allies at the Big Three meetings in Tehran and Yalta. There had been differences of opinion but no real clash. The Allies had vowed to punish the guilty and prevent a military resurgence of Germany.[3] In all Allied camps there had existed strong sentiment for erasing Germany forever from the map of Europe. Moderation gained few adherents as the war progressed into the German homeland, revealing the incredible machinery for the grotesque final solution. The gas chamber, the death camps, the heaps of pitiful cadavers, the whole apparatus of genocide nauseated the soldiers. Added to the ruins of Coventry and London, the years of occupation, the dead—in Russia's case over twenty million—there had been no doubt as to the nature of the enemy. However crudely the Russians behaved in their occupation of Eastern Germany, however difficult they became in negotiation, they remained Allies, often co-operative and even enthusiastic. The Germans, on the other hand, were a people damned, a race cursed with the Nazi virus.

To make final provision for the hated Germans, the Allies had met at Potsdam outside Berlin in July 1945. As usual Premier Josef Stalin represented the Russians, but President Harry Truman had replaced Franklin Roosevelt and in the midst of the conference Clement Attlee had taken over Winston Churchill's chair as the result of Labour's upset electoral victory. One or two minor tiffs aside, the meetings progressed genially. Stalin had been sufficiently co-operative so that there had been either general agreement on most points or, occasionally, a temporary postponement. The over-all American policies of denazification, demilitarization, democratization, and decentralization found ready favor although the details of implementation remained vague. Specific solutions on reparations, boundaries or the future German government had to be foregone for the time being. By the end of the conference, control of Germany had passed over to the Four-Power Control Commission, which now included a French representative. Many of the problems left unsolved by the Potsdam meeting would presumably be worked out in the quadripartite government of Germany centered in Berlin.

The city of Berlin, where the Control Commission set up headquarters, had been given a special status. When the occupation zones for Germany had been fixed, the Allies had agreed that in view of Berlin's status as Hitler's capital the city would come under three-power occupation. Later a sector for the French had been added. When the war ended in May 1945, Berlin as expected had fallen to the Red Army. Not until June 5, 1945, a month later, did the first formal four-power meeting of the Allied military commanders take place in Berlin. On June 17, the first American column started for the German capital.

After a long delay, following the Russian insistence at the checkpoint on a prior "agreement" restricting the number of American troops, the trucks had been allowed through. Even then the Russians directed them into a guarded compound near Potsdam. The Russians soon made it plain that they had no intention of allowing Americans to take over their zone in Berlin until the Americans evacuated the parts of Saxony and Thuringia which belonged in the Soviet zone. Despite some individual reluctance to give up the rich lands of Saxony and Thuringia for a few square miles of bomb ruins, Washington had every intention of honoring the agreements with Russia. On June 30, when the Americans agreed to turn over the two areas in return for ready access into Berlin, the Russians ended their blockade tactics. On July 1, General Floyd Parks and Colonel Frank Howley, the American commanders, finally got into the city. On the next day they met with the Russian commander, Colonel-General Gorbatov, to complete final arrangements. On July 4, the Americans formally took over their sector in a ceremony attended by General Bradley and complete with artillery salutes.[4]

The Western Powers soon found that the Russians had not spent idly the months since the capture of Berlin. Almost as soon as the shooting had ended, Soviet teams had moved into the burning rubble of Berlin and begun to dismantle the city. Not only industrial equipment, machine tools and military supplies had disappeared eastward, but also plumbing fixtures and dairy herds. The confiscations had taken place so hurriedly or so crudely that much of the loot would only be of use for scrap when it reached the Soviet Union. While these informal reparations continued, individual Russian soldiers had run amok in the captured city, looting, raping and terrorizing the shell-shocked inhabitants. Simultaneously a more constructive program of absorption had taken place. Since the Western Allies had not appeared, the Four-Power government for the city, the *Kommandatura*, with only the Russian representatives present, passed a series of basic laws. The police force had been established and its ranks filled with carefully selected recruits. The banking industry, the ration bureau, and the newspapers and radio station had been organized on Soviet terms and staffed by hand-picked German Communists. On June 10, Zhukov unilaterally allowed the formation of German political parties in the Eastern Zone. In Berlin under Soviet authorization a single trade union under Communist control began to function, as well as four political parties. Uninterested at first in the Soviet penetration of Berlin, the Western Allies in general had remained intent on denazification and demilitarization. On July 7 and July 11, the full *Kommandatura* met and agreed that there would be no change in the unilateral Russian organization of Berlin without the unanimous agreement of the *Kommandatura.* Despite some friction and occasional disagreement, the joint occupation of Berlin had begun in an atmosphere of friendship and optimism.

The summer of 1945 had been a halcyon time of Allied co-operation. On June 10, Marshal Zhukov visited General Eisenhower at Frankfurt where compliments and toasts were exchanged, culminating in Zhukov's joining a troupe of Negro performers in a bilingual rendition of "Old Man River." Between August 10 and August 15, in his turn, Eisenhower made an official trip to Moscow as a guest of the Soviet Government. A round of state dinners, buffets, and tours had followed. In Moscow the American diplomats Averell Harriman and General John Deane remained unimpressed with the extravagant Soviet reception. They explained to Eisenhower's Deputy Military Commander in Germany, General Lucius D. Clay, that even during the war no real co-operation had developed with the Russians. They did not feel that any would be possible in the future. Surrounded by an aura of military fellowship, Eisenhower and Clay, however, remained skeptical of the Embassy's pessimism. As Clay later wrote:

> *General Eisenhower and I agreed that we had enjoyed our trip and that we had found a sincere friend in Marshal Zhukov. The Allied Control Council was established, and our friend Zhukov was the Soviet representative. We had the Potsdam Protocol, agreed to by at least three of the occupying powers, including Russia, to serve as the directive for our future actions. There seemed to be no further reason why quadripartite government could not be made to succeed. General Eisenhower and I determined to do our part.*[5]

By the time of the V-J Day parade even a brief exposure to Soviet officers and Soviet policies had made many Americans and British less optimistic. The friction with the Russians had increased and seemed likely to continue. The Soviet-controlled press and radio had begun to harangue the West. The Russian officials never seemed interested in moderation or compromise. Yet despite this harassment, there did not appear to be sufficient reason to give up hope. In November 1945, for example, agreement was reached on three specific air corridors into Berlin and the final agreement was signed early in January 1946.[6] A similar agreement on road, rail and canal control was assumed to be unnecessary in view of the oral agreements between Truman and Stalin of June 14 and June 18, 1945. Thus, with the air corridor agreement in January, the new year came into Berlin on the wings of hope.

If the Western occupying powers foresaw 1946 as a year of hope, the Berliners surely did not. During most of the year, the attention of the people was limited to finding enough food, a room, and, during the winter, a little heat. The bleak and dismal city showed few signs of recovery as the Berliners struggled among the ruins not so much to put their lives back together as just to exist. Except for the dedicated German Communists, carefully maintained by the Russians, few had time or heart for politics. The momentary elation at the arrival of the Anglo-American Occupation Forces in July 1945 had dissolved into apathy when the Germans realized that the Allies saw all Germans tainted with Hitler's curse and all Russians as friends. Yet, even in the face of Russian hostility and Western indifference or opposition, there were those Germans who, after twenty-five years, rushed to fill the vacuum in Berlin's political life. Historically the strongest party in Berlin, Germany's most anti-Nazi city, had been the Social Democrats (SPD). In 1946, using their long-buried organization, the SPD leaders began to reconstruct their party amid the ruins of Berlin. These first tentative efforts to loosen the Communist grip on the institutions of the city immediately attracted the attention of the Russians, if not of the Western powers.

In an effort to emasculate any potential political opposition, the German Communists urged a merger on the SPD. For some time it appeared as if the SPD leadership would succumb to a combination of threats and promises, for the ideal of a United Front and the reality of Soviet might were a powerful combination. In the most difficult circumstances, with little sympathy from the Western powers and ominous opposition from Russian, the antimerger forces managed to postpone their party's absorption on February 14. Through March and April a series of intraparty votes finally prevented the absorption of the SPD by the Communist-dominated SED party except in the Russian Zone. There the Russians banned the "illegal" SPD. The Western Sectors of the city, however, presented other problems. After passing the decision up to the Control Commission for Germany and receiving it back in the *Kommandatura*, the Russian delegate finally agreed with the West that the SPD should be permitted to exist in Berlin. This meant that in the first free elections in Berlin since the advent of Hitler, the Russian-backed SED would have to compete openly with the SPD and the other democratic parties. It is difficult to tell if the Russians really felt that their heavy-handed support of the SED during the electoral campaign would prove effective or if they were, in 1946, unwilling to antagonize the West openly by preventing the Berlin elections. In any case, their SED did very poorly indeed, polling just under 20 per cent of the votes while the three democratic parties received the rest, with the SPD getting almost 49 per cent. Despite all their efforts to aid the SED and impede the democratic parties, the Russians had suffered a humiliating blow. Even worse, 1946 had marked a change in Soviet policy toward Germany which made this limitation on Soviet control of Berlin even more frustrating.

Although analysis of Russian motives occupies a secure niche in Western scholarship, much of the results remain speculative or tenuous, for the Russians seldom publish memoirs, reveal disagreements, open archives or allow relevant interviews. Yet, from a variety of evidence, it seems reasonably clear that in 1945 Stalin had intended to crush the Germans once and for all. Neither he nor any of the Russians ever again wanted to face the German menace. Unilaterally, the Russians absorbed East Prussia, expelling or liquidating the inhabitants. Moscow saw to it that their satellite Poland occupied substantial sections of historic Germany to the east of the Oder-Neisse line. Sometime early in 1946, because of the variety of unexpected options, Stalin's ambitions apparently expanded. The West seemed unaware of the almost total exhaustion of the Russian nation or of the awesome inhibitions of the atomic bomb. Instead, the Americans in particular dismantled their military machine, withdrew their presence from Europe, and continued to offer their naïve friendship. The Russian absorption of Eastern Europe had taken place with very little opposition and had aroused little interest except from the frustrated exiles isolated in the West. The way seemed open to continue Soviet aggrandizement beyond the lines reached by the Red Army. Without need to heed domestic criticism, Stalin could drive his exhausted country on to a position of hegemony over Europe.

The immediate prospects were inviting. In Czechoslovakia a coalition government tottered along from day to day. In Greece a strong pro-Communist partisan movement needed only further encouragement to produce civil war. Finland remained isolated and friendless, open to pressure. More important, the shattered economic structure of Western Europe opened up "legal" possibilities for the powerful Communist parties of Italy and France. The key to further expansion, however, revolved around Russian policy in Germany. In Poland or Rumania little attention had been given to the population when the Soviet system had been imposed intact and unmodified by any local considerations. In a divided Germany, Stalin could not risk antagonizing the Western half of Germany by a continuation of his policies of spoliation or by the sudden imposition of Soviet institutions on the East Zone. Thus, in order to improve the Soviet position, the Russians began, occasionally haphazardly, to compete for the Germans' favor. Their new and hamhanded tactics during 1946 had not produced the expected results. While all the reports from France and

Italy indicated a rapid growth in Communist membership and prospects, the Germans in Berlin had bluntly turned down the Russian SED by four to one. As long as the Germans were given a free choice, any substantial gain for the SED seemed unlikely. Soviet policy in Germany increasingly sought to prevent the conditions which would make such a choice possible: the Eastern Zone was to be part of the Soviet Empire, the city of Berlin absorbed, and the Western Zones dominated or debilitated.[7]

Within Berlin, Soviet activities had to be more cautious than in the distant reaches of the Eastern Zone, but even there the Russians made only transparent efforts to conceal their intention of retaining a grip on the city's political and economic structure. When the SPD majority leaders attempted to remove Lord Mayor Ostrowski, a man seemingly willing to co-operate with the Communists, the Russians used their veto in the *Kommandatura* to prevent his elected successor, Ernst Reuter, from taking office. Reuter, an ex-Communist, made no secret of his feelings about Soviet ambitions in Germany. The long Lord Mayor wrangle revealed to the interested the object of Russian intentions—control of Berlin. The Soviets struggled to retain their grip on the police through their man Paul Markgraf, captured before Stalingrad and converted to Communism in prison camp. Every institution of Berlin, the university, the radio, the newspapers, the unions, became battlefields as the Russians tried to hold on to their creatures. During 1947, despite all their efforts to retain their predominant position in the city, Russian power declined.[8]

In Germany at large, the brief post-Potsdam honeymoon had ended in 1946. Efforts in the Allied Control Council for united agreement, particularly four-power economic control, met with evasions and delays. In many cases, the French refused to accept Anglo-American proposals which would strengthen the German economy. Paris was content with a prostrate, enfeebled Germany.[9] Russia was content to let France take the lead in weakening Western Germany. On the highest level, the Council of Foreign Ministers, the Anglo-American diplomats found the Russians uninterested in decisions on Germany. Acting as they chose in their own zone, they refused co-operation on a variety of legal pretexts. In May 1946, General Clay had finally halted the dismantling of German plants for shipment to the Eastern Zone. If the Russians would not agree to a German economic policy, there seemed no point in further American appeasement. In July, Secretary of State James Byrnes sent identical notes to Britain, France and Russia asking for an agreement on a joint economic administration for Germany. London agreed. Paris remained noncommittal, for the French continued to take a jaundiced view of any moves to re-establish a viable Germany. A shattered and starving Germany stirred few Frenchmen to pity. The Americans and British, however, had found that their occupation of a destroyed Germany cost money, a great deal of money, close to 600,000,000 dollars a year. The Russians, well aware of the Western dilemma and division, as expected, refused to participate. In Washington the essential issue had been faced that without widespread changes in the economic structure of Occupied Germany, or at least in the Anglo-American zones, more and more money would have to be pumped in merely to keep the Germans from starving. By the winter of 1946–1947, conditions had reached an appalling state. In Berlin 200 people froze to death; schools and factories closed, and the population stayed home, wrapped in tattered clothes in rooms without heat, existing on a diet inadequate to sustain human life.[10] Moscow, obviously, was content with a weakened West Germany divided into three artificial units and subject to Russian veto. On June 25, 1947, Secretary Byrnes asked for centralized German economic agencies to control economic unification and for a provincial German government. His proposals led directly to the unification of the American and British Zones, Bizonia, on July 30, despite Russian opposition and French suspicion. On June 25, 1947, the German Economic Council met for the first time at Frankfurt. A first step at least had been taken to drag Western Germany back from an abyss of starvation and degradation.

By 1947, the American Government had reluctantly come to the conclusion that Franklin Roosevelt's grand design for the postwar world had been based on wishful thinking. Some still had hopes for personal diplomacy; some, like Henry Wallace, still had faith in the Russians. Most of the members of Truman's Administration had come to view Churchill's Iron Curtain speech of 1946 not as reactionary pessimism but prophetic realism. The regular meetings of the Foreign Ministers had proved fruitless. All personal proposals, private negotiations, general statements and hopeful overtures had been barren. The Russians preferred delay and the consequent decay of the Anglo-American position in Germany. The decision to institute Bizonia had simply been one piece of evidence of the growing split with Russia. The failure of agreement at the Moscow Foreign Ministers Conference simply underlined the hardening of the Soviet position. The Russians seemed smugly determined to absorb the devastated continent.

Even the unexpected Anglo-American venture in Germany seemed to have come too late. Europe was prostrate, its industrial plant smashed, its economic structure shattered. Shortages, rationing, malnutrition, labor unrest, Communist infiltration and governmental instability haunted almost all of Western Europe during the cold bleak winter of 1946–1947. During these months sentiment grew in favor of what its chief proponents called containment, the stemming of the Russian advance. On March 12, 1947, President Truman instituted an aid program to Greece and Turkey to prevent a Communist takeover on the withdrawal of the British. On June 5, 1947, in a broad effort to turn the tide, to create a viable Europe capable of resisting Communist subversion, the new Secretary of State, George C. Marshall, in a speech at Harvard University proposed that the United States help reconstruct the economy of Europe with a massive aid program. In July Washington informed General Clay that he should prepare to integrate West Germany into the European Recovery Program. The American public, still largely unmoved by the Germans' plight, did not hear of this until the formal announcement in December. The Germans, too, had no idea that help of a sort might be on the way.

As summer faded into fall, Clay and his administrators began to fear that the aid might be too late. The German economy, what there was of it, ground slowly to a halt as winter came. By January 1948, food stocks had fallen below the danger level. Three years after the war, life in Germany reached its nadir. Few Germans could follow the intricate diplomatic negotiations over their fate. Few could understand what the Americans intended; if, in fact, Washington had a real policy at all. In a maze of cross-purposes, industrial plants were still being dismantled, harbor installations destroyed, and coal exported as reparations. At the same time the Germans were supposed to contribute to a prosperous Europe by creating a stable and productive Germany. All the while the Russian menace loomed in the East. Worst of all, during the previous summer the Germans had experienced the severest drought in recent history. The harvest had been poor. By midwinter the Germans seemed close to extinction; theirs was now a bleak land of ruined cities, cold rooms, starvation diet, ragged clothes, despair and bitterness.

Even then, the great latent pool of suspicion and rancor remained in the West. The Germans had only themselves to blame. Any discussion of rebuilding German industry or revitalizing Germany always met with opposition, vindictive or reasoned, from a wide spectrum of political opinion. Three years of misery for the Germans seemed little enough. The haunting remembrance of Hitler's instant rearmament in the thirties haunted some. The death of six million Jews could not be forgiven by others. Thus many experts preferred to ignore the fact that European recovery without Germany was impossible and that without an immediate economic renaissance Russia would scoop up the remains.

Even those who saw the alternatives most clearly still hoped that the Russians would relent and participate in the controlled rebuilding of Germany. In August 1947, for example, Clay made one "last" effort to achieve a united quadripartite currency policy; for a sound currency in Germany had become essential for the country's recovery.[11] In

February 1948, Clay was still trying to achieve agreement. By then, the Russians began to suspect that their standard tactics of delay, obstruction and vituperation had not proven sufficient. The steps toward Bizonia made it clear that Britain and the United States would not indefinitely allow their proposals to be vetoed in the Council of Foreign Ministers, in the Allied Control Council and in the *Kommandatura*. Apparently Stalin decided to probe further, to exploit the seeming Anglo-American uncertainty, to go over to the offensive, to stir up the troubled waters of Europe.

For the Russians, 1948 boded well. Much of Eastern Europe had been absorbed. Western Germany lay prostrate. Italy faced an election in April which many observers felt the Communists could win in a free and open vote. France continued to be torn by bitter political disagreement as one government after another struggled under the menace of the Communist Party. Great Britain remained sunk in shortages, exhausted by war. America appeared to be led by a confused little man who scarcely had the backing of his own party. The West was divided, weakened and uncertain. Only the existence of the American atomic bomb lent any substance to the Western posture, and perhaps Washington preferred not to risk an all-out atomic war.

The tentative maneuvers began at the West's most vulnerable spot, the city of Berlin. Isolated deep within the Russian Zone, totally dependent upon supply lines completely controlled by the Red Army, Berlin was an ideal pressure point. If the West did not respond firmly and immediately to the first tentative probes, then the Russians could grow more daring. If the West resisted, then further thought could be given to an open rupture. During January 1948, the Russians interfered with interzonal rail traffic. Planted rumors, directed news and repeated hints began to appear in the controlled press of the Russian Zone to the effect that the Western Powers would soon withdraw from Berlin. In February, General of the Army Vassily Sokolovsky, the Russian representative on the Control Council, indicated that it was the Russian view that Berlin was really part of the Soviet Zone. In the same month, the growing maze of restrictions on travel in and out of Berlin was first imposed and then removed. The three-pronged offensive—the rumors of withdrawal, the proposal of Soviet legal rights, and the iron hint of a blockade—had one obvious and ominous direction: the imposition of a "legal" siege.

The realization that the Western Powers had no written guarantee of entry into Berlin except for the January 1947 protocol on the three air corridors had begun to loom larger in the American analyses of the German problem. In Washington, where Truman had piecemeal assumed the leadership of the West's resistance to continued Communist expansion, the sporadic Russian probing in Berlin had to take a back seat to a horde of urgent problems. The Administration had to shepherd the European Recovery Program through Congress, seek the creation of a unified military establishment, secure universal military training, begin the negotiations leading toward a Western European military alliance, all in addition to the bitter struggle for Truman's domestic policies. As always in an election year, counsels were divided, criticism abundant. Never in so short a period had so many vital decisions piled up on a President's desk. Everywhere in the world, there were growing demands on America's limited military and economic resources. Crisis followed crisis in Europe and in Asia. China seemed to be sliding toward communism. Palestine was gripped in an undeclared war. Italy tottered. Then on February 24, 1948, one more unexpected and devastating shift in the balance of power occurred. In Czechoslovakia, in a brutal and violent *coup d'état,* the Communists swallowed up one more country. Although the Czech Republic for two years had been cruelly strained by internal Communist conspiracy and external Russian pressure, the sudden disappearance behind the iron curtain of Eastern Europe's only democracy came as a bitter surprise. Unwilling simply to influence, Moscow demanded subservience. The Russian Bear had again broken down the unmanned ramparts and run wild in the fold.

The meetings of the Allied Control Council had more and more become the platform from which Sokolovsky delivered vitriolic tirades on the evil motives and diabolic methods of the Western Powers. With the decline of Soviet restraint there had come a rise in specific harassment: inspectors boarded military trains, the confiscation of former Secretary of State Byrnes' book *Speaking Frankly,* and the constant rumormongering of the Eastern Zone press. In February, Yugoslavia, Czechoslovakia and Poland met in a staged three-power conference primarily to castigate the West's German policy. Then, on March 5, a bombshell arrived in Washington in a top-secret telegram from General Clay.

> *For many months, based on logical analysis, I have felt and held that war was unlikely for at least ten years. Within the last few weeks I have felt a subtle change in Soviet attitude which I cannot define but which now gives me a feeling that it may come with dramatic suddenness. I cannot support this change in my own thinking with any data or outward evidence in relationships other than to describe it as a feeling of a new tenseness in every Soviet individual with whom we have official relations. I am unable to submit any official report in the absence of supporting data but my feeling is real. You may advise the Chief of Staff of this for whatever it may be worth if you feel it advisable.*[12]

In Washington the evidence that the world was moving toward the brink of a major crisis began to build up rapidly. On March 10, Jan Masaryk, Foreign Minister of Czechoslovakia, fell or jumped to his death. Rumors circulated of Soviet pressure on Norway to sign a pact similar to the one Moscow was urging on Finland. On March 18, the Soviet puppet People's Congress in East Germany met to call for German unification on Russian terms. On the same cold and rainy day, some 70,000 West Berliners demonstrated on the 100th anniversary of the liberal revolution of 1848. Ernst Reuter told them, "It was Prague's turn, Finland was next, whose turn is it now? It will not be Berlin's turn."[13] Athough the American intelligence estimate had come through two days before that there would be no war for sixty days, Clay's concern had obviously been based on fact and not on fantasy. Meanwhile Clay had cabled the War Department and his civilian counterpart Robert Murphy had cabled the State Department, both urging the use of a "small combat force" to clear the highway to Berlin recently closed for "repairs" and guarded by two Mongolian soldiers. Murphy was particularly insistent that the Russians were bluffing. Washington refused to gamble.[14]

Ignoring Reuter's rhetoric and relying on Washington's uncertain response, the Russians continued to probe. On March 20, in a carefully arranged display of spontaneous indignation, Marshal Sokolovsky delivered one more tirade against the Western Powers, this time for refusing to inform his Government of the results of their three-power conference in London concerning a currency reform for West Germany. He then stalked out. They now knew that "quadripartite government had broken up and that the split in Germany . . . had taken place."[15] The collapse of the sterile forum of the Control Council removed the one arena of constant high-level confrontation. Considerable uneasiness existed in Washington that the next arena would not be as peaceful; but attention wavered as the constant flow of problems, decisions, conferences and position papers continued. The future of Palestine, the collapse of Nationalist China, the final passage of ERP absorbed the diplomats and administrators. Washington moved from crisis to crisis and Berlin was neglected.

On March 31, the German problem returned with a vengeance. Another telegram arrived from Clay reporting that Soviet General M. I. Dravotin had announced a new system of inspection for Allied personnel entering the Russian Zone. A series of nonstop conferences began, culminating in a major meeting of Truman, Defense Secretary James Forrestal, Generals Eisenhower, Spaatz and Bradley, and a variety of other high officials from the State and Defense Departments. Word then arrived that the British were putting armed guards on their trains. Clay, whose position remained more confident and more militant than that of Washington, received permission to bar Russians from the American trains. It was a risk but a small one and, furthermore, the British had already made the decision for the West. In retaliation the Russians began to halt American trains at border points. Clay's response, in turn, was to send in an armed train. The Russians frustrated his ploy by shuttling the train off to a siding where it sat for a few days before trundling back into the Western Zone. In the meanwhile, on April 1, several loads of food for the occupation forces had been flown into the Western Sectors of Berlin by a small, hastily organized airlift. Clay continued to urge a stronger stand. He felt that the Russians were bluffing and would back down. He insisted that there was no need to evacuate American women and children; in fact, to do so would prejudice the West in the eyes of not only the Germans but also the Italians, who were about to vote in Europe's most crucial election. Washington agreed. The Allied occupation force would remain in Berlin supplied by air if need be. Within a few days other crises again drew attention elsewhere. Germany and Berlin may have been battlefields in a new kind of war but few watched them regularly or closely in a world of strange, new battlefields.[16]

The Russians gradually began cutting off access to Berlin because of "technical difficulties." In April, they expelled the United States Signal Corps team stationed in East Germany to keep communications open. In Washington Soviet Ambassador Alexander S. Panyushkin probed Robert A. Lovett and Charles E. Bohlen of the State Department as to what the United States' position toward the Soviet Union really was. In May the Russians imposed a complicated system of documentation on freight shipments into Berlin. Practically every day further regulations on road, rail and water traffic were announced or were repealed. Border security tightened up. New rules which were on one day and off the next interrupted the flow of traffic into the city. All during this not-too-subtle pressure, the West remained stoically calm except once. On April 5, a stunting Soviet fighter plane hit a British transport in midair, killing everyone concerned. The British immediately announced that fighters would accompany their transports. The United States followed suit. The Russians hastily apologized and the crisis soon degenerated into the usual name-calling; but henceforth Soviet efforts to limit air traffic never took the form of actual interference.

In other areas the creeping blockade, always justified by the ever-present "technical difficulties," continued so that by June Berlin had nearly been cut off from the Western Zones. The Russians held up civilian supply trains or "lost" freight and mail cars. At the same time the Eastern Zone press noted the low food supplies in Berlin, the impossibility of an airlift to supply the needs of 2,500,000 people, and the imminent withdrawal of the Western Powers. In June at Warsaw, Russia and the Eastern satellites met in a Foreign Ministers Conference to formulate a "common" German solution. The Warsaw Declaration demanded, in effect, a permanent Soviet veto over German economic affairs and a powerful if not pre-eminent position in any German government. The Soviet position had been made clear. On June 16, the Soviet delegates walked out of the Berlin *Kommandatura*. The time for tirades had passed. The flash point for Germany again seemed quite near.

The increasing Soviet concentration on Germany was partially the result of the marvelous opportunities presented by the Western presence in a Berlin hopelessly isolated in the Eastern Zone. Secondly, a Soviet success was needed in view of the failure of the glowing promises of January. Neither Greece nor Finland had succumbed to infiltration in one case and intimidation in the other. In Italy De Gasperi's Christian Democrats had won well over 40 per cent of the vote and forced the strong Communist Party into a permanent negative exile. In France the fate of the Communist Party had been the same. On March 17, the Treaty of Brussels had taken the first steps in the creation of a Western European defense system. On April 3, Truman had signed the European Recovery Program and almost immediately the effect became noticeable in Western Europe's economy. Week by week the West seemed to draw together and grow stronger rather than weaker in the face of Russian threats. Perhaps worst of all, the dread plague of heresy had been introduced into the monolithic Communist empire: Tito had taken Yugoslavia out from under the heavy-handed control of Russia in the name of National Communism. In January, Russia had seemingly been on the very crest of the wave of the future. In June, six months later, Stalin must have had some concern that the tide might be ebbing.

In Germany, however, the Allied position seemed so fragile that pressure on Berlin, once it had been assured that general war would not result, could only be successful. At most the Russians wanted a dominant position in Germany, and, at the least, control of Berlin. In order to retain their foothold in Berlin, either the Allies would have to permit Soviet penetration of the institutions of Western Germany or else they would have to recognize that their continued presence in Berlin depended upon Russian toleration. Thus Russia would soon have a consolidated and communized Eastern Germany with Berlin as its capital or, even better, a stranglehold on all Germany.

Early in June, prominent East Zone leaders had been brought to

Soviet headquarters in Potsdam to be told that the West would be out of Berlin by the fall. The Russians told the Peoples' Congress to be prepared to transform itself into an East Zone Parliament. Lavrenti Beria arrived in Berlin, possibly to begin the organization of a German police army. As a result, rumor of a great diplomatic victory spread through satellite diplomatic circles.[17]

Although they needed no particular excuse to extend their traffic restrictions to the Western Zone civilians, the Soviets decided to make the pending Western currency reform the final straw. On June 1, France reluctantly joined the Anglo-American currency program. Final arrangements for the introduction of the joint Western currency then took another three weeks. On June 18, the Allies announced that in two days their new currency would go into use in the three Western Zones but not in Berlin. The Russians immediately began stopping freight and passenger cars at the Eastern Zone border. On June 24, they ended all rail traffic into Berlin. Inside Berlin, they cut off all electric power into the Western Zone. Eastern newspapers rushed into print with tales of chaos, rioting and anarchy. Over a trumped-up issue and still using technical excuses, the Russians had finally made their move. Western Berlin had been sealed off.

Despite the obvious and elaborate Soviet preparations for just such a blockade, Washington still had no ready response, no prepared position. On June 25, the first meeting between Truman, Forrestal, Secretary of the Army, Kenneth C. Royall and Under Secretary of State Lovett dealt solely with the legal position of the West. Clearly this line of thought was of little use. On the next day, a Sunday, a large meeting in Royall's office in the Pentagon of military personnel and State Department officials informally ran over the various alternatives.[18] This group, which bypassed the formal decision-making agencies, the National Security Council, the War Council and even the Central Intelligence Agency, passed on its suggestions to the President. The most militant suggestion was to consider the possibility of transferring the two B-29 squadrons at Goose Bay to bases in Great Britain. The group had not discussed either the possibility of an airlift or the use of the atomic bombs. On June 27, Truman examined their suggestions, but made no decision. For the next several days conferences in Washington continued, as the experts repeatedly ran over the unpleasant alternatives. Once again Washington had neither the desire nor the capacity for war; once again America's prestige demanded a strong stand. If the United States was unable or unwilling to fight in June 1948, still Washington could not allow Berlin to be abandoned. In the main, Washington decided to do nothing and stall for negotiations. Truman authorized a temporary and limited airlift. "In this way we hoped that we might be able to feed Berlin until the diplomatic deadlock could be broken."[19] Much in the same way that imperial powers had once sent gunboats to frighten the unruly natives, Washington prepared the way to send the B-29 squadrons to Great Britain and to Germany. The planes, known as A-bomb carriers, were about the only mobile American military reserves. They were not, however, sent as a first step in an impending atomic war. After three years, confusion still reigned on the question of atomic warfare. No decision had yet been made even on the theoretical usage of atomic bombs; much less had anyone as yet mentioned their application to the Berlin situation. The Americans did not envision an atomic war, but some sort of negotiations. With their hopes plaintively on discussion, Washington and London waited and watched for some sign from Moscow.

In Berlin, on his own hook, General Clay's response to the full blockade had been far more rapid and immeasurably more productive. On the morning of June 24, he had called General Curtis LeMay, American Air Force Commander in Europe, and had asked for an immediate airlift of food and fuel. Clay planned to maintain 3,000 American troops, 3,000 British and 1,500 French and all of their dependents. He hoped 500 tons a day would be sufficient. Clay estimated that a daily average of 4,000 tons would sustain a minimum economy for the German people. The Air Force would have some leeway in building up to this for West Berlin had food for thirty-six days and coal for forty-four. On June 25, the first C-47 flew into Berlin with a load of food for the German civilians. East or West, very few experts had any hopes for the airlift other than as a temporary expedient, but it was *something*. Simultaneously with his efforts in Germany, Clay continued to urge a strong stand on Washington. He insisted that the Russians did not want a war—"the possibility was remote." He insisted that the German people were willing to suffer the shortages and discomforts of the future in order not to fall into the Soviet Zone. Clay, in fact, stressed the "amazingly courageous resistance of the Berlin population," which was a rather remarkable reversal of form for the overlord of an evil and odious former foe. The slow tentative American-German rapprochement began to speed up. Meanwhile, Clay had found, as he had predicted, that negotiations with the Russians from a position of weakness would be hopeless. Efforts to solve the blockade locally collapsed on July 3, when Sokolovsky had brazenly informed the three military governors that the "technical difficulties" would remain as long as the West continued their plans for a West German government. Washington decided to switch negotiations from Berlin to Moscow.[20]

On July 6, the three Western Allies sent almost identical notes to the Soviet Union protesting the blockade and outlining the West's legal rights. In their own good time, the Soviets replied on July 14, with a variety of justifications and an offer to discuss all German conditions. It was apparent that the Russians believed time was on their side. Berlin could never be supplied by air, certainly not during the winter. Even if the West wanted to remain, they could not do so in the face of 2,500,000 starving Germans, who would on their own part demand a Western accommodation with Russia. Just what specific accommodation Stalin had in mind was not at all clear; but that at least he would expect substantial concessions by the West or even evacuation of West Berlin was considered very possible. In July his victory seemed almost a certainty to all but the Pollyannas. All that needed to be done was to delay until the West realized the facts. If, of course, it faced up to its defeat sooner, fruitful negotiations could begin at once. While Stalin waited, the Americans agonized and went over the same ground again and again. On July 19, Truman met with Secretary of State Marshall and Defense Secretary Forrestal and outlined his position, "We would stay in Berlin until all diplomatic means had been exhausted in order to come to some kind of accommodation to avoid war."[21] It was a highly unsatisfactory decision, since the Russians had already repulsed American diplomatic overtures in Berlin and no one could foresee actually fighting a war.

Two days later Clay flew into Washington bringing with him the first hint of optimism. In the National Security Council meeting he pointed out that the airlift was already bringing in enough food, and with seventy-five more C-47s it could deliver the necessary tonnage of coal as well. Clay urged the transfer of the big C-54s, which could carry ten tons instead of the C-47s' two and a half. Clay's calm and confidence encouraged Truman, who was more inclined to take a strong position than were many of his diplomatic and military advisors. The President, however, did not feel disposed to accept Ambassador Murphy's position that the Soviet Union should be openly challenged. Instead Truman seized on an expanded airlift as the best possible temporary policy. He pressured reluctant General Hoyt Vandenberg, Air Force Chief of Staff, to switch the limited American transport force to Germany. Truman insisted that to supply Berlin by land convoy held the danger of war if the Russians resisted. Then the unprepared Air Force would be in even more desperate straits. Thus it was better to concentrate the transport in Germany and avoid an immediate showdown. Vandenberg accepted Truman's order and promised that the Air Force would "devote its every energy to carrying out"[22] the airlift. With an expanded airlift assured, Clay, accompanied by Bohlen, carried instructions for the next Western diplomatic maneuver in the time gained by the airlift.

Thus, by July, the Americans had arrived at a policy of sorts. It is difficult to believe that for over six months, while the Russians tightened their unofficial blockade and then sealed off Berlin except for the fragile air corridor, the United States had prepared no response. The decision, to stay and to negotiate, superficially appeared firm, even daring, but few had any conviction that the airlift would give more than a short breathing space. Then the Russians would have to be appeased. To stay simply meant postponing the unpleasant future for a while in hopes of some sort of miracle. The Americans in Germany, particularly Clay and Murphy, had stressed that unless Washington put up a show of determination in the face of the Russians' squeeze, the West's position would continue to deteriorate. Few listened. War had become too great a risk. The United States had dismantled its military establishment. In June, after the full blockade, open defiance seemed even more dangerous. Washington had refused to gamble. All during these extended conferences, the one real American bargaining point, the final trump card, the atomic bomb, had scarcely been mentioned. In retrospect, after years of detailed analysis on the nature of thermonuclear war, it is difficult to realize that by and large the American President and the National Security Council continued to think of war in conventional terms. They were far more concerned with the horde of Russian divisions poised in Eastern Europe than with the possible fears and anxieties of Stalin facing an atomic holocaust. That such an uncertainty existed in Moscow seems certain in view of the number of doors left open behind the Russian advances. Roads were closed for "technical" reasons, limitations imposed because of "violated" agreements, walkouts made on negotiable points. The one immediate show of force in April, when the British threatened to fly fighters in support of their air transports, apparently was sufficient to keep the Russians out of the air corridors. Washington did not intend to bluff with the bomb; in fact, never even considered the possibility. Other than the empty gesture of the B-29s, the West would depend upon diplomacy.

On July 28, Bohlen and the American Ambassadors to Great Britain and Russia, Lewis Douglas and Walter B. Smith, reached an agreement with British and French diplomats for a simultaneous protest to Moscow. The scene had now definitely shifted from war warnings to open negotiation. In Moscow, after some obviously contrived delay, Foreign Minister V. M. Molotov met with the Western ambassadors on July 31. He agreed to arrange a conference with Stalin. At nine o'clock on the evening of August 2, they were ushered in to meet an affable and genial Stalin, the Uncle Joe of old. For two hours, Stalin discussed the Berlin difficulties in a reasonable tone. He insisted that the core of the dispute was the currency problem. All agreed that a variety of compromises existed and that further talks with Molotov would produce a solution. The further talks with a cold, unbending Molotov produced nothing. The talks had to be broken off.

The next move was up to the West. The British had backed the Americans to the hilt, accepting enthusiastically the B-29 squadron. Labour Foreign Minister Ernest Bevin now insisted to Ambassador Douglas that the Western ambassadors in Moscow take a strong line and demand to see Stalin again. The British feared the West would be outnegotiated and forced to a crippling compromise. Such a loss of face might open up the Middle East to Communist penetration. Washington agreed to a second attempt. Once again, on August 23, the three ambassadors saw Stalin, hoping for a crack in the Soviet intransigence. Once again, Stalin proved most helpful. He produced a compromise plan not unlike that devised by the Western ambassadors. Some disagreement occurred over the wording. Ambassador Smith felt the Russian formulation would undermine German confidence in American intentions. Both sides agreed that further talks with Molotov would produce a solution.

As soon as the ambassadors met with Molotov they found the Russian unyielding. The broad general principles that had seemed so clear with Stalin became impossible to define in specifics. The so-called Moscow Agreement with Stalin produced not agreement but an endless source of quibbles with Molotov. Both in Germany and Washington there was growing concern that Smith had weakened in his talks with Stalin, that he had not included a clause on Western judicial rights in order to achieve agreement. In Moscow nothing reasonable seemed to lead to an agreement. Finally, on August 27, the three ambassadors and Molotov decided that they would give the military governors in Berlin one week to find a way to end the blockade and introduce Russian currency into Berlin under Four-Power control. The idea that if the men at the top were unable to find a solution, then their subordinates would be able to do so was a novel, if sterile, innovation. From August 31 to September 7, the four military governors met seven times. After lengthy technical discussions, agreement was reached on the currency changeover in Berlin. Then, with time running out, Sokolovsky suddenly expanded the discussion with demands for control over commercial aircraft. The West refused to consider the Soviet demand, which had played no part in the Moscow Agreement, and all discussion ended.[23] The Moscow Agreement had been simply a movement in delay. The West had been given a chance to concede gracefully during the month of high-level negotiations and had not taken advantage of the opportunity. The week of conferences in Berlin had been doomed from the start. The Russians would wait until the West fully realized its impossible situation.

The Western ambassadors' difficulties with Molotov and Stalin were by no means unusual. The course of Western-Soviet negotiations had never really run smoothly. Still the Americans, particularly, persisted in believing that real co-operation and reasonable compromise with the Russians were not only desirable but possible. Trained in debate, practiced in reasoning together, inveterate believers in personal relationships, the American diplomats, professional and amateur, long resisted the notion that the strategy and tactics of Soviet negotiation had little relation to Western norms. The British and French, with a longer exposure to Communist diplomats, tended to be more cynical. The Americans would not believe that their opposite numbers were truly manipulated puppets or dedicated enemies. The more effective Americans proved to be those who had for one reason or another suspended their American predilection for fair play and simply assumed, whether true or not, that all Russians were devious, dishonest and unscrupulous. Only if one were always skeptical, constantly suspicious of agreement, and totally uninterested in personal overtures, could a negotiator hammer out agreements of any kind with Stalin's diplomats. Even as late as September 1948, the Americans were not fully aware of the diplomatic realities, preferring to believe, instead, that two months of negotiation had some substance in reality.

The most optimistic Soviet prognosis of the crisis had foreseen an immediate break in German morale and the collapse of the Western position in Berlin. This would be followed by an ignominious Western withdrawal. When the Germans did not crack and the West did not give way, Stalin had opened the talks in Moscow to acquire his pound of flesh more leisurely. When the West complained about his price and haggled over his methods, he had settled back to wait. On September 6, Forrestal met with Generals Bradley and Gruenther to discuss the amazing Soviet duplicity. There was even some talk that the Russians might not want an agreement. On the next day, the National Security Council suggested an approach to the United Nations if the stalemate continued. On September 8, Secretary Marshall and the Joint Chiefs of Staff met to go over the same old ground. On September 9, the Cabinet met again and Marshall explained that Bevin preferred to go back to Stalin rather than appeal directly to the United Nations. By this time all concerned in the dispute had been driven close to a state of exhaustion.[24]

On September 14, the West presented an aide-mémoire to the Soviet Government stating that the Berlin debacle had been a result of Sokolovsky's refusal to follow the Moscow directive. On September 18, the Soviet Government replied, placing all the blame on the West. To add insult to injury, on September 24, the Soviet Government released to the public a statement presenting its position in a mixture of "half-truths, distorted facts, and malicious charges."[25] Reluctantly some American diplomats came to recognize the Soviet position and accept the fact that time was on Moscow's side. Just as Stalin's point finally seemed to be getting through to the awkward Americans, others less deeply involved in the world of diplomacy felt differently. Where Stalin had an apparently unassailable position in June, when the crisis began, by September the situation was quite different. If diplomacy had stood still, the situation in Berlin had not.

While the long weeks of sterile negotiations had dragged on in the chancellories and embassies of the world, the cause and the core of the crisis, the city of Berlin, had changed its role in many eyes. Suddenly, the ruined capital of the Nazi empire had been unexpectedly transformed into an outpost of Western freedom. Even if the situation was not as sudden or as exaggerated as some journalists indicated, a very real change in the attitude of the occupying powers had occurred and had spread to their civilians at home. For obvious reasons neither the British nor the French had any particular time for Germans of any variety. The Americans, too, had tended to regard all Germans as equally guilty of mass murder and aggressive war. Then, in Berlin, the isolated and often hampered efforts of some Germans to create free institutions and to protect them against the Communists had gradually created a sharper vision of the nature of the German people. This was particularly true for the Americans, who had less to forgive and thus were better able to discriminate among the varieties of Berliners. That many of the German men and women who sought to build a democratic political party or a free trade union had suffered exile, imprisonment and torture under Hitler helped to convince many Americans that some Germans at least had Western values. Now the Berliners refused to knuckle under to the Russian blackmail. Many in the West were impressed in spite of themselves. Even if the outlook for the winter was gloomy, even in the face of Soviet bribes and warnings, the Berliners resisted Russian pressure. Their faith in the promises of the West and their stubborn determination to hold out awakened American sympathy. This metamorphosis from pariah to ally had far-reaching effects first on the Western policy in Berlin and then in Europe.

As the first planes in the airlift droned overhead, the German struggle for the city took a form different from negotiations or conferences. Although the Soviets were simply waiting for the West's compliance, they continued their efforts to erode the West's position in Berlin by a complex variety of maneuvers: kidnapings, rumors, propaganda, and bribes. All proved amazingly ineffective. In a city-wide display of solidarity only 60,000 of West Berlin's population of 2,500,000 accepted the Soviet offer to allow anyone to purchase food in the Eastern Sector. Instead, smuggling became a patriotic gesture. For many the blockade was not simply a matter of waiting it out. Many had to defend their jobs and their institutions, for the Soviets tried to seize control of all city-wide organizations. Government departments were torn apart, officials intimidated, and mob scenes staged at the Berlin City Hall. On September 6, a Communist-directed mob took over the City Hall and forced the city government minus the tame SED into the Western Zone. Western protests, private or public, had no effect. The Russians intended to absorb their half of the city immediately. They erased one by one the last vestiges of city-wide institutions, splitting East Berlin away, isolated and free of contamination.

On September 9, the people of Western Berlin answered the Russians' tactics by a mass meeting. For two months these monster meetings had been held, but in view of the staged riots on September 6, the democratic parties and unions decided to hold another. The protest was planned for September 9 in front of the ruined Reichstag. The reluctant British had to be persuaded to allow a demonstration so close to the Russian Zone. Finally they agreed. For two days the Radio in the American Sector (RIAS) announced the rally. By mid-afternoon on September 9, it seemed as if all Berlin had begun to move toward the Reichstag. By five o'clock, as far as the eye could see, 300,000 Germans spread out until they merged and faded into the distance. Franz Neumann, leader of the SPD, and Ernst Reuter, the SPD mayor, spoke of Berlin's meaning for the world. As speaker followed speaker, some of the crowd grew reckless just as the British had feared. They rushed toward the Russian troops at Brandenburg Gate. The Russians fired into the surging crowd and the British barely managed to prevent an ugly incident from turning into a massacre. Even if marred by Russian shots, the September 9 meeting revealed the extent of the Berliners' commitment to the West and the depth of the Russian alienation. The Germans had opted for democracy even when the success of the airlift remained problematical to the Americans in Washington.[26]

At first, of course, the civilians of Berlin doubted the airlift. But, while the experts in America took almost six months to be convinced, the Berliners by necessity had to believe sooner. The airlift was their only hope of avoiding absorption into the bleak and brutal Russian empire. As long as the planes flew in, Berlin would be safe. "The roar of the airplanes became the recurring motif of the resistance and the pulsation of the life in the besieged city." Even with maximum plane loads, which did not come for many months, the airlift could barely maintain life in the city. Gas and electricity were available only a few hours a day, and often those hours came in the middle of the night. Most public transportation had to be severely curtailed; buses were rare, and the subway did not run at night. Without raw materials or fuel many factories closed, and all commercial activity except smuggling dwindled away.[27] To prevent total collapse and maintain Clay's estimated minimum tonnage needed for subsistence, an Air Lift Command under American Major General William H. Tunner was created. He immediately began a program to get more tonnage into Berlin by speeding up plane maintenance, accelerating flight frequency and, above all, creating an organization which would, under optimum conditions, put a plane down in Berlin every three minutes.

Tunner and the West began to create the vast, far-flung system necessary to land planes in Berlin as a regular, routine matter. A wide network of repair and maintenance stations spread across Europe and to America. In the Great Falls Air Force Base in Montana a complete mockup of the Berlin air corridors allowed pilots to practice without risk. The pilots went through 133 hours of training, including three landings with a C-54 loaded with 70,000 tons of sand ballast. These pilots then joined others from Guam and Panama, Mobile, San Antonio, and the Azores, who flew into Germany with their planes. Into Berlin, in five levels, they came and went on a round-the-clock schedule, touching down only for a few minutes while the highly trained German ground groups swiftly unloaded the food and coal on a split-second schedule. The British flew in Sunderland flying boats on the Wannsee River. In the French Zone at Tegel still another airport was built. Scheduled for its first flight on January 1, work went so well the date was moved up to December 15. Actually the airport received its first plane on November 5, two months early. The whole complicated operation of the airlift, including weather stations far at sea and the 200-hour inspections and maintenance in the center at Burtonwood in England, gradually fell into routine. As Tunner was later to point out, the value of all this experience to the American Air Force was beyond price.

> *If we gained nothing from the lift . . . it would still be worth while for what it has taught us in the techniques of using masses of big airplanes in a concentrated operation.*[28]

To the German civilians in Berlin it was their immediate salvation that remained of interest, not the long-term knowledge of techniques. As long as the planes flew in and out, they could feel secure.

Elsewhere there remained those who still considered the airlift nothing more than postponing the inevitable. The tonnage did climb, particularly with the arrival of the larger C-54s, but many doubted if it could last. On August 13, Black Friday, an unexpectedly heavy fog cut visibility to ground zero. The lift was hampered so badly that only 1,500 tons reached Berlin. This was the all-time low. By early September, General Tunner had produced an operation as regular as a clock. On September 9, the daily average had climbed to 4,000 tons, and Secretary of Air Stuart Symington told the National Security Council that this figure would soon be 5,000 tons. When Secretary Marshall left for Paris on September 19, to attend the European session of the United Nations, he left with the knowledge that on the previous day, American Air Force Day, the lift had flown in 7,000 tons. With a determined Berlin population for whom was felt increasing empathy and responsibility, and an airlift that could deliver 7,000 tons a day, the West's assets had increased.

After the Russian note of September 18, the American desire to go before the United Nations became the only diplomatic gambit remaining. In Paris the Foreign Ministers of France and Britain met with Secretary Marshall to work out the details. Although the chances of a sudden Soviet concession seemed slight, an appeal to the United Nations would transfer the sterile discussions held in secret to an open forum and display the West's justifiable grievances to world opinion. On September 29, in identical notes, the Western powers asked Secretary-General Trygve Lie to call a Security Council meeting to consider the threat to peace posed by the Berlin blockade. Although Lie was pretty much aware of the hopelessness of a settlement in the Security Council where the Soviet veto would swiftly end discussion, he did feel there was a chance for quiet mediation and began using members of the Secretariat staff to maintain contacts with the official American and Soviet delegations. The Americans Abraham Feller and William H. Stoneman and the Russian Arkady Sobolev felt out their countrymen. As Lie foresaw and as the West expected, the Soviets responded angrily to the demand for a Security Council meeting, claiming that the United Nations had no jurisdiction. Despite Soviet delegate Andrei Vishinsky's ultimatum that Russia would take no part in the discussions, on October 5, the Security Council included the dispute on its agenda.[29]

At the meeting on October 5, one by one, the three Western delegates—Dr. Philip Jessup of the United States, Sir Alexander Cadogan of Great Britain and Alexandre Parodi of France—carefully outlined the West's legal rights and the Russians' unilateral violations. The six other Security Council nations—self-defined neutrals, Argentina, Belgium, Canada, China, Colombia and Syria—immediately began independent efforts to find a solution. Under the chairmanship of Argentina's Foreign Minister Juan Bramuglia, they sought a formula for compromise. At the same time Lie had been meeting with Jessup and Sobolev seeking his own "independent formulation of a proposal for four-power control and use of Soviet currency in Berlin." All contacts remained doubtful of any solutions. The Soviet Union apparently insisted on introduction of the currency before the problems of four-power control had been completely solved. The United States demanded further clarification after the lifting of travel restrictions. In effect the Russians demanded full control of the currency of Berlin, which would be not only a considerable propaganda victory but also assure them of a dominant position in Berlin. This was not as much as had been hoped for in June but would still be a "victory." Then, too, if need be, the blockade could always be tried again. On their part, the West seemed willing to negotiate, but unwilling to pay off the Russians in any acceptable form for lifting the blockade. On October 22, the six-power neutral committee presented a resolution to the Security Council on which it felt a solution could be based. Although it would make the Eastern mark the only currency in Berlin, the plan called for real four-power control. Vishinsky found this unacceptable. The Soviet Union was interested in concessions, not compromises. Russia vetoed the plan on October 25.[30]

After this subtle maneuver, the West was skeptical of further negotiations. Cadogan informed Lie that Foreign Secretary Bevin remained unmoved by the prospect of informal negotiations. On November 3, the United Nations General Assembly approved an appeal to the Great Powers to renew efforts to compose differences and establish a lasting peace. Although the West wanted no more direct negotiations and saw no hope of indirect ones, they saw no disadvantage in allowing Bramuglia's neutrals to carry on conversations. On November 13, Lie and Dr. Herbert V. Evatt of Australia, President of the General Assembly, addressed an unheralded and unexpected letter to the four major powers asking for a summit meeting. The request received an icy Western reply, since such a meeting could lead nowhere but to a further impasse. Russia took full advantage of Lie's well-meant opening to accept immediate conversations, but the Russian note made no mention of lifting the blockade. The summit meeting had to be discarded. With all the arrows from his diplomatic quiver now gone, Lie fell back on the neutrals who had organized a special committee. They had appointed Dr. N. Kaldor as Secretary and Gunnar Myrdal of Sweden as the expert on economic affairs. As the committee met to piece together one more report, the blockade dragged on. Officially all diplomatic avenues but the neutrals' detour into committee work had been blocked.[31]

Lie was not so easily discouraged. He maintained his contacts, East and West, despite the chilly atmosphere of the deadlock. He met with Andrei Vishinsky to feel out the Russian position. He met with Philip Jessup and Dean Rusk to find out the Americans' feelings. There had been no thaw. Soviet diplomacy seemed to be suffering from something of a time lag as the situation changed faster than the Soviet diplomatic position. By November even the doubters and scoffers had to accept the airlift. The successive washout dates, the day of evacuation for Berlin, had passed one after another while the heavily loaded transports continued to roar into Tempelhof and Gamov. On October 15, the Combined Airlift Task Force on a joint Anglo-American basis under General Tunner had created the permanent bureaucratic superstructure necessary for modern success. When Clay flew to Washington a week later, he learned of the approval of the National Security Council for sixty-four more C-54s to replace the old C-47s. Clay knew that these "with the British contribution would successfully carry us through the winter."[32] The Russians did not know it or would not admit it. On November 2, Philip Jessup told Lie of the "transports arriving like pearls on a string."

The Russians were out of date. Time was no longer on Moscow's side. The surprising election victory of President Truman underlined the continuity of the American policy of holding on in Berlin. Washington and London, somewhat amazed at the effectiveness of the airlift, prepared for a long and exhaustive test of wills with the Russians. They even tentatively moved over to the offensive in the German arena. By mid-September increasingly severe new Western border measures had created a mild form of counter-blockade. With the counter-blockade, the militancy of the Berliners had grown.

Regardless of the new strength of the Allied position, however, the diplomatic deadlock continued in the United Nations and in all the official and private contacts between East and West. The Russians would not admit the changed circumstances. They continued to plug the holes in the walls around Berlin so that by late fall they had so far as possible sealed off the city from the surrounding Eastern Zone. At the same time, their efforts to dominate the Berlin *Magistrat* were increasingly producing split departments. The Western parties would not allow a *coup d'état* by stages and the Russians could not tolerate any free political institutions. All through October and into November, the struggle continued, with the result that the Russians split Berlin in two. On November 30, they recognized the de facto schism by acknowledging an East Sector *Magistrat*.[33] The boundless Russian prospects of June had narrowed considerably. Publicly, in the corridors of world diplomacy the Russians remained calm and sure, but in Berlin they had been obliged to ensure at least half of the city by the use of force and violence.

The West's confidence and enthusiasm grew week by week. The

airlift's only real crisis came during November when for two weeks absolutely impossible weather cut flights to a minimum. While there was sufficient food stockpiled in the city, the coal supplies soon were endangered. When the weather broke, Clay decided to fly in only coal at first and live on the food stocks. The gamble paid off. By December the daily average flown in had reached 4,500 tons. By January this climbed to 5,500. The Soviet blockade had become not a threat but an irritant; this irritant, however, went far toward producing a pearl.

On October 20, the West German Parliament Council had met at Bonn to draft a constitution for West Germany. The success of the Berliners in creating their own democratic institutions in the face of Russian terror and Western apathy, along with the growing Allied sympathy with the population, had created an atmosphere of mutual faith and understanding between the Germans and the occupying powers, particularly the Americans, which would have seemed impossible a year before. In the face of the Russian threat, Britain and even France were more willing to concede far broader self-government to the Germans than had been their original intention. That such confidence had been well placed became abundantly clear on December 5 when Berlin voted overwhelmingly for the democratic parties despite Soviet demands for an election boycott. On their part, the Germans' bitterness and despair resolved into hope. More than anything else the example of Berlin did much to alleviate the black and general guilt and national disgrace which had been Hitler's legacy for many.

Politically, then, Soviet pressure in Berlin had resulted in a hardening of German opposition to the Communist system. As a byproduct it bolstered the future West German Government which the Germans felt had been earned and not imposed. As a corollary, there was an increased Western acceptance of expanded German self-government and self-expression in light of Berlin's response to the blockade. Economically, life for the Berliners remained bleak, cold and monotonous, a grim affair among the ruins; but the infusion of ERP funds and, more important, the impact of a stable currency had revitalized West Germany. Instead of a prostrate defeated nation, torn into pieces and living on handouts, West Germany had taken sufficient steps along the road to recovery that some of the more optimistic had already begun to talk of a "miracle." By December, then, Germany was well on the road to being incorporated into the anti-Communist Western European politico-economic system. The blockade had not worked; the pressure in Berlin had not worked; in fact, the results had boomeranged.

At first tentatively, certainly reluctantly, the Russians had to reconsider not only their German policy but also their prospects in Europe generally. Crude intimidation, armed coups and semilegal

Communist takeovers backed by the presence of the Red Army could no longer be counted upon to expand Soviet influence. The economic conditions which bred chaos in Western Europe were disappearing. Even with most of the chips in their hands in Berlin, efforts to swallow up the *Magistrat* and through it the city had produced only a divided city. Without the physical presence of the Red Army, any further Communist expansion was thwarted in Europe. Although the nature of Soviet decision-making remains enigmatic, there is some evidence that, by December, Stalin had decided on a switch of emphasis to a "peace" campaign. The division of Berlin had been completed and a tame East Sector *Magistrat* created. Shift of policy or not, the blockade remained, the East German press kept up a shrill anti-Western barrage, and the kidnapings of anti-Communist Germans continued.

In the West, therefore, few in December could see any softening of the Soviet stand. Still, for Berlin, it was the best December and the best Christmas since the war. Vice President-elect Alben Barkley, the ubiquitous Bob Hope, the Secretary of the Army, the Secretary of Air, Irving Berlin, and a host of others flew into the city for the holidays. The airlift flew Operation *Santa Claus* bringing in Christmas packages. Everyone from Bob Hope to General James Doolittle told the Berliners they had earned their place in the West. Clay had nothing but praise for them.

> *The determination of the people did not falter. They were proud to carry their burden as the price of their freedom, and though the price was high it brought them something in return that had become dear. They had earned their right to freedom; they had atoned for their failure to repudiate Hitler when such repudiation on their part might have stopped his rise to power.*[34]

Just before Christmas the neutrals' committee, in particular the two experts Myrdal and Kaldor, had presented their formula for the solution of the currency problem. Although the French and British were inclined to accept the report as a basis for discussion, Washington felt that the situation in Berlin had deteriorated so greatly as to make adjustments to the Moscow Agreement of August no longer particularly useful. The Americans felt that the report had been constructed so that it appeased the Russians who had caused the crisis. In January, when the experts of the four powers met in Paris, the United States presented a counter-formula which would have allowed the Eastern mark into the Western sectors of Berlin as the sole currency, but only under Western control. At last the Americans could afford to be uncompromising. As expected, the Russians rejected this repeated offer of nothing. In turn, the three Western powers after some delays then rejected the neutrals' formula which Russia had accepted. Even this

Russian "acceptance," obviously solely for propaganda purposes, was hedged about by massive reservations. If the West no longer had to consider appeasing the Russians, the Russians for a time had to continue demanding concessions in order to keep face. With the failure of the neutrals' formula and the continued diplomatic stalemate, Washington demanded that the Western mark be circulated in the three Western Zones of Berlin until the city could be reunited. On February 11, the Committee of Neutrals informed the President of the Security Council that further work would not be useful.

On a different level, however, further maneuvers had begun. During January, after the United Nations delegates had returned to Lake Success, Lie mentioned to the Soviet delegate, Jacob Malik, that he might talk privately to Professor Jessup if the Soviet Union wanted a settlement. Malik remained noncommittal. Then, on January 31, Stalin replied to a variety of questions addressed to him by J. Kingsbury Smith of the International News Service. Later, as the American Kremlinologists pored over his answers, they noted that Stalin had not specifically referred to the currency problem in discussing Berlin. This might mean that Russia had decided to give up negotiating on the basis of the moribund Moscow Agreement. On February 15, Jessup casually asked Malik while they stood chatting privately in the delegates' lounge if Stalin's omission had been accidental. Malik said that he would find out. There for a month the matter rested.[35]

While the Russians had by February formally begun their peace campaign, Moscow seemed in no hurry to terminate the blockade or their firm stand in Berlin. What seemed to be going on was a gradual shift with the Russian hard and soft approaches mingling in some confusion. An anti-American speech was canceled on January 28, but, on February 9, an independent union official was reported missing since January 31 and assumed abducted by the Soviet police. The Eastern Zone press reported on February 15 that a German peace petition with five million signatures was to be forwarded to the United Nations. At the same time, the Russians instituted stricter control of the border and cut down on the number of permissible checkpoints. On the Western side of the checkpoints, the situation improved by leaps and bounds. Airlift tonnage increased, and even Prime Minister Clement Attlee flew in to see the city. Ernst Reuter made a triumphant tour to France, Great Britain and the United States. He came home to a hero's welcome, the symbol of the new Germany. Russia's hard line had obviously long since reached the point of diminishing returns. On March 15, Malik sought out Jessup to reveal that Stalin's lapse had been intentional; in other words, the Russians had given up hope of getting anything at all out of the blockade.

The blockade had indeed become a farce. The airlift had moved into high gear. The planes flew in vast tonnages not only of flour and coal but also steamrollers, a fire tender, three-and-a-half-ton girders, electric generators, even a goat, and two million pine seedlings to replace the trees cut for firewood. On April 16, "the Easter Parade," almost 1,400 aircraft landed 12,940 tons. Huge new planes like the Douglas C-74 *Globemasters* or the Lockheed C-119 *Constellations*, along with sophisticated new all-weather equipment, had turned the airlift from a ramshackle patchwork operation into a symbol of American technical and scientific superiority. Every new flight made the Russians look increasingly foolish. For a variety of reasons, Moscow realized that the time had come to extract themselves from the rigid posture created by their Berlin position but not without a face-saving display of negotiations.

Even the formalities of contemporary diplomacy are complex. Although Malik and perhaps Jessup realized the charade, new highly secret and very intensive discussions began. Jessup and Malik met secretly at the Soviet delegation's Park Avenue headquarters and once at Lie's Forest Hills home. Although the negotiations were a tightly kept secret, the United States on March 21 introduced the West mark into Berlin. This sealed the division of the city and ended any slight possibility of appeasement. On the following day, Malik informed Jessup that if a definite date could be fixed for a Foreign Ministers' conference, then the blockade could be lifted even before the meeting. In the meanwhile the Soviets intensified their new look: the Cultural and Scientific Conference for World Peace, the first in a dreary series, met in New York; a second later met in Paris and simultaneously in Prague for those refused French visas. On April 19, the day the peace conference opened in Paris, the East Zone marked the event with decorations, slogans and the ringing of church bells. By this time, the British and French had been drawn into the Jessup-Malik discussions. A few rumors began to sift out, but not even Clay had as yet been informed.

On April 26, the Russian news agency Tass published an account of the discussions. On May 5, the three Western powers issued a joint statement announcing that the blockade would be lifted on May 12 and that a meeting of the Council of Foreign Ministers subsequently would take place. The proposed conference was "to consider questions relating to Germany and problems arising out of the situation in Berlin, including the question of currency in Berlin." All of which translated out to be a Russian retreat. Moscow gave up the blockade for a momentary propaganda forum at Paris. It could hardly even be considered a face-saving gesture. At midnight on May 11–12, the Russian General

Chuikov formally lifted the blockade. Chuikov, the hero of Stalingrad, had replaced Sokolovsky in March just in time to see the end of another Russian siege. On the morning of May 12, the streets of Berlin were filled with released school children, mass meetings and endless celebrations. The first trucks arrived bedecked with flowers. Overhead the planes of the airlift droned on. The following day an American plane landed with the one millionth ton of coal. In the twelve months of the blockade, United States planes had logged 189,844 flights and the British 87,884.[36] They had flown in 1,952,660 tons at the cost of forty-eight lives. No one could have foreseen the incredible growth of the airlift nor the implications for Berlin, for Germany, and for the entire world balance of power.

The Russian decision to cut their losses in Berlin and give up the blockade without receiving any concessions has never been analyzed to the satisfaction of all. In view of the minimal cost to the Russians and the very heavy expenditure of Western talent, equipment, and money, the Russians must have had compelling reasons. These could hardly be the rather limited counter-blockade, annoying but hardly more, or the propaganda impact of the massive airlift, embarrassing but nothing more. Both could have been tolerated in return for the continued commitment of Western strength to cargo carrying. Rather, two general interrelated factors persuaded the Russians that the time had come for a change. As had so often happened in Russian history, a check in Europe which temporarily thwarted further expansion had produced a quickening of interest in Asia. If all the news from Europe had been bad during 1948 and 1949, the reverse had been true in the Far East. The Chinese Communists, little understood and often discounted in Moscow, had exceeded Russia's wildest expectations. Their string of military victories had culminated in the capture of Shanghai. Asia had been transformed. A whole variety of options had opened in Korea, Japan, Manchuria and Mongolia for Soviet penetration. In Asia the hard line, seemingly outdated in Europe in 1949, might still be used to advantage. In Europe the switch to the soft line could go on with a flurry of peace conferences and a demand for a popular front. There was no real point in holding out over Berlin.

As a result Russia suddenly had shown an interest in real negotiations and a rapid settlement. Heretofore all the various bodies from the Security Council to the August meetings with Stalin, all the lower level approaches, the informal conversations, the "unofficial" mediations and public airings had proved futile in that no grounds for discussion existed. Although the twelve months of conversation may have reduced tensions somewhat, seldom did the discussions deal with realities. The endless technical talks on currency had simply masked a Soviet demand for hegemony in Berlin, hardly a subject on which technicians, however skilled, could find a satisfactory formula. When all hopes of real Western concessions had faded, the Soviet initiated secret negotiations more to create an aura of concession than to secure any material benefits. Stalin did not have to worry about the effect of a defeat on his own people; either they would not be told or they would believe the official explanation. On the other hand, the new and generous Soviet concession might influence the uncommitted. Thus not only were the Russians affable about the details of lifting the blockade but they even made several gestures as signs of good will, such as returning 4,000 freight cars to West Germany. Acid and gall had not worked, so honey was offered instead.

While the awkward switch to sweetness and light did little to impress the recently awakened and alarmed leaders of the West, it was warmly received by Soviet sympathizers and the new neutrals. The attempt to disarm the West had come much too late to affect any but the gullible. Hardened suspicions, sincere disagreement, even historical antagonism had all given way in Western Europe before the awesome threat of Soviet aggression. A quick switch in Berlin and 4,000 freight cars were not going to make any difference. On April 4, 1949, the North Atlantic Treaty Organization pact had been signed by President Truman. On May 8, the Parliamentary Council at Bonn had adopted a new basic law for Western Germany.

The West, despite all its internal contradictions and encrusted distrust, had united in a military confederation that in time would obviously include the infant German Republic. The transformation of Germany from criminal to cohort would take time but the process had been immeasurably accelerated by the example of the Berliners. Perhaps as important as the Western countermoves or rearmament and realignment had been the hothouse year of Berlin, which if it had not saved Germany's soul had at least opened the door to salvation. Whatever lingering susceptibility to authoritarianism might remain in Germany, however much evasion of the shared guilt of Hitler critical observers might find in Germany, there would remain the legend of Berlin. For the Germans a new life began on that bleak, rainy day when, stretching as far as the eye could see before the burnt-out Reichstag, the cold and ragged population of Berlin had shouted their defiance in the face of the Communists with no assurance of victory except their own faith in democracy.

8 A Summary of Sieges

> The worse policy is to attack cities. Attack cities only when there is no alternative. —SUN TZU

SEVEN sieges do not make a summation of all sieges at all times, not even modern sieges, nor need seven battles reveal the nature of a war, not even a recent one. Still, the scholar and the soldier both hope that the failures of the past need not be repeated, at least not regularly. Few generals or historians have ever doubted that a study of the past should in time produce broad wisdom. For the professional soldier the assimilation of the general maxims and the choice axioms of former wars and ancient writers is considered essential. That a grasp of the past does not produce contemporary perfection is all too apparent; for, if the rules of war could be learned as are those of grammar, there would be no losing generals. The difficulty is in the application of generalities in the heat and uncertainty of battle. While Sun Tzu is meaningful, even valid, after 2,000 years, his works would have been of dubious worth to a corps commander outside Stalingrad. It often seems that the greater the wisdom shown by the writer, the more difficult a sly battlefield application. On the highest level the timeless verities of war are as beautifully wrought and universally valid as the admonitions of a mystic and just about as ambiguous in daily application. On the other end of the scale, the essential techniques of war must be learned, hence taught, before practiced. The preparation of fields of fire, the construction of earthworks, the use of a lance should be pursued to automatic perfection. These skills, traditional or fresh, are more the province of the drillmaster and less that of the historian. Techniques are not so much the gift of the past as the practice of the present.

The real lessons of military history—often overestimated, regularly misunderstood, seldom of immediate aid—are neither absolute nor infallible. Generals and schoolboys, often in time interchangeable, have pored over the records for pleasure as much as for profit. As an art form alone military history would retain its charm, its universal attraction; but it is the possible insight into the future battles, rather than into the nature of man, that holds out the greatest appeal. Even if the past is seen as through a glass darkly, a window smudged by pride and *prejudice, too often reflecting the viewer, no one as yet has given up hope that former battles may somehow give insight into future wars. If there is a common thread in contemporary sieges, then a contrast or comparison of the seven cities may shed some light on a surprisingly common variety of contemporary battle.*

In general the course of modern warfare has indicated that, just as in Sun Tzu's time, attacks on cities are best avoided. A dedicated and determined population, militia or professional, properly motivated and inured to suffering, hedgehogged into the rubble of a modern city, is one of the most formidable opponents imaginable. The nature of the motivation is not essential. It may be patriotism, class hatred, fatalism; it is only necessary that the motive be sufficiently intense to ensure that the population prefer the siege to surrender. So dedicated and so protected by the crumpled remains of a great city, a ferocious and lengthy battle is assured. Only time, massed fire, the weight of iron, and the daily exchange of life for a few yards of cinders has proved successful. Once sealed within the city, the defenders seem to grow not despondent but defiant, resisting intensely all pressure with inflexible resolution. Even the noncombatants at their lowest ebb retain a sullen reluctance to surrender.

No general, however contemptuous of his opponent or confident of his own army, should engage in such a battle without the most overwhelming military and political reasons. Often, of course, a battle within a city is unavoidable without risking a deterioration of the entire war, as was the case at Warsaw in 1944. At times, however, the siege develops almost independently of the commander's original intention, as was the case at Stalingrad in 1942. To recognize the dangers before the battles, as Glubb did in Jerusalem, or to withdraw from the risks in time, as Franco did in Madrid, requires some courage and considerable judgment. At times the heat of battle and the hope of sudden victory prevent a general from easily giving up the initiative. To assess the possibilities in preparation of the assault, as did Yamashita at Singapore, requires an iron army and supreme confidence; even then, as Paulus found, success is not always assured. In most cases, prudence tends to pay greater virtues to the besieger than daring; but once the advantages of victory have been coldly weighed against the inevitable costs, the techniques for success are available. No city in isolation, no matter how determined, can withstand superior force forever, even if resistance is pursued to the final death as in the Warsaw Ghetto. On the other hand, no assault, whatever its technique, can assume unlimited time and permanent isolation, as the Russians discovered in Berlin. Ideally, as Sun Tzu pointed out, those skilled in war capture cities without assaulting them, but since ideal conditions seldom exist during wartime, sieges have been and still are a traditional form of warfare.

In the case of Madrid in 1936, no one had anticipated even the theoretical possibility of a siege. To the Nationalists, the city had been envisaged as a goal, never a battleground. The city had no real capacity for defense: no fortifications, no civilian defense, no professional army, apparently even no effective leadership. That such a city could resist was never seriously considered during the summer. That it could be defended was not seriously considered until November. Then the effectiveness of the militia pushed back into a natural fortification of ruined buildings became all too clear to Franco. Fighting within the University City for the first time indicated that long training and refined skills need have no place in modern city fighting. A Nationalist officer, no matter how highly trained, crouched in a basement of a burning building proved no more effective than an equally brave but totally untrained Spanish peasant. The nature of modern construction, the immense complexities of urban building on a variety of levels with imperishable materials, gave all the advantages to the defender. Efforts, limited by the nature and number of the weapons available, to terrorize the city into surrender proved only that the civilians had a greater capacity for suffering than had been anticipated. There proved to be no easy victory at Madrid, and Franco pulled back, preferring indirect attacks on the flanks to costly and sterile frontal assaults. Once the center of gravity had shifted elsewhere, the professional observers, fascinated with new weapons and new techniques, tended to discount the events of November 1936. Few felt there was any general application in the short and brutal grappling within the University City. Despite the Spanish experience, the siege remained obsolete.

The attack on London from the air was considered by all as the ultimate means of warfare, a difference in kind from all previous battles. Alone, unaided by ground troops, the great attack of September 9, 1940, might well end the war in holocaust and panic. Actually, the German air attack proved to be a new form of artillery bombardment which to some degree eliminated the distance barrier but by no means changed the whole nature of warfare. Once the battle had been joined, the Germans could punish the civilians of London and hamper the economic life of the city with their flying artillery, but they could not do sufficient destruction to demolish London nor could they create sufficient panic to terrorize the population. The limited bomb loads narrowly determined the possible damage, so narrowly that the official British misgivings proved misplaced. London could function under the bombs. It is now apparent that an immense quantity of high explosives is necessary to batter down a modern city.

A far more effective method of destruction was to be found in the monster fire storm which, when properly stoked, could burn out whole cities. Even then, such a disaster did not always totally erase a city's economic capacity and seldom broke civilian morale despite the incredible number of casualties. Attack from the air, like bombardment by artillery, can seldom win a siege alone if the civilians are willing to suffer and to die. Since the normal reaction of a civilian population, whether British or Japanese or German, to bombing is renewed dedication, strategic bombing can succeed only when the nation as a whole is unwilling to continue the suffering pointlessly. In London, in 1940 and 1941, the civilian response was such that Great Britain could continue the war. If as Churchill pointed out, the German bomb capacity had been greater, then the Government would have had to reconsider; it is unlikely, however, that even then civilian terror would have forced Britain's decision. London revealed that not only does a great city take a long time to destroy but that a determined population can take a great deal of punishment.

In the case of Singapore, the factors which made defiance and defense possible in London and Madrid did not exist or did so only in an abortive form. The civilian population, particularly the British, and to some extent the military, assumed their inviolate superiority over any attacker, especially the Japanese. Where the people of London and Madrid feared the enemy, Singapore scorned him. Safe with its illusion of invulnerability, it believed sacrifice would be unnecessary and even undesirable. Once the true nature of the Japanese threat had been made clear, very little time remained to respond. The power structure of the city dominated by a thin layer of authority, based more on tradition and class than loyalty, proved completely inflexible. Divided by race and religion, sheltered by class and prejudice, with no experience in unity and few common loyalties, only a revolutionary effort instigated by inspiring leadership could have succeeded. Instead, until the last, the tried and true colonial formulas long outdated elsewhere found favor with the military and civil authorities. Thus the potential of the Asiatic population was ignored, their energies went unharnessed, their loyalty, if any, unclaimed. The British control mechanism under strain revealed that the Empire's efficacy had been no more than a myth. Once the military and material failures of the Empire had been revealed to the Asians, the British could find no replacement. The small complacent minority ruling an alien mass in traditional ways thus proved incapable of rising to a new challenge in a new manner. In London the British people had made their blood, sweat, tears and toil into historic virtues. In Singapore these were symbols of weakness or class failure. Instead of defiance before certain defeat, the British accepted disgrace first and assumed it was defeat.

Even after the Japanese landings on the island, if the population had been inspired to suffer and to die, to ignore the lack of water and *the threat of bombs, to fight for each house, the possibility of at least a stalemate and perhaps even victory still existed. Although the Japanese position may not have been as precarious as Yamashita later indicated, the problems of taking a defiant city with an army limited in size were real enough. Instead, the British Army seized upon civilian suffering as sufficient cause of surrender. After the illusion of British invulnerability passed never to return, the civilians accepted the Japanese punishment stoically. How much more effective British resistance would have been if the civilians had been properly inspired and properly organized remains, of course, problematical, but a defiant population might well have inclined the army to fight to protect them rather than to surrender to save them. There is no doubt, however, that the collapse of the illusion of Fortress Singapore and the debilitating effect on the British was merely a reflection of the limitations of an antedated class structure. Such limitations might not have been insurmountable if a Churchill or a MacArthur had appeared, but Singapore in 1941 proved no breeding ground for defiance in adversity. The ultimate fate of Singapore might have been that of Bataan, but in subsequent years the British would not have had to return to Asia with the heavy albatross of ready capitulation hanging about their necks. As it was, all the individual bravery and personal sacrifice went for naught because the traditional methods could not mold the huge and divided city into a fortress which might have turned aside the Japanese lance.*

At Stalingrad the techniques of modern siege warfare were honed and perfected. The use of massed fire, the methods of holding a house or taking a room, the flexible perimeter, and the value of snipers became part of a textbook routine. After Stalingrad, all modern military academies and special training schools could teach city fighting as they once had taught artillery placement or tank deployment. At times during the next few years, various formations would have to relearn the lessons of the Sixth Army or the tactics of Chuikov, but the new text would be the same even if the language differed. City fighting had been absorbed into the curriculum of war. On a tactical level the battle of Stalingrad became a military event of supreme pedagogical importance, evoking explanation, detailed analysis, vindications and reasoned reviews. For the Germans the trauma had to be understood to be absorbed; for the Russians the victory had to be elaborated to be appreciated; for all soldiers the battle had to be incorporated into the copybook just as had Waterloo or Gettysburg. For siege warfare the most significant factor was the very long lapse between the beginning of the battle in late August 1942 and the realization by the Germans of the existence of a siege. For much too long, the command of the Sixth Army felt that one more battalion would do the trick. For nearly two months, despite growing uneasiness, the Sixth Army felt certain that Stalingrad could be taken with one more frontal attack. While many have pointed out Hitler's strategical shortcomings during the campaign, less attention has been paid to the misguided confidence and consequent crudity of maneuver on the part of the battlefield commanders. On all levels the Germans felt that they had operational initiative when in effect all their mobility had long been lost. To become entangled and not accept the predicament with innovation led to disaster.

On a strategic level, to recognize the dangers of a siege and withdraw as Franco did or to accept the risks and advance as Yamashita did, seems essential. Although Hitler's insistence on the capture of the city without reference to the rest of the front now appears in error, the German generals conducting the battle failed to respond to the new conditions. In those ideal chessboard campaigns so beloved by German military historians, the Russians, with a basic superiority in manpower, could have funneled men into Stalingrad in sufficient quantity to defend the city to doomsday. All the individual superiority of the German soldier with his superb training and disciplined skills was canceled out in the ruins of the city. The capture of a well-defended modern city requires a very considerable advantage in men and material on the part of the attacker. The Germans simply did not have this and refused to acknowledge the fact. Even when the position was reversed and the Sixth Army isolated, supplied only by an ineffectual airlift, the Russians required over two months to extinguish German resistance. Once the siege mentality is implanted, whether by lack of choice or by political commitment or even by innate stubbornness, a long and grueling battle is assured. The failure to perceive this had the most disastrous consequences for the entire German effort on the Eastern Front.

At Warsaw, in 1943 and 1944, the Germans had an opportunity to use the techniques and tactics brought back from the East. Even then, the fantastic difficulties of beating down a determined defense within a city were not fully appreciated. Although the Jews within the Ghetto managed to create a coherent defense for only one day, their armed resistance went on beyond the bounds of belief. Since the threat of death held no terror but rather a certain attraction, the Germans were forced to kill every defender, to murder or to drag off bodily every civilian. In order to reach the Jews it proved necessary to destroy the entire Ghetto, burning it out and tearing it down. Even then a tiny number of Jews managed to survive in the rubble. In the 1944 rising, the Germans could, with all the techniques of attack perfected on the Jews, crush the rebellion with the slow and costly routine necessary. With the unexpected time at their disposal and a massive superiority, the Germans found that the agonizing procedure of attack, although effective, was an unbelievable drain on the limited resources of the German Army. If the Polish Home Army had not decided there was some immediate advantage in surrender, for the civilians at least, the struggle could have dragged on for months.

In all the sieges the capacity of man to suffer had been grossly underestimated by his leaders. Though the Polish population, unlike the Jews, was not prepared for extinction and the Polish Home Army had none of the control apparatus of the Russians at Stalingrad or the British in London, nevertheless the Poles resigned themselves to endure. Apparently the necessity for formal civil control declines in relation to the exterior pressure. Polish patriotism, Spanish class hatred, traditional British determination—all these proved more significant than the efficiency of a governmental structure or a party control. In Singapore, of course, the Imperial ideal was quite insufficient and no one could produce an alternative loyalty or even a shared hatred. Once the ring is closed, the trapped population, if given any opportunity at all, chooses to endure rather than to submit. In Warsaw this reflex was writ large. Merely to suffer courageously does not prevent defeat. In isolation, sieges could be prosecuted successfully. The Germans were given the time by the Russian withdrawal in 1944 and had perfected the techniques learned in 1942 and 1943. While an insurrection within a city has immense initial advantages for the defenders, unless ultimate, if not immediate, relief arrives, a superior force employing appropriate techniques can at cost crush the rising. The Budapest revolt in 1956 merely underlined the lessons of Warsaw. There, once the Russians were assured of sufficient time, the same dreary routine of Warsaw achieved the same ultimate results. No amount of Hungarian bravery or ingenuity could deny the Russians. Sieges had become routine.

In Jerusalem the most obvious contrast was that neither the Arabs nor the Jews had the overwhelming superiority necessary to achieve an uncontested success within a major city. Only at the Jewish Quarter of the Old City could the Arabs concentrate the mass of their unskilled volunteers and the firepower of the elite Arab Legion. Once again the step-by-step demolition and destruction ended in capitulation, but the fate of the Jewish Quarter need not have been that of the Warsaw Ghetto. The Arabs did not have unlimited time. Relief, however, was undoubtedly bungled because of other pressing demands, because of the agony of the moment, and surely because of the amateur nature of the Jewish military force in Jerusalem. In any case, at the opening of the struggle the Arab Legion did not have the manpower or even the firepower to force its way into the New City. Glubb, more than *anyone else in the Jerusalem area, knew the risks of city fighting for a small army trained in movement. Only the overweening ambition of King Abdullah forced the commitment of the Legion in the city. Even to Abdullah, however, the dangers of continued frontal attacks soon became clear. Once the fighting had shifted to the surrounding country, the Legion was again able to operate effectively, but on the defensive rather than in the sweeping attacks anticipated. After the first truce the Jews were no longer isolated or unarmed, although their numerical relation to the Arab mass remained the same. The Jews, apparently far more deeply motivated and certainly more inventive, swung over to the offensive. The Arab posture collapsed. Only the presence of the highly disciplined Arab Legion in the Jerusalem area prevented a total collapse.*

At this point the Arabs faced some of the difficulties which had plagued the British at Singapore, not the least of which was an archaic class structure unsympathetic to contemporary war. Even when the promise of easy victory changed into the presence of defeat, all might not have been lost even if the Jews had been given more time by international events. An enthusiastic, untrained peasant "army" might have managed within Jerusalem as well as the Spanish militia did within Madrid, but by this stage of the struggle the Arabs were no longer enthusiastic. It is true, however, that in other battles the Arab, once enveloped and entrapped with the hope of retreat gone, proved a determined if poorly led opponent. The opportunity for the Arab to undergo a siege in Jerusalem never came, however, for the United Nations and Israel's limited resources prevented the final battle.

If Berlin is considered a siege by other means, as it was by many at the time, the most significant aspect is the gradual development of civilian determination in the Western Zones. The Germans within Berlin developed the siege mentality more slowly, freed as they were from the forcing chamber of blood and fire. With only recent and uncertain civil institutions, with a heritage of guilt and defeat, and with their ultimate salvation dependent upon the whim of apathetic or antagonistic former enemies, nevertheless the population managed to reach a consensus to defy the Russians. Individually and collectively, the people of Berlin gambled their own and their city's future at most unappealing odds. Apparently physical isolation, universal vulnerability and a distasteful enemy can produce a spirit of defiance even without exterior control and in the face of the hard facts of the moment. Berlin did produce its own leaders, but often with only minimal power. Berlin did have hope of relief, but often with only minimal evidence. The regular drone of the expanding airlift and the daily softening of Allied distaste played a strong role, but long before the success of the airlift or the firm gestures of Western unity, the population had taken immense risks to prevent a Russian success.

Stalin had never anticipated the slow ripening of the crisis. From a flash challenge to be followed by immediate Western concession, the Russians allowed the affair to continue into a trial of will by blockade. Diplomatically, Stalin made the same error in Berlin that Paulus and Hitler had made at Stalingrad: refusal to recognize the advantages of the defense and the possible effect of the passage of time. At the very time when flexibility might have paid dividends in Europe, Stalin had become wedged into a hard position in Berlin. The Russians might have backed out in the early fall by accepting the potential of the airlift, but having gone so far Stalin preferred to push forward in the face of increasing risks. The Russians gambled that the airlift could not supply the city during the winter. Even by October, this was a risky assumption. Worse, even if true, the crisis would be bound to drag on for several months, unifying the West and alienating the Germans. The blockade reached the point of diminishing returns, with the maximum gain being the bleak, evacuated ruins of West Berlin. By the time Moscow accepted failure, the possibility of lulling the West into complacency in Europe had long passed, and any faint hopes of bullying or converting the Western Germans had gone aglimmering. The Russians had produced a defiant defense within Berlin and were denied the means to suppress it. If the Russians had absorbed the military lessons of Stalingrad, they also revealed that the translation into diplomatic terms had been ignored. To recognize the past in the present, to see the usefulness of yesterday's battle, is obviously not an automatic response of even a trained mind.

The sieges in these seven cities underline the fact that the defense of a populated city is by no means an obsolete maneuver, but, rather, that such a battle is as common as any other in contemporary warfare. With the passage of time the means for both defense and offense have been absorbed and codified. To some degree such means are self-apparent. For the untrained civilian of Budapest, the possibilities available could be seized without first reading the relevant texts. For the determined professional army, also without text, the opportunities were even more obvious, as the bitter Japanese last-ditch defense of Manila proved to the Americans. That cities will be attacked in future wars is readily accepted now that the margin between atomic war and world peace has been broadened. Despite the massive atomic armories and the development of ballistic delivery systems, battles are still being fought with conventional weapons, more refined and sophisticated but still the descendants of the immediate past. Obviously atomic weapons of whatever magnitude are the ideal siege artillery since they would *eliminate the lengthy and costly destruction of the city. Even with atomic weapons, unless the city is totally vaporized and the earth enameled with glazed rock, some sort of defense despite the obvious dangers might be possible. Still, in an atomic war the capacity to eliminate cities would surely prohibit their defense; but then an atomic war would perhaps be the war of a different kind so often foreseen in the past: unlimited, total and final. If a limited atomic war could occur, a possibility so distressing to some that even its name is anathema, any concentration in a prime target would be suicidal and the siege truly obsolete. The probability of an atomic war—limited, which is unlikely, and total, which is unthinkable—has not as yet inhibited the pursuit of narrower aims with more conventional means. The Americans did not use atomic weapons in Korea nor, despite some consideration, did they lend them to the French to break the siege at Dien Bien Phu. The siege-blockade of Cuba came and passed without atomic war, and the fighting in Viet Nam has as yet produced little pressure for atomic commitment. While a nuclear disaster is always a possibility so long as the weapons exist, the present field of battle, particularly among the great powers, seems to be limited both geographically and operationally by mutual self-interest. As a result besiegement remains a continuing possibility.*

The siege, despite its prevalence, has not been in vogue for some time. After the hopes for tanks and airplanes had proven somewhat ill-founded, the fashion in war turned to the fruits of the new scientific technology, the giant bombs and the complex weapons systems. When wars continued to be fought in ways not strange to Napoleon and with weapons not unfamiliar to Rommel, the opportunities of guerrilla warfare attracted the military mind. It would appear that tactics and even weaponry, after Hiroshima, moved backward through history, as the Korean War was fought with the weapons of the previous war and culminated in two solid lines of deep earthworks running across the peninsula in a manner reminiscent of a still earlier war. In the case of Viet Nam the Americans have seemingly retrogressed to the Indian campaigns despite the presence of helicopters and jet bombers. The siege has been left somewhat in the middle ground between the mathematical systems and war games on one side and the ideological analysis of wars of national liberation on the other. Obsolescence does come to weapons and tactics: the bow and arrow have only limited application at the moment and the cavalry charge may for the time being be outmoded. Yet in warfare the nature of battle remains much the same, and battles have always been fought for cities. Despite Sun Tzu's most cogent admonition that to attack cities is the worse policy, sieges have always occurred. To ignore a real and present possibility of war is to give up a pawn without gaining position. If, for example the American presence in Saigon were viewed from the point of view of a siege by guerrillas, certain insights if not revelations might be forthcoming. Whatever critical response the particular seven cities under siege may evoke, the chronicles of old battles retain a fascination which cannot be wholly divorced from the next and future war.

Notes and Sources

AS is almost always the case with any phase of modern history, any list of sources must be selective or there would be room for little else. Since there has been no attempt at scholarly omniscience in the text, it would be pointless to introduce the concept in the bibliography. I have, instead, merely outlined the major materials more or less readily available and the notes I felt minimally necessary to avoid plagiarism, legal or moral. At times references may be made in the notes to sources not contained in the bibliographical section.

Madrid

Few wars in recent times have produced as partisan or as extensive a literature as the Spanish Civil War. Until recently the vast outpouring consisted mainly of journalism, special pleading, or memoirs of dubious value. Apparently no one involved, general or clerk, has remained out of print. As a result the war has remained hidden in a cloud of printed controversy. In the last decade with the receding of passions and the availability of documentation, the war has attracted the interest of less involved scholars who have produced a new and more balanced literature of the period. Because of the opening of the German Foreign Office archives after the Second World War and access to State Department documents for the period, the prospects of the diplomatic historian have brightened. Beginning with P. A. M. van der Esch's *Prelude to War* (The Hague, 1951) and continuing through Dante Puzzo's *Spain and the Great Powers* (New York, 1962), the international aspects have been thoroughly covered; but the specific involvement of the great powers in the war has been less thoroughly investigated. David C. Cattell in *Communism and the Spanish Civil War* (Berkeley, 1955) and *Soviet Diplomacy and the Spanish Civil War* (Berkeley, 1957) has produced what appears to be for the foreseeable future the definitive account of Russian involvement. Manfred Merkes has begun the job for Germany, but other powers, Italy, in particular, remain uninvestigated. For the political and military aspects of the war, two most valuable works are Stanley G. Payne's *Falange* (Stanford, 1961) and Robert Colodny, *The Struggle for Madrid: The Central Epic of the Spanish Conflict (1936–1937)* (New York, 1958). Several of the earlier general syntheses of the war and its background remain useful, particularly:

Gerald Brenan, *The Spanish Labyrinth*, New York, 1943.
Salvador de Madariaga, *Spain*, New York, 1943.
E. Allison Peers, *The Spanish Tragedy, 1930–1936*, New York, 1936.

The two most recent general studies in English have been Hugh Thomas's *The Spanish Civil War* (New York, 1961) and Gabriel Jackson's *Spanish Civil War and Republic, 1931–1939* (Princeton, 1965).

All of these, early and late, have examined, digested and organized the chaos of sources available; but nothing more clearly reveals the present state of the military history of the war than the fact that in Colodny's work the pages of notes explaining, qualifying, or defining, are almost equal to the number of pages of text. If international aspects, the fate of the exiles, the impact on the intellectuals and the response of public opinion have been organized, the same simply cannot be said for the military aspects. This is true despite the regular appearance in a variety of languages of volumes hopefully titled and encrusted with past errors. Colodny's work, then, is almost a pioneer study, since much of the "history" of the war has been and to some extent still is based on guessing games, post-facto memories, and dubious sources.

Notes

1. Robert Payne in *The Civil War in Spain* (New York, 1962), pp. 17–19, an anthology of contemporary accounts (which is in Premier paperback editions and hence readily available), quotes from the Spanish Government's vast lawsuit of 1953 (which is not so readily available).
2. The best account in print of the *coup,* still obscured in time and myth, may be found in Stanley G. Payne's *Falange* (Stanford, 1961), pp. 101–118. *Cf.* Robert Alan Friedlander, July 1936 Military Rebellion in Spain (unpublished Ph.D. dissertation, Northwestern University).
3. The Spanish Army had developed into a most curious institution by 1936. Its purpose remained unclear, its military capacities negligible, and its future uncertain. The vast officer corps, a form of occupational relief for the middle and upper class youth, was poorly paid, perpetually restless and often resentful. Its size in relation to both the enlisted ranks, with one officer for six privates, and to the Spanish population, with one general for every 15,000 Spanish males, was ridiculous. (Lawrence Dundas, *Behind the Spanish Mask,* London, 1939, p. 2.) The enlisted men were ill-trained, poorly armed, and badly disciplined, barely capable of garrison duty and an occasional parade. At the time of the rising, these soldiers, confused and often cut off from their weapons, were unable to resist their officers. For the purposes of war the only effective part of the army became the officer corps. The enlisted men, without weapons or training, simply wandered off to join militia or return home, leaving a small, dedicated band of armed and determined rebels.
4. Hugh Thomas, *The Spanish Civil War,* New York, 1961, p. 143.
5. An excellent account of much of this period in Madrid can be found in the exciting and lightly fictionalized account by Arturo Barea in *The Forging of a Rebel,* "The Clash" (London, 1946), cf. pp. 519–520.
6. Although there has been one limited study in Germany by Manfred Merkes on German involvement, there is as yet no authoritative source. Most figures are the result of probably quite reasonable estimates. In the case of Germany, aid was sufficiently extensive to give considerable qualms to the conservative leaders of the army. In time the constant drain of gold and blood would become a source of despair to many of Italy's leaders.
7. There is a considerable body of work in Spanish on the military developments, usually but not always by former participants (López Muñiz, Zugazagoita, de Villegas, Aznar, *et al.*) as well as the massive thirty-five volumes of the *Historia de la Cruzada Española.* Along with these, almost every nationality is represented in a general survey. In English, Colodny's *The Struggle of Madrid* represents the new analytical approach and Frank Jellinek's *The Civil War in Spain* (London, 1938), a deeply involved presentation—in this case Republican. Thomas's *The Spanish Civil War* presents an excellent synthesis of most campaigns.
8. The Montreal *Star,* October 30, 1936 (Thomas, *Spanish Civil War,* p. 289) reported that Durruti, the leading anarchist "general" early in the war,

replied to some "military" suggestions by the Soviet writer and correspondent Ilya Ehrenburg in such a way as to reveal the anarchist mind at war: "You mean officers should be appointed? Orders should always be obeyed? An interesting idea, difficult to introduce. . . ." *Cf.* Ilya Ehrenburg, *Memoirs, 1921–1941* (New York, 1964), pp. 326–364. George Orwell in *Homage to Catalonia* (Boston, 1952) felt that "revolutionary" discipline was more effective than might be expected and in any case gave raw, undisciplined troops the only effective order possible. Orwell, however, may have been an anarchist at heart, while Ehrenburg was, on proper occasion, a Stalinist. Generally the all-anarchist units did not function particularly well in Spain despite individual bravery and great general elán.

9. Despite considerable effort on the part of the present Spanish Government to document in detail the extent of the Red terror, no final estimate for formal and informal executions on either side can be more than an educated guess. Thomas, *Spanish Civil War,* pp. 169, 173, gives the round figures of 75,000 for the Republicans and 40,000 for the Nationalists, although, of course, the latter added a considerable number to their score after the war. The Spanish soul has never been noted for either moderation or restraint, and the Civil War with its injection of ideology and class hatred into the ancient regional feuds of Spain presented an unequaled opportunity for vengeance. From Fredrico García Lorca, Spain's great modern poet, shot apparently for no good reason, to the naive parish priest, shot because he wore the clerical habit, the terror wanton or intentional touched all.
10. Barea, *Rebel,* p. 536.
11. Despite the fine studies by David C. Cattell (*Communism and the Spanish Civil War* and *Soviet Diplomacy and the Spanish Civil War*), a mass of myths concerning Communist plots and programs remains undemolished (*Cf.* Burnett Bolloten, *The Grand Camouflage, The Communist Conspiracy in the Spanish Civil War,* London, 1961). The most persistent is that the Spanish Communist Party planned a *coup* before the Army and that they dominated, owned and operated the Republic as a front organization. With some exceptions due to "faulty" ideology on the part of some Spanish party members or an excess of national patriotism, the Communists wanted what Stalin wanted: a conservative united front policy which would extend the Republic's life. There is little doubt that with their domination of the army the Communists could have brought off a *coup* any time after the summer of 1937, but only at the expense of Stalin's united front program and with the likelihood of destroying Republican resistance. Thus the Party sought to dominate rather than operate the government by means varying from polite blackmail to outright assassination.
12. The siege of the Alcázar had all the drama of a classical medieval battle: the little band of true believers, the great horde of frustrated infidels and, finally, the last-minute relief by the forces of light. In the very substantial literature of the siege, present Spanish writers often portray the battle in terms of a morality play; the Alcázar has become a Nationalist shrine complete with guided tours. Although the Republicans were incredibly inefficient, Moscardó's resistance was in truth a remarkable and highly courageous feat. *Cf.* (as a start) H. P. Knickerbocker, *The Siege of the Alcázar,* London, 1938; Rodolphe Timmermans, *Heroes of the Alcázar,* London, 1937; and Geoffrey McNeill-Moss, *The Epic of the Alcázar,* London, 1937; Manuel Aznar, *The Alcázar Will Not Surrender,* New York, 1957; Cecil Eby, *The Siege of the Alcázar,* N.Y., 1965.
13. The extent of Russian aid to the Republic is most thoroughly analyzed in Cattell's *Communism and the Spanish Civil War* and *Soviet Diplomacy and the Spanish Civil War.* For a survey of the nature of the military aid see D. C. Watt, "Soviet Military Aid to the Spanish Republic in the Civil War 1936–1938," *The Slavic and East European Review,* xxxviii, no. 91, pp. 536–538.
14. The International Brigade produced a massive literature—not only the vast spate of propaganda and prejudicial publications of the time but also the later memoirs, recollections and histories. Seemingly every member, if he lived, felt called upon to detail his adventures. Among the Italians alone, Luigi Longo wrote a history; Pietro Nenni, a history; Blasco Grandi, a survey of Togliatti in Spain; Pacciardi, a history of the Garibaldi Bat-

talion, and so on down a long list. There is not yet, however, a balanced, definitive monograph on the brigades.

15. Thomas, *Spanish Civil War,* pp. 316–317.
16. Colodny, *Struggle for Madrid,* p. 34.
17. Neurath to José Rovira Armengol (Draft Note), Berlin, November 1936, *Documents on German Foreign Policy, 1918–1945,* Series D, vol. III, p. 125.
18. Barea, *Rebel,* p. 589.
19. There is still a very considerable air of mystery about just which Russian officers were in Spain under what aliases. Reportedly Rokossovsky, Koniev and Malinovsky, all to be marshals, and Stern, Meretskov and Rodimtsev, who would be generals, served in Spain. During the war an often bitter behind-the-scenes struggle took place between Stalin's secret police, special agents, and the army. For many of the Soviet advisors, their return to Russia in 1937 and 1938 was merely a way station to exile in Siberia or death. Some are still being posthumously pardoned; for example, on March 2, 1965, the Soviets suddenly paid tribute to Semyon P. Uritsky, who served in Spain and then organized in Moscow the military and civilian aid for the Republican forces.
20. Colodny, *Struggle for Madrid,* p. 55; Kol'tsov's memoirs have been published in Russia but are not yet translated into English.
21. Geoffrey Cox, *Defence of Madrid* (London, 1937), p. 121.
22. Foreign Minister Neurath to the Legation in Portugal, Berlin, November 17, 1936, *German Documents,* Series D, vol. III, p. 132.
23. There are no really official figures for losses. Most writers choose the several most reliable sources and perform a sort of numbers game which results in an averaged-out figure. With primitive records and many of them long since strayed, at present it is impossible to be more precise.
24. In Spain the potential of the German 88-mm. gun as something other than an antiaircraft weapon was fully explored for the first time. The result was the best tank killer of the Second World War. Perhaps the best tank, the Russian T-34, in prototype as the T-26, was also tried out in Spain.
25. The American formations, the Abraham Lincoln Battalion (or Brigade) and the George Washington Battalion were first used at Jarama. The American volunteers, by and large, were less exotic than their European counterparts. Although Ring Lardner's son was killed at the battle of Ebro, most of the members have remained fairly anonymous despite a flurry of interest during the McCarthy era. The more notable Americans tended to be correspondents, professional or amateur, such as Herbert Matthews, Hemingway, Dos Passos, Capra. *Cf.* John Hohenberg, *Foreign Correspondents: The Great Reporters and Their Times* (New York and London, 1964), pp. 309–318.
26. One of the odd groups now incorporated into the Nationalist army of Moors, Legionnaires, Falangists and officers was a delegation from Ireland. On February 16, they fought a brief battle with what turned out to be a Nationalist unit from the Canary Islands. They never really proved worth the expense and trouble and were shipped back to Ireland with thanks. Although there were a few volunteers to the Nationalist cause, the Irish were the only group comparable to the International Brigades. *Cf.* E. O'Duffy, *Crusade in Spain,* Dublin, 1937. Francis McCullagh, *In Franco's Spain,* London, 1937.
27. Gustave Regler, *The Owl of Minerva* (London, 1959), pp. 305–310.
28. *Ibid.,* pp. 305–310.
29. Spanish Embassy Washington, *The Italian Invasion of Spain, Official Documents and Papers Seized from Italian Units in Action at Guadalajara* (Washington, 1937), p. 289.
30. *Ibid.,* p. 289.
31. Ernest Hemingway, "The Spanish War," *Fact,* London, July, 1938, p. 12.
32. John Dos Passos, *Journeys Between Wars* (New York, 1938), pp. 362–363.
33. Just what effect the Russian experience in Spain had on their tactics during the Second World War is not fully clear except in the area of armor. Here the "lesson" of the Spanish war was that tanks should be scattered about, not concentrated. It took the German panzer blitz for the Russians to unlearn this lesson. Pavlov's difficulty with his tanks may have been because of the targets he chose—infantry or fortified positions where his armor proved inappropriate and highly vulnerable. In any case, his subsequent career proved no greater success. He avoided the purges which carried off so many of his colleagues only to be shot in 1941 for "ineffi-

ciency"—*i.e.*, losing. Alexander Werth, *Russia at War* (New York, 1964), p. 154. *Cf.* also B. H. Liddell Hart, *The Soviet Army* (New York, 1950), pp. 316–317.

34. The most coherent, even if obviously biased, account of the final days of Madrid may be found in Segismundo Casado, *The Last Days of Madrid* (London, 1939), p. 147.

35. There is even a small bibliography of books and articles, titled in a variety of languages, ranging from military lessons (Helmut Klotz, Vincent Usera or General Duval) to the lessons for anarchism (Richards).

London

The air war over London has been most thoroughly and persistently covered by official and unofficial historians, participants and victims, commissions and organizations. If there is one lack, it is a single volume encompassing the very considerable German material which has as yet not been dispassionately evaluated, although regularly incorporated in other studies. Fortunately for the general reader and the historian as well, the huge mounds of source materials have been analyzed, digested and presented in the quasi-official British histories of the Second World War. The Military Series, edited by Sir James Butler, is detailed, accurate and definitive. The other official military histories are of like value.

Sir James Butler, *Grand Strategy, September 1939–June 1941*, London, 1957.
Basil Collier, *The Defense of the United Kingdom*, London, 1957.
Denis Richards, *The Royal Air Force, 1939–1945*, vol. I, London, 1953.

The series of Civil Histories are equally indispensable, in particular:

Terence O'Brien, *Civil Defense*, London, 1955.
Richard Titmuss, *Problems of Social Policy*, London, 1950.

While many of the others like M. M. Postan's *British War Production* (London, 1952) or C. M. Kohan's *Works and Buildings* (London, 1952) should be consulted, they do tell more about works or food or production (three volumes) than most readers want to know. Other than the great serial histories, practically every organization or institution involved has its own record (*Cf.* Guy Morgan's *Red Roses Every Night* [London, 1948], a survey of the London cinema under the blitz). A sample of the most useful would be:

Major A. B. Hartley, *Unexploded Bomb*, New York, 1959.
Sir Aylmer Firebrace, *Fire Service Memories*, London, 1949.
Geoffrey Blackstone, *History of the British Fire Service*, London, 1957.

The Battle of Britain has been more than adequately chronicled. A very considerable percentage of the participants, from the Prime Minister to the pilots, have come out in print, ranging from Dowding's "The Battle of Britain," a Despatch Supplement to the *London Gazette*, 1946, to Lewis Whitnell's "autobiography," *Engines over London* (London, 1949) which turned out to be a hoax, a sure sign of popular interest. For over-all surveys of the air war, consult the more recent:

Alexander McKee, *Strike from the Sky, The Story of the Battle of Britain*, London, 1960.
Derek Wood and Derek Dempster, *The Narrow Margin, The Battle of Britain and Rise of Air Power, 1930–1940*, New York, 1961.
Edward Bishop, *The Battle of Britain*, London, 1960.

As is to be expected, other than the memoirs and histories, there are detailed accounts of air bases, airplanes, radar, night defenses, and every phase of air defense (*Cf.* Sir Frederick Pile, *Ack-Ack, Britain's Defense Against Air Attack During the Second World War* [London, 1949]). On the German side the most useful memoirs are:

Werner Baumbach, *The Life and Death of the Luftwaffe,* New York, 1960.
Adolf Galland, *The First and the Last,* New York, 1954.
Albert Kesselring, *Kesselring: A Soldier's Record,* New York, 1954.
Werner Kreipe, "The Battle of Britain," *The Fatal Decisions* (eds. Seymour Freiden and William Richardson), New York, 1956.

Göring did not have the opportunity to begin his memoirs and his biographers reveal little new.

For the Battle of London, Constantine FitzGibbon's *The Winter of the Bombs* (New York, 1957) is a general account quite superior to Drew Middleton's *The Sky Suspended* (New York, 1960). Richard Collier in *The City That Would Not Die* (New York, 1960) has detailed the great raid of May 10. There are, usually earlier, accounts of specific areas under the blitz: William Sansom, *Westminster in War* (London, 1947) or Ben Thomas Tinton, *War Comes to the Docks* (London, 1942), even accounts of specific buildings: Walter Robert Matthew, *St. Paul's in Wartime* (London, 1946). Finally there are the blitz diaries, for apparently everyone kept a diary and published it in one form or another, so that we know the impact of the attacks on air-raid wardens, nurses, strolling journalists, and firemen. Much of this material in one way or another has been incorporated in the surveys of air war's effect on civilians: Stanford Research Institute, *Impact of Air Attack in World War II,* 3 vols. (Washington, 1953), and Irving Janis, *Air War and Emotional Stress* (New York, 1951).

Notes

1. Alexander McKee, *Strike from the Sky,* London, 1960, p. 215; Constantine FitzGibbon, *The Winter of the Bombs* (New York, 1957), p. 41.
2. By the time the *Luftwaffe*'s General Staff Historical Branch compiled *The Douhet Theory and Its Application to the Present War* in November 1944, the Germans were considerably less enthused about the instant effect of strategic bombing.
3. The multi-objective, uncertainly motivated, attack on September 7 was typical of the entire German air effort during August and September with shifting emphasis and conflicting demands. *Cf.* Ronald Wheatley, *Operation Sea Lion* (Oxford, 1958), pp. 52 ff.; Derek Wood and Derek Dempster, *The Narrow Margin* (New York, 1961), pp. 409–410.
4. The whole nature of the relation of Operation *Sea Lion* to the *Luftwaffe* is examined in both Wheatley's *Operation Sea Lion* and Peter Fleming's *Invasion 1940* (London, 1957). The background of Hitler's ambivalent policies vis-à-vis Great Britain may be found in Walter Ansel, *Hitler Confronts England* (Durham, 1960).
5. Wheatley, *Sea Lion,* p. 73.
6. *Ibid.,* p. 74.
7. Adolf Hitler (ed. Trevor-Roper), *Blitzkrieg to Defeat* (New York, 1965), pp. 37–38.
8. Wheatley, *Sea Lion,* p. 74; Wood and Dempster, *Margin,* pp. 330–332.
9. Asher Lee, *Blitz on Britain* (London, 1960), p. 70.
10. D. M. Crook, *Spitfire Pilot* (London, 1942), p. 66.
11. FitzGibbon, *Winter,* p. 45.
12. *Ibid.,* pp. 43–55; G. V. Blackstone, *History of the British Fire Service* (London, 1957), p. 411; Sir Aylmer Firebrace, *Fire Service Memories* (London, 1949), pp. 165–169.
13. FitzGibbon, *Winter,* p. 55.
14. *Cf.* Kenneth Poolman, *Zeppelins Against London* (New York, 1961).
15. Terence O'Brien, *Civil Defense* (London, 1955), pp. 385–396; Richard Titmuss, *Problems of Social Policy* (London, 1950), pp. 257–258. *Cf.*

E. Mira, "Psychiatric Experiences in the Spanish War," *British Medical Journal,* vol. I, 1939, pp. 1217–1220. The British tended to accept the example of Barcelona where panic did occur rather than Madrid where it did not. *Cf.* I. Janis, *Air War and Emotional Stress* (New York, 1951), pp. 99–100. Also based on Spanish "experience," the conclusion was reached that unexploded bombs would be no problem.

16. FitzGibbon, *Winter,* p. 76.
17. McKee, *Strike,* p. 216.
18. Denis Richards, *Royal Air Force,* vol. I (London, 1953), p. 203.
19. Winston Churchill, *The Second World War,* vol. II, *Their Finest Hour* (Boston, 1949), p. 330.
20. The figures on tonnages, weights, sorties, casualties and practically any aspect of the war can be found entabled in the various appendices of the Civil and Military Histories of the Second World War. Making use of German figures and correlating a variety of sources, often overlapping and conflicting, the individual authors have come to what must be considered as near the definitive figures as possible.
21. Adolf Galland, *The First and the Last,* New York, 1963, p. 45.
22. The arduous struggle to protect St. Paul's is detailed in W. R. Matthew, *Saint Paul's Cathedral in Wartime 1939–1945* (London, 1946). Davis and Wyle were, for their efforts, the first recipients of the George Cross.
23. Frances Faviell, *A Chelsea Concerto* (London, 1959), p. 104.
24. Franz Halder, *Diaries,* vol. IV, pp. 194–195.
25. The question of the use of massed squadrons, the wing, against the Germans developed into the key tactical dispute, and the discussion since has often been acrimonious. Since Dowding and Park succeeded, the question revolves about how much more or less effective the wings would have been. In time the powers that be seemingly were convinced by Leigh-Mallory, for after the battle Dowding and Park were removed and assigned elsewhere to somewhat less imposing jobs. The removal "was not perhaps the most impressive immediate reward that might have been devised for the victory of one of the world's decisive battles" is the comment of Richards in the history of the Royal Air Force (Richards, *RAF,* p. 195). The former RAF pilots have chosen sides as well, with no clear majority in sight for either position.
26. For those with the time, the reading of the war diaries—of which there are scores—reveals much of the general attitude. There is seldom much mention of invasion and a surprising uniformity of reaction. These memoirs, along with much else, formed the grist for the statistics mills of the social scientists judging the impact of the raids on the civilians in scholarly postwar studies. Their conclusions, undoubtedly far more detailed and far more arcane, were regularly prefigured by contemporary accounts of air-raid wardens and literate ladies.
27. Churchill, *World War,* vol. II, p. 372.
28. Basil Wood, *Hell Came to London* (London, 1941), p. 66.
29. There is a feeling in many contemporary accounts, often admittedly by authors predisposed to Labour anyway, that the resentment of the people coupled with the crumbling of the rigid class system under the stress of the raids, indicated a postwar revolution of some sort. Thus, in their own way, the German raids may have played a part in the Labour Party's 1945 victory.
30. Titmuss, *Social,* p. 261.
31. Janis, *Air War,* p. 170.
32. Ben Robertson, *I Saw England* (New York, 1941), p. 131.
33. Kingsley Martin, "Reflections on Air Raids," *Political Quarterly* (London, 1941), vol. 12, p. 79.
34. Barbara Nixon, *Raiders Overhead* (London, 1943), p. 36.
35. James Pope-Hennessy, *History Under Fire* (London, 1941), p. 45.
36. Churchill, *World War,* vol. II, p. 359.
37. Wheatley, *Sea Lion,* p. 188.
38. Galeazzo Ciano, *Diaries, 1939–1943* (New York, 1947), pp. 298–299.
39. A. E. Clouston, *The Dangerous Skies* (London, 1954), pp. 145–157.
40. Richards, *RAF,* p. 209.
41. Wood and Dempster, *Margin,* p. 385.
42. Richards, *RAF,* pp. 205–206.
43. Halder, *Diaries,* vol. IV, pp. 220, 245.
44. Richards, *RAF,* p. 209.
45. A. B. Harley, *Unexploded Bomb,* New York, 1959, pp. 58–60.
46. FitzGibbon, *Winter,* p. 207.
47. *Ibid.,* p. 178. *Cf.* C. F. Rawnsley and Robert Wright, *Night Fighter,* New York, 1957
48. Werner Kreipe, "Battle of Britain," *The Fatal Decisions,* New York, 1956, p. 23.
49. Richards, *RAF,* p. 217.

50. The raid is presented in detail by Richard Collier in *The City That Would Not Die* (New York, 1960).
51. O'Brien, *Civil Defense*, p. 688.
52. Alexander Werth, "The Burning of the Temple," *The 1943 Saturday Book* (London, 1942), pp. 47–48.
53. Churchill, *World War*, vol. II, p. 266.
54. Titmuss, *Social*, pp. 558–560, 251–303.
55. Kreipe, "Battle," p. 28.
56. Werner Baumbach, *The Life and Death of the Luftwaffe* (New York, 1960), p. 82.

Singapore

As is the case in all the campaigns in which the British fought, there are extensive semiofficial histories. The appropriate volume for the army is Major-General Stanley Woodburn Kirby, C. T. Addis and others, *The War Against Japan*, "The Loss of Singapore," vol. I (London, 1957–1961). (*Cf.* George Weller, "Operations of Malayan Campaign, from 8th December 1941 to 15 February 1942.") The Australian equivalent is Lionel Wignore's *The Japanese Thrust* (Canberra, 1957); and for the Indian Army there is K. N. Sastri and K. D. Bhargava, *Official History of the Indian Armed Forces, Second World War*, "Campaigns in South-east Asia: 1941–1942," vol. 3 (Calcutta). For the war at sea, the volume in the United Kingdom series is Captain S. W. Roskill's *War at Sea 1939–1945*, vol. I (London, 1954). On the Japanese side there is nothing comparable, in or out of English. Saburo Hayashi's (collaboration with Alvin D. Coox) *Kògun, The Japanese Army in the Pacific War* (Quantico, 1959) touches only briefly on Singapore. The most useful of all Japanese sources is Masanobu Tsuji's *Singapore, The Japanese Version* (New York, 1961): *Cf.* Saburo Sakai, *Samurai* (New York, 1963), and M. Okuniya and J. Horikoshi, *Zero* (New York, 1961).

Recent efforts have been made through interviews and the application of Japanese sources to develop the other side of the Singapore story, in particular by John Deane Potter's biography of General Yamashita, *The Life and Death of a Japanese General* (New York, 1962), and John Toland in *But Not in Shame* (New York, 1961). The Japanese side, except for Tsuji's book, has translated nothing comparable to the memoirs and reports of the British; *cf.* A. E. Percival, "Operations of Malaya Command," Despatches, *London Gazette*, 20 February 1948, or *The War in Malaya* (London, 1949) or Sir Archibald Percival Wavell's "Operations in South-west Pacific," 15 January 1942–25 February, 1942," Despatches (August, 1942), much less individual participants like Angus Rose, *Who Dies Fighting* (London, 1944), or A. G. Donahue, *Last Flight from Singapore* (New York, 1943).

There are several over-all histories of the Malayan campaign:

Kenneth Attiwill, *Fortress*, New York, 1960.
Frank Owen, *The Fall of Singapore*, London, 1960.
Edwin Maurice Glover, *In Seventy Days*, London, 1946.

For naval affairs see:

T. J. Cain (collaborator A. V. Sellwood), *H.M.S. Electra*, London, 1959.
Captain Russell Grenfell, *Main Fleet to Singapore*, New York, 1952.
Bernard Ash, *Someone Had Blundered*, New York, 1961.

Three detailed studies of widely varying scope are:

Eugene Herbert Miller, *Strategy at Singapore*, New York, 1942.
Sir George Maxwell, *The Civil Defense of Malaya*, London, New York, 1944.
I. McA. Stewart, *History of the Argyll and Sutherland Highlanders, 2nd Battalion*, London, New York, 1947.

Two of the more interesting accounts by correspondents are O. D. Gallagher, *Retreat in the East* (London, 1942) and Cecil Brown, *From Suez to Singapore* (New York, 1942). Other useful accounts of observers are Lord Strabolgi's *Singapore and After* (New York, 1942); Ian Morrison, *Malayan Postscript* (London, 1942), Compton MacKenzie, *Eastern Epic* (London, 1951).

An interesting if not necessarily significant bibliographical side-note is that solely by a list of book titles in the area of what might be called interpretive history the development of the Singapore campaign and its impact can be followed:

John Sharp, *Impregnable Fortress*
Russell Brandon, *The Naked Island*
S. E. Field, *Singapore Tragedy*
Dorothy Crisp, *Why We Lost Singapore* and/or
H. Gordon Bennett, *Why Singapore Fell*

At present the only inappropriate title would appear to be G. A. Weller's *Singapore Is Silent.*

Notes

1. E. H. Miller, *Strategy at Singapore* (New York, 1942), traces the intricate tale of the position of Singapore in British prewar strategy. The major confusion in the minds of both the civilians and military men was the unwarranted assumption that the island of Singapore was a fortress capable of withstanding a land assault. Miller was not immune to the Fortress Myth: "It had been prepared in advance with elaborate fortifications and supplies to withstand a long siege. Its land and aerial defenses had been strengthened for protracted resistance . . ." (p. 136); however, Miller's book was published in 1942 when detailed information was secret, apparently even from the Prime Minister.
2. O. D. Gallagher, *Action in the East* (New York, 1942), p. 95; Cecil Brown, *Suez to Singapore* (New York, 1942), p. 282, also quotes Brooke-Popham, although in different words.
3. Brown, *Suez to Singapore,* p. 240.
4. Not only were the British planes few in number and poor in quality, many with speeds under 100 miles an hour, but the official British estimation of Japanese air capacity was wildly erroneous. The British had a fairly accurate idea about the number of Japanese aircraft but they judged the pilots to be only 60 per cent as effective as British pilots and the planes to be second-rate. On the last point, there was little excuse in view of a report which had arrived in Singapore on July 26, 1941, detailing the capabilities of the Japanese *Zero.* Unfortunately "this valuable report remaining unsifted from the general mass of intelligence information" (*i.e.,* unread) meant that the British air strategy was badly handicapped. Kenneth Attiwill, *Fortress* (New York, 1960), p. 34; Russell Grenfell, *Main Fleet to Singapore* (New York, 1952), p. 75.
5. Winston Churchill, *The Second World War,* vol. III, *Grand Alliance* (Boston, 1950), pp. 615–616.
6. The wording of the communiqué was solely to bluff the Japanese, but it proved a fruitless ploy. Although the Japanese intelligence in Malaya was not as omniscient as the British would later believe, it had known of the two battleships since a sighting in November. Strangely enough, while they had identified the *Repulse,* it was not until the British communiqué that they knew the other battleship was the *Prince of Wales* and not the *King George V.* Masatake Okumiya and Jiro Horikoshi, *Zero* (New York, 1961), p. 62.
7. One of the Churchill strategic decisions most often criticized, then and since, was his willingness to ship equipment to British allies, Greece and Russia, before shipping it to Singapore.
8. Angus Rose, *Who Dies Fighting* (London, 1944), pp. 31–32.
9. Masanobu Tsuji, *Singapore, The Japanese Version* (New York, 1961), p. 40.
10. For the development of the military campaign in both Malaya and Singapore, I have depended upon the highly detailed official histories balanced by Tsuji's Japanese version. While these volumes reveal an almost hour-by-hour description of the campaign, their scope is often limited to the nearest

regiment's next move; nevertheless, although room for analysis remains, the official histories are the definitive sources.

11. Attiwill, *Fortress,* p. 26. Curiously this Order of the Day had been prepared six months before so that it could be translated into the various Oriental languages.
12. Bernard Ash, *Someone Had Blundered* (New York, 1961), p. 209.
13. Okumiya and Horikoshi, *Zero,* p. 68.
14. Brown, *Suez to Singapore,* p. 328.
15. Tsuji, *Singapore,* p. 110.
16. As early as December 18, the Chief of the Imperial General Staff, Lord Alanbrooke, had doubted Malaya's holding out for a month, and the day before he wrote "I do not feel that there is much hope of saving Singapore." It took longer than ten days to convince Churchill or the Malayan commanders. Arthur Bryant, *The Turn of the Tide* (Garden City, New York, 1957), pp. 228, 236.
17. Churchill, *World War,* vol. IV, p. 49.
18. Attiwill, *Fortress,* p. 77.
19. *Ibid.,* p. 113.
20. John Deane Potter, *The Life and Death of a Japanese General* (New York, 1962), p. 80.
21. Ian Morrison, *Malayan Postscript* (London, 1942), p. 146.
22. Frank Owen, *The Fall of Singapore* (London, 1960), p. 140, quotes the *Straits Times,* "The announcement is about two and a half years late."
23. Attiwill, *Fortress,* p. 126.
24. *Ibid.,* p. 174. *Cf.* Douglas Bailey in *We Built and Destroyed* (London, n.d.), pp. 85–86, ". . . I saw a file of men walking, stumbling, dragging along the grass verge in the direction of the Bukit Timah Road—some were bootless, some shirtless, and a few had not even trousers. One had a tommy-gun, very few had rifles, none had kits on their backs. They were covered with mud from head to foot, scratched and bleeding, exhausted, beaten."
25. John Toland, *But Not in Shame* (New York, 1962), p. 229.
26. Attiwill, *Fortress,* p. 189.
27. Toland, *Shame,* p. 230.
28. *Ibid.*
29. Attiwill, *Fortress,* pp. 205–206.
30. Toland, *Shame,* p. 238.
31. Potter, *Japanese General,* p. 88.
32. Toland, *Shame,* pp. 240–241.
33. Compton MacKenzie, *Eastern Epic* (London, 1951), p. 401.

Stalingrad

The historiography of the battle of Stalingrad has moved through several well-defined periods as the sources for the siege became available. At first the accounts tended to be based on the Russo-Allied patriotic wartime literature (V. S. Grossman, *Stalingrad Hits Back,* Moscow, 1942; or Alexander Werth, *Stalingrad,* New York, 1947). Then came the far more detailed agonizing reappraisals of the Germans ranging from Field Marshals' bestsellers (Erich von Manstein, *Lost Victories,* Chicago, 1958) to professional military accounts squirreled away in the *Marine Corps Gazette.* Finally, with the tentative beginnings of Russian revelations, ranging from the bleak official histories to the recent release of memoirs, a more balanced scholarly judgment has been possible.

For the Russians, the publication of memoirs is always politically motivated: Soviet history does not so much reveal the past as explain the present. Chuikov or Zhukov must write for a contemporary purpose which by necessity may warp the old world to buttress up the new. Still, by 1965, the Russian generals have begun to indulge in the battle of the books, and the process inadvertently reveals much that the stolid official history ignores. The basic book is V. I. Chuikov's *The Beginning of the Road* (London, 1963). A. I. Yeremenko's *Stalingrad* has been translated into French, but as yet is not available in English. Zhukov, long in and out of disgrace, is now in the process of publishing his memoirs. The Germans—or, rather, those who survived—have given the public an almost total if occasionally contradictory picture of their side of the battle down to the regimental level. A mere sampling is listed here:

Adolf Hitler (ed. H. R. Trevor-Roper), *Blitzkrieg to Defeat, Hitler's War Directives, 1939–1945*, New York, 1965.
E. von Manstein, *Lost Victories*, Chicago, 1958.
Walter Goerlitz, *Paulus and Stalingrad*, New York, 1963.
Franz Halder, *Diary* (mimeographed).
Kurt Zeitzler, "Stalingrad," *The Fatal Decisions*, eds. Seymour Freidin and William Richardson, New York, 1956.
F. W. Mellenthin, *Panzer Battles 1939–1945*, London, 1955.
Walter Warlimont, *Inside Hitler's Headquarters*, New York, 1964.

There is a very considerable scholarly literature on both the nature and tactics of the German and Soviet armies; for example:

German

J. W. Wheeler-Bennet, *The Nemesis of Power*, London, 1953.
Telford Taylor, *Sword and Swastika*, New York, 1952.
B. H. Liddell Hart, *The Other Side of the Hill*, London, 1948.
F. Hinsley, *Hitler's Strategy*, Cambridge, 1951.

Russian

V. D. Sokolovsky (ed.), *Military Strategy and Soviet Doctrine and Concepts*, New York, 1963.
B. H. Liddell Hart, *The Red Army*, New York, 1958.
Raymond Garthoff, *Soviet Military Doctrine*, New York, 1953.
Louis B. Ely, *The Red Army Today*, Harrisburg, 1949.
John Erickson, *The Soviet High Command, 1918–1945*, London, 1962.

Earlier balanced efforts such as W. E. D. Allen's *The Russian Campaign of 1941–1943* (London, 1944) gradually incorporated more German sources.

United States Military Academy, *The War in Eastern Europe*, West Point, 1952.
George E. Blau, *The German Campaign in Russia*, Washington, 1955.

The three best recent syntheses are Alexander Werth's *Russia at War, 1941–1945* (New York, 1964), making use of personal experience, Russian sources, and an enthusiasm for the accomplishments of the Soviet army; Paul Carrell's *Hitler Moves East* (Boston, 1964), using a great number of German sources, including divisional and unit histories; and, finally, Alan Clark's *Barbarossa, The Russian-German Conflict, 1941–1945* (New York, 1965), the most balanced account so far.

Perhaps, as is often the case, the most accurate account of what it was like to be in Stalingrad is fiction, Konstantine Simonov's *Days and Nights* (New York, 1945) for the Russians and on the German side Theodor Plievier's *Stalingrad* (New York, 1948).

Notes

1. The most concise account of Hitler's strategy for the summer offensive may be found in George E. Blau, *The German Campaign in Russia—Planning and Operations (1940–1942)*, (Washington, March 1955), pp. 109–142.
2. Adolf Hitler (editor H. R. Trevor-Roper), *Blitzkrieg to Defeat* (New York, 1965), p. 129.
3. *Ibid.*, p. 130.
4. Halder later published his analysis of Hitler as a military leader (*Hitler as Warlord*); needless to say he was strongly critical as have been most of the generals. *Cf.* Blau, *German Campaign*, p. 134, for Jodl's caution.
5. In recent years there has been a gradually developing examination of Hitler's historical position in Europe, in particular his responsibility for the

war and his relation to the German background. There would seem to be a considerable body of evidence, as yet unworked, that he was far more conservative and traditional than his contemporaries believed. Whatever the historians' ultimate uncertain judgment may be, the German generals misunderstood him from the first and have often misrepresented him.

6. At almost every stage of the Russian campaign, there had been ample speculation as to what would have happened if an alternative policy had been followed. For example, the possibility that Stalingrad could have been occupied without resistance during the summer if Hitler had not tinkered with the original battle plan is a pet proposal. The most apt comment on this postwar German analysis may be found in Alan Clark's *Barbarossa* (New York, 1965), p. xxi: "Which is more absurd—to allow, with the wisdom of hindsight, an immaculate German campaign against a Russian resistance still plagued by those blunders and follies that arose in the heat and urgency of battle, or to correct both and to reset the board in an atmosphere of complete fantasy, with each side making the correct move like a chess text, when 'white must win'?"
7. V. I. Chuikov, *The Beginning of the Road* (London, 1963), pp. 13–43.
8. Winston Churchill, *The Second World War* (London, 1951), vol. IV, pp. 425–451.
9. Chuikov, *The Beginning,* p. 249.
10. *Ibid.,* p. 61; Clark, *Barbarossa,* pp. 217–218.
11. Chuikov, *The Beginning,* p. 284, admits the lack of preparations as does Yeremenko.
12. Paul Carrell, *Hitler Moves East 1941–1943* (Boston, 1964), p. 562.
13. Russian sources vary from year to year, depending upon the political needs of the moment, as to the part played by Khrushchev at Stalingrad. *Cf.* "The Military Adventures of a Civilian General" in Lazar Pistrak's *The Grand Tactician, Khrushchev's Rise to Power* (New York, 1961), pp. 208–225.
14. Chuikov, *The Beginning,* p. 90.
15. Alexander Werth, *Russia at War, 1941–1945* (New York, 1964), p. 483.
16. Chuikov, *The Beginning,* p. 135, quotes from Major-General Hans Doerr's account (*Der Feldzug Nach Stalingrad,* Darmstadt, 1955).
17. Chuikov, *The Beginning,* p. 308. For a detailed account of the new tactics, *cf.* pp. 268–343.
18. Walter Warlimont, *Inside Hitler's Headquarters* (New York, 1964), pp. 252–264; Franz Halder, *Diary,* "The Campaign in Russia, Part II," pp. 387 ff.
19. Kurt Zeitzler, "Stalingrad," *The Fatal Decisions,* eds. Seymour Freidin and William Richardson (New York, 1956), p. 134.
20. Erich von Manstein, *Lost Victories* (Chicago, 1958), p. 294; Walter Goerlitz, *Paulus and Stalingrad* (New York, 1963), p. 229.
21. Chuikov, *The Beginning,* p. 182.
22. *Ibid.,* p. 191.
23. *Ibid.,* p. 197.
24. *Cf.* Mathew P. Gallagher, *The Soviet History of World War II, Myths, Memoires and Realities* (New York and London, 1963).
25. For Soviet doctrine, see Raymond Garthoff, *Soviet Military Doctrine* (New York, 1953), pp. 67–72, 97–138.
26. A detailed account of the first days of the German encirclement may be found in Goerlitz, *Paulus,* pp. 215–235; for Jeschonneck's report, see Carrell, *Hitler Moves,* p. 591. Clark in *Barbarossa,* p. 256, stresses Paulus' delay in requesting permission to break out and his other somewhat curious reactions.
27. Zeitzler, "Stalingrad," *Decisions,* p. 166.
28. Goerlitz, *Paulus,* pp. 224–225.
29. Garthoff, *Soviet Doctrine,* pp. 106–116; Clark, *Barbarossa,* pp. 257–258.
30. Goerlitz, *Paulus,* p. 241. In time the Germans would lose 500 JU-52s in the Stalingrad airlift.
31. Manstein, *Lost Victories,* p. 320.
32. A detailed account of the battles on the Chir River during December, battles that eliminated Manstein's dual option, may be found in F. W. von Mellenthin's *Panzer Battles* (Norman [Oklahoma], 1958), pp. 175–184.
33. Manstein, *Lost Victories,* p. 336.
34. Chuikov, *The Beginning,* p. 254.
35. Goerlitz, *Paulus,* p. 251. The *Luftwaffe* supplied an average of 137.7 tons a day from December 12 to December 31, then the totals declined rapidly.
36. Warlimont, *Hitler's Headquarters,* p. 286.
37. Manstein, *Lost Victories,* p. 360.
38. *Ibid.,* p. 362.
39. Warlimont, *Hitler's Headquarters,* pp. 300–307.

Warsaw

In general the Polish campaigns during the Second World War with the possible exception of the Ghetto uprising in 1943 have not attracted a great deal of Western scholarly interest, as a group of sketches by Kazimierz Wierzynski entitled *The Forgotten Battlefield* (New York, 1944) suggests. Thus, there is an extensive German and Polish literature on the September 1939 campaign but little in contemporary works in English other than J. Bryan's *Siege*, published in 1940 and C. Hollingworth's *The Three Weeks War in Poland,* published in the same year. At the same time, a variety of patriotic pamphlets were produced which shed little light.

Peter Jordan, *First to Fight*, London, 1943.
Dominik Wegierski, *September 1939*, London, 1940.
Ksawery Pruszynski, *Polish Invasion*, London, 1941.

Even many late memoirs (*cf.* Marta Korwin-Rhodes, *The Mask of Warriors, The Siege of Warsaw, September 1939*, published in 1964) are of little use. There are various short accounts, often in odd places, which are in one way or another useful if not readily available.

T. Dodson Stamps and Vincent J. Esposito (eds.), *A Military History of World War II*, West Point: USMA, 1956.
Alfred H. Burne, "The Polish Campaign," *The Fighting Forces*, vol. XVI, pp. 374–381.
Alexander Polonius, *I Saw the Siege of Warsaw,* Glasgow, 1941.
Lieutenant-General Mieczyslaw Norwid-Neugebauer, *The Defense of Poland,* London, 1942.
F. B. Czarnomski (editor), *They Fight for Poland,* London, 1941.
Von Wedel, "The German Campaign in Poland," *Field Artillery Journal*, vol. XXIX, November–December, 1939, pp. 488–497.

The Polish government gave its own account of the German victory in the Ministerstwo Informacji's *The German Invasion* (The Black Book), vol. I, London, 1942.

In view of the fearful and highly efficient methods of Hitler's final solution, the natural assumption would be that those source materials relating to the Polish Jews in general and those in the Ghetto in particular would be limited. If anything, the reverse is true. When the Nazis' intentions became clear, one of the first and most widespread reactions was to write down and preserve accounts of Ghetto life. Emmanuel Ringelblum organized a special group, the *Oneg Sabbath,* to chronicle the times, and he also wrote an extensive daily commentary (Emmanuel Ringelblum, *Notes from the Warsaw Ghetto,* New York, 1958). His archives, buried in two places, were unearthed in September 1946 and December 1950. Subsequently the survivors' stories were collected and preserved. The result has been an unexpected if incomplete mass of raw data scattered in a variety of libraries and institutions on three continents. So extensive and so diverse had been the examination that Mark Bernard, the director of the Institute of Jewish History at Warsaw, has written an interpretive article on "Problems Relating to the Study of the Jewish Resistance Movement in the Second World War" (*Yad Washem Studies*, Jerusalem, vol. III, 1959). In Jacob Robinson and Philip Friedman, *Guide to Jewish History under Nazi Impact* (New York, 1960), six bibliographies solely concerned with the Warsaw Ghetto are listed and in an earlier Friedman bibliography 740 items, including 100 books, are noted. There is not in English, however, a definitive history of the Ghetto (*Cf.* Leonard Tushnet, *To Die with Honor*, New York, 1965); rather there are several chronological anthologies, containing first-hand accounts.

Meyer Barkai and Izhak Zuckerman, *The Fighting Ghettos*, Philadelphia and New York, 1962.
Albert Nirenstein, A *Tower From the Enemy*, New York, 1959.
Leo W. Schwarz, *The Root and the Bough*, New York, 1949.
Philip Friedman, *Martyrs and Fighters*, New York, 1954.

Several of the memoirs are lengthy and revealing, particularly David Wdowinski's recent *And We Are Not Saved* (New York, 1965). Two solid over-all studies are Joseph Tenenbaum's *Underground* (New York, 1952) and Gerald Reitlinger's *The Final Solution* (New York, 1953). There have also been detailed studies of various aspects of Ghetto life such as Joseph Tenenbaum's article in Louis Falstein (editor), *The Martyrdom of Jewish Physicians in Poland* (New York, 1964) or Nathan Feinborg, "On the Underground Press in the Warsaw Ghetto," *Yad Washem Studies* (Jerusalem, vol. I, 1957). For the German side the so-called Stroop Report (Bernard Mark, editor), *The Report of Jurgen Stroop* (Warsaw, 1958), or *Nazi Conspiracy and Aggression* (Washington, 1946, vol. III, pp. 718–774), as expanded by his testimony included in the Nuremberg Trial reports (International Military Tribunal, *The Trial of the Major War Criminals Before the International Military Tribunal* [Nuremberg, 1947–1949]), is all but sufficient; for obvious reasons subsequent German publications have not been extensive.

Although there is a wide and continuing literature published in Polish concerning the 1944 uprising (*Cf.* Adam Borkiewkz, *Powstanie Warszawskie 1944* [Warsaw, 1957], republished in 1964, and Jerzy Kirchmayer, *Powstanie Warszwskie* [Warsaw, 1964]), there is no authoritative study in English other than the brief *Sixty-three Days* (London, 1945). There is a very considerable collection of memoirs of participants and by far the most thorough is that of the military commander Bor-Komorowski, *The Secret Army* (New York, 1951).

Jan Karski, *The Story of a Secret State*, New York, 1944.
S. Mikolajczyk, *The Rape of Poland*, London, 1948.
Stefan Korbonski, *Fighting Warsaw*, London, 1956.
Irena Orska, *Silent is the Vistula*, New York, 1946.
Z. Stypulkowski, *Invitation to Moscow*, London, 1951.
Waclaw Zagorski, *Seventy Days*, London, 1957.
Anna Zajaczkowska, *The Underground Struggle*, Swatantrapur, Aunph, 1945.

Notes

1. Alfred H. Burne, "The Polish Campaign," *The Fighting Forces*, vol. XVI, no. 5, December 1939.
2. T. Dodson Stamps and Vincent J. Esposito (eds.), *A Military History of World War II* (West Point: USMA, 1956), I, 1–8.
3. Lieutenant-Colonel von Wedel, "The German Campaign in Poland," *Field Artillery Journal*, November–December, 1939, pp. 488–497.
4. Gerd Von Rundstedt, as quoted in *Military History*, p. 23.
5. Franz Halder, *Diaries*, vol. II, "The Polish Campaign," Part II, p. 8.
6. F. B. Czarnomski, *They Fight for Poland* (London, 1941), p. 96; Julien Bryan, *Siege* (New York, 1940), pp. 31–34.
7. *Military History*, p. 23.
8. Poland, Ministerstwo Informacji, *The Black Book*, "The German Invasion," vol. I (London, 1941), p. 70.
9. Halder, *Diaries*, vol. II, Part II, p. 16.
10. Czarnomski, *Poland*, p. 99.
11. Jan Karski, *The Story of a Secret State* (New York, 1964), p. 56.

12. Radio SWIT broadcasts actually emanated from London with information relayed by a small underground transmitter in Warsaw. See Stefan Korbonski's *Fighting Warsaw* (London, 1956).
13. Albert Nirenstein, *A Tower From the Enemy* (New York, 1959), pp. v–ix.
14. David Wdowinski, *And We Are Not Saved* (New York, 1965), p. 41.
15. Nirenstein, *Tower*, pp. 4–5; Mordecai Lenski, "Problems of Disease in the Warsaw Ghetto," *Yad Washem Studies*, vol. I (Jerusalem, 1959), pp. 283–294; Wdowinski, *Saved*, pp. 38–40; Philip Friedman, *Martyrs and Fighters* (New York, 1954), pp. 31–116; Nathan Feinborg, "On the Underground Press in the Warsaw Ghetto," *Yad Washem Studies*, vol. I (Jerusalem, 1957), pp. 67–84; Emmanuel Ringelblum, *Notes From the Warsaw Ghetto* (New York, 1958).
16. Friedman, *Martyrs*, pp. 122–123.
17. Wdowinski, *Saved*, pp. 61–78.
18. *Ibid.*, pp. 78–79.
19. Karski, *Secret State*, p. 321.
20. Nirenstein, *Tower*, p. 62.
21. Zivia Lubetkin quoted in Meyer Barkai and Izhak Zuckerman, *The Fighting Ghettos* (Philadelphia and New York, 1962), p. 22; Nirenstein, *Tower*, pp. 72–73.
22. Isaac Schwarzbart, *The Story of the Warsaw Ghetto Uprising* (New York, 1953), p. 6. The Irgun group did get some arms through the security corps of the Home Army. R. Ainsztein, *Jewish Observer & Middle East Review*, XIV No. 24, June 12, 1964, pp. 16–17. Alexander Donat in "Our Last Days in the Warsaw Ghetto," *Commentary*, vol. 35, No. 4, April 1963, p. 378, also suggests the Irgun under Frenkel was the best armed group.
23. The commander of the Polish Home Army Tadeusz Komorowski ("Bor") in *The Secret Army* (London, 1951) explains the Polish underground's position plausibly, but still that "49 revolvers" has a mean and ignoble sound about it.
24. Nirenstein, *Tower*, pp. 117–119.
25. *Ibid.*, pp. 59–60, 102–103, 212.
26. The German action is presented in lavish, if slightly inaccurate, detail in Jurgen Stroop's own *Report* (edited by B. Mark, Warsaw, 1958), supplemented by his testimony at Nuremberg. The various Jewish accounts vary in detail and in the excitement of the moment are somewhat exaggerated. This is particularly true in the question of casualties. Zuckerman contends that the Germans lost 200 killed and wounded on the first day (Joseph Tenenbaum, *Underground*, New York, 1952, p. 105), while Stroop gives the total German losses for the entire action as sixteen killed and ninety wounded. The Polish clandestine press reported 400 dead and 1,000 wounded, the lowest of anti-German figures, for the whole rising. In any event, as Anielewicz wrote, the important thing had been the revolt, not its effectiveness.
27. Friedman, *Martyrs*, p. 184.
28. *Ibid.*, p. 118.
29. Nirenstein, *Tower*, p. 122.
30. Josef Goebbels, *Diaries*, New York, 1948, p. 244.
31. Leo W. Schwarz, *The Root and the Bough*, New York, 1949, p. 62.
32. Nirenstein, *Tower*, p. 119.
33. Wdowinski, *Saved*, p. 95.
34. Barkai and Zuckerman, p. 78.
35. Life among the rubble is revealed by Leon Najberg, "A Fragment of the Diary of the Rubbish Men," in Tenenbaum, *Underground*, pp. 130–146.
36. *Ibid.*, p. 146.
37. Komorowski, *Secret Army*, p. 201.
38. Alexander Werth, *Russia at War*, p. 879.
39. K. M. Atholl, *The Tragedy of Warsaw* (London, 1945), p. 6. It is noteworthy that some English translations quote Bor as saying the Russians "will" cross the Vistula, while in others he is quoted as saying that they "may" cross.
40. Winston Churchill, *The Second World War*, vol. VI, "Triumph and Tragedy" (Boston, 1953), p. 129.
41. Komorowski, *Secret Army*, pp. 201–237.
42. Z. Stypulkowski, *Invitation to Moscow* (London, 1951), p. 123.
43. As is often the case, the underground was divided politically, with not only a small Communist action group, Communist Peoples' Army (AL) but also a pro-Communist group, Polish Peoples' Army (PAL) and a far Right splinter force, the Nationalist Armed Forces (NSZ). These three small groups co-operated only at times with the Home Army (AK), tending to carry out independent operations. Even communication with the Home Army was limited.
44. Stypulkowski, *Invitation*, p. 124; Komorowski, *Secret Army*, p. 214.
45. Werth, *Russia at War*, p. 873.
46. Heinz Guderian, *Panzer Leader* (New York, 1952), p. 285.

47. Stanislaw Mikolajczyk, *The Rape of Poland* (New York, 1948), pp. 70–78.
48. Churchill, *World War,* vol. VI, p. 131.
49. Andrzej Pomian, *The Warsaw Rising* (London, 1945), p. viii.
50. Most of the Poles connected with the exiled government in London or with the Home Army in Warsaw see the Russian withdrawal as a plot. The Communist writers tend to gloss over the problem or plead military difficulties. Two later, less committed writers, Alan Clark (*Barbarossa*) and Alexander Werth (*Russia at War*), disagree with the plot thesis.
51. Irena Orska, *Silent is the Vistula* (New York, 1946), p. 12.
52. Incredible as it may seem at this late date in the tragic history of Polish Jewry, enough Jews had survived to form a Jewish unit in the Home Army. On August 3, 1944, Izhak Zuckerman issued an appeal to arms in behalf of the Jewish Fighting Organization of the Home Army.
    "To the Defenders of the Warsaw Ghetto!
    To the Jews who remain alive!"
    There were few left to come out of hiding and fight the Germans. That there were any is amazing. Barkai and Zuckerman, *Fighting Ghettos,* p. 97.
53. Komorowski, *Secret Army,* pp. 208–209; *Sixty-three Days,* London, 1945, pp. 33–34.
54. Komorowski, *Secret Army,* p. 216.
55. Pomian, *Rising,* pp. 1–4; Komorowski, *Secret Army,* pp. 221–225; Atholl, *Tragedy,* pp. 15–17; Waclaw Zagorski, *Seventy Days,* London, 1957, pp. 33–34.
56. Orska, *Silent,* p. 69.
57. Komorowski, *Secret Army,* p. 253.
58. Zagorski, *Seventy Days,* pp. 52–60; Pomian, *Rising,* pp. 4–6.
59. Stypulkowski (*Invitation,* p. 125) quotes German General Dittman that the suppression of the rising was "one of the luckiest military successes of 1944."
60. Mikolajczyk, *Rape,* p. 69; Komorowski, *Secret Army,* p. 250; Clark, *Barbarossa,* p. 391.
61. Churchill, *World War,* vol. VI, p. 132.
62. Stefan Korbonski, *Fighting Warsaw* (London, 1956), p. 367.
63. Komorowski, *Secret Army,* p. 304. *Cf.* Bor's "Sewer Warfare in the Warsaw Uprising," *The Nineteenth Century,* CXLVIII, no. 881, July 1950, pp. 24–31.
64. Orska, *Silent,* p. 149.
65. Korbonski, *Fighting Warsaw,* pp. 370–372.
66. Churchill, *World War,* vol. VI, pp. 131–141.
67. Clark (*Barbarossa,* p. 418) quotes a postwar Zhukov statement, "we could not see how we could get beyond the Vistula unless the German forces on our front were considerably weakened."
68. Korbonski, *Fighting Warsaw,* p. 386.
69. In an interview during 1944 (Anna Louise Strong, *Inside Liberated Poland* [New York, 1944]), General Korczys of the First Polish Army revealed that his first contact with the Home Army had been through two women messengers on September 12. A radio man had been dropped into the city in order to spot artillery for him, but there had been no direct contact with General Bor. When the landing by Berling's troops on the west bank was made, Korczys claimed that Radoslaw and his officers avoided contact and withdrew through the sewers. This, as of 1944, was the "official" Russian explanation of Bor's difficulties in making contact. Undoubtedly, the Russians did have their troubles in setting up liaison with the Home Army but mainly because they were not interested—at least not to the point of using a radio.
70. Komorowski, *Secret Army,* p. 343.
71. Korbonski, *Fighting Warsaw,* p. 379.
72. *Sixty-three Days,* p. 73.
73. Pomian, *Rising,* p. 29.
74. *Ibid.,* p. 35; Komorowski, *Secret Army,* pp. 362–366.
75. Clark, *Barbarossa,* pp. 392–395.
76. Churchill, *World War,* vol. VI, p. 144.
77. *Ibid.,* vol. VI, p. 145.
78. Mikolajczyk, *Rape,* p. 90.
79. Komorowski, *Secret Army,* p. 382.
80. *Sixty-three Days,* p. 99.

Jerusalem

While few recent events have produced as many and varied responses, many of them in print, as the establishment of Israel, there is a surprising paucity of material on the military history of the conflict. There are several good studies, but there has not been any outpouring of memoirs and diaries, even to any great extent in Hebrew. *Cf.* Patricia Rose, *The Siege of Jerusalem,* London, 1950; Harry

Levin, *Jerusalem Embattled*, London, 1950; Shmū'el Bazaq, "In the City of David" in *The Captivity of the Legion*, Jerusalem, 1949 (Hebrew); Devora Hyrkanos-Ginzburg, *Jerusalem War Diary* (Israel), 1950. This is partially due to the conspiratorial background of the Jewish Army and the consequent habitual reluctance to reveal too much to their self-declared Arab enemies. This automatic secretiveness is such that Netanel Lorch in his excellent *The Edge of the Sword* (New York, 1961) originally included no proper names. For the Arabs, the chronicling of a lost war, the major humiliation in contemporary Arab history, holds little charm. A collection of three brief Arab memoirs has been published in Hebrew (*Through the Eyes of the Enemy*, Tel Aviv, 1955). The most authentic Arab account is by the former British commander of the Arab Legion, Sir John Bagot Glubb, in *A Soldier with the Arabs* (New York, 1957). While detailed and, at times, disinterested work has been done on Palestine during the Mandate and on some areas of Israeli history, particularly the Suez crisis in 1956, the siege of Jerusalem has not drawn the outside investigation of scholars. One reason may very well be that Dov Joseph's *The Faithful City, The Siege of Jerusalem, 1948* (New York, 1960) has gone a long way toward presenting a complete picture of the Israeli side of the battle.

For the period of the Mandate, the orthodox British view of the Middle East may be found in the highly authoritative Royal Institute of International Affairs volumes: *Great Britain and Palestine 1915–1945* (London, 1942) and *The Middle East, 1945–1950* (London, 1950). The Zionist equivalent is the ESCO Foundations' *Palestine—A Study of Jewish, Arab, and British Policies*, two volumes (New Haven, 1947). The best scholarly survey is undoubtedly J. C. Hurewitz, *The Struggle for Palestine* (New York, 1950), which includes a twenty-five-page bibliography. A later, if less exacting, work is John Marlowe's *The Seat of Pilate* (London, 1959). Of the host of books on Palestine in particular and the Middle East in general, Jon Kimche's *Seven Fallen Pillars, the Middle East, 1945–1952* (New York, 1953) is most readable. For the military campaigns, Lorch's *The Edge of the Sword* is perhaps the best of a rather solid collection.

Jon and David Kimche, *A Clash of Destinies*, New York, 1960.
E. O'Ballance, *The Arab-Israeli War, 1948*, London, 1956.
Harry Sacher, *Israel—The Establishment of a State*, New York.

There are some detailed accounts of the war, but few touch on Jerusalem (*Cf.* Moshe Pearlman, *The Army of Israel*, New York, 1950) although Zeev Sharef's *Three Days* (Garden City [New York], 1962) is an excellent and detailed account of the actual establishment of Israel. There are diaries, memoirs and reports from the siege period, but they range from David Ben Gurion, *Rebirth and Destiny of Israel* (New York, 1954) and *Years of Challenge* (New York, 1963) through Arthur Koestler, *Promise and Fulfillment, Palestine 1917–1949* (New York, 1949), down to some very immediate journalism.

Notes

1. The whole complicated tale of British responsibilities and rights in Palestine is covered in J. C. Hurewitz, *The Struggle for Palestine* (New York, 1950).
2. The Labour Government's policy in Palestine or lack of one would appear to have been the responsibility of Foreign Secretary Ernest Bevin, whom the Jews felt was anti-Zionist at best and anti-Semitic at worst. Whatever the Foreign Secretary's personal feelings grew to be, the ancient British policy of muddling through was in Palestine carried to new lengths. When no viable solution appeared,

the Labour Government, harassed by scores of critical problems, tended to let nature and the men on the spot run their course.

3. For the military developments of the siege the most dependable source, even if reticent, is Netanel Lorch, *The Edge of the Sword* (New York, 1961), although Jon and David Kimche, *A Clash of Destinies* (New York, 1953), contains several revealing passages. For the Arabs, the historian is stuck with odds and ends and Glubb's *A Soldier with the Arabs* (New York, 1957).
4. "Memorandum presented by the Jewish Agency to the United Nations Palestine Commission, 1947," p. 6.
5. Dov Joseph, *The Faithful City, The Siege of Jerusalem 1948* (New York, 1960), p. 6. Joseph's book is the prime source for the events of the siege on the Israeli side. Harry Levin's *Jerusalem Embattled* (London, 1950) is rather highly colored. *Cf. Experiment in Anarchy* (London, 1949) by R. M. Graves, the last mayor of the city before partition.
6. Zeev Sharef, *Three Days,* New York, 1962, p. 255; D. Knohl, *Siege in the Hills of Hebron* (New York and London, 1959).
7. John Roy Carlson, *Cairo to Damascus* (New York, 1951), p. 350.
8. Glubb, *A Soldier with the Arabs,* pp. 124–125.
9. Lorch, *The Edge of the Sword,* p. 185.
10. *Ibid.,* p. 187.
11. *Ibid.,* p. 188.
12. Ted Berkman, *Cast a Giant Shadow* (New York, 1962), p. 278.
13. Kimche and Kimche, *Clash of Destinies,* p. 200.
14. David Ben Gurion, *Rebirth and Destiny of Israel* (New York, 1954), p. 260.
15. Joseph, *The Faithful City,* pp. 236–237.
16. *Ibid.,* p. 247.
17. Glubb, *A Soldier with the Arabs,* p. 187.
18. Joseph, *The Faithful City,* p. 263.

Berlin

No definitive diplomatic history of the Berlin blockade will be possible until the opening of some diplomatic archives, which in the West will occur in the fullness of time, and a deeper insight into Soviet decisions, which is a remote possibility at best. Despite the lack of full diplomatic documentation, there exists a vast body of material from which a reasonably clear understanding of the development of the Western powers' position can be obtained. The most vital sources are the published memoirs and diaries of the participants rather than the extensive collections of nonsecret documentation. The actual train of events can be followed in the most intimate detail through official chronologies (Office of Military Government of the United States, *Chronological Tables on Germany, 1947–1949* [n.p., 1949]), histories (Oliver J. Frederiksen, *The American Military Occupation of Germany, 1945–1953,* History Division, Headquarters United States Army, Europe, [Darmstadt, 1953]), and surveys (Royal Institute of International Affairs, *Survey of International Affairs, 1947–1948* [London, 1952]), as well as in the increasing number of scholarly monographs (Frank Willis, *The French in Germany, 1945–1949* [Stanford, 1962]).

As must be apparent from the text, the entire Berlin crisis floated upon a sea of paper, official gazettes of the Control Council, recorded debates in the Security Council, four-power protocols, State Department Bulletins, Proceedings of the Council of Foreign Ministers, Parliamentary Debates *et al.* All of this has been hoarded, much of it has been published, and little of it is of interest but to the most dedicated historian. The United States State Department has published several relevant collections, such as:

Documents on Germany, 1944–1959, Washington, 1959.
The Berlin Crisis: A Report on the Moscow Discussions, Washington, 1948.
Germany 1947–1949: The Story in Documents, Washington, 1950.

A *Decade of American Foreign Policy, Basic Documents, 1941–1949* (Senate Document), Washington, 1950.

The British and Russians have published their collections as well; for example:

Great Britain, Ministry for Foreign Affairs, *Germany No. 2 (1961) Selected Documents on Germany and the Question of Berlin, 1944–1961*, London, 1961.

———, *An Account of Events Leading up to a Reference of the Berlin Question to the United Nations*, London, 1948.

Union of Soviet Socialist Republics, Ministry of Foreign Affairs, *The Soviet Union and the Berlin Question*, vol. I, Moscow, 1948.

There are even private collections such as that of the Royal Institute for International Affairs or those of American scholars.

Beate Ruhm von Oppen, *Documents on Germany under Occupation 1945–1954*, London, 1955.

J. K. Pollock, James H. Meisel, and H. L. Bretton, *Germany under Occupation, Illustrative Material and Documents*, Ann Arbor (Michigan), 1949.

Collections of lesser scope or narrower interest have also been published.

United States, Office of Military Government, United States Sector, Berlin, *Berlin Sector: A Four Year Report, July 1, 1945–September 1, 1949*, Berlin, 1949.

Great Britain, British Control Commission for Germany, *Notes on the Blockade of Berlin, February, 1949.*

The most relevant memoirs are really of more interest than the foregoing mound of undigested materials to the general reader. Unfortunately the definitive biographies of several significant figures, drawing on private papers, have not yet been published. Several others could not or did not write their impressions.

Willy Brandt, *My Road to Berlin*, Garden City (New York), 1960.

Lucius D. Clay, *Decision in Germany*, New York, 1950.

———, *Germany and the Fight for Freedom*, Cambridge (Mass.), 1950.

James Forrestal (Walter Millis, ed.), *The Forrestal Diaries*, New York, 1951.

Frank Howley, *Berlin Command*, New York, 1950.

Trygve Lie, *In the Cause of Peace*, New York, 1954.

Robert Murphy, *Diplomat Among the Warriors*, New York, 1965.

Walter Bedell Smith, *My Three Years in Moscow*, Philadelphia and New York, 1950.

Harry S. Truman, *Memoirs*, vol. II, New York, 1965.

For the diplomatic background to the crisis there are the ubiquitous collections of documents on Tehran, Yalta, and Potsdam; but the balanced studies of several scholars are more meaningful.

John L. Snell, *Wartime Origins of the East-West Dilemma over Germany*, New Orleans, 1959.

John Lukacs, *A History of the Cold War*, Garden City, 1961.

Herbert Feis, *Between War and Peace: The Potsdam Conference*, Princeton, 1960.

For the German question in general:

Eugene Davidson, *The Death and Life of Germany: An Account of the American Occupation,* New York, 1950.
Drew Middleton, *The Struggle for Germany,* London and New York, 1950.

For a contrast, the Soviet position is explained by the rabid W. G. Burchett, *Cold War in Germany* (Australia, 1950). For works on Berlin in particular see the following diverse group:

Lowell Bennet, *Bastion Berlin,* Frankfurt, 1951.
Max Charles, *Berlin Blockade,* London, 1959.
W. Phillips Davison, *The Berlin Blockade,* Princeton, 1958.
Curt Reiss, *The Berlin Story,* New York, 1952.
Philip Windsor, *City on Leave,* London, 1963.

Special studies like Willis, *The French in Germany;* J. P. Nettl, *The Eastern Zone and Soviet Policy in Germany, 1945–1950* (London, 1951); and Franz Neumann, "Soviet Policy in Germany," *Annals of the American Academy of Political and Social Sciences,* vol. CCLXIII, May, 1949, pp. 165–179; L. C. Green, "Berlin and the United Nations," *World Affairs,* January 1949, pp. 22–42 are useful but not always readily available.

For the airlift proper see:

Berlin *Magistrat, Airlift Berlin,* Berlin, 1949.
Great Britain, *Berlin Airlift.*
United States Air Force, Europe, *Berlin Airlift,* U.S. Air Force, Europe, 1949.
Charles J. V. Murphy, "The Berlin Airlift," *Fortune,* vol. xxxviii, no. 5, November 1948, pp. 89–93, 218 and pages following.
"Operation Vittles," *Aviation Operation,* April 1949, vol. 11, no. 5, supplement, pp. 1–120.

Notes

1. Frank Howley, *Berlin Command* (New York, 1950), pp. 74–76.
2. *Ibid.,* p. 76.
3. Two excellent books on the period are Herbert Feis, *Churchill, Roosevelt, Stalin,* Princeton, 1957, and J. L. Snell, *The Meaning of Yalta,* Baton Rouge, 1956.
4. Howley, *Berlin,* pp. 27–35, 41–48.
5. Lucius D. Clay, *Decision in Germany* (Garden City [New York], 1950), p. 50.
6. Document on Air Corridors, 22 November 1945, also enclosures of November 22, 27 and 30, 1945, Great Britain, Ministry of Foreign Affairs, *Germany No. 2 (1961), Selected Documents on Germany and the Question of Berlin 1944–1961* (London, 1961), pp. 60–64. Similar citations, some even more exotic, could be made for every single oddment of paper mentioned in the text.
7. W. Phillips Davison, *The Berlin Blockade* (Princeton, 1958), pp. 37–47.
8. *Ibid.,* pp. 47–62.
9. For the over-all French policies in postwar Germany *cf. Frank Willis, The French in Germany, 1945–1949* (Stanford, 1962).
10. Eugene Davidson, *The Death and Life of Germany* (New York, 1959), pp. 157–159.
11. Jack Bennet, "The German Currency Reform," *Annals of the American Academy of Political and Social Science,* vol. CCLXVII, January 1950, pp. 43–54.
12. James Forrestal (ed. Walter Millis), *The Forrestal Diaries* (London, 1952), pp. 367–368.
13. Willy Brandt, *My Road to Berlin* (Garden City [New York], 1960), p. 188.
14. Robert Murphy, *Diplomat Among the Warriors* (New York, 1965), pp. 349–351.

15. Clay, *Decision,* p. 357.
16. *Ibid.,* pp. 358–361; Murphy, *Diplomat,* pp. 351–352; Harry S. Truman, *Memoirs* (New York, 1965), vol. II, p. 147; Forrestal, *Diary,* pp. 424–428.
17. J. P. Nettl, *The Eastern Zone and Soviet Policy in Germany, 1945–1950* (London, 1951), pp. 105–109; Drew Middleton, *The Struggle for Germany* (New York, 1949), p. 121.
18. Forrestal, *Diary,* pp. 424–428.
19. Truman, *Memoirs,* p. 148.
20. Clay, *Decision,* pp. 362–368.
21. Forrestal, *Diary,* p. 431.
22. Truman, *Memoirs,* pp. 149–151. Vandenberg's reluctance to increase the airlift was apparently only equaled by his desire to avoid a war for which the United States seemed unprepared. Apparently the American Air Force is not always as bellicose in private as the journalists claim in public.
23. Walter B. Smith, *My Three Years in Moscow* (Philadelphia and New York, 1950), pp. 237–250; Clay, *Decision,* pp. 369–371; Forrestal, *Diary,* pp. 440–441, 449–450.
24. Forrestal, *Diary,* pp. 450–454.
25. Clay, *Decision,* p. 375.
26. Davison, *Blockade,* pp. 90–144, 162–182. For the September 9 meeting *cf.* David Shub, *The Choice* (New York, 1950), pp. 142–158, *Berlin Chooses Freedom* (Berlin, 1948).
27. Brandt, *Berlin,* pp. 196–199.
28. Charles J. V. Murphy, "The Berlin Airlift," *Fortune,* vol. xxxviii, no. 5, November 1948, p. 90.
29. Trygve Lie, *In the Cause of Peace* (New York, 1954), pp. 200–201.
30. *Ibid.,* pp. 202–204; Max Charles, *Berlin Blockade* (London, 1959), pp. 99.
31. Lie, *Peace,* pp. 203–215.
32. Clay, *Decision,* p. 385.
33. Davison, *Berlin,* pp. 195–228.
34. Clay, *Decision,* p. 388.
35. Davison, *Berlin,* pp. 247–249, 254–255; Lie, *Peace,* p. 216.
36. The figures for flights, tonnages and the length of the siege vary depending upon the starting and ending dates. Berlin *Magistrat, Airlift Berlin* (Berlin, 1949), p. 102; Charles, *Blockade,* p. 137.

Index

J. Bowyer Bell

J. Bowyer Bell was born in New York City on November 15, 1931. His education has been extensive. In 1953 he received a B.A. in history from Washington and Lee University, where he graduated with Honors with Exceptional Distinction. He then went on for a Masters in Modern European Diplomatic History at Duke University, followed by a Fulbright at the Universitá a Roma. Here Dr. Bell worked on the dissertation which earned for him a Ph.D. in 1958, again from Duke University.

The author has taught at a variety of schools, including the Gow School in South Wales, N.Y., Georgia State Teachers' College, and Trinity School in New York. Presently he is an associate professor at New York Institute of Technology, where he teaches European and American History, American Government, and the History of Science.